CYBERSECU~~~~

INCIDENT MANAGEMENT

MASTERS GUIDE

Volume 1
Preparation, Threat Response, &
Post-Incident Activity,
Second Edition

Colby Clark

www.CyberSecurityMastersGuides.com

CYBERSECURITY
MASTERS GUIDES

www.CyberSecurityMastersGuides.com

ISBN: 9798874027414

V1.E2.R1

DEDICATION

This book is dedicated to my tremendously patient wife and not-so-patient children, who have endured decades of my information security and incident response/management career with the long hours and the traveling lifestyle associated with it. My career has enabled us to live how and where we want and take incredible trips together. However, as a result, I have missed many important family events. I would not have been able to pull this off without their love and support.

ABOUT THE AUTHOR

Colby Clark is a senior information security professional with over 24 years of experience and leadership in security-related fields, including computer incident response, management, and command; digital forensics, malware analysis, eDiscovery, cybersecurity architecture, regulatory compliance, technical writing, curriculum development, software designer, and other security-related fields.

Colby received a Master of Science in Cybersecurity and Information Assurance from Western Governors University and graduated Cum Laude with a Bachelor of Science in Business Administration from the University of Southern California. He maintains industry-relevant certifications, including CISA, CISM, CISSP, EnCE, CEH, CHFI, GCCC, GCFA, GCWN, GREM, GCIH, GNFA, GDAT, GDSA, and GLEG.

He has taught advanced computer forensic and incident response techniques at the Computer and Enterprise Investigations Conference (CEIC), Techno Security Conference, Enterprise Security Solutions Summit (ES3), Secure World, and other venues.

He has performed time- and threat-relevant eminence and security evangelism activities, including writing whitepapers, posting blog entries, and performing speaking engagements regarding information security and incident response topics.

Colby has published other works in addition to the "Cybersecurity Incident Management Masters Guide" series, as an author and/or co-author of various genres. He also collaborated on various other information security works, such as Hacking Exposed Linux, 3rd edition, and was a developer of the Open Source Security Testing Methodology Manual (OSSTMM) by the Institute for Security Open Methodologies (ISECOM).

CONTENTS

PART 1 – INCIDENT MANAGEMENT PREPARATION

1 INTRODUCTION TO INCIDENT MANAGEMENT

The State of the State

The current reality is that even a single vulnerability on either a system accessible from or connecting to and browsing the Internet could potentially become an attack vector that could lead to a security breach. It has the potential to affect more than just the compromised endpoint but could also subsequently result in the full-blown exposure of the corporate environment and everything therein. In a worst-case scenario, any application or operating system vulnerability could result in privilege escalation that leads to credential harvesting, lateral movement, and ultimately to unfettered network and resource access. This could enable attackers or malware to achieve their objectives of compromising the target environment, resources, and data, as well as maintaining persistence for later use. As such, the stakes in cybersecurity are very high.

Clearly, an undetected attacker or malware can have a catastrophic impact on an organization if not quickly detected. The consequences of an attack include legal actions, regulatory compliance issues, reputational loss, theft of intellectual property, and subsequent financial impacts. Any one of these consequences could cause debilitating results to an organization and potentially result in long-term consequences. All of them hitting at once could be catastrophic and result in its demise.

When it comes to attackers vs. defenders, except for isolated circumstances (like companies having no Internet connection whatsoever), attackers typically have the advantage. Attackers only have to get it right once, but defenders need to get it right every time. Information security professionals face well-armed and funded attackers freely targeting infrastructure that cannot always be fully patched or at least not patched in time.

Moreover, employees and personnel are typically not security professionals and will never be fully trained to avoid social engineering or to successfully thwart attacks. It is unrealistic to expect finance people in charge of sending ACH transactions to perform a forensic review of email headers to look for anything suspicious that might identify email spoofing. As such, it should be expected that security controls will sometimes fail, and attackers will get through. This is where incident response and management capabilities become critical.

In today's threat model, the most reasonable detection and response approach to take is that of advanced persistent threats (APT). This model includes an inherent assumption that there are dedicated personnel assigned to infiltrate and maintain persistence within the security practitioner's organization and that they will be successful in breaching security controls and gaining access to the environment. This obviously comes off as very paranoid, but it is, unfortunately, true. "Just because you are paranoid doesn't mean they aren't out to get you."

Considering the amount of money to be made or saved by cybercrime, espionage, and the ability to steal rather than build or grow, there is a lot of motivation and financial backing. This has led to significant demand, which has created an international market and various dark web marketplaces for exchange to meet that demand. According to CyberCrime Magazine, cybercrime "cost the world ~$8 trillion in 2023." This markedly overshadows the amount of money spent on cybersecurity in 2023, which is estimated at between $160 and $225 billion, depending on the accuracy of the various sources. Long story short, the attackers have a lot more money to spend than the defenders.

All of this money available to the global hacking community has created thriving malicious marketplaces for information, goods, and services. Just like any service industry, there are freelancers that operate alone, teams that collaborate, large organizations with the resources to function like armies, and clandestine nation-states that get involved and have actual armies. All these entities want to be the first to gain access to key organizations and their respective systems, accounts, and data.

The security practitioners and responders must assume that try as they might, they will not successfully be able to thwart all attacker advances and that the attackers will eventually pierce the company's defenses and gain a foothold. Either that or they must assume that the attackers already have some level of a foothold within the organization that they are looking to maintain or increase. As such, a strong focus must be maintained on the detection and response of unauthorized or malicious activity to enable security personnel to discover and stop it before it becomes a serious problem.

Enabling Factors

In order to protect themselves from well-funded and highly organized hacking groups and nation-states, it is necessary for companies to implement a well-organized and exercised approach, including people, processes, and technology, to enable timely and effective detection and response to cyber-attacks. As such, the responders must take an attitude that they are performing continual incident response, looking for how the attackers have gained access to the organization and preparing to vanquish every foothold that is discovered.

Moreover, the security practitioners and responders must learn from attacker tools and command & control methods identified through the process to identify other tools and footholds extant elsewhere. Once all malicious hosts and attacker methods have been identified, the responders will attempt to block attackers and remove all attacker presence from the organization in a single, fluid motion. This includes blocking all attacker accounts, backdoor access, C2 methods, and eradication of any attacker footholds on compromised resources.

To be successful at incident management, security teams need to have adequate staffing; supporting policies, processes, and procedures; and the right technological capabilities to provide visibility and blocking within the environment. Success in cybersecurity requires a holistic plan covering all angles, providing capabilities for combatting the evolving threat landscape.

Regarding people, success in incident management will require adequate staffing to facilitate incident management, incident response, and underlying information security workflows. Each organization will need to determine the critical mass of internal personnel required to support incident management activity, which requires subject matter experts for systems or environments being investigated.

Personnel needs will vary from organization to organization, but without dedicated internal personnel, the program will lack continuity of vision. Internal personnel can be augmented by specialized contractors or service providers to reduce excessive full-time headcount, augment incident management skillsets, reduce learning curves, and speed up the time for completion.

However, outside resources need to be able to utilize internal tools and follow and comply with prescribed internal policies, procedures, and playbooks. Moreover, outside resources need to comply with required SLAs and meet SLOs, or there can be policy violations potentially exposing the company to regulatory compliance and/or legal risks.

Without supporting policies, procedures, and playbooks, people will not be required to support the cybersecurity or incident management workflows, and they will not even know how to perform them when the situation arises. Essentially, if it is not defined, funded, mandated, trained, and measured, security and response programs are nothing but hopeful wishes. These types of programs are expensive in time, money, and manpower. Programs without the right level of leadership backing will be doomed to fail. Success will be as elusive as unicorn hunting.

Success in cybersecurity and incident management programs starts from the top down. It comes in the form of leadership commitments for the funding of technology, personnel, policies/processes, and time required to fully develop and implement an incident management program and the supporting cybersecurity infrastructure to support it. If not for all of these supporting elements, it will never obtain the traction it needs.

Senior management support combined with written documentation demonstrating a holistic plan composed of adequate people, processes, and technology will make the incident management program viable. There are a lot of requirements nested in that last sentence, which will be fully explored throughout this book.

Standard incident management workflows must be created, tasks need to be tracked, individuals must be assigned, progress must be measured, and assigned individuals need to be held accountable by policy to enable success. All of this requires approval, funding, support, and enforcement from the highest levels of the company. Unless all these factors are in play, the program will fail at different points.

Regarding incident response technology requirements, the technology must enable full visibility and control in the three critical analysis and response target areas. These consist of the following, which in turn provide insight into the activity related to all processes, accounts, files, or other objects:

1. Network traffic
   a. All Ingress/egress traffic from all network points of presence (PoPs)
   b. Traffic between and within critical or sensitive network segments (this may include server VLANs, PCI/PII/PHI networks, DMZs, or other sensitive networks)
   c. Traffic to/from affected systems, including all internal or external traffic
2. Endpoints – Including workstations, servers, virtual machines, cloud systems, and sensitive or critical devices. For the sake of rapid response, endpoint detection and response (EDR) agents should be installed everywhere possible for immediate use. If one has to deploy these for use after an incident, precious time is lost, and deployment activity may alert attackers that responders are aware of them.
3. SIEM/log analysis – Including onboarding, integration, and correlation from all critical environments, security devices/applications, EDR technologies, antivirus/anti-malware systems, IAM systems, servers, services, applications, and

workstations should have their logs collected, aggregate, correlated, and analyzed against detection rules and threat feeds.

Malicious activity can hide, but it will leave fingerprints in one or more of these key areas that can be used for detection and response. The better these three system types are integrated and correlated, the better the detection and response capabilities will be.

Enabling security practitioners and incident responders to quickly identify, investigate, and resolve security issues requires a combination of technologies and analysis processes. It is most easily and comprehensively accomplished by utilizing Endpoint Detection and Response (EDR) solutions, combined with network traffic analysis and blocking solutions, and all relevant log data aggregated into a SIEM for automated correlation, analysis, and alerting.

If designed, implemented, and maintained properly, technology capabilities will enable the incident response and incident management processes. However, incident response and incident management extend well beyond what has been discussed and include deep-dives into other technical, soft-skill, and procedural areas.

Incident Response vs. Incident Management

Incident response and incident management are often confused with each other or conflated, but they are actually quite different. Like many terms in cybersecurity, incident response and incident management are often used interchangeably. However, they exist at different levels of related activity and are part of a somewhat overlapping continuum of the same.

Incident response is the term best applied to the technical deep-dive that takes place during an incident. Conversely, incident management performs an oversight function for an incident, as well as planning, follow-up, and reporting tasks related to incident response.

To complicate matters, both terms have evolved significantly over time. Up until the advent of cybercrime, when technical people referred to "incidents," they were typically referring to infrastructure failures and outages that impacted uptime and service delivery. This still happens frequently today, especially when talking to dedicated operations people. They often have to ask people to define what they mean by an "incident."

However, in today's threat landscape, the term "incident" usually refers to a cybersecurity breach that threatens or has compromised the confidentiality, integrity, and/or availability of environments, systems, services, applications, accounts, and/or data. While it would be possible to distinguish this as a "security incident" as opposed to a "service delivery incident," a security incident usually causes a service delivery incident, and the two are hopelessly intertwined. For the rest of this book, the term "incident" will refer to a "security incident" that may or may not cause a "service delivery incident."

2 INCIDENT RESPONSE REQUIREMENTS

Description

Incident response (as distinguished from incident management) is a highly specialized technical field, which is actually composed of numerous nested specialties. They are seldom held by a single individual, and having most or all of them would make one a "renaissance man" of cybersecurity. The role is essentially a roll-up of advanced skill sets in many other highly technical fields. The more specialties that responders can perform, the more versatile and valuable they are in performing incident response.

For these reasons, being an incident responder is often a senior-level stage in one's career path that requires significant background in prerequisite fields to be successful as a sole practitioner. However, more often than not, a successful incident response engagement requires a well-equipped team with diverse and overlapping skill sets rather than a single, clever individual. While it is true that there are ninja rockstars out there who can run an incident response engagement alone, just because you can doesn't mean you should. A team, even if it is only two people, and one of them is a project manager, is still preferable.

So, now for the details. Following is a list including many of the skills that are most commonly found or used on an incident response team, depending on the needs of the investigation. This list is far from comprehensive, and new or esoteric needs that need to be navigated come up all the time. Moreover, new versions of existing technologies create additional challenges, as there are often modifications in storage, configuration methods, file structure, file systems, file formats, encoding, encryption methods, etc.

Each of these things may need to be figured out on the fly or have staffed resources back in the lab to assist. The common denominator is that people with incident response and investigation experience, or the ability to reverse engineer and map out changes and identify relevant details, need to be available onsite or remotely to assist. It is critical for the success of response activity that the Incident Commander staff engages with personnel who have the right skill sets. The following sections will go through the roles, skill sets, and rationale.

Key Incident Responder Skillsets

- Technical troubleshooting
- Threat research and analysis
- Project management
- Systems administration and engineering
- Network administration and engineering
- Network forensics
- Computer forensics
- Evidence handling
- Regex/GREP/other query languages
- Shell, API, and application scripting
- SQL scripting
- Computer science and programming
- SIEM queries & log analysis
- Memory analysis
- Malware analysis
- Cryptography
- Data recovery
- Information security
- Vulnerability assessment
- Penetration testing
- Application security
- Database security
- Security gap assessment
- Reporting

Technical Troubleshooting

Technical troubleshooting is a key skill to begin with during an incident. You typically cannot accept at face value any conclusions you are told at the outset of an incident unless you have been told them by a seasoned, trusted party. However, even then, initial conclusions should always be vetted. Oftentimes, customers, end-users, or operations personnel think they have a security incident when, in fact, they just have an operating system, application, network configuration, or hardware issue.

Quite often, a disruption in service or some sort of misunderstood anomaly is perceived as the result of a security incident. It is important not to jump immediately into incident response workflows when anomalous problems are reported.

Rather, begin by trying to identify if there is a non-malicious technical issue that could explain it. It is not uncommon for an application error, resource/sharing conflict, browser plug-in crash, network slowness, or an unexpected error message to raise suspicions or create alarm with users. Due to security training and news headlines, personnel are becoming increasingly suspicious of hacking and malware, but they typically don't have enough technical breadth or depth to fully assess the situation. It will save a tremendous amount of time if false incidents can be avoided through proper troubleshooting prior to escalating an incident.

In order to perform satisfactory troubleshooting, knowledge of the affected and supporting technologies as relevant to the situation is required. In most cases, this usually includes some combination of operating systems, applications, databases, networking, web services, cloud services, supporting security technologies, and subject matter experts for each. It sometimes takes a village.

Threat Research and Analysis

Once the responders have obtained sufficient information about a particular security incident, it is important to understand what type of threat they may be facing and how best to respond to it. Usually, threats take place in campaigns that are seen over and over again across various industry verticals. This may happen one at a time or sometimes everywhere all at once until the malware authors have moved on to a new campaign.

This often manifests as waves of attacks against organizations with similar infrastructure that are vulnerable to the same exploits. Examples are those with similar payment system types, hardware, software packages, etc. For instance, it manifests with clusters of attacks against retail chains, all having similar payment systems. Later, similar attacks occur in other industry verticals with related technology and infrastructure, such as across healthcare environments with similar systems. Banking environments and insurance agencies are also common targets that are often compromised in waves of attacks.

Through adequate threat research and analysis, security practitioners and responders will be able to see these campaigns coming, put security controls in place ahead of time (usually rules to identify and block IOCs), and know what to look for to ensure quick detection and response. Moreover, having integrated threat feeds from multiple sources that feed network, endpoint, and log analysis solutions is key for efficacy and efficiency. With the volume of threats that are being developed, it is no longer feasible to maintain this type of endeavor manually. The human resource cost for research and development would be highly prohibitive and not very competitive. Long story short, a custom-developed solution is much more expensive and less reliable than fully integrated, automated services that crowdsource and aggregate data from numerous environments.

Project Management

A very important aspect of incident response is the ability to manage the overall incident response process, especially if there is no designated incident commander involved. In lieu of an Incident Commander, it is key that the lead incident responder identify and track required objectives, workflows, action items, technical steps, and people involved.

It is very seldom that incident response is performed independently by a sole practitioner without any assistance. Usually, there is a team involved, especially from the customer's side, including representation for security, network, server, workstation, management, legal, and/or compliance teams. Also, it is advisable that each incident involving a significant outbreak involving multiple systems and/or analysis types should have multiple dedicated incident responders that divide workstreams and analysis types.

However, a single individual with both incident response technical skills and project management experience needs to assume the incident command role. This role is essential to the success of the investigation. The individual in this role is required to develop an understanding of the issues.

This includes working with subject matter experts to perform troubleshooting and incident validation. It will involve identifying the required people and technology resources, mapping out the evidence universe, laying out the overall plan for the investigation, clearly defining objectives, and assigning/tracking the investigation's progress.

The most common method to do this is by physically or virtually gathering all subject matter experts (SMEs) together in a war room surrounded by whiteboards. This can be bolstered by an open incident bridge for remote participants with teleconference/screen-sharing displaying a digital method to track and report the action items and status to ensure everyone is on the same page.

Further, due to the demands placed on this role, it is ideal to have a dedicated Incident Commander. It is very difficult to have the "heads-down" focus required for the technical aspects of incident response and simultaneously perform the "heads-up" role, which is the project management (incident management) function for incident response. Usually, people trying to fulfill both roles at once will find themselves failing at one or the other or find themselves lacking somewhat at both.

Systems Administration and Engineering

Most people who become good at computer forensic analysis have a strong background in systems administration/engineering. They possess an understanding of the ins and outs of how systems and applications function, where changes are made by software/malware, where artifacts could exist, what logs are most relevant, and how to lock systems down. This type of knowledge is absolutely essential to performing expedient and effective incident response.

Additionally, multi-platform knowledge is key. All devices, systems, operating systems, services, and applications have the potential to be breached. Every common technology type has had its share of exploits associated with it. No technology is immune, so knowledge of as many system types as possible is important. The more a practitioner knows about each type of system and how to perform investigation, containment, and remediation on them, the more value they provide to the incident response team, and the more likely they are to be engaged in response activities.

Network Administration and Engineering

Most people who are successful at incident response have a healthy amount of network administration and/or engineering background. In most cases, performing a successful attack means exploiting operating systems or applications, installing malware, moving laterally, stealing data, and maintaining persistence. There will always be network components on both ends of that spectrum, as well as different places in the middle. Networking knowledge and access are key at all phases of an investigation.

Incident Commanders and responders need to be comfortable with network devices, understand the type of data to look for and provide instructions on what data to collect and how to go about it, how to handle that data, and how to implement or advise upon network inspection and containment controls. This often involves changes to the network to enable the identification of malicious activity, collection of data, and subsequent containment or remediation processes.

Network Forensics

Network forensics has a significant overlap with network administration and engineering, but it is a deep dive into the network traffic stream to perform analysis at various levels. This portion of the investigation is very important as it will help identify evidence of infiltration, exfiltration, lateral movement, malware download/communication, C2, and other artifacts that may only be available if captured from network traffic.

Considering the complexity of network traffic analysis and the need to reduce the dataset to enable deep-dive investigations, performing network forensics begins with analyzing flow data to identify endpoints and traffic of greatest relevance. From there, network traffic is dissected to in as much depth as necessary to achieve investigative goals. Typical analysis steps include identifying all hosts involved and methods of communication, decoding/decrypting the traffic streams to view the contents, carving out and reconstructing relevant evidence (communications, files, usernames, passwords, keys, etc.), and developing a list of items to search for on affected hosts or in other network traffic captures.

Computer Forensics

Most incident response investigations having a legal or compliance concern will ultimately turn to computer forensic investigation to analyze endpoints and artifacts to identify evidence related to the compromise and sensitive information that could have been exposed. There are a wide variety of tools to perform this – both local and remote. Having responders skilled in this is essential to address many of the most pressing concerns and related workflows involved in an incident. These include root cause analysis, identification of all compromised hosts, malware samples/artifacts, and the identification of compromised sensitive data.

Ultimately, this information will serve the customer by helping them develop an understanding of how to restore their data and better protect their environment. Moreover, it could positively determine whether the incident is reportable and who needs to be notified.

Specific findings from computer forensic analysis can make the difference between 1) over-reporting due to lack of clarity or specific findings or 2) not having to report because analysis proved it was unnecessary. Additionally, having both computer and network forensic analysis findings can create a much more conclusive case as the two findings validate each other.

Evidence Handling

Forensically sound evidence handling per the Federal Rules of Civil Procedure is something that should always be performed by default to ensure personnel always handle evidence properly. It should not be an extra step that practitioners try to bolt on by request but something that is always done by documented policy, procedure, and practice. If it is not a common practice, people will make mistakes, and there will be gaps in the chain of custody, or evidence will not be handled in a forensically sound manner. Response personnel need to take care to do this as any case could end up in court and possibly become a criminal case.

More specifically, it is essential that each evidence item is properly collected, verified, documented, handled, transported, and stored with a complete chain of custody. If any of these steps are missed or not completed properly, it provides wiggle room in a court of law for the opposing side to invalidate evidence and the respective analysis findings and conclusions based on it. As such, it could be considered the "fruit of the poison tree" simply because a basic step was overlooked in an otherwise perfectly executed investigation.

However, most incident response cases do not go to court for the purpose of litigation against perpetrators, as attacks are usually initiated by entities in foreign countries. Moreover, it is not usually feasible to successfully perform attribution without assistance from federal law enforcement agencies, and they seldom get significantly involved in most hacking cases. More often, if cases do go to court, it is due to a civil lawsuit against the affected organization from customers whose data was impacted.

Regex/GREP/Other Query Languages

A key part of the analysis is attempting to identify when, how, and by whom malicious activity happened and what specifically was affected. A responder needs to be able to tell the full story, and primary tools enabling the discovery of this information are the various methods of searching (common or proprietary functions) for specific content. These usually include, but are not limited to GREP, keywords, exact data, partial data, stemming, expressions, patterns, simple conditions, compound conditions, Yara rules, IOCs, Boolean logic, SQL queries, forensic hashes, fuzzy hashes, or other matching criteria.

There is no single way to accomplish this when performing incident response, as content comes from various sources and is consumed and analyzed using different solutions. As such, having a strong understanding of how to search for, locate, and extract desired content using a variety of methods and toolsets is key to the success of an incident response investigation.

Shell, API, Application Scripting

To simplify the process of parsing structure data, scripting in all of its forms is critical. It is frequently used for decoding or decrypting data, performing searches, collecting evidence, formatting output, and automating the overall forensic process.

Moreover, the ability to perform shell scripting on different operating systems and/or use native scripting languages in applications is critical. Frequently, the process of gathering desired evidence artifacts is highly laborious and best suited to a scripted process, inasmuch as it can be defined. Weblogs are a good example of this, as they are often completely full of noise. However, if you can carve out (for example) SQL injection statements using a scripted process, you can quickly see what happened in an attack.

Every operating system has its own scripting language(s) that are either native or at least supported. As operating systems progress, so do the power and utility of the scripting languages, which are either native to or supported by them, and the APIs used to access them.

Moreover, applications have their own native scripting languages to parse and process information. These are included in most forensic tools, which provide a wide variety of scripted functions supporting automated analysis operations within the tool. Moreover, in most cases, many of the functions of the forensic tools, particularly compound or sequential analysis functions, are only accessible via scripting languages, as there is no method to perform such functions within the interface.

Cloud services are also well known for possessing scripting functionality that can significantly automate the process of performing all phases of incident response, as well as containment and remediation within the cloud. These environments can be profoundly large and complex yet simultaneously lack support for conventional endpoint or application collection and analysis methods. As such, the native or supported scripting languages within cloud environments are vital to the success of incident response activities.

Lastly, during the process of evidence gathering, files will be collected that cannot immediately be searched, as they need to be decrypted, decoded, merged, separated, sanitized, interpreted, and/or otherwise converted to a friendlier format for searching. Utilizing scripting languages as appropriate to manipulate the content and format it for analysis will simplify the incident response workflow and reduce the time required to complete the analysis.

SQL Scripting

We live in an increasingly database-driven world. Gone are the days when websites and file shares fully resided in directories on disk, and they can be easily enumerated and identified with file system-based forensic tools. By and large, even simple websites with what may appear to be static content are now held in databases, such as WordPress, which is the most popular and probably the easiest-to-use tool for people to create websites.

Moreover, many file-sharing and archival tools are really just databases storing files in blobs in databases. As such, the ability to search, identify, retrieve, and analyze information from databases is critical to investigations. Unfortunately, performing database forensics using automated graphical tools is not currently reliable or feasible. There have been several proof-of-concept tools released that attempt to do database forensics and focus on specific SQL languages, but there is nothing mature or reliable. As such, it is necessary to utilize the native SQL language variants for the respective database types to search and identify relevant content and perform evidence collection. This typically requires a lot of trial and error.

Computer Science and Programming

Unfortunately, shell and database scripting languages will only take analysis so far. For some incident response challenges, formal computer programming skills are required. For the sake of clarity, this does not normally require the development of applications – although sometimes that happens, as well.

The point of this is that computer science and programming skills will provide the ability to understand and interact with functions, APIs, or interfaces, as well as to decompile and analyze malicious applications. More specifically, the ability to unpack, decrypt, decode, disassemble, or otherwise reverse engineer and reveal the functions and operations of malicious scripts or applications can be key to handling an incident.

These skills are often outsourced by customers to external, on-demand contractors. However, having to rely on external service providers for incident response generally results in delays that complicate investigations, potentially impacts reporting deadlines, and strains customer relationships. As such, it is beneficial to have these skill sets on an internal incident response team. It is beneficial even if resources are not deployed but are shared resources in a lab utilized by multiple teams.

SIEM Queries & Log Analysis

Performing SIEM queries and log analysis is a very broad, complicated, and dynamic space. While some logs are documented, and certain events are well-known indicators, many log sources are highly esoteric and mysterious. Depending upon the log configuration, detailed logs may help identify the smoking gun. Conversely, having the default, minimal log settings will leave you scratching your head and deriving new methods to determine what happened.

There are many types of logs within the evidence universe, and they provide varying levels of value and support to investigations. As stated previously, default log settings seldom capture enough information to tell the story.

On the other hand, something as voluminous as C2 audit logging on databases can bury responders in log data that will require tremendous amounts of searching and analysis. Moreover, C2 logging is so noisy that it will likely impair system and application stability and availability in the process. It can be helpful in corroborating evidence under the right conditions, but it is typically too noisy to be useful and too much data to be successfully captured and stored.

Multiple types of logs, formats, and output options are captured for each operating system, service, and application. Having the right configuration implemented for the associated use cases (or misuse cases) is crucial to enabling an investigation and identifying suspicious or malicious activity.

It is crucial at the outset of investigations to be able to quickly identify and then capture and preserve relevant log sources to prevent content from being lost, such as being deleted by the attackers or overwritten based on time or volume. All logging has limitations, and default log settings typically overwrite and spoliate data fairly quickly. Following the preservation of logs begins the process of identifying methods of extraction to provide meaningful content responsive to the investigation's needs.

As such, it is required that incident response teams have the capabilities to analyze logs for all network/security devices, servers/workstations, operating systems, platforms, services, applications, and log aggregation/SIEM solutions to correlate and enrich data relevant to an investigation. The volume of logs that are potentially available can be massive, frequently totaling dozens or hundreds of terabytes of data.

These logs will usually have non-standardized field names across different log sources containing similar information. Having the ability to correlate and normalize log fields/data and parse/cull the log content during a preliminary filtering phase prior to more in-depth analysis is critical to incident response investigations. It is not feasible to manually analyze all the logs that typically exist, and the majority of log content consists mostly of noise.

Memory Analysis

Due to the evolution of attacks and the nature of current threats, memory analysis has become the primary method of triage and the first stage of analysis when performing incident response. This is because modern threats move so quickly and can be so polymorphic and dynamic that there is no time to perform formal disk-based forensic analysis, nor would it be of much help in stopping an attack. This is the typical focus of Endpoint Detection and Response (EDR) tools.

It is not uncommon for hundreds or thousands of systems to be infected within minutes, and the fastest way to identify attacker and malware characteristics is through memory metadata combined with network activity and retrospection to daisy chain the history into a succinct timeline. This includes the identification of infiltration/exploit, spreading, communication, exfiltration, and persistence mechanisms. Utilizing this quickly accessible data, security practitioners and responders can put in place containment controls to stop the threat from spreading and effectively preserve the environment in its current state for additional analysis.

In addition to the analysis of memory metadata, analysis of memory contents can provide a great deal of information about malware in memory and related artifacts. These include DLL injection, API injection, hollowed processes, fileless malware, scripted malware, credentials, key exchanges, strings, stolen content, communication, commands, etc.

Malware, whether packed executable binaries or encoded/encrypted scripts, is hard to analyze if collected from the network or on disk. However, it is easier in memory. It needs to be decoded in memory to perform its functions. Therefore, analysis in memory is the best and easiest way to harvest and truly profile the malware.

Malware Analysis

This is a task that is usually divided into different layers requiring significantly different levels of skill. They are most easily separated into 1) behavior analysis and 2) static analysis/reverse engineering.

The behavioral analysis portion is relatively easy. These days, it can be performed very quickly. In the early days, we used to step through this by hand, and it took a significant amount of time and extensive steps to perform manual or semi-automated comparisons.

Fortunately, those days are gone, and it is a task that is best automated, considering the vast array of automated tools and services available that simplify the process and provide adequate results. However, sometimes malware is aware it is being analyzed by automated tools and will not display the same behavior.

In such cases, a more manual approach may be required unless the automated process has options to trick the malware adequately. Static analysis/reverse engineering is a step-by-step, highly manual process that is not reliably automated, as you may have to figure out how to outsmart the malware's anti-reverse-engineering checking methods along the way. It typically requires advanced programming and assembly skills, including the ability to analyze the code in a debugger and walk each operation to identify malicious functions and artifacts.

This functionality is often outsourced by customers to an incident response provider through a retainer agreement, as it is difficult to keep individuals with these skill sets busy and their skill sets relevant in most customer environments. However, every incident response services provider should have this capability internally, without the need to outsource, as there is an expectation of availability, speed, and efficiency.

Cryptography

A large percentage of attacks use some sort of encryption to mask network traffic or malware artifacts. Encryption helps prevent detection by network and endpoint data inspection and security devices/controls, as well as reverse engineering of components.

Encryption methods vary depending on the attacker and purpose. The encryption strength may or may not be robust, as the focus of most encryption is typically the avoidance of detection rather than truly safeguarding the content, with the notable exception of ransomware. As such, to evade inspection methods, a simple XOR key is usually sufficient to enable the attacker to avoid being detected, but not impact speed or system performance.

Therefore, in order to perform malware analysis, identify capabilities, or determine what data may have crossed the network or been exfiltrated, the ability to perform cryptographic analysis is essential. Making an affirmative determination regarding what data was exfiltrated and who specifically was affected is very important for legal and compliance purposes, as it will help prevent the need to over-disclose. Without conclusive proof, companies are often forced to speculate about who "could have been affected," which is typically overly broad and damaging to the company's reputation.

These skills are typically held by those with reverse engineering knowledge as part of the malware analysis workflows. However, considering the simplicity of many of the encryption algorithms used, team members with advanced scripting capabilities are often adequate.

Data Recovery

Incident response is a highly layered process, and data recovery comes into play at several stages throughout the process and for different reasons. Commonly, to get to the bottom of what occurred during an incident, there are many prerequisites and follow-up steps.

Being as attackers will often delete malicious artifacts and stolen content at various stages, the incident responders may need to utilize a forensic process to recover files, memory fragments, or other artifacts of exploit or data compromise to identify what happened. There is not necessarily a simple path or standard way to do this. The method used to search, identify, and recover the desired content is determined on a case-by-case basis, depending on the data set and how it was deleted.

Some forensic tools do go through a standard process consisting of multiple stages that may or may not prove fruitful in an effort to give responders a good starting place, but it is just that. A fairly common process includes a starting point of identifying unallocated, deleted, and partially overwritten fragments of files to enable responders to determine what attackers may have attempted to delete.

Data elements that are often deleted and require recovery either for investigation or restoration include malicious exploit scripts, downloader files, malware install files, stolen data repositories, affected user-created documents, etc. Moreover, as part of the restoration process during incident response, practitioners may be called on to recover data that cannot otherwise be restored from backups.

Information Security

Information security is the underlying basis of incident response, incident management, and all of the related activity at every stage. The gaps in information security posture and weak or missing controls create opportunities for attackers to breach environments and gain unauthorized access to systems and data.

The actions involved in the detection, response, containment, and blocking of security incidents utilize information security concepts, technologies, and related resources. They are used to perform analysis and effect changes on networks, endpoints, applications, accounts, and logs. Findings and recommendations following a breach are centered around the strengthening of security controls related to people, processes, and/or technology. As such, incident responders must be exceptionally well-versed in information security concepts, tools, capabilities, configurations, and architecture and have the ability to discuss them in detail.

Most security incidents include multiple phases where solutions need to be identified and developed to inform containment, mitigation, and remediation activities. Moreover, there are (or should be) post-incident lessons learned where the Incident Commander collaborates with affected parties to assist in developing solutions and countermeasures. An incident without performing after-action lessons learned with some solutions development to prevent future foreseeable intrusions is a significant missed opportunity.

Vulnerability Assessment

This may seem a little counterintuitive, but if you have no better place to start, performing vulnerability assessments during incident response can provide insight into security gaps in devices, systems, services, and/or applications. Every investigation needs a starting point, and if it is expected that an incident may be related to an external attack and there are no good indicators identifying the entry point, a vulnerability assessment may provide one. It also helps drive mitigation and remediation efforts.

Identification of these security gaps will identify how the technology could have been breached and may provide a starting point for artifact collection and analysis. This can be very useful, as it provides the ability to narrow the scope and establish an entry point for analysis. This can greatly expedite an investigation, leading to quicker root cause analysis and the ability to put in place containment or mitigation controls. It also helps drive after-action discussions, lessons learned, and recommendations.

Having said that, just because a vulnerability scanner identifies that technology has specific vulnerabilities, it does not mean that the vulnerabilities used to exploit the technology were the same as those detected. While it is certainly possible, all findings need to be validated, and it must also be determined if there were multiple exploits against a system.

On systems that have not been properly maintained for an extended period of time, it is common to find multiple critical vulnerabilities and potential points of entry. In these circumstances, it is often common to find multiple overlapping compromises that occurred at different points in time. They often occur in one or more ways and step on each other, thus trampling the respective evidence and timeline artifacts. It is not uncommon to see systems with vulnerable versions of WordPress that have dozens of web shells installed by various waves of attackers that compromised the system over time.

Penetration Testing

Having knowledge of penetration testing for incident response is very helpful, but it is not mandatory. The benefit is derived by understanding attacker techniques in exploiting systems or applications, the ability to identify what is affected during the exploitation, awareness of persistence mechanisms that can be deployed, and determining where breach artifacts may exist as a result of a successful compromise.

Basically, by understanding what attackers target and how they exploit those targets, security practitioners and responders will be more proficient in their jobs. They will understand the attacker or malware activity, know where to look for evidence of exploitation, and understand the types of controls that need to be implemented for containment, mitigation, and remediation activity. Simply put, awareness of attack strategies makes the entire security and response team more proficient.

Application Security

Having knowledge of application security can be important for incident response when investigating breaches of services and applications. These types of breaches can be highly specialized and require in-depth knowledge of coding and application security concepts.

It is highly valuable to response activity if practitioners possess the ability to identify vulnerabilities in web application code, understand where artifacts of exploitation would manifest, and have the knowledge to identify and implement compensating or mitigating controls. However, considering many applications are proprietary or custom-coded, it usually requires assistance from various members of the application and database teams involved in the creation and maintenance of the application. It is critical to have access to SMEs that are familiar with the proprietary application, its content, and its logs.

Database Security

Security in databases is something that is often overlooked. It is a skill set that is particularly important when investigating and responding to database breaches. It is unfortunately common for data/content access security to be handled by the web application accessing the database content, rather than provided by the database server itself. This exposes the database, its functions, and its content to significant risk if the application controls are bypassed.

This means that the attackers could obtain free reign of the database and other resources if they bypassed the application controls or gained control of an account used by the application. It is entirely possible for the attackers to exploit the lack of database controls to leverage its functionality for lateral movement, both on systems and across the network.

For example, the underlying operating system could become compromised using database functions, command shells, or admin utilities. This would expose the server's file system content and may also enable it to make network connections to other systems within the compromised environment.

SMEs having strong technical knowledge of database security, the ability to identify gaps, and the aptitude to recommend containment or mitigation controls are critical during a breach response. It will expedite the process of bringing systems back online in a secure manner.

Security Gap Assessment

To state the obvious, security breaches have causes, and those causes need to be enumerated. As such, there is a need to perform a security gap assessment for each breach and identify missing security controls. At the very least, the response team (with input from appropriate SMEs) should perform a gap assessment of the failed controls that led to the security breach.

However, to ensure attackers do not re-enter via other vulnerabilities, it is advisable to expand the gap assessment to enumerate all likely intrusion methods and recommended controls to secure the environment. If done right, this will avoid playing whack-o-mole with intruders and enable the security team to fully contain the environment and/or affected resources. Even if it is not possible to plug the gaps and implement recommended or temporary compensating controls during the response process, all gaps and recommendations should be captured as lessons learned in a final report.

After all, if the gaps weren't known ahead of time and aren't enumerated and documented as part of the investigation or recovery and security validation, then when would they be discovered? Don't miss the opportunity to lay all the problems out on the table and hold resource owners accountable.

Reporting

Every incident involving a bypass of security controls that gets detected and investigated should have a report that accompanies it. It must document the details of the incident, the actions of the investigators, the findings of the investigation, and the recommendations that come from it. This is very important for regulatory compliance and legal concerns that may arise in either the short or long term. Incident responders need to perform their investigation in such a way as to build toward that report and gather all relevant content to support it.

Further, the final report will outlive the incident. It is the only exposure that some individuals (such as customer executives) will have with the incident or the respective incident response team. As such, the report should be well-written and stand on its own or have supporting documents called out within the report and provided along with it. Supporting documents usually include lists of exposed content, accounts, regulated data, or analysis documents.

Subject Matter Experts (SMEs) for Affected Resources

Regardless of how qualified an incident response team the Incident Commander is able to build, there will always be a need for dedicated subject matter experts who support the environment(s) in question. They are usually dedicated blue-team personnel who perform a development or administrative function.

Having those resources engaged in response activity will save a tremendous amount of time as they can more easily answer questions regarding "how is the system intended to work?" and can help spot anomalies that might be related to an incident or provide guidance on how responders can obtain the data they need to analyze.

However, it is also important to recognize that these individuals may also have contributed to the problem, and it is best to use them in an advisory function and have the incident response personnel gather and process all artifacts (as much as possible) from a conflict-of-interest perspective. Moreover, sometimes subject matter experts might inadvertently (or deliberately) stomp on or delete evidence due to a lack of familiarity with forensic processes or a desire to suppress the knowledge of the root cause.

Further, if these individuals are part of an insider threat scenario, their involvement can significantly compromise an investigation. So, the Incident Commander must always use the best rationale when engaging SMEs and determining how to use them. This is always a judgment call that should be considered carefully.

3 INCIDENT MANAGEMENT REQUIREMENTS

Leading or performing incident management is also highly technical and very advanced, similar to incident response, but not to the same degree or in the same way. With incident management, the Incident Commander or Incident Manager does not need to maintain as deep of technical skills as are required for incident response investigators. However, the Incident Commander or Manager still needs to be intimately familiar with all of the incident response concepts in order to guide the overall investigation and gauge the efficacy or accuracy of findings. The Incident Commander/Manager typically must rely on other technical resources to perform deep-dive investigation and analysis tasks.

The reason for this is that the Incident Commander cannot simultaneously be "heads-up" performing the incident management role and "heads-down" doing technical deep-dives needed for incident response. During cybersecurity incident investigations, it is difficult, if not impossible, to function in a technical capacity (performing deep-dive analysis) and an incident command capacity (incident management and oversight) simultaneously.

In most cases, the Incident Commander/Manager will lead a team of technical experts focused on the analysis and security posture of specialized and/or overlapping areas within the evidence universe. This will be used to accomplish investigative actions, containment needs, and/or remediation objectives identified by legal/compliance teams, executive leadership, customer needs, or the overall needs of the investigation according to best practices.

Finding the right person to perform the incident command role is very hard to do, as it is challenging to find all of these skill sets in one person. Being lucky enough to identify people with technical skills who can resist the urge to dive into the depths of an investigation and ignore everything else is hard enough. However, it is even harder to identify people with project management and executive communication skills who can assess, understand, and guide the technical aspects of an investigation. When you are trying to hire for this, you might feel like you are trying to find a bigfoot who has extensive experience with riding and training unicorns.

The skill sets required include knowledge of conducting investigations, containment, vulnerability mitigation, and full remediation of networks, services, applications, logs, content, and the underlying system types and data elements. Without a firm foundation in technical skills, it is not possible to drive the incident management process forward to a successful conclusion or to accomplish and/or validate all of the required workstreams along the way.

Further, in addition to a strong background in incident response and incident management, acting as an Incident Commander/Manger requires a long list of more business- and executive-friendly soft skills. The bullet points below enumerate many of the skills that are most commonly found or used by the CyberSecurity Incident Commander/Manager for the purposes of full lifecycle incident management. This extends well before and after a cybersecurity incident and requires a holistic program with a continuity of vision. This list is far from comprehensive, and there should be a flashing neon sign for "other duties undefined." Each one of these skill sets and justifications will be explored individually.

Key Incident Commander/Manager Skillsets

- Program development
- Incident management framework
- Product evaluation framework
- Program management
- Compliance requirements/guidelines
- Laws, ordinances, and guidelines
- Security best practices
- Executive presence
- Strong communication skills
- Extreme patience

Program Development

Incident management ideally starts prior to the occurrence of a security incident and includes planning for threats the organization will likely face. In actuality, for most organizations, incident management begins after an organization has experienced a breach and people begin running around in a panicked state. Following that, they realize they need a better plan and hopefully start developing one.

This should involve developing an incident management program that will include detailed plans for the people, processes, and technology within the customer environment and partner or connected vendor environments. This plan must evolve and be updated with the evolving threat landscape, changes in capabilities, and/or lessons learned from future incidents that identify the need for changes in the program.

Incident Management Framework

Because implementing and managing the full lifecycle cybersecurity incident management process is so detailed, complicated, and individualized per organization, incident management program development should utilize a framework to guide all phases from end to end. From a very high level, this includes the planning, development, implementation, execution, program evolution, and all intermediary sub-processes, workflows, and components.

There are many incident management frameworks in existence, as well as generic incident management plans that theoretically work for fictional generic companies. However, to be effective, everything needs to be customized to an organization for it to fit like a glove and function optimally. Developing a program is very complex and combines multiple disciplines that might not be fully fleshed out unless a comprehensive program is utilized. This book utilizes a 13-step Incident Management Framework (IMF) to thoroughly map out the threat landscape, customer environment, and all of the content, capabilities, and needs for incident response and management.

Product Evaluation Framework

There is often the need to have the Incident Commander/Manager involved in product evaluations to determine the viability of solutions for detection, response, investigation, or other security needs. This is common with respect to incident planning or follow-up to acquire security products or services to fill known gaps.

When performing vendor selection to identify technologies and capabilities to facilitate incident response, the evaluation team should develop a product evaluation framework. It should enumerate all requirements and the key functions, features, methodologies, and capabilities of all of the respective products.

It is very common for vendors to claim comprehensive capabilities and complete victory over various workflows and security threats. There are many claims of being a "market leader" of a certain capability, even if they only kind of do it in a limited capacity. Moreover, products will often address the same need using completely different methods, some of which have greater efficacy than others. In fact, the best way to tell if vendors are lying is to watch them closely and see if their lips are moving. Of course, your mileage may vary, and discernment is absolutely critical.

As such, it is very important to independently assess if products or services can or will be successful. To do this, the participants must distinguish whether the methods used by the individual tools would be successful under the intended conditions in which they would be applied and how they would perform in comparison to other options. The volumetric scale of usage is also an important consideration in that some products function very well on a small scale of 1-500 but will completely fail on a large scale of 100,000 – 250,000.

Program Management

Incident management includes the planning and oversight of multiple projects and/or responses, often simultaneously. Quite frequently, a single incident will spawn multiple distinct responses with different groups representing different technologies or data sets.

The Incident Commander/Manager is the individual holding all of these response activities together and rolling up the findings and statuses to leadership. This type of activity will involve coordination with numerous departments, personnel, resources, technologies, prerequisites, and timelines. It is critical that the team has one or more individuals experienced with performing program management, cross-project correlation, and orchestration activities to keep everything in sync.

Regulatory Compliance Requirements and Guidelines

To effectively plan for incidents and drive them to successful completion, the Incident Commander/Manager or supporting member of the compliance team must understand the regulatory compliance requirements, guidelines, and respective reporting timelines associated with them as they pertain to incident management concerns. The regulatory compliance requirements differ and sometimes overlap and/or conflict by industry vertical, payment methods, data types, regions, and other factors. Overlaps and conflicts usually pertain to reporting timelines or security requirements.

Companies are generally safe if they go with the strictest requirements. However, knowing what those are is an essential requirement, and new regulations come almost every year and could apply at various levels (location, data type, industry, etc.). While a lot of regulatory ink has been written, it is still very much a nascent space. It lacks holistic alignment between different regulatory requirements and the specificity of controls needed to keep systems secure and data safe.

Laws and Ordinances

Just like with regulatory compliance, the Incident Commander/Manager or supporting member of the legal team must understand the applicable laws and ordinances that would influence the incident management program development or drive the incident response investigation itself. This becomes particularly dynamic when it comes to case law, which evolves quickly, particularly in the information security space. Moreover, there are many laws on the books that have never been tested in court, which may or may not be interpreted differently based on a ruling in a court case.

It is critical to have a well-informed member of the legal team to help drive the investigation and keep the company and practitioners out of trouble. Laws differ by jurisdiction, company type, industry vertical, data types, region, and other factors. This could mean having various individuals who are knowledgeable about the various geographic areas.

Laws are particularly complicated outside of the United States, and it becomes difficult when trying to do investigations in foreign countries. Some countries like Great Britain, Germany, or anything in the EU can be problematic. Without the right people involved, these laws and ordinances are fraught with danger.

Security and Investigative Best Practices

Part of developing incident management programs, implementing containment/mitigation controls, or deriving lessons learned and follow-up actions from incidents is possessing an awareness of best practices in applicable areas. As such, Incident Commanders/Managers or assigned team members must always have their heads up, their eyes forward, and drive toward applicable security best practices or reasonable compensating controls to develop robust programs and better secure compromised environments. This part is harder than it sounds. Business needs often get in the way of implementing security best practices, and team members have to make tough decisions about implementing compensating controls to protect porous environments.

Executive Presence

An Incident Commander/Manager is the voice of the investigation and must be prepared to present and authoritatively provide guidance to groups at any level within the organization relative to all phases of incident response/management. These groups may range from senior leadership or board of directors down to technical teams or anywhere in between.

As such, Incident Commanders/Managers need to be able to speak various dialects of technical, business, legal, compliance, and any other communication style that may be required. Each of these groups of stakeholders will require their own communication style and level of technical details. All of the target audiences require the Incident Commander/Manager to have an executive presence to build credibility and instill confidence that what is being presented or proposed is the right course of action.

Strong Communication Skills

In addition to being able to adapt one's communication styles to different audiences, the Incident Commander/Manager must be strong in all areas of communication and presentation. These include creating and conveying information using any common method or format. Communication and presentation skills will be used to convey the agreed-upon vision amongst the various groups and are key for the program management and reporting functions to obtain alignment. A critical element of this is being able to translate between the various parties, which is mostly translating technical-speak to leadership-speak or vice versa.

These communication delivery methods include verbal communication, written documentation, visual diagram creation, flowchart workflow creation, and any other method used to share the incident management vision. Moreover, the Incident Commander/Manager must be experienced and comfortable summarizing distilled concepts or expanding technical details as appropriate for the various audiences and their respective needs. Considering the wide variety of audiences the Incident Commander/Manager must present to, it is critical not to be too technically detailed. Successful communication at that level must summarize or distill the content yet be able to expand into technical details and substantive proof as requested.

Extreme Patience

By way of warning, every workflow under the incident management umbrella (from planning to execution to follow-up – which, by the way, means even more planning) involves a significant degree of change. It usually happens under expedited timeframes and has a high potential for conflict. Quite often, emergency changes need to be made to block ongoing malicious activities, and there may be no time to test the impact of making these containment-related changes and results.

Sometimes, there are unintended consequences, and business processes are inadvertently impacted when trying to block malicious activity. Change-induced problems caused by rapidly implemented containment measures often lead to conflicts with business units and leadership. This can be a no-win situation.

Further, every incident has a cause. Oftentimes, during the process of responding to an incident, it is identified that entities involved in the response or managing the compromised infrastructure are culpable for the breach, either due to inaction or error. These types of situations can be embarrassing and tend to create a stressful environment. This can easily put people on edge, considering all of these potential risks, the possible impact on the customer, and the personal and professional jeopardy to those involved with the affected technology or failed security controls.

It is the Incident Commander's responsibility to set the correct tone for the incident management and response activity. It is extremely important that blame never be discussed and that the Incident Commander and all incident management/response staff generate extreme patience, even when others may be behaving at their worst. If done properly, this will carry over to the rest of the group and help prevent tense situations from turning into hostile ones. Think of it as high-stakes adult babysitting.

4 ESSENTIAL SOFT SKILLS & COMMUNICATIONS

Value Proposition

The value of Soft Skills during incident management cannot be understated. It is critical to remember that the response team is often walking into a hostile environment laced with political landmines, and all the technical skills in the world are not enough to make the response completely successful. In order to bring it all together and make the response effort a success, the Soft Skills that are needed to pull this off include everything in the following list, each of which will be discussed in detail:

- Providing leadership
- Establishing trust
- Fostering good relationships
- Never play the blame game
- Let facts speak for themselves
- Set reliable expectations
- Continuity of vision
- Continuous improvement

Providing Leadership
Methodology

To set the stage from a fundamental level, the customer is requesting assistance with incident response and management activity. They need leadership on how to respond to or prepare for computer security incidents or the threat of the same. Customers are not professional incident managers or responders, have a narrowly focused view, and usually do not have the experience, resources, or skill sets necessary to handle incidents themselves.

Even if customers do have internal incident response and management capabilities, their view is mostly limited (except external threat intel) to what happens inside of their environment. As such, they have myopic visibility to only the campaigns, malware, and specific threats they face, rather than exposure to a broad customer base and having fought similar campaigns in multiple customer environments. Except in large environments, most internal response capabilities are roles that fall on IT members for which they are typically ill-equipped and ill-suited. Long story short, this is why the incident response/management fields exist.

For incident response/management consulting divisions, it is common for response teams to respond to the same threat again and again across the country at different customer sites. This typically happens in various waves of customer industry verticals, such as insurance companies, credit unions, other banks by size, retailers, healthcare providers, etc. Each time teams respond to the threat, they become more proficient and quicker at stomping it out.

The attacker methodology is to create an attack campaign for a particular type of environment and then use it everywhere that is similar. Following that, they will modify it to suit a different slightly purpose and start the process over again. As such, experience with responding to the specific threat is critical in leading the customer through the process in an expedited manner.

Moreover, response personnel need to be recognized as the smartest and most trusted people in the room at all times. This includes always having a plan and showing how each action relates to the entire process and provides value individually or as part of the whole.

This is a very tall order and requires the people in this role to always be at the top of their game. The customer needs to see the response team as a unified, one-stop resource to address any question, concern, or request. This means that they do not deflect requests, but instead, they must make note of requirements and make sure they are accomplished.

Setting the Right Tone

More than just providing methodology, establishing the right tone is important. Customers are often scared, confused, panicked, and quite possibly angry. They will feed off the response team members' queues. When providing leadership, it is important to provide a sense of confidence and reassurance – not to be mistaken for arrogance. Convey an attitude of "You have successfully beat this before, and you will partner with the customer and respective personnel in their environment to do it again."

Some people will see response personnel as their savior. However, no matter what response team members do, others may see them as a threat to their jobs. Those who perceive response personnel as a threat often do so because responders might identify evidence that they did something wrong, which could place them at blame for the intrusion.

Response personnel need to be able to navigate a wide variety of complicated factors during an engagement. These include challenging situations like handling difficult personalities, remaining calm under pressure, navigating response needs vs. business needs, directing the customer personnel, and avoiding interpersonal drama and political pitfalls. It may seem at times like performing highly technical babysitting in a war zone.

As such, response personnel must always be recognized as respected and impartial subject matter experts who can authoritatively speak to the current status of an investigation and articulate the entire process. They are there to lead the customer through the response process, which includes minimizing drama.

Collaboration and Communication

Successful incident response engagements require collaboration between incident management/response personnel and customer personnel – AKA the consultant and the customer. Customers understand and can navigate their environment better than outside parties, regardless of how smart they are.

It is important for response personnel to focus on providing leadership to customer personnel and guide them on how to detect and respond to threats within their environment. More specifically, the response team should focus on what investigative strategies need to take place, and the customer personnel should carry out the instructions and provide results from the respective data sources.

In addition to knowledge of the environment, response personnel cannot usually make changes themselves. They typically can (and should) only recommend actions or changes to the environment that need to be carried out by knowledgeable customer personnel.

It is highly inadvisable for the incident response team to make changes to the environment directly as they are likely to result in business impact if not executed with proper consideration for business-critical dataflows. Oftentimes, collateral damages from changed-induced outages are perceived as worse than the incident itself – don't be that guy.

Interestingly, in most environments, people are more likely to be fired due to a change-induced outage than a cybersecurity incident. So, earning customer respect and obtaining their insight and cooperation is essential to the success of any response. After all, they know their environment, systems, applications, and other resources better than the response team does or would ever need to. Insight from customer SMEs is critical to all phases of the response process.

The most important Incident Management skill is communication and being able to develop and convey a plan in a way all involved parties can understand and execute. It is one thing to share it, but a completely different thing for people to understand your plan or vision.

Usually, this involves visual aids, such as a whiteboard (actually many whiteboards) – the more, the better. It has been said many times that a whiteboard is the most powerful incident management tool ever made. It is critical to get all of the key players in a room, looking at the same whiteboard and nodding their heads at the same time.

The objective is to visually lay out the environment and critical components, threats, capabilities, and resources. This includes the entire evidence universe, key objects of investigation, response tools, and all of the details of the investigation. The incident management components include action items, owners, prerequisites, roadblocks, statuses, all steps, etc.

- Affected networks – It is important to know what is in-scope and what is not, as it drives the response, investigation, and containment activities.
- Compromised systems – It is critical to know what must be immediately contained to prevent spread and leakage.
- Critical assets – It is critical to identify the highest priorities for monitoring and protecting and to determine the focus of containment, mitigation, or initial remediation processes.
- Network chokepoints – The response team needs to identify anywhere network monitoring and blocking controls should exist or need to be implemented.
- Ingress/egress locations – It is essential to understand every way that attackers, malware C2, and data can come and go in or out of or between networks.
- Security/investigative devices – The response team must develop an understanding of all of the security capabilities that they have to work with and determine what needs to be added.
- Investigative plan – The Incident Commander/Manager needs to lay out the steps of the overall plan so everyone knows what to expect and prepare for.
- Action items – Clearly detail each step, purpose, affected resource, prerequisite, roadblock, & estimated time of completion.
- Task assignments – Identify teams, accountable parties, accountable leaders for escalation, and related programs or projects.
- Respective statuses – Always maintain up-to-date statuses for all tasks in real-time, so they can be provided (if asked) without research

Incident Management requires coordination and organization of investigative resources, tasks, communications, and the overall messaging. The Incident Commander/Manager should be the central point of this organization, and communication related to the incident (both from the customer and the consultants) should be needed to accomplish the documented or improvised steps within the incident management playbooks or ad-hoc based on investigative needs.

The Incident Commander/Manager must collaborate with the customer to identify the required resources, respectively, for playbook steps, data sources, investigative capabilities, constraints, etc. Having the Incident Commander/Manager manage the communications and resources will ensure a central, organized flow to the investigation and communication in alignment with guidance from leadership and the needs of the investigation.

It will also avoid the all-too-common problem created by the fog of war where participants try to act on competing or conflicting requests they have received from multiple sources. There should be one message delivered in a consistent format at a reliable time frame that everyone uses to obtain the current investigation status and investigative needs.

Remember, providing clear guidance/training, articulating steps, and keeping customer resources engaged are essential to the customer experience. It is not enough to be heard. The Incident Commander/Manager and responders must make sure they are understood. This means that they need to learn the customer's communication style and speak their language.

The only person one really controls is oneself. It is easier for the Incident Commander/Manager to learn the customer's communication style and speak their language than for the customers and their team members to do the same.

If the customer's personnel do not understand the requested task(s), are not fully engaged, or begin to doubt the response personnel, the engagement will likely begin to experience problems. When this happens, the outcome of the response activity will be in doubt, and customer satisfaction will be at risk. This could have a negative impact on the customer relationship in both the short and long term.

Establishing Trust

Establishing lasting trust within a team in any situation always starts with an environment of mutual respect and camaraderie among team members. One of the first things an Incident Commander/Manager should do, especially to get past big egos, is to admit that 1) He/she cannot do this alone, 2) The team holds the keys to success as they understand how the systems work and can access the needed content, and 3) Ask for everyone's help as the response team is going to sink or swim together.

The biggest trick is getting a bunch of alpha players with big egos and various biases to set them aside and listen to other people's ideas so that the group can collaborate on identifying and resolving issues. Unless there are significant confidentiality concerns, and there is a need to drastically restrict communications to a small set of need-to-know individuals, responding to incidents is an all-hands-on-deck scenario for technical personnel and stakeholders.

The response process functions best by giving people their own assignments for which they are best suited out of a larger pool of work. Each person or group should have their individual tasks and deliverables suited to their skill sets and responsibilities, which tasks are chosen from a common pool of tasks that the whole group works down.

However, avoid separating tasks or teams in any way that could create "us vs. them" mentalities that become barriers to communication and sometimes result in blame and hostility. If you are not careful, this may happen.

While it is true that temporary alliances, kind of like gangs, are built with divisive mentalities, it is not productive in the long term. This is especially true when you need all team members from various groups to rely on each other and work together during extended hours and weekends.

In order to get all the right ideas and information out on the table, it is critical to encourage the sharing of ideas and potential concerns. Sometimes, people with the most information about affected resources are the quietest, as they have the most risk. Moreover, people may be afraid to speak up for safety reasons, and most people are reluctant to be the first.

Getting past that usually involves asking sample questions or potential negative observations (even if silly, outlandish, or humorous) to get the conversation started and make it safe for people to share ideas they might be reluctant to come right out and express. Sometimes, you have to overtly pull feedback out of people to get the discussion started by calling them by name and asking if they have any thoughts or concerns.

Most importantly, when people do speak up, even if they are off base, try to find the validity in their viewpoints and recognize that everyone provides value. If you shut people down for whatever reason, it will discourage anyone else from speaking up.

Irrespective of whether incident management resources are internal to an organization or come in from the outside as consultants, the best approach is to treat the business or other entity that they work for as a valued customer. Throughout this book, we will refer to the entity for whom incident management/response or other information security services are being performed as the customer. This is really important to remember, as the customer ultimately has all the power and must choose to follow the guidance of the incident management team. Keep in mind that the business teams are the customers, and the response teams are the consultants. If the customers "aren't buying," the project cannot be successful.

Security professionals literally have to find ways to sell the customer on the value of incident response, security controls, and stopping the spread of malware or data loss affecting their business-critical systems and applications. Even if the security team has the authority to force security controls and policy/procedure into being, it does not mean the customer will actually follow them. The customer must choose to make good decisions and obey security requirements.

It is key to remember that without customer cooperation and participation, incident response, containment, remediation, and mitigating security security controls will fail. A successful response requires access to customers' personnel, systems, knowledge, authorization, or other resources to make it successful. The security and response teams cannot be successful without customer support and participation, as the resource owners must live with it and pay for it.

While it is easy to say or intend to maintain good relations with the customer, it requires a careful plan and constant diligence. Long story short, incident management and response personnel need to stay above the interpersonal fray and always remain a neutral, objective, authoritative source of information. Succinctly stated, it is essential to do four things, which will be covered in more detail:
1. Foster good relationships
2. Never play the blame game

3. Let facts speak for themselves
4. Set reliable expectations.

Fostering Good Relationships

During incident response activity, access to critical resources is not inherently assumed or granted and is typically earned by developing and maintaining good relationships with the customer. It is incredibly helpful to have these relationships and processes established ahead of time.

The customer needs to feel safe that response personnel are there to help them and not throw them under the bus. The Incident Commander/Manager should make a specific point of stating that there is a "no throwing people under the bus rule."

Situations arise where people are closely tied to failures, which are often closely aligned with specific people, processes, and/or technology. It may become the case that inadequacies or incompetence become clear. As such, it is always helpful to give the affected parties an "honorable out" (or an assumed reasonable explanation). This will help avoid their embarrassment and enable the response team and subject matter experts to focus on solving technology and process problems, provide required workarounds, develop compensating controls, and communicate or escalate as necessary.

Be aware that security and particularly response personnel may inherently have a lot of influence, particularly after a significant incident. Long story short, their words will carry weight, and the words spoken need to be chosen carefully.

Information security and particularly incident management/response personnel are often greeted with suspicion, and customers may be reluctant to provide access to anything that could place them at further risk or make them look bad. Sometimes, the customer may not provide the response team with any access at all if they feel it is in their best interest not to.

On a personal note, the author once spent a week on an IR engagement sitting in the company lobby because the security team wanted a qualified external expert to prove the IT team was not doing their job, and it led to a security breach. The IT team objected and would not let the author past the lobby, and he sat there for a week at $350 per hour as neither side would give in.

Security incidents never happen because customers have perfect security controls and processes. Incidents usually happen as a result of a lapse in security (whether people, processes, and/or technology) and generally some sort of combination of at least 2 of the 3. Moreover, there is often a cascading effect resulting from an incident that goes well beyond the initial attack vector.

Long story short, the existing controls and processes did not work. Just as there should be defense-in-depth to protect environments and data, incidents are caused not only by individual security gaps but also by the lack of depth of security controls. Said another way, security-gaps-in-depth is the opposite of defense-in-depth and leads to security breaches.

As such, this results in the need to implement additional technology to provide visibility and blocking controls (typically network, endpoint, or log aggregation) to augment the failed visibility and blocking controls. These will also facilitate the investigation, containment, and remediation steps of the incident response activity.

Not only is someone responsible for the existence of the security gaps, but they are likely also needed to implement the solution. It is not helpful to discuss their culpability or create embarrassment that would alienate them during the incident. The response team needs to partner with them to design and implement the solution(s).

As the incident's root cause is identified and security gaps are enumerated, the accountability and responsibility for the incident will become clear. People will often begin to start pointing fingers. This is a perfect opportunity to listen and observe rather than get involved.

Also, try as they might, do not let anyone use your fingers to point at them. Stick to the facts of the case, diligently document observations and findings, and stay out of the drama. The middle of an investigation or response activity is not the time to assign or discuss blame.

Regarding capturing investigative findings, all observations of capabilities, gaps, and subsequent recommendations should be documented within the case notes and broken down into strengths, weaknesses, and recommendations pertaining to people, processes, and technology. But, in doing so, you are going to have to call somebody's baby ugly.

Make a point to let people know ahead of time if you are going to bring something up as a recommendation that might make them, their department, or technology look bad. It is helpful to invite them to contribute to the discussion and the contents of the report and to use the investigation findings to help them get more support and additional resources.

This means helping them use the incident to improve their situation. Frame gaps as opportunities and support for their security program for which the response team can help them gain support. Make sure they are aware that the response team can help them use the incident findings and recommendations as justifications to make necessary changes in people, processes, and technology. The customer SMEs probably already know they need to improve their security posture, but they have not been able to justify it. Ensure the customer knows that the response team's intention and focus is the customer's success and supporting their security endeavors. This may be the opportunity they need to improve their security.

Never Play the Blame Game

Incidents are inherently stressful situations, and reputations, careers, money, and the survival of businesses are on the line. It is entirely likely that if a significant breach occurs and notable gaps reveal blatant errors, then somebody may get fired. Some incidents and investigative findings can be career-destroying or even company-ending events.

Quite literally, a severe security incident involving sensitive data loss combined with the culpability for regulatory non-compliance may be the beginning of the end for victim companies. They could lose customer confidence and will likely face significant fines from multiple sources and other legal actions. It is common for large companies to face lawsuits and penalties from the following sources:

1) The Security and Exchange Commission – For companies that are publicly traded
2) State Attorneys General/Department of Justice agencies – Usually involves the attorneys general from each state for all states having affected customers
3) Federal Trade Commission (FTC) – Consumer protection and misrepresentation
4) Health and Human Services (HHS)/Office of Civil Rights (OCR) – Applies to companies affected by a compromise of HIPAA data
5) Banks and payment card providers can impose fines and processing restrictions if financial instruments are affected
6) Customers may file individual or class-action lawsuits

All included, per the 2023 Ponemon Institute/IBM Cost of a Data Breach Report, the average cost per record involved in a data breach was $165 across all industry types. The average total cost of data breaches reached $4.45M across all industries, with the average healthcare breach tipping the scales at $10.93M. This is an increase of over 53% since 2020. If large numbers are involved, these costs can be devastating to a company or organization, especially if they are larger than average. (IBM, 2023)

These are very high-stakes situations, and the potential impact of large breaches may range from severe to catastrophic. There is an extreme tendency within rival factions of companies (usually between IT operations teams and information security teams) or between stressed-out leaders to immediately start blaming each other during incidents. It is not unheard of for fistfights to break out over security incidents and the stresses involved.

Sometimes, opposing entities will attempt to use incidents to score political points and related findings as a sword, a shield, or both. Response teams need to be aware that various people or groups may try to engage incident response personnel or their findings to support their assertions and bolster their arguments. Responders should try to reserve their comments to avoid being taken out of context.

While it can be tempting and somewhat natural to slip into the blame game and assign responsibility for an incident, it is extremely unwise. It will almost always backfire and result in a lack of cooperation within the company that could complicate the investigation. It will also impair the team's ability to develop and implement containment, mitigation, recovery, and remediation solutions. As Einstein said, "It is not possible to prepare for war and peace simultaneously," and there is no way to unify a team by building walls in the middle of one.

Incident participants need to feel they are in a no-judgment environment. The best way to do this is to remain focused on the technical aspects of the response efforts and identify specific recommendations to improve the situation, but not dig into who is at fault. Usually, people inherently know that anyway, so there is no reason to focus on it.

To be quite candid, once that line is crossed, there is really no going back, and the cross-collaboration team that the Incident Commander/Manager and responders worked so hard to create will begin to unravel. Placing blame and choosing sides results in an irredeemable loss of the unbiased status, trust, and credibility that was previously established, particularly with anyone on the receiving end of that blame.

Moreover, others will also wonder if they are next. At this point, the response team might be perceived as a threat and will undoubtedly begin to encounter resistance. The group that weaponized the response team will certainly be very supportive, but it will begin to be more difficult to get needed support from other groups.

The only way to win this game is not to play in the first place. Walk away and keep the response team's unbiased, 3rd party status from being impacted. It is as easy as saying, "Let's not discuss blame at this stage." If pressed on it at a later stage or in reporting, you can just say, "The facts speak for themselves," and then focus on the specific deficiencies within people, processes, and/or technology, but stay away from implicating specific parties.

Let Facts Speak for Themselves

The best strategy to remain a trusted, unbiased third party is to find definitive evidence and let facts speak for themselves. More specifically, the most reliable way to build and maintain the level of credibility and trust required to successfully complete an incident management engagement is to affirmatively establish the facts and root cause(s) of the case through the identification of conclusive, corroborated evidence.

Then, let that evidence tell the story and support the narrative. In that way, the customer can trust evidence instead of relying upon opinion.

Conversely, the best way to lose credibility is to make assumptions or push unfounded theories that turn out to be wrong! Opinions are not facts, and they usually just create drama.

Facts are what truly matter, and they stand on their own if properly revealed. When performing in an investigative role, it is important not to speculate, opine, blame, or jump to any unfounded conclusions. Using facts to tell the story also helps avoid situations where investigators could make assumptions or draw unfounded conclusions.

Focusing on facts also helps by avoiding placing unnecessary focus on the people/victims involved in an incident. Instead, it focuses attention on the evidence artifacts, indicators of compromise, and threat vectors, which leads to the identification and enumeration of root cause(s), containment actions, and remediation items.

More specifically, if people are the victims of an incident and not the perpetrators (such as if they happen to be malicious actors), it is not overly productive to focus on them as the subject of investigation and ongoing discussion.

It is true that investigators need to explore their access, identify what could have been compromised using their account(s), and reset their passwords. However, overly focusing on victims rather than security gaps and methods of exploitation is unnecessary and creates needless drama. It often creates embarrassment and comes off like bullying to those on the receiving end of it. If they are malicious actors, however, then focus away as it will become critical to understand the full scope and implications of their access and activity.

Something else to consider and another reason it is not a great idea to focus on victims is that sooner or later, everyone will be a victim. Social engineering, waterhole attacks, and other advanced cybersecurity threats can be very sophisticated and could affect anyone.

Everyone is a target. Given unpatched or zero-day security vulnerabilities, everyone could be a victim. As such, it is best to focus on the facts of the case, which involve security threats, attack vectors, and deficiencies that allowed them, as well as preventing future exploits.

Focusing on facts is especially important in incident communications. These succinct, factual statements will outlive the incident and may drive a host of changes for some time to come. Make sure these statements convey the story that should be remembered from the incident and provide justification for needed changes.

A couple of examples are in order. Example 1 – an undesirable way to represent the findings from an incident would be to state the following, even if true: "

> *It is the fault of David from Sales, who fell for a phishing email scam and clicked on a link that downloaded and executed malware that spread all across the environment and stole data that has regulatory implications and may require public disclosure."*

Example 2 – a better way to state the specific facts of the case would be to stipulate the following details:

> *"Corp-WS-0354, a vulnerable workstation in sales – used by David, was the point of origin. The attack vector was a malicious link contained in a phishing email to the corporate email account. When clicked, the link accessed a malicious JavaScript exploit from the affected system. The JavaScript downloaded a malicious PowerShell script, which deployed the encoded, embedded malware that replicated across the environment. The malware then searched, identified, and exfiltrated all files with .xls(x), .doc(x), and .pdf extensions. Some of these files have sensitive information with regulatory compliance impact and may require a public disclosure."*

So, let's identify key strengths, weaknesses, and potential for problems with each example. Example 1 is inflammatory and provides little factual evidence. It is almost assured to result in embarrassment and bad feelings. This will lead to needless drama and obstacles.

Example 2 provides actionable information that identifies the root cause, attack vector, and exploit method. It provides a clear path for containment and remediation. This method is more powerful as it is fact-based and inherently drives the need for remediation through enumeration of the gaps and providing a starting place for recommendations. Moreover, it tells a way better story.

Set Reliable Expectations

All throughout an incident, but especially at the beginning, there will be pressure to provide definitive information at expedited timeframes. The customer's leadership needs to report to senior executive leadership, such as the board of directors. They need status updates with appropriate findings data from the incident management team to do it.

It may initially make the customer happy if the investigator provides ambitious estimates according to customer desires. However, if the information turns out to be wrong or the expedited timelines are not met, it will quickly turn into a bad situation that erodes credibility. Members of the response team can go from hero to zero with a single missed expectation or false report.

It is always better to provide a reasonable, realistic timeframe by which analysis can be completed. It is even better to pad the time estimates a little, just in case there are delays or other problems, which are very common. As the saying goes, it is better to under-promise and over-deliver than be perceived as unreliable for missing deadlines, which would quickly erode trust.

Customers and leadership will set expectations based on the Incident Commander's or responder's estimates. If they are not met, everyone looks bad, and trust has evaporated. It is always better to set realistic expectations and defend them. Even if customers don't like it at first, they will respect you for it later, and they will know they can trust you. More specifically, identify the tasks in progress, reasonable times of completion for each task, current investigative findings and observations, and then stand by them.

In addition to providing reasonable estimates for individual analysis tasks, also make sure to avoid being over-presumptive on timing for overall incident resolution. At the beginning of an incident, you don't know what you don't know, and you really have no idea what you are getting into without fully exploring the evidence universe and determining the impact. More specifically, until the full scope of an incident is known, all affected nodes and threats identified are contained, and potentially compromised datasets are identified, it is unrealistic to provide reliable estimates for investigation completion.

Once it is all laid out on the table, and there is the ability to affirmatively establish the full scope of work remaining, then it is possible to provide final estimates. Just as with any form of program or project management, there is a need to enumerate all of the steps, prerequisites, or roadblocks.

It is also critical to make sure they are visible to customer leadership. In doing so, be specific. Identify and describe each of the "who, what, when, why, and how" questions. Leadership visibility of prerequisites and roadblocks often leads to additional resources or leverage to enable and/or expedite their resolution.

The speed of the investigation is always dependent on the ability to gather and analyze data. Based on the number of systems, the aggregate data size, storage media types, and the search or investigation type, it is mathematically possible to calculate how long individual systems or data sets will take to process. Some types of analysis are fairly consistent when it comes to searching and processing. Given adequate time and experience, any type of analysis will result in fairly consistent, average times for that type of analysis. For example, using experienced resources, full forensic analysis takes about 8-12 man-hours per affected system; volatile data analysis only takes about 2-3 hours per system; etc.

Huge surprises and delays can come about involving the time it takes to make evidence ready for shipping (compression and encryption), transport time, decryption/extract, data conversion, data import/acquisition, etc. Complications can arise from any task in the workflow, and these complications translate to more time. This is particularly true with large datasets or anything requiring some sort of decoding or translation. Essentially, complications involving these considerations can result in derailing estimate accuracy and result in blown timelines.

Continuity of Vision

One of the most essential soft skills for full-lifecycle incident management is providing continuity of vision across the entire incident management lifecycle, as well as the information security program as a whole. They are intertwined and inseparable. This starts with the proactive incident management preparation process, continues through reactive activity, and feeds lessons learned back into the proactive process, which augments the information security program.

The full scope of incident management begins well before an incident occurs and extends far beyond threat containment and reporting. It is essential for consistency, efficacy, and continued relevance of the incident management program, which is a continuous cycle. At all phases of full-lifecycle incident management, the Incident Commander/Manager should be looking for improvement items for any or all information security controls or response mechanisms.

A comprehensive incident management program ensures proper planning, deployment, testing, and maintenance of incident management functions and capabilities that are customized to address the customer's specific threat landscape, business needs, technology roadmap, and extant limitations.

A well-thought-out plan involves coverage for each of the people, processes, and technology sufficient to identify and respond to threats in the customer environment and all requirements to support it. Each of the categories within people, processes, and technology are significantly packed and complex. From a high level, they include the following nested sub-categories for which continuity of vision must be maintained:

People:
- Employees
- Contractors/consultants
- Partners/vendors

Processes:
- Policies
- Standards
- Procedures
- Plans
- Playbooks
- Workflows

Technology:
- Accounts
- Network
- Endpoint
- SIEM/Log correlation and threat feed integration

In order to provide a holistic, functional solution, the incident management program cannot be simply downloaded from a template on the Internet and directly applied to the customer. Long story short, it likely will not fit.

There is also a temptation to borrow a well-built incident management program from another company, and while there are similarities and many concepts carry over, it also will not fit. Each environment is unique, and a relevant incident management program cannot just be used, borrowed, begged, stolen, or otherwise repurposed from a template or another organization and used as-is.

A functional program demonstrating continuity of vision requires customization to the customer environment. It must be tailored to provide visibility, analysis, and response functions/capabilities across in-scope infrastructure and resources for all likely threats and use cases.

More specifically, a working incident management program must be fitted to the customer environment to properly respond to likely threats within their environment. It needs to be designed to protect a company's assets in alignment with business needs, regulatory requirements, and security capabilities.

A comprehensive incident management program demonstrating continuity of vision can be created utilizing the 13 domains in the Incident Management Framework (IMF), which will be discussed in more detail throughout this book:

13 Domains of the IMF
1. Identification – Identify critical assets, systems, user data, respective threats, attacks, and security capabilities.
2. Communication – Identify the ability to communicate and escalate/resolve action items.
3. Immediate Response – Identify the ability to immediately respond to and investigate identified threats using internal or external resources.
4. Containment – Identify capabilities to perform network and/or endpoint containment for identified threats.
5. Evidence Collection – Identify capabilities to collect all evidence types from the evidence universe.
6. Analysis – Identify the ability to perform analysis of all evidence types using internal or contracted personnel.
7. Mitigation – Identify the ability to patch, fix, or otherwise close vulnerabilities that resulted in a successful attack vector.
8. Legal counsel – Identify processes and access to legal counsel and the use thereof to protect communications.
9. Eradication – Identify the ability to affirmatively eradicate threats and related artifacts from the environment.
10. Reporting and Lessons Learned – Identify processes, capabilities, content, and maturity of reporting.
11. Remediation and Continuous Improvement – Identify capabilities for resolving issues and applying lessons learned.
12. Documentation – Identify quality and completeness of policies, procedures, plans, playbooks, and environment documentation.
13. Training and Testing – Identify the quality and completeness of the training program for users, admins, executives, and related threats.

Continuous Improvement

Even after an incident management program has been custom-crafted for the customer environment, it is not finished. It will always be a work in progress and in continual flux. Due to the evolution in the threat landscape, advancements in technology, changes within the customer environment, and findings from lessons learned identified in each incident, the incident management program must be updated to remain relevant. The longer it remains stagnant, the less relevant it will become.

It is critical to remember that continuous improvement applies to more than just technology or configuration changes. It is necessary to consider the need for changes within any or all of the people, processes, and/or technology. Changes in each of these categories involve a lot of time and usually money. Each one of these areas has its own respective challenges requiring planning, collaboration, and funding to overcome.

- People – Making changes or additions to human resources is a significant change that involves leadership at all affected levels, human resources, recruiting, and funding to pay for it all.
- Processes – Making changes or additions to the company processes require extensive collaboration, coordination, notification, training, and auditing to ensure changes are put in place without significant impact or risk to the organization.
- Technology – Depending upon the state of technology within the affected environment and the extant ability or inability to implement needed detection and blocking controls, this can become very expensive. New or replacement hardware, software, and licensing can be very expensive, often totaling 7, 8, or even 9 figures. Sometimes, these changes involve years of architecture, budgeting, planning, testing, implementation, and training.

For example, there are multiple entry points that drive changes. If it begins with threats, new threats may require additional capabilities, configurations, and playbooks for successful detection and response. This means that the threats have driven the need for changes in technology to detect them as well as the process for doing so. This, in turn, will drive the need to obtain personnel to staff the tasks or workflows identified within the new playbooks, which may be considered a drain or overtasking of existing resources.

If the starting point is new security and investigative capabilities, they require configuration and tuning that will enable deeper insights into malicious activity across the evidence universe. This results in the need for more use cases that will drive more detections, more response needs, and more people to staff them.

If the starting point is lessons learned, it drives the need for new capabilities in each of people, processes, and technology and the interrelation between the three. If done right, this is a continual cycle of changes, tuning, tweaking, and updating. It is basically a game of spy vs. spy.

Until the industry is in a situation where computers and automated responses can stop automated threats, there will be a continual arms race involving the need for an ever-increasing quantity of people, processes, and technology to respond to emergent threats.

5 INTRODUCTION TO THE INCIDENT MANAGEMENT FRAMEWORK (IMF)

While it is ideal to proactively create a thoroughly planned, architected, vetted, and tested incident management program before an incident, it seldom happens that way. Usually, the need to develop one is identified during or after a significant incident, when it becomes perfectly obvious to everyone that the response would have gone a lot better if there had been proper planning.

Further, based on the author's over 24 years of information security and incident response consulting experience involving thousands of entities of all sizes and markets, most companies are not prepared. Typically, if incident response or management plans exist, they are usually ad-hoc and incomplete. In general, they tend to be focused more on recovery than truly addressing cybersecurity threats or the incident management lifecycle.

Unless designed holistically, incident response/management plans often only address a limited subset of known problem points encountered during incidents at various times by the entity. As such, they almost always lack the end-to-end maturity that can be provided through the use of a holistic plan based on likely critical assets, personnel, threat scenarios, sources, misuse cases, and associated workflows.

A robust Incident Management Framework (IMF) that will be covered at a high level in this chapter is fully explored in Volume 2 of the Cybersecurity Incident Management Master's Guide series, which details the processes involved in incident management program development and evaluation. All of the incident response/management concepts included in this book will be framed in the context of the IMF and will conform to IMF requirements to facilitate best practices.

What is Needed

The IMF introduced in this section has been developed and enhanced to meet the aggressive threat and regulatory landscapes that have evolved over the last few decades. It has further been adapted through lessons learned in thousands of consulting engagements to meet business drivers, investigative needs, security best practices, and regulatory requirements. The IMF is a structured framework that can be used holistically to evaluate and plan full lifecycle incident management capabilities, with a focus on each of the four critical analysis and response target areas: 1) Accounts, 2) Networks, 3) 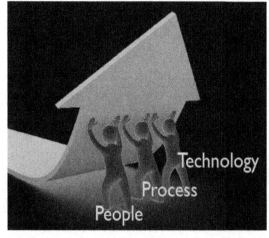 Endpoints, and 4) SIEM/logs. Further, Technology is broken down into three critical analysis and response target areas: Network, Endpoint, and SIEM/log analysis.

The IMF is ideal for use by entities involved in processing, storing, or transmitting any form of sensitive or proprietary information or having access to any environments with the same. It enables them to create and implement a robust information security program, including detection, response, investigation, eradication, remediation, operations support, and training capabilities that are compliant with all regulatory requirements (HIPAA, PCI-DSS, GLBA, SOX, FACTA, FERPA, FISMA, etc.), as well as audit frameworks and security best practices (NIST, ISO, COBIT, and others). Leveraging a structured program such as the IMF is the key to implementing security frameworks and best practices to meet or exceed regulatory requirements and protect the entity against modern cyber threats.

13 Incident Management Framework (IMF) Domains

The IMF methodology will cover the requirements needed to adequately detect and respond to cybersecurity incidents in today's evolving and persistently threatened landscape. The scope of the methodology includes mature guidance to enable preparation, testing, rapid detection, response, containment, mitigation, remediation, and recovery from actual breaches and to guide the processes throughout. The IMF is broken down into 13 separate domains, and an entity's information security and incident response capabilities are measured or designed against the same.

Following is a list and high-level explanations of the 13 IMF domains:
- Identification
- Communication
- Immediate Response
- Containment
- Evidence Collection
- Analysis
- Mitigation
- Legal and Compliance
- Eradication
- Reporting and Lessons Learned
- Remediation and Continuous Improvement
- Documentation
- Training and Testing

Identification Domain

The focus of the identification domain encompasses everything that is information security or incident response-related, or that affects the respective considerations, capabilities, and requirements within the entity's environment. This includes enumeration of key assets, people, processes, and technology within the customer environment, as well as anything that poses a risk or adversely affects it.

Inside the customer environment, this typically includes identification

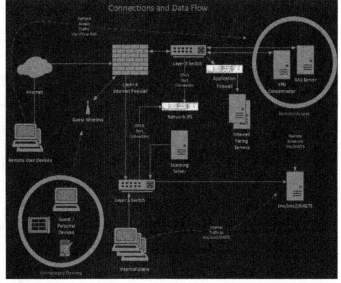

of all locations, policies, procedures, key networks, systems, services, applications, workstations, personnel, and data, as well as the security and monitoring controls in place to provide visibility, inspection, and protection of the same. Identification of threats includes a comprehensive look at internal or external threats, threat actors, capabilities, motivations, methods, malware, and the ability to detect related activity.

Communication Domain

The focus of the communication domain is the processes, protocols, contact lists, resource ownership lists, and escalation capabilities that the entity possesses and utilizes to communicate and respond to security and/or compliance events and incidents. The communication and escalation capabilities include those that are either internal or external to the organization. External communications include vendors, third-party service providers, law enforcement contacts, regulators, or others necessary for reporting requirements.

The workflows include the entity's ability to effectively communicate, assign responsibilities, escalate for the resolution of problems, and track all aspects of an incident from identification through resolution. This must also involve the identification and tracking of action items, lessons learned, and remediation tasks all the way through resolution and closure. This will usually extend far beyond the active phases of incident response.

Immediate Response Domain

The focus of the Immediate Response domain is the entity's ability to quickly respond using either internal or external resources and technologies to investigate a potential incident and ascertain the potential for malicious activity. Unless all monitoring and response are outsourced and integrated, internal resources are typically quicker, as external resources typically come with an SLA that is 4 hours or greater (sometimes much greater) – that is a long time.

Incidents can move very quickly, and without the ability to respond rapidly, they can quickly get out of hand and possibly compromise the entire environment. The longer the threat goes without a response, the greater the risk to the confidentiality, integrity, and availability of systems, services, and data within the affected environment. Some threats (like malicious GPO pushes in Active Directory) can take out the entire environment in a matter of hours or even minutes if the situation is right (maybe wrong is a better word). In any case, time really is of the essence.

Containment Domain

In order to be effective, immediate response needs to be followed by containment of compromised systems and malicious activity as quickly as possible. The focus of the Containment Domain is the entity's ability to quickly respond using either internal or external resources and technologies to contain/halt an incident and keep it from continuing and/or spreading.

This prevents further unauthorized physical or digital access to locations, environments, systems, devices, applications, users, and data. It typically involves disconnecting affected systems from the network, resetting affected account passwords, isolating clean environments from affected ones, blocking access to malicious external hosts, and stopping malware wherever it is found.

The quicker the containment, the less the risk that malicious applications and actors will obtain a foothold within the organization or compromise sensitive data. Quick containment protects the security posture as well as the regulatory compliance impact.

Evidence Collection Domain

The focus of the Collection domain is the entity's ability to effectively collect and preserve evidence from the entire evidence universe. This includes visibility into all physical locations and their respective data sources, such as network traffic, endpoints, services, applications, and their respective evidence artifacts.

Typical evidence artifacts and data types typically include network traffic captures, memory dumps, volatile data, registry data, file system data, user information, database content, logs, etc., for all affected resources and evidence repositories. This also includes the procedures the customer has for collecting and preserving evidence. Typical considerations are acquisition, verification, chain of custody, documentation, storage, non-repudiation, retention, and disposal.

Analysis Domain

Once evidence has been collected from the various sources, the next step is to perform analysis to identify indicators of compromise, malicious artifacts, root cause, compromised data, affected users or other individuals, etc. The focus of the Analysis domain is the entity's ability to analyze any or all collected evidence, identify targets or risks, build an incident timeline, and enumerate all relevant facts pertaining to the incident. This will involve analysis of suspicious applications or malware, endpoint activity, network activity, log analysis, and unauthorized access.

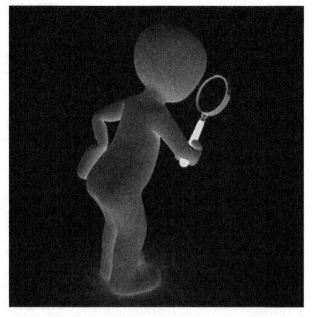

This includes the ability of an entity to detect security risks. Can they 1) identify unpatched attack vectors, security blind spots, or other security control gaps, and 2) determine the associated impacts and make recommendations? Activity at this stage of incident response is where most of the content for the subsequent lessons learned report is identified.

Mitigation Domain

The focus of the Mitigation domain is the entity's ability to eliminate threats or vulnerabilities that caused the incident. This is performed either directly through patching or required configuration changes or through compensating controls if the primary mitigation method cannot be performed.

This includes the entity's procedures, capabilities, and technology for patching, reconfiguration, hardening, applying relevant compensating controls, or

otherwise eliminating or blocking vulnerabilities that permitted or led to the exposure or attack. It also includes the testing and validation of successful mitigation controls. No mitigation effort is complete without successful validation that the vulnerabilities have been resolved.

Legal and Compliance Domain

The focus of the Legal and Compliance domain is the entity's ability to engage and utilize legal counsel appropriately to resolve problems effectively. Somehow, this is often one of the most underused capabilities that can have the greatest impact as the result of a security breach.

Engaging legal counsel throughout all stages of a security breach and subsequent response for guidance and protection of communications is essential to protect the entity, responders, and the outcome of the investigation. This includes the entity's procedures and capabilities for engaging legal counsel for all reasons pertinent to an investigation. There are many facets of an investigation that require an attorney or are best directed by one, including:

- Protection of communication and work product – Responders must direct sensitive communications to or through attorneys and have the right labeling in the subject line and/or body of communications.

- Setting legal objectives and boundaries for an investigation – Attorneys may require special steps or operations to be performed or restrict responders from performing certain actions.

- Identifying legal and compliance pitfalls that pose risks – Attorneys may be aware of actions or situations to avoid based on recent case law or compliance changes.

- Implementing litigation holds – Attorneys need to direct litigation holds and preserve communications and evidence pertinent to investigations and regulatory compliance.

- Engaging external entities – Attorneys often engage outside legal counsel for specialized legal concerns.

- Reviewing and negotiating contracts – Attorneys should review and bless all contracts and ensure appropriate language is included to facilitate and comply with legal and regulatory requirements.

- Executing non-disclosure agreements ("NDAs") – Attorneys should make sure appropriate NDAs are in place for all external and internal entity types, as appropriate for the circumstances.

- Guiding the handling of electronically stored information – Attorneys need to make sure evidence is handled properly and in accordance with the Federal Rules of Civil Procedure and local requirements.

- Performing breach notification – Attorneys will take the lead on breach notification to external entities and regulators.

Eradication Domain

The focus of the Eradication domain is the entity's procedures and capabilities to fully eradicate malicious activity, malicious applications, compromised user accounts, inappropriately stored information, or any threats related to the compromise. In a nutshell, eradication should remove anything from the environment and related systems that should not be there.

This pertains to artifacts either placed there by the attacker or from another source that need to be

cleaned up related to a finding from the investigation. This could include vulnerable, sensitive content that should have been better secured and which was accessible to the attacker due to insecure storage, lack of controls, or accidental disclosure. The environment, networks, systems, services, applications, and accounts should be returned to a known good state.

Reporting and Lessons Learned Domain

The focus of the Reporting and Lessons Learned domain is the entity's procedures and capabilities to adequately capture content for all aspects of incident reporting and after-action activity. This includes identifying relevant gaps and findings associated with cybersecurity incidents, as well as formulating plans of action based on those findings to improve the entity's security posture.

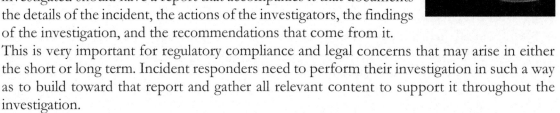

Even if it is not possible to plug the gaps and implement recommended or temporary compensating controls during the response process, all gaps and recommendations should be captured in the lessons learned in a final report. Every incident that gets investigated should have a report that accompanies it that documents the details of the incident, the actions of the investigators, the findings of the investigation, and the recommendations that come from it.

This is very important for regulatory compliance and legal concerns that may arise in either the short or long term. Incident responders need to perform their investigation in such a way as to build toward that report and gather all relevant content to support it throughout the investigation.

Further, the final report will outlive the incident, and it is the only exposure some (such as customer executives) will have to the incident or the respective incident response team. As such, the report should be well-written and stand on its own or have supporting documents called out within the report and provided along with it.

Remediation and Continuous Improvement Domain

The focus of the Remediation and Continuous Improvement domain is the entity's procedures and capabilities to apply lessons learned and make changes to fix identified gaps or findings in people, processes, and technology to improve the entity's security posture. This includes the entity's ability to resolve security flaws that  permitted the incident to happen or at least apply interim compensating controls while longer-term action plans are in process.

Even after an incident management program has been custom-crafted for the customer environment, it is not finished. It will always be a work in progress in continual flux.

Due to the evolution in the threat landscape, advancements in technology, changes within the customer environment, and findings from lessons learned identified in each incident, the incident management program must be updated to remain relevant. The longer it remains stagnant, the less relevant it will become.

Documentation Domain

The focus of the Documentation domain is the comprehensiveness and quality of an entity's documentation pertaining to various security-related topics, including:

- Information security – The root of everything
- Incident response/management – Planning for breaches
- Environment and capability diagrams – Knowing the environment
- Asset and activity ownership – Define who to contact for affected devices
- Management support – Defined leadership mandate and measurement
- Vendor support – Ascertain vendor capability to follow security & response
- Strength of contract language – Requires security & response elements

This includes the quality, efficacy, and comprehensiveness of all types of policies, procedures, and processes that guide response-related activity within the entity in accordance with the

IMF. Typical documents include:

- Principles – High-level, broad ideals that govern behavior and articulate enterprise strategies and direction
- Policies – A high-level, broadly applied document describing strategic guiding principles, roles, responsibilities, and governance.
- Standards – A high-level, specifically applied document describing strategic guiding principles, roles, responsibilities, and governance.
- Processes – The flow of tasks, activities, transactions, and data through various procedures to accomplish the desired outcome.
- Procedures/Plans/Playbooks/Workflows – All of these are the detailed, tactical steps that guide and describe how one or more policies, standards, and/or processes are executed, including the use of controls to accomplish the desired outcome. The main difference is the comprehensiveness of the scope, the breadth of the scope, the specificity of the language, and the method of delivery. Plans, playbooks, and workflows are all types of procedures, but plans are typically comprehensive for an entire theme (like an incident response plan), playbooks are typically very specific to a task, and workflows are typically visualizations of a playbook task.
- Guidance – Details specific parameters of security and compliance requirements and their application to assist personnel in understanding and effectively meeting them.
- Baselines – Minimum security requirements for systems, applications, and controls

Training and Testing Domain

The focus of the Training and Testing domain is the comprehensiveness, appropriateness, and efficacy of the entity's training program, testing functions, and tabletop mock drills to evaluate the readiness, adequacy, and proficiency of the entity's information security, threat detection, and incident response processes and capabilities. It also evaluates the entity's capabilities and plans to perform vulnerability assessments, penetration tests, and application security evaluations of key resources within the environment.

6 REGULATORY AND LEGAL REQUIREMENTS

Evolution

Over the past couple of decades, information security controls and associated detection and response capabilities have evolved from being information technology concerns into regulatory compliance concerns and now into key business drivers. Regulatory requirements are increasing in complexity and specialization and often overlap within organizations.

Simply to stay in business, entities must successfully pass the regulatory compliance audits that are required for their industry, payment methods, and data types that they store, process, or transmit. Companies in all regulated sectors performing regulated transactions and/or possessing regulated content need to have at least an acceptable minimum baseline of security controls and incident response capabilities.

When developing information security and incident management programs, the common theme in complying with the security component of all of these regulatory requirements is having a defensible and well-documented security, detection, and response posture. It must be compliant with all applicable requirements. It should also be reviewed, updated, and tested at least annually. In fact, compliance requirements have become the primary driver for information security controls.

While it may sound like a positive development that compliance is driving greater security, it also creates a notable gap. If compliance does not require it, entities may not implement it, even if there is a known deficiency. Security spending is commonly driven by compliance requirements, and other areas not in the compliance focus may suffer.

Security ≠ Compliance

To be clear, there is a huge difference between being compliant and being secure. A company can be audited and found to be compliant but also be insecure and suffer a breach before, during, or after the compliance audit.

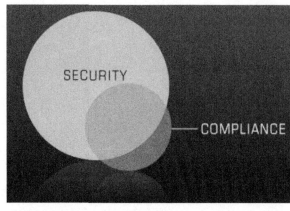

Although there are overlaps between compliance and security, they need to be considered and evaluated separately. Compliance should never be the only driver for security. Although it is true that if an environment is completely secure, it will be mostly compliant – but not entirely. Compliance and security are quite distinct, and security is a much larger endeavor than compliance if done right.

Further, considering most regulatory requirements are purposefully vague, it leaves a lot of room for interpretation and evolution. Many of the regulatory compliance standards are over a decade old, and their vagueness has enabled them to remain without significant alteration.

Moreover, the vagueness and subsequent interpretation is a double-edged sword. It is usually not specific enough to tell entities what they need to do in order to be secure. However, it can also be interpreted by regulators to make the case that entities were not in compliance with it; therefore, they were breached. It is really easy for regulators to say, "We cannot tell you specifically to do it. However, if you got breached, you clearly weren't doing it right…"

Regulations With Teeth

If regulators find that companies are not in compliance with applicable compulsory standards and requirements or if there has been a security breach of regulated content due to non-compliance, it could result in fines, restrictions on performing business functions, and/or limitations on accepting credit card payments. Highly regulated sectors, data types, and/or enforcement groups that are commonly encountered include the following.

1. HIPAA, HHS, and OCR (medical records)
2. PCI-DSS/card brands (payment cards)
3. GLBA (banking)
4. SOX (publicly traded company financials)
5. FACTA (Consumer credit)

6. FERPA (educational rights and privacy)
7. FISMA (Federal information security)
8. FERC & NERC (energy security)
9. FTC (Consumer protection)
10. Multi-State AGs/DoJs (Consumer protection)

HIPAA, HHS, and OCR

HIPAA (medical records) – The Health Insurance Portability and Accountability Act of 1996 is a federal law that has been amended to the Internal Revenue Code of 1996. It was designed to improve the portability and continuity of health insurance coverage in both group and individual markets.

HIPAA has been updated several times, and the later revisions significantly enhanced patients' privacy protections. The updates provide new rights to individuals for their health information, and it strengthens the government's ability to enforce the law. The previous requirements focused more on healthcare providers, health plans, and entities that process claims. The revisions extend requirements to business associates (such as contractors or subcontractors) of healthcare, health plan, and claim processing entities that receive, process, or store protected health information (PHI).

Unlike other compliance regulations that focus primarily on the "Confidentiality and Integrity" of data, HIPAA extends its reach into the "Confidentiality, Integrity, and Availability" (CIA triad) of data used for patient care, with "Availability" being the key difference. As such, if attackers or malware compromise any of the CIA triad, the entity is in non-compliance with HIPAA and HHS requirements.

The Health and Human Services (HHS) Office of Civil Rights (OCR) Ransomware Fact Sheet takes this aggressive interpretation of the CIA triad a couple of steps further by stipulating that ransomware activity against patient data is considered to be a breach. Specifically, it stipulates: 'Whether or not the presence of ransomware would be a breach under the HIPAA Rules is a fact-specific determination. A breach under the HIPAA Rules is defined as "…the acquisition, access, use, or disclosure of PHI in a manner not permitted under the [HIPAA Privacy Rule] which compromises the security or privacy of the PHI." See 45 C.F.R. 164.402.6

When electronic protected health information (ePHI) is encrypted as the result of a ransomware attack, a breach has occurred because the ePHI encrypted by the ransomware was acquired (i.e., unauthorized individuals have taken possession or control of the information) and thus is a "disclosure" not permitted under the HIPAA Privacy Rule.'" As such, the HHS Ransomware Fact Sheet is taking the rather extreme and technically counterintuitive position that privileged content that never left the system it was stored on, but was encrypted by ransomware, is considered to have suffered "disclosure." (HHS, 2013, p. 1)

Apart from the guidance in the Ransomware Fact Sheet that goes into very specific detail about the impact of ransomware, the rest of the guidance requires significant interpretation to translate its requirements into technical information security concepts. However, the AAPC has assembled a very informative compliance self-assessment checklist based on HIPAA security and HITECH compliance (HIPAA Security and HITECH Compliance Checklist). It enumerates implementation specifications, provides guidance, and guides assessment methodology.

PCI-DSS/Card Brands (Payment Cards)

The Payment Card Industry Security Standards Council (PCI-SSC) maintains card payment regulations for all of the card brands, which are consolidated into the PCI DSS. Per the DSS, "The Payment Card Industry Data Security Standard (PCI DSS) was developed to encourage and enhance cardholder data security and facilitate the broad adoption of consistent data security measures globally.

It provides a baseline of technical and operational requirements designed to protect account data. It applies to all entities involved in payment card processing—including merchants, processors, acquirers, issuers, and service providers. It also applies to all other entities that store, process, or transmit cardholder data (CHD) or sensitive authentication data (SAD).

The DSS is updated frequently compared to most of the regulatory compliance standards/requirements. Since its inception in 2004, it has been updated every 1 to 3 years. This has helped it remain the most relevant and functional of all compliance requirements.

An interesting caveat is that the PCI-SSC is not the entity that pursues legal action when a security breach occurs that compromises cardholder data stemming from the merchant's PCI DSS non-compliance. Instead, the credit card brands (Visa, Mastercard, American Express, etc.) themselves impose fines and restrictions.

The DSS provides a "High-Level Overview" consisting of the following summary data, as well as highly detailed requirements, testing procedures, and guidance. In fact, it is one of the most prescriptive, specific, and detailed of all existing regulatory requirements today.

There are 12 high-level areas for which PCI provides highly detailed security requirements and governance, as follows. (PCI SSC, 2018, p. 1)

1 and 2 identify how to Build and Maintain a Secure Network and Systems
> 1. Install and maintain a firewall configuration to protect cardholder data
> 2. Do not use vendor-supplied defaults for system passwords and other security parameters

3 and 4 identify how to Protect Cardholder Data in transit or at rest

3. Protect stored cardholder data

4. Encrypt transmission of cardholder data across open, public networks

5 and 6 identify how to Maintain a Vulnerability Management Program

5. Protect all systems against malware and regularly update anti-virus software or programs

6. Develop and maintain secure systems and applications

7 – 9 Identify how to Implement Strong Access Control Measures

7. Restrict access to cardholder data by business need to know

8. Identify and authenticate access to system components

9. Restrict physical access to cardholder data

10 and 11 identify the need for Regularly Monitoring and Testing Network controls

10. Track and monitor all access to network resources and cardholder data

11. Regularly test security systems and processes

12 identifies the need to Maintain an Information Security Policy

12. Maintain a policy that addresses information security for all personnel

GLBA (Banking)

The Gramm-Leach-Bliley Act was established in 1999 and applies very broadly to banking requirements. The Security sections are 501 and 505(b)(2), which in the text are very high-level, and one might not immediately identify that they actually apply to security controls.

The Electronic Code of Federal Regulations, Title 16, Chapter 1, Subchapter C, Part 314 – Standards for Safeguarding Customer Information provides implementation guidance for the GLBA security sections, which is more applicable to designing a security program. The Standards for Safeguarding Customer Information provide better detail on what is required for an information security program.

However, it talks more about the concept of developing a program to protect against anticipated threats or hazards to the security, integrity, and confidentiality of customer information and the unauthorized access thereof that could result in substantial harm or inconvenience. It does not go into detail regarding the specifics or the implementation of such.

In summary, the Standards for Safeguarding Customer Information uses a lot of words to address the need to develop a comprehensive and accessible information security program to implement safeguards across applicable areas appropriate to the scale, complexity, and scope appropriate to protect customer information against anticipated threats and designate personnel to support it. Specifically, Standards for Safeguarding Customer Information stipulates the following. (US Government, 1999, p. 1):

§314.3 Standards for safeguarding customer information.
(a) Information security program. You shall develop, implement, and maintain a comprehensive information security program that is written in one or more readily accessible parts and contains administrative, technical, and physical safeguards that are appropriate to your size and complexity, the nature and scope of your activities, and the sensitivity of any customer information at issue.

Note that there is nothing in this requirement about what specifically to do or how to do it. It essentially says, "Just do it and make sure it works." It is like a coach saying, "OK, go win the game!" Good examples of this are the objectives, which come next in the document:

Such safeguards shall include the elements set forth in §314.4 and shall be reasonably designed to achieve the objectives of this part, as set forth in paragraph (b) of this section.
(b) Objectives. The objectives of section 501(b) of the Act, and of this part, are to:
(1) Ensure the security and confidentiality of customer information;
(2) Protect against any anticipated threats or hazards to the security or integrity of such information; and
(3) Protect against unauthorized access to or use of such information that could result in substantial harm or inconvenience to any customer.

The Elements section stipulates that you have to designate people to be in charge of it and develop the program and further breaks out the items that need to be secured in greater detail, including systems, networks, software, information processing, storage, transmission, and disposal.

§314.4 Elements.
In order to develop, implement, and maintain your information security program, you shall:
(a) Designate an employee or employees to coordinate your information security program.
(b) Identify reasonably foreseeable internal and external risks to the security, confidentiality, and integrity of customer information that could result in the unauthorized disclosure, misuse, alteration, destruction or other compromise of such information, and assess the sufficiency of any safeguards in place to control these risks. At a minimum, such a risk assessment should include consideration of risks in each relevant area of your operations, including:
(1) Employee training and management;
(2) Information systems, including network and software design, as well as information processing, storage, transmission and disposal; and
(3) Detecting, preventing and responding to attacks, intrusions, or other systems failures.
(c) Design and implement information safeguards to control the risks you identify through risk assessment, and regularly test or otherwise monitor the effectiveness of the safeguards' key controls, systems, and procedures.
(d) Oversee service providers, by:
(1) Taking reasonable steps to select and retain service providers that are capable of maintaining appropriate safeguards for the customer information at issue; and
(2) Requiring your service providers by contract to implement and maintain such safeguards.
(e) Evaluate and adjust your information security program in light of the results of the testing and monitoring required by paragraph (c) of this section; any material changes to your operations or

business arrangements; or any other circumstances that you know or have reason to know may have a material impact on your information security program.

In addition to the previous sections, TITLE 15 of US CODE COLLECTION, CHAPTER 94, SUBCHAPTER I, Sec. 6801 also identifies the need to protect the security and confidentiality of customer content, but it does not list any additional specifics for information security controls or requirements:

> *Protection of nonpublic personal information (a) Privacy obligation policy It is the policy of the Congress that each financial institution has an affirmative and continuing obligation to respect the privacy of its customers and to protect the security and confidentiality of those customers' nonpublic personal information. (b) Financial institutions safeguards In furtherance of the policy in subsection (a) of this section, each agency or authority described in section 6805(a) of this title shall establish appropriate standards for the financial institutions subject to their jurisdiction relating to administrative, technical, and physical safeguards - (1) to ensure the security and confidentiality of customer records and information; (2) to protect against any anticipated threats or hazards to the security or integrity of such records; and (3) to protect against unauthorized access to or use of such records or information which could result in substantial harm or inconvenience to any customer.*

Securities and Exchange Commission (SEC)
17 CFR Parts 229, 232, 239, 240, and 249; Regulations S-K, S-T

On September 5, 2023, the SEC adopted new rules to require current disclosure about material cybersecurity incidents and periodic disclosures about a registrant's processes to assess, identify, and manage material cybersecurity risks management's role in assessing and managing material cybersecurity risks, and the board of directors' oversight of cybersecurity risks. Disclosures must be presented in Inline eXtensible Business Reporting Language ("Inline XBRL").

SOX (Publicly Traded Company Financials)

The Sarbanes-Oxley (SOX) Act of 2002 and subsequent updates established standards for publicly traded companies in the United States. SOX is administered by the Securities and Exchange Commission (SEC), which handles compliance, rules, and requirements for US public companies.

From a high level, SOX requirements stipulate that a publicly traded company must be able to certify its financial reports, and it mandates the creation of internal procedures designed to ensure accurate financial disclosure. Everything else related to information security is an interpretation.

Sections 302 and 404 are those from the SOX regulatory requirements that have the most direct impact on computer information security and incident management. Both sections require some interpretation to convert into information security concepts. Neither section specifically identifies computer systems, digitally stored data, or cybersecurity in the text, and if all information was stored on paper, the content would equally apply.

However, as most companies use computer information systems to collect, process, store, and report financial information, the focus is not only on the accounting/financial accuracy but also on the security controls within and surrounding the information systems and respective networks. Therefore, SOX is indirectly a driver for information security and incident management.

Section 302

Mandates internal procedures designed to ensure accurate financial disclosure, including an assessment of controls that protect the financial reporting process from unauthorized modification. It also places the responsibility for the accuracy of financial reporting, and thus the security controls that protect it, at the highest levels of corporate management.

As such, CFOs and CEOs now face possible criminal fraud liability for security gaps that result in unauthorized modifications and subsequent inaccuracies of company financial reports. However, section 302 does not stipulate the controls that must be assessed.

Section 404

Stipulates that access controls should be maintained, reviewed, and periodically reported. It requires management and external auditors (which are required) to assess the efficacy of internal controls protecting company financials and report the assessment findings annually to the SEC.

FACTA (Consumer Credit)

The Fair and Accurate Credit Transactions Act (FACTA), which was instituted in 2003 and then subsequently updated several times, is actually an amendment to the Fair Credit Reporting Act (FCRA) of 1970. FACTA is enforced by the Board of Governors of the Federal Reserve System, the National Credit Union Administration, the Office of the Comptroller of the Currency, the Office of Thrift Supervision, the Federal Deposit Insurance Corporation, and the Federal Trade Commission (FTC).

FACTA was created to implement requirements for financial institutions and creditors to develop and implement a written Red Flag ID theft detection and prevention program. Specifically, the Red Flag Rules are intended to "detect, prevent and mitigate identity theft in connection with the opening of certain accounts or certain existing accounts" and must be appropriate for the "size and complexity of the financial institution or creditor and the nature and scope of its activities."

As is typical, the requirements require interpretation to apply to information security and incident management concepts and will vary based on differences in workflows and data across organizations. Under the FACTA rules, a Red Flag is defined as any pattern, practice, or activity that indicates possible identity theft.

FACTA stipulates that the Red Flag Rules must include reasonable policies and procedures that:
- *Identify red flags that may arise in its employees' handling of consumer data;*
- *Detect those red flags when they occur;*
- *Respond appropriately to prevent and mitigate identity theft; and*
- *Ensure periodic updates (including the red flags) that reflect changes concerning the risks of identity theft, including the ability of the financial institution or creditor to protect customers against identity theft.*

Red flags are categorized as follows:
- *Warnings from consumer reporting agencies or service providers;*
- *Suspicious documents;*
- *Suspicious personal identifying information;*
- *Suspicious accounts or other suspicious activity related to a covered account; and*
- *Notice or alerts of possible identity theft from customers, law enforcement, or other persons.*

In the process of identifying red flags, entities must consider the risk factors associated with each type of covered account, methods used to open the account, account access, and the sources of red flags. The FACTA regulations provide examples of ways to respond to red flags upon detection, which make really good action items for incident management, as appropriate for the situation:
- *Monitor an account for evidence of identity theft;*
- *Contact the customer;*
- *Change any passwords, security codes, or other security devices that permit access to the customer's account;*
- *Reopen a covered account with a new account number;*
- *Not open a new account;*
- *Close an existing account;*
- *Not attempt to collect on an account or not sell the account to a debt collector;*
- *Notify law enforcement; or*
- *Determine that no response is warranted under the circumstance.*

Identity Theft Programs must:
- *Initially be approved by the financial institution or creditor's board of directors, or an appropriate committee of the board;*
- *Be overseen by the board, or an appropriate committee of the board, or senior management;*
- *Provide for appropriate training of staff; and*
- *Exercise appropriate oversight over service vendors.*

FERPA (Educational Rights and Privacy)

The Family Education Rights and Privacy Act was introduced in 2000 and has been updated several times since. It stipulates very high-level requirements for the protection of Personally Identifiable Information (PII) according to several key use cases. However, like many regulatory requirements, it does not go into specific detail about how the protections should be implemented.

The US Department of Education established the Privacy Technical Assistance Center (PTAC) as a resource for education stakeholders to obtain information about data privacy, confidentiality, and security practices related to student data and information systems and compliance with FERPA requirements. Two notable guidelines are 1) Integrated Data Systems and Student Privacy and 2) the Data Security Checklist.

The high-level protection requirements specified in FERPA that are most applicable to information security and incident management include:

99.2 – Purpose of regulations

- *"confidentiality of information relating to children with disabilities who receive evaluations, services, or other benefit"*
- *"confidentiality of information requirements regarding children and infants and toddlers with disabilities and their families who receive evaluations, services, or other benefits"*
- *"Confidentiality of information requirements that apply to personally identifiable data, information, and records collected or maintained"*
- *Conditions [that] apply to disclosure of information for Federal or State program purposes*

99.35 – Conditions that apply to the disclosure of information for Federal or State program purposes

(v) Establish policies and procedures, consistent with the Act and other Federal and State confidentiality and privacy provisions, to protect personally identifiable information from education records from further disclosure (except back to the disclosing entity) and unauthorized use, including limiting use of personally identifiable information from education records to only authorized representatives with legitimate interests in the audit or evaluation of a Federal- or State-supported education program or for compliance or enforcement of Federal legal requirements related to these programs.

(b) Information that is collected under paragraph (a) of this section must—

(1) Be protected in a manner that does not permit personal identification of individuals by anyone other than the State or local educational authority or agency headed by an official listed in §99.31(a)(3) and their authorized representatives, except that the State or local educational authority or agency headed by an official listed in §99.31(a)(3) may make further disclosures of personally identifiable information from education records on behalf of the educational agency or institution in accordance with the requirements of §99.33(b); and

(2) Be destroyed when no longer needed for the purposes listed in paragraph (a) of this section.

(c) Paragraph (b) of this section does not apply if:

(1) The parent or eligible student has given written consent for the disclosure under §99.30; or
(2) The collection of personally identifiable information is specifically authorized by Federal law.
(Government Publishing Office, 2018, p. 1)

FISMA (Federal information security)

The Federal Information Security Modernization Act was established in 2003 (and updated in 2014) to produce key security standards and guidelines required by Congressional legislation. The FISMA publications are developed by NIST in accordance with its statutory responsibilities under the Federal Information Security Modernization Act (FISMA) of 2014, 44 U.S.C. § 3551 et seq., Public Law (P.L.) 113-283.
f
The NIST publications that are the basis for FISMA security requirements are very prescriptive and used as a standard by which other security requirements, standards, and guidelines are judged. Moreover, although the NIST publications and FISMA security requirements directly apply only to government entities, they are also adopted by private industry and used for security development and audit standards.

The vision of FISMA is to provide security guidance for the following:

- Standards for categorizing information and systems by mission impact – These assist with prioritization for designing and implementing controls as well as performing response
- Standards for minimum security requirements for information and systems – These establish a minimum baseline for security controls for which all systems must at least comply.
- Guidance for selecting appropriate security controls for systems – These guidelines are usually contextual by use case.
- Guidance for assessing security controls in systems and determining security control effectiveness – This involves assessing security controls through some form of security testing or audit process.
- Guidance for the security authorization of systems – This involves validating systems for access to environments and production use.
- Guidance for monitoring the security controls – This involves the ongoing security monitoring processes.

Per nist.gov, "NIST is responsible for developing information security standards and guidelines, including minimum requirements for federal systems, but such standards and guidelines shall not apply to national security systems without the express approval of appropriate federal officials exercising policy authority over such systems." Special Publications specifically applicable to FISMA include FIPS 199, FIPS 200, and NIST Publications 800-18, 800-53, 800-59, 800-60, 800-137, and 800-160. Supporting Special Publications include 800-37, 800-39, 800-53A, 800-171, 800-171A, and NIST Interagency Report 8011. Additional security standards and guidelines are also being produced by the

Computer Security Division in support of FISMA.

Understanding the applicability of FISMA required NIST publications for performing incident management on government entities is essential to success. Moreover, familiarity with the NIST publications is important for all information security professionals as they provide a strong starting place for program development, audit functions, and overall security best practices.

FERC & NERC (energy security)

In 2006, the Federal Energy Regulatory Commission (FERC) certified the North American Electric Reliability Corporation (NERC) as the Electric Reliability Organization (ERO) that will enforce its reliability standards, which were developed and certified by FERC. Further, the mission of NERC is to ensure the reliability of the North American bulk power system. This includes the cybersecurity and related assets that are essential to the operation of the electric grid. NERC operates in conjunction with government agencies, the electric industry, and electricity consumers to provide a coordinated and comprehensive effort to address electricity grid cybersecurity threats.

NERC has developed FERC-approved Critical Infrastructure Protection (CIP) reliability standards, which were approved in 2008 and subsequently updated, most recently in 2018. They are one of two sets of mandatory cybersecurity standards in place for the United States' critical electric infrastructure. NERC also developed a three-level alert system that informs the electrical industry and makes recommendations for preventative actions for cyber vulnerabilities and related threats.

The 2018 Revised Critical Infrastructure Protection Standard (CIP-003—7 – Cybersecurity – Security Management Controls – Summary identifies the following cybersecurity scope:

> *The Federal Energy Regulatory Commission (Commission) approves Critical Infrastructure Protection (CIP) Reliability Standard CIP-003-7 (Cybersecurity – Security Management Controls), submitted by the North American Electric Reliability Corporation (NERC). Reliability Standard CIP-003-7 clarifies the obligations pertaining to electronic access control for low impact BES Cyber Systems; requires mandatory security controls for transient electronic devices (e.g., thumb drives, laptop computers, and other portable devices frequently connected to and disconnected from systems) used at low impact BES Cyber Systems; and requires responsible entities to have a policy for declaring and responding to CIP Exceptional Circumstances related to low impact BES Cyber Systems. In addition, the Commission directs NERC to develop modifications to the CIP Reliability Standards to mitigate the risk of malicious code that could result from third-party transient electronic devices.*

FTC (Consumer Protection)

The Federal Trade Commission (FTC) was established in 1914 by the Federal Trade Commission Act and is an independent agency of the United States government. The primary mission of the FTC is the advocacy of consumer protection and the elimination or prevention of anticompetitive business practices.

When it comes to cybersecurity breaches, the department of the FTC that affected companies are most likely to run afoul with is the Bureau of Consumer Protection. The Bureau of Consumer Protection has a mandate to protect consumers against unfair or deceptive acts or practices in commerce.

The Bureau attorneys enforce federal laws related to consumer affairs and rules promulgated by the FTC. The Bureau's functions include enforcement actions, investigations, and consumer/business education. Most notably, the areas of principal concern for the Bureau of Consumer Protection are advertising/marketing practices, financial products/practices, telemarketing fraud, and privacy/identity protection.

Under the FTC Act, the Commission has the authority to bring legal actions in federal court through its own attorneys. In some consumer protection matters, the FTC appears with or supports the U.S. Department of Justice.

The FTC has established a long history of prosecuting companies compromised by cybersecurity breaches for having a privacy statement on their website but not protecting customer data with reasonable, appropriate, and expected security controls. Companies prosecuted by the FTC for such offenses typically receive a consent decree, which results in a 20-year sentence characterized by bi-annual security assessments from an outside entity to provide independent validation of effective security controls. It is quite possible that someone could commit murder and be tried, convicted, and serve their full prison term before a company has served the full term of their consent decree.

Multi-State AGs/DoJs (Consumer Protection)

In recent years, groups of state attorneys general and state departments of justice have banded together to file a combined lawsuit against companies affected by a security breach. This provides a huge advantage to them as they are able to share the costs of the lawsuit as well as leverage the privacy laws of the strictest state.

More specifically, if a company has customers in 12 states and it suffers a data breach, all 12 of those state attorneys general may have standing to sue and will make their choice of law that of the state having the strictest privacy laws – usually California or Massachusetts. Litigation is typically filed under the context that the victim company "failed to take adequate and reasonable measures to ensure their computer systems were protected." To assist in making their case, the states typically hire information security or incident response service providers to evaluate the pre-breach security controls of the victim company, as well as the method of breach, and determine whether the security controls were adequate and reasonable.

The California Attorney General's Office has even gone so far as to release a data breach report with a listing of safeguards they believe constitute reasonable information security practices. These are as follows:

- Inventory of Authorized and Unauthorized Devices
- Inventory of Authorized and Unauthorized Software
- Security Configurations for Hardware and Software on Mobile Devices, Laptops, Workstations, and Servers
- Continuous Vulnerability Assessment and Remediation
- Controlled Use of Administrative Privileges
- Maintenance, Monitoring, and Analysis of Audit Logs
- Email and Web Browsing Protection
- Malware Defenses
- Limitation and Control of Network Ports, Protocols, and Services
- Data Recovery Capability
- Secure Configurations for Network Devices such as Firewalls, Routers, and Switches
- Boundary Defense
- Data Protection
- Controlled Access Based on the Need to Know
- Wireless Access Control
- Account Monitoring and Control
- Security Skills Assessment and Appropriate Training to Fill Gaps
- Application Software Security
- Incident Response and Management
- Penetration Tests and Red Team Exercises
- Implement Multi-Factor Authentication for Online Accounts
- Encrypt Personal Information on Portable Devices

(Kamala D. Harris, 2016, p. 39)

Cyber Incident Reporting for Critical Infrastructure Act (CIRCIA)

In March 2022, CIRCIA was signed into law requiring the Cybersecurity and Infrastructure Security Agency (CISA) to develop and implement regulations requiring covered entities to report covered cyber incidents and ransomware payments to CISA. These reports are intended to allow CISA to rapidly deploy resources and render assistance to victims suffering attacks, analyze incoming reporting across sectors to spot trends, and quickly share that information with network defenders to warn other potential victims.

White House Federal Acquisition Regulation (FAR)

A combination of United States federal agencies, including the Department of Defense (DoD), the General Services Administration (GSA), and the National Aeronautics and Space Administration (NASA), proposed a ruleset change by Executive Order 14028 (Signed May

2021) to FAR to include sweeping regulations for federal contractors to promote "Cyber Threat and Incident Reporting and Information Sharing." The stated intent of the agencies' proposal for FAR is to implement security policies, provide access to federal agencies, and establish rapid notification and reporting timelines. The *"proposed rule supports implementation of the National Cyber Strategy by strengthening and standardizing contract requirements for cybersecurity and by providing mechanisms to help ensure that entities or individuals that knowingly put U.S. information or systems at risk, but violating these cybersecurity requirements, are held accountable."* Specific provisions that have been identified as significant concerns include the following. The proposal is still under review and, as of January 2024, is in the public commentary phase.

- *52.212-5 – Contract Terms and Conditions Required to Implement Statutes or Executive Orders – Commercial Products and Service usage of new clause 52.239-ZZ, including flow down subcontracts.*
- *52.239-ZZ*
    - *(a) Regulatory familiarization.*
    - *(b) 52.239–ZZ, paragraph (b), for contractors to support security incident reporting, including: providing information regarding reportable incidents to CISA at https://www.cisa.gov/report, and to affected agencies, and any updates until eradication or remediation activities are completed.*
    - *(c) 52.239–ZZ, paragraph (c)(1), for contractors to support incident response by conducting data preservation and protection and providing to the Government, if requested.*
    - *(d) 52.239–ZZ, paragraph (c)(2), for contractors to support incident response by developing, storing, and maintaining customization files, and providing to the Government, if requested.*
    - *(e) 52.239–ZZ, paragraph (c)(3), for contractors to support incident response by developing and maintaining a software bill of materials (SBOM) and providing or providing access to the SBOM (and its updates) to the Government.*
    - *(f) 52.239–ZZ, paragraph (c)(4), for contractors to support incident response by providing to the Government and any 3rd party authorized assessor all incident and damage assessment information identified in clause paragraphs (c)(1)–(3), if the Government elects to conduct an incident or damage assessment.*
    - *(g) 52.239–ZZ, paragraph (c)(5), for contractors to support incident response by, if applicable, submitting malicious code samples or artifacts to CISA using the form at https://www.malware.us-cert.gov within 8 hours of discovery and isolation of the malicious software.*
    - *(h) 52.239–ZZ, paragraph (c)(6), for contractors to support incident response by providing access (see (c)(6)(i)) to additional information or equipment necessary for forensic analysis, upon request by the Government, and time to cooperate with the Government on ensuring effective incident response, corrections, or fixes, and time (see(c)(6)(ii)) to confirm validity of request from CISA by contacting the CISA Hotline and notifying the contracting officer.*
    - *(i) 52.239–ZZ, paragraph (d)(1), for contractors to support incident response by subscribing to the Automated Indicator Sharing (AIS) capability or successor technology during the performance of the contract.*
    - *(j) 52.239–ZZ, paragraph (d)(2), for contractors to support incident response by sharing*

cyber threat indicators and recommended defensive measures in an automated fashion using AIS during the performance of the contract.

- o *(k) 52.239–ZZ, paragraph (e) for contractors to support incident response by implementing delta capabilities required for moving to IPv6 for ICT products and services using internet protocol (capabilities in NIST SP 500–267B).*
- o *(l) 52.239–ZZ, paragraph (e) for contractors to provide a corresponding supplier's declaration of conformity in accordance with the USGv6 Test Program (see NIST SP 500– 281A). (m) 52.239–ZZ, paragraph (e) for contractors, for which the agency CIO has approved a waiver of IPv6 requirements, to develop and provide an IPv6 Implementation Plan to the Government that details how the contractor plans to incorporate applicable mandatory capabilities recommended in the current version of NIST SP 500– 267B into products and services provided to the Government.*
- o *(n) 52.239–AA, paragraph (b) for offerors to represent that they have submitted all security incident reports in a current, accurate and complete manner; and represent that they have required each lower-tier subcontractor to include the requirements of paragraph (f) of FAR clause 52.239–ZZ in their subcontract.*

- *52.239-AA – Security Incident Reporting Representation, is proposed to be added to require offerors to represent that they have submitted all security incident reports in a current, accurate, and complete manner and represent whether they have required each lower-tier subcontractor to include the requirements of paragraph (f) of FAR clause 52.239-ZZ in their subcontract.*
- *52.244-6 – Subcontracts for Commercial Products and Commercial Services, is proposed to be revised to add the subcontract flow down prescription for commercial product and service usage of new clause 52.239-ZZ*

References

HHS.(2013). Summary of the HIPAA Security Rule. Retrieved from: https://www.hhs.gov/hipaa/for-professionals/security/laws-regulations/index.html

HHS.(2017).Cyber Attack Checklist. Retrieved from: https://www.hhs.gov/sites/default/files/cyber-attack-checklist-06-2017.pdf

HHS.(2018). FACT SHEET: Ransomware and HIPAA. Retrieved from: https://www.hhs.gov/sites/default/files/RansomwareFactSheet.pdf

AAPC.(2011). HIPAA Security and HITECH Compliance Checklist. Retrieved from: http://aapcperfect.s3.amazonaws.com/3f227f64-019f-488a-b5a2-e864a522ee71/93474f1d-58b3-4364-b060-790f48531f8a/71e98110-fafe-4880-8449-bddfbef5efa6.pdf

PCI SSC.(2018).PCI DSS. Retrieved from: https://www.pcisecuritystandards.org/documents/PCI_DSS_v3-2-1.pdf?agreement=true&time=1548655486397

US Government.(1999). Gramm-Leach-Bliley Act. Retrieved from: https://www.govinfo.gov/content/pkg/PLAW-106publ102/pdf/PLAW-106publ102.pdf

Government Publishing Office.(2018). Electronic Code of Federal Regulations Part 314 Standards of

Safeguarding Customer Information. Retrieved from: https://www.ecfr.gov/cgi-bin/text-idx?c=ecfr&sid=1e9a81d52a0904d70a046d0675d613b0&rgn=div5&view=text&node=16%3A1.0.1.3.38&idno=16

Association of Corporate Counsel.(2011).The Fair and Accurate Credit Transaction Act (FACTA). Retrieved from: https://www.acc.com/legalresources/quickcounsel/tfaacta.cfm

PTAC.(2018).Data Security Checklist; Retrieved from: https://studentprivacy.ed.gov/sites/default/files/resource_document/file/Data%20Security%20Checklist_0.pdf

PTAC.(2018).Integrated Data Systems and Student Privacy. Retrieved from: https://studentprivacy.ed.gov/sites/default/files/resource_document/file/IDS-Final_0.pdf

Government Publishing Office.(2018). PART 99—FAMILY EDUCATIONAL RIGHTS AND PRIVACY

Retrieved from: https://www.ecfr.gov/cgi-bin/text-idx?rgn=div5&node=34:1.1.1.1.33

NIST.(2016).FISMA Background. Retrieved from https://csrc.nist.gov/projects/risk-management/detailed-overview

Energy Central.(2011). FERC versus NERC. Retrieved from https://www.energycentral.com/c/iu/ferc-versus-nerc

FERC.(2018). Revised Critical Infrastructure Protection Reliability Standard CIP-003-7 – Cybersecurity – Security Management Controls. Retrieved from https://www.ferc.gov/whats-new/comm-meet/2018/041918/E-3.pdf?csrt=2699639746415147935

IBM.(2023). 2023 Cost of a Data Breach Study. Retrieved from https://www.ibm.com/reports/data-breach?utm_content=SRCWW&p1=Search&p4=43700077723822555&p5=p&&msclkid=f58baa3e6ec71908 4226cfa87d85cc4f&gclid=f58baa3e6ec719084226cfa87d85cc4f&gclsrc=3p.ds

Kamala D. Harris (2016). California Data Breach Report. Retrieved from https://oag.ca.gov/sites/all/files/agweb/pdfs/dbr/2016-data-breach-report.pdf

7 IMPACT OF REGULATORY NON-COMPLIANCE

What Does It Cost?

In relation to cybersecurity incidents, the potential costs and business impacts can be very high and will come from various places. The consequences of a successful attack typically include immediate costs as well as residual costs. The breach aftermath and associated expenses can drag on for years due to multi-year remediation projects. Any of these could result in a cascade of problems that may cause a significant impact on an organization  and potentially even result in its untimely demise.

Immediate Costs

Immediate costs and impacts include the predictable costs of responding to a large or significant incident, which often involves all hands on deck for information security, IT, and investigative personnel. This usually also includes consulting resources and generally licensing costs for required tools, some of which are related to the specific consulting companies. Cheap immediate costs start around the low-to mid-tens of thousands and could range up into the millions or tens of millions, considering the size, scope, complexity, and the products or services purchased.

Residual Costs

Common residual costs and impacts of security and regulatory non-compliance related to or that could result in a successful breach are much more varied than the immediate costs. These commonly include the following:

- Lawsuits – There can be many lawsuits that follow a security breach, and they come from various different directions, some of which may come off as unexpected.
- Penalties/fines – Regulatory/government agencies and card brands may impose penalties or fines of various types.

- Restrictions – Oftentimes, restrictions on operations or payments may be imposed by outside agencies on an affected company that hamper business processes and interfere with generating revenue.
- Negative company evaluation – This impact and residual cost is derived from the fact that customers who have their own regulatory requirements and who may need to perform vendor security audits could see the affected company as a risk, or it may fail their audit outright due to a successful breach and discovery of critical vulnerabilities.
- Reputational loss – This impact and residual cost involves a loss of consumer confidence that the affected company's customers (and the street overall) have in the affected company overall.
- Intellectual property loss – This cost occurs if the affected company loses its crown jewels, secret sauce, or whatever it is that the company derives its value from when that knowledge becomes "free" to everyone on the Internet or perhaps the affected company's competitors or customers.
- Improvement costs – The costs associated with making improvements to people, processes, and/or technology in order to detect, respond to, or prevent additional/future cybersecurity breaches and regulatory non-compliance.

Lawsuits, Penalties, Restrictions, and Fines

A significant cybersecurity breach that impacts regulated data will almost certainly lead to lawsuits, penalties, restrictions, and fines, followed by a mandate to put in place the detection and response capabilities that should already have been extant, resulting in additional residual costs. It is common for large companies to face lawsuits, penalties, restrictions, and fines from one or more government or regulatory agencies, credit card brands, or other sources. These usually include:

1) The Security and Exchange Commission (SEC) – This pertains to companies that are publicly traded.
2) Federal Trade Commission (FTC) – This affects companies that fail in their duty to protect customer data, do not live up to published claims, commitments, and policies related to the same, and/or suffer a breach of any regulated data type. The FTC may get involved and impose a consent order.
3) Health and Human Services (HHS) – Affects companies suffering a loss of HIPAA-regulated data – Protected Health Information (PHI)
4) State Attorney Generals (AGs) and Departments of Justice (DoJs) - In recent years, groups of state attorneys general and state departments of justice have banded together to file a combined lawsuit against companies affected by a security breach under the laws of the strictest state.
5) Banks and payment card providers can impose fines and processing restrictions – If financial instruments are affected, the card brands are particularly aggressive about this. The Payment Card Industry Security Standards Council (PCI-SSC) maintains card payment regulations for all the brands, but the card brands themselves impose fines and restrictions.
6) Customers – They may file individual or class-action lawsuits.

7) Investors – They can hurt affected companies in different ways. Problems may include lawsuits, pulling their investments, devaluing the company, or even forcing leadership changes if they have enough support from other investors and the board.

The threat of regulatory actions and fines is not purely theoretical, nor is it an idle threat. All included, per the 2023 Ponemon Institute/IBM Cost of a Data Breach Report, the average cost per record involved in a data breach was $165 across all industry types. The average total cost of data breaches reached $4.45M across all industries, with the average healthcare breach tipping the scales at $10.93M. This is an increase of over 53% since 2020. (IBM, 2023)

If large numbers are involved, these costs can be devastating to a company or organization, especially if they are larger than average. However, government fines for individual breaches of other regulated data types have gone a lot higher. Consider the following recent fines from various global regulatory agencies:

1) Didi Global – Fined $1.19B by the Chinese Cyberspace Administration in 2022
2) Amazon – Fined $877M by Luxembourg National Data Protection Commission (CNPD) in 2021
3) Equifax – Fined $575M by a combined lawsuit by multiple United States consumer protection agencies in 2019

Negative Company Evaluation

Customers are increasingly sensitive to regulatory compliance requirements, which mandate controls that assure the confidentiality, integrity, and availability of systems and content. This includes ensuring vendors and business partners with access to and control of data meet at least the minimum security and response capability baseline that the customer is subject to.

It is no longer acceptable to outsource and transfer risk. The company contracting the service is still ultimately responsible for the data security of their customers and themselves. If companies are unable to provide an acceptable level of security, they either need to come into compliance quickly, or customers will be forced to take their business elsewhere.

More specifically, companies will ultimately lose business in the RFP discovery process or renewal processes. They simply will not meet the requirements without adequate, documented capabilities, controls, and testing of the same.

Reputational Loss

If consumers do not believe that the vendor or related service(s) they use are secure, or they have a valid reason to think their data may be unsafe, they can and will take their business elsewhere. Many alternatives exist for more secure and regulatory-compliant services and/or products. It is easy to find alternatives, and most of them promise to be both secure and compliant. If it is identified that a company lost its customers' data in a security breach or if it were made public that it failed a compliance audit, it is very likely to result in the loss of additional customers.

Once reputational loss occurs and loyalty is eroded, it is likely that it will not easily be regained, if such is even possible. A security incident exposing consumer information, particularly if it is sensitive and damaging, is very likely to lead to an immediate reputational loss. Some good recent examples include:

- Equifax, which in 2017 saw a 27% drop in net income following their reported breach. (USA Today, 2017, p.1)
- Target announced a 46% drop in profit following their 2013 breach (New York Post, 2014, p.1)

According to identiyfinder.com, the following are statistical averages for customers avoiding breached organizations:

- 33 percent of consumers will shop elsewhere if their retailer of choice is breached
- 30 percent of patients will find a new healthcare provider if a hospital/doctor's office is breached
- 24 percent of consumers will switch bank/credit card provider if the institution is breached
(Identity Finder, 2014, p.1)

Intellectual Property Loss

Intellectual property is a common target of espionage and cybercrime – everyone is looking for an edge and to keep competitors from having one. The threat of intellectual property loss is a significant business driver and common casualty in cybersecurity breaches. It has become commonplace for countries like China to hack for industrial and military secrets and harvest intellectual property from companies along the supply chain, as well as hacking prior to investing in foreign companies to gain an edge on company profitability, resources, and other intelligence prior to investment or purchase.

Long story short, hacking intellectual property and confidential information gives the attackers a competitive edge and often negates the desire or need for purchase or investment, and it creates undue competition. As a specific, single example, the FBI reported that China stole plans for the F22, F35, and 32 other top-secret projects in 2014. This put China decades ahead in its fighter jet program, as well as other defense projects. China went from having no fighter jet capabilities to 5th generation fighter jets with similar specifications to US counterparts. (The Washington Times, 2014, p.1)

Improvement Costs

These are the costs associated with making improvements to the customer environment in order to reliably detect, respond, or prevent additional/future cybersecurity breaches and avoid regulatory non-compliance. They are expensive and very time-consuming but always cheaper than the fully loaded cost of a breach, especially considering putting these in place will be required following a breach.

Developing an adequate program to address cyber threats, successfully pass all audits, and avoid the risk of non-compliance involves addressing all required elements of People, processes, and technology. In summary, these include:

- People – Identify and develop all necessary functions to support processes and technology related to cyber defense; develop and maintain contact lists of all key technical personnel, department heads, approvers, network/system/application owners, legal representatives, compliance team members, and anyone else needed to assist with incident response and management.
- Process – Develop and maintain security, response, business continuity, and disaster recovery plans, programs, playbooks, workflows, and relevant diagrams.
- Technology – Document and diagram the entire environment (including all locations), ingress/egress PoPs, crown jewels, sensitive data, and the security, monitoring, and response technologies that exist. In doing so, identify gaps and architect necessary controls to remediate them.

Regarding incident response technology requirements, the technology must enable full visibility and control in the three critical analysis and response target areas, consisting of:

- Account management
    - Implement IAM controls for all accounts, whether on the domain, local system, service, or application.
    - Employ and validate least privileged access and separation of duties to mitigate security and regulatory risks.
    - Utilize MFA and/or password vaulting controls for elevated accounts.
    - Utilize MFA or OTP for all remote access.
- Network traffic
    - Implement monitoring, inspection, detection, and blocking controls for egress traffic to prevent access to malicious or unauthorized locations and unauthorized content from leaving.
    - Implement monitoring, inspection, detection, and blocking controls for ingress traffic to prevent access from malicious or unauthorized locations or unauthorized access on external-facing resources.
    - Implement lateral (east/west) network traffic between and within critical or sensitive network segments – these may include server VLANs, PCI or PHI networks, DMZs, or other sensitive networks.
- Endpoints
    - Implement endpoint security controls/agents on workstations, servers, virtual machines, cloud systems, and sensitive or critical devices.
    - For the sake of rapid response, endpoint detection and response (EDR) agents should be installed everywhere for immediate use.
    - If one has to deploy these for use after an incident, precious time is lost and may alert attackers that responders are aware of them.

- SIEM/log analysis
  - Implement centralized logging and monitoring in all critical environments for security devices/applications, antivirus/antimalware/EDR systems, IAM systems, servers, services, applications, and workstations.
  - Data sources should have their logs aggregated, correlated, and analyzed against detection rules and threat feeds.

Malicious activity can hide, but it will leave fingerprints in one or more of these key areas that can be used for detection and response. The better these three system types are integrated and correlated, the better the detection and response capabilities will be. Combining all of these strategies will create a defensible posture not only against threats but also against auditors and regulations of all types. Implementing a customized, holistic, integrated solution is what it takes to avoid the negative side effects of regulatory non-compliance and the pain that comes with it.

References

IBM.(2023). 2023 Cost of a Data Breach Study. Retrieved from https://www.ibm.com/reports/data-breach?utm_content=SRCWW&p1=Search&p4=43700077723822555&p5=p&&msclkid=f58baa3e6ec71908 4226cfa87d85cc4f&gclid=f58baa3e6ec719084226cfa87d85cc4f&gclsrc=3p.ds

USA Today.(2017). Equifax data breach hacks away at credit-monitoring firm's third-quarter profit. Retrieved from https://www.usatoday.com/story/money/business/2017/11/09/equifax-data-breach-hacks-away-credit-monitoring-firms-third-quarter-profit/849193001/

New York Post.(2014) Target's profits down $440M after data breach. Retrieved from https://nypost.com/2014/02/26/targets-profits-down-46-after-data-breach/

Identify Finder.(2014). Sales Drop as Corporate Data Breaches Rise According to New Study from Identity Finder. Retrieved from https://www.prnewswire.com/news-releases/sales-drop-as-corporate-data-breaches-rise-according-to-new-study-from-identity-finder-257140751.html

The Washington Times.(2014). FBI: Chinese hacker accessed god mine of data on F-22, F-35, and 32 U.S. military projects. Retrieved from https://www.washingtontimes.com/news/2014/jul/16/fbi-chinese-hacker-accessed-gold-mine-data-f-22-f-/

8 SECURITY STANDARDS AND BEST PRACTICES

Evolving Standards

There are numerous security standards, and they have evolved over the years. They primarily started in the public sector and then moved into the private sector. In this chapter, we will go over some of the most commonly referenced security standards that come up during incident management and security audits or are frequently identified as authoritative in government requirements, regulatory standards, or seen as best practices.

Security Standards

- NIST CSRC – The National Institute of Standards and Technology Computer Security Resource Center was established in 1994. It is a division of the US Department of Commerce and offers free information security guidance. It develops and maintains an extensive collection of standards, guidelines, recommendations, and research on the security and privacy of information and information systems.
- ISO – International Organization for Standardization is an independent, non-governmental international organization with a membership of 164 national standards bodies. It brings together experts to share knowledge and develop voluntary, consensus-based, market-relevant international standards that support innovation and provide solutions to global challenges. The ISO content is paid per publication. The ISO 27002 standard came into being in 2007, but it was adapted from a long history of other, earlier standards that will be covered in more detail.
- ITIL – Formerly an acronym for Information Technology Infrastructure Library, is the best-known set of detailed practices for IT service management. It dates back to 1989 and has been owned and managed by several different entities under different structures. It focuses on aligning IT services with business needs. ITIL version 4 content is available for pay.
- COBIT – Control Objectives for Information and Related Technologies was first

released in 1996. It is a good-practice framework created by the Information Systems Audit and Control Association (ISACA), which is an international professional association for information technology (IT) management and IT governance. It has been through 5 major revisions, and COBIT content is free for ISACA members.

- OWASP – The Open Web Application Security Project is a non-profit organization and open community established in 2001. It is dedicated to enabling organizations to conceive, develop, acquire, operate, and maintain applications that can be trusted. All OWASP resources, such as tools, documents, forums, and chapters are free and open to anyone interested in improving application security.

NIST CSRC

Believe it or not, NIST has been around since 1901, and it has always been involved in establishing standards within the sciences. In 1994, NIST got into cybersecurity guidance with the Computer Security Resource Center (CSRC). Since then, they have developed a steady stream of computer and cybersecurity-related standards and practice guides that continue to grow and cover an ever-increasing library of information security-related topics.

The purpose of NIST cybersecurity standards was originally focused on government security controls. However, they are also considered industry benchmarks, providing common sets of security standards at varying baseline levels to be used across any industry vertical or security target. NIST frameworks provide highly detailed, technically sound, and broadly applicable sets of controls for information systems and procedures.

They are robust enough to satisfy security and auditing controls from legal and regulatory requirements. They also provide a sound basis to establish the confidentiality, integrity, and availability of systems, applications, and information being processed, stored, or transmitted. Best of all, the NIST content is free! It is available to anyone for public or private use!

There are 2 different NIST CSRC Special Publication families that are most relevant to computer and cybersecurity topics. These include the SP 800 and SP 1800 families:
- SP 800 – Computer security guidelines for various focus areas, most notably for incident response/management:
    - 800-61 – Computer Security Handling Guide
    - 800-53 – Security and Privacy Controls for Information Systems
    - 800-83 – Guide to Malware Incident Prevention and Handling
- SP 1800 – Cybersecurity practice guides, including various secure configuration guidelines

The NIST information security frameworks are guidelines for organizations to develop their own certification programs. However, they are not certification programs in and of themselves. Neither people nor companies are certified under NIST.

ISO

The ISO/IEC 27000-series standards have a long and deep history and evolution. They are descended from a corporate security standard donated by the Royal Dutch Shell Company (AKA Shell) to a UK government initiative in the early 1990s. The Shell standard was developed into British Standard BS 7799 in the mid-1990s and later adopted as ISO/IEC 17799 in 2000.

The ISO/IEC standard was revised in 2005 and renumbered ISO/IEC 27002 in 2007 to align with the other ISO/IEC 27000-series standards. It was later revised again in 2013. As such, ISO/IEC 17799, ISO/IEC 27002, and ISO/IEC 27001 were derived from the original British Standard BS 7799, which was adapted from the Shell corporate security standard.

It applies to organizations of all types in any sector (public or private, profit or non-profit) that have a need to process, store, transmit, and/or protect confidential or sensitive information. It provides guidance for companies trying to implement common information security controls in established or developing industries and/or environments. It includes guidance for policies, procedures, and technical controls affecting the people, processes, and technology.

The framework is designed for organizations to use as a reference for selecting controls within the process of implementing an Information Security Management System (ISMS) based on ISO/IEC 27001. It provides very broad-based guidelines for the development of policies and respective security, business, and regulatory-related controls within an organization. It is very high-level, and it requires those applying it to already have an in-depth understanding of information security and know how to apply it within an organization. The guidelines are tantamount to placeholders for security controls and are neither detailed nor prescriptive. It reads like the table of contents for a book about security controls and processes but lacks all of the details required to design or implement them.

The fact that it has not been revised since 2013 makes it a little stale. However, considering it is non-technical and non-specific about controls, it affords the framework somewhat of a buffer bolstering its relevance.

Organizations can be certified under ISO/IEC 20000. It presents a specification for IT service management for which selected ITIL processes can be used as guidance documents. Note that ISO 27001/2 complies with the security requirements of ISO/IEC 20000.

ITIL

ITIL is the first standard that comes to mind regarding IT change management and providing consistent system baselining. ITIL ownership and responsibility have shifted a few times since its inception. However, since July 2013, ITIL has been owned by AXELOS, which is a joint venture between Capita and the UK Cabinet Office.

AXELOS licenses entities to use the ITIL intellectual property, accredits licensed examination institutes, and manages updates to the framework. Entities that wish to implement ITIL internally do not require this license to do so.

The ITIL 4 Foundation Book, containing the most recent revision, was released on February 18th, 2019. In the former version (ITIL v3, AKA ITIL 2011), ITIL was published as a series of five core volumes. Each volume covered a different IT Service Management (ITSM) lifecycle stage. Although ITIL underpins ISO/IEC 20000 (previously known as BS 15000), there are some differences between the ISO 20000 standard and the ITIL framework.

There is no formal, independent third-party assessment available for ITIL compliance in an organization. Moreover, certification in ITIL is only available to individuals. The goal of ITIL is the development of a vendor-neutral approach to service management. The ethos behind the development of ITIL was the recognition of increased dependence on IT services that must be managed by high-quality IT processes.

In its application, ITIL describes the various types of procedures and guidelines, which are not specific to technologies, companies, or organizations. The guidance can be applied by any entity when establishing integration with their respective strategy, delivering value, and maintaining a minimum level of competency and change control.

The guidance allows the organization to establish a baseline from which it can plan, implement, and measure the efficacy of its program, the respective information technology controls, and their respective changes. ITIL does not attempt to cover the entire breadth of IT management or governance. However, the respective guidance and compliance are the first considerations in change management.

COBIT

COBIT is usually implemented to address the need for IT and related services standardization, unification, and alignment with business objectives and/or external requirements or regulations. The goal of the COBIT guidance is "to research, develop, publicize and promote an authoritative, up-to-date, internationally accepted IT governance control framework for adoption by enterprises and day-to-day use by business managers, IT professionals and assurance professionals."

It is a strong framework with broad coverage, providing alignment and a measure of maturity between governance and regulatory requirements against business objectives and required resources. COBIT contains no technical details included within the framework. Therefore, it is generic and non-specific.

COBIT is typically used for the purposes of self-auditing and assessment against control objectives, and there is no certification process for organizations. The COBIT 5/2019 framework is based on 5 key principles:

- Principle 1: Meeting stakeholder needs – It focuses on meeting stakeholder objectives by enabling business value creation through the use of information technology. Entities can customize it to suit their individual context through the cascade of goals, which translates the high-level enterprise goals into manageable, specific, IT-related goals that map to specific processes and practices.
- Principle 2: Covering the Enterprise End-to-end – It integrates Information Technology goals and the enterprise goals overall. It accomplishes this by addressing all functions and processes within the enterprise, not limited to IT, and treats information and related technologies as any other asset within the enterprise. IT-related governance and management are considered enterprise-wide enablers for business objectives and stakeholder goals.
- Principle 3: Applying a single integrated framework – Because there are many IT-related standards or best practices that provide guidance at various levels, COBIT 5 provides an over-arching ability to align with other relevant standards and frameworks at a high level and form the mesh between them.
- Principle 4: Enabling a holistic approach – It seeks to provide the efficiency and effectiveness of a holistic approach for governance and management of enterprise IT considering all of the interacting components. The COBIT 5 framework defines the following seven categories of enablers to support the holistic approach:
  - Principles, Policies, and Frameworks
  - Processes
  - Organizational Structures
  - Culture, Ethics, and Behavior
  - Information
  - Services, Infrastructure, and Applications
  - People, Skills, and Competencies
- Principle 5: Separating governance from management – It distinguishes between governance and management as disciplines that require different types of activities, different organizational structures, and serve different purposes. It distinguishes between them as:
  - Governance is the activity that ensures stakeholder and regulatory considerations are evaluated to identify, facilitate, and monitor the achievement of balanced objectives.
  - Management develops and monitors activities in alignment with the direction set by the governance body to achieve the agreed-upon objectives.

OWASP

OWASP has become the de facto authority of web application security standards. It is deeply technical and is utilized by both red-team and blue-team activities, including the following:

- Application development
- Software architecture
- Information security technical writing
- Vulnerability assessment
- Application security assessment
- Penetration testing

OWASP currently has over 93 active projects that provide security controls, secure code/function examples, guidelines, and assessment procedures/utilities for all web-related languages, applications, and technologies. OWASP projects are collections of related tasks, having defined roadmaps and team members. The project leaders are responsible for providing the vision, roadmap, tasks, promotion, and building the team for their respective projects.

OWASP provides a Top-10 reference standard identifying the most critical web application security risks as of the date of publication, which is updated every few years. Adopting the OWASP Top 10 should be considered a minimum baseline for all web applications. The OWASP Top 10 – 2017 publication contains the following items:

A1:2017-Injection

A2:2017-Broken Authentication

A3:2017-Sensitive Data Exposure

A4:2017-XML External Entities (XXE)

A5:2017-Broken Access Control

A6:2017-Security Misconfiguration

A7:2017-Cross-Site Scripting (XSS)

A8:2017-Insecure Deserialization

A9:2017-Using Components with Known Vulnerabilities

A10:2017-Insufficient Logging & Monitoring

9 RESPONDER READINESS

Knowledge Requirements

When it comes to Incident Commander/Manager and responder readiness, there are many components that need to be taken into consideration to create a well-prepared team. As usual, the plan involves developing the right people, processes, and technology to make it successful. The following are some of the primary considerations areas and details.

Knowledge of the Current Threat Landscape

To remain relevant, team members must maintain awareness of the current cybersecurity threats, specifically attacker/malware applications, functions, capabilities, and methods. This requires a significant dedication to staying up to date with threat intelligence, vulnerabilities, attacker TTPs, malware, and evolving trends. Be warned, this is an eternal treadmill of learning that never ends. Maintaining awareness involves researching and documenting the evolving elements that are typically organized, grouped, and applied in relation to a mature framework, such as the Lockheed Martin Kill-Chain. It provides a good structure for discussing what attackers are doing at each stage, which can then be translated into actions that defenders need to apply to detect, block, or otherwise respond to it, as follows:

- Reconnaissance
  - Attacker – Selects targets of interest (any people, processes, and or technology) to case the environment, profile technologies, identify vulnerabilities, and develop a plan of attack.
  - Defender – Perform actions to prevent disclosure of sensitive information and detect/block casing activity.
- Weaponization
  - Attacker – Develop tooling, malware, backdoor, and delivery methods to successfully deploy exploits based on extant vulnerabilities against targeted resources.
  - Defender – Develop knowledge and detection capabilities of the attacker's Tactics, Techniques, and Procedures (TTPs). This includes all of their known toolsets, malware, delivery methods, artifacts, and related indicators.
- Delivery
  - Attacker – Launches attacks against victims over vulnerable people, processes, and/or technology. These commonly include phishing emails, malicious websites, infected USB drives, worms, automated exploit kits, etc.
  - Defender – Develop and implement training and countermeasure capabilities to detect and block expected delivery methods. This will be a combination of people, processes, and technology, all of which leverage knowledge of weaponization and delivery techniques. Training should be provided for technical teams, leadership, and standard users, as appropriate.
- Exploitation
  - Attacker – Develop exploit methods that can compromise vulnerabilities and deliver weaponized payloads on the victim's devices, systems, or applications. These will likely include multiple exploits that are targeted to the victim's environment and resources of interest.
  - Defender – Develop detection capabilities, hardening techniques, countermeasures, and compensation controls against exploit methods. These include deploying some or all of the following as appropriate:
    - Network devices
    - Endpoint agents
    - Centralized logging aggregation, correlation, and analysis/SIEM
    - Resource hardening (all types)
    - Least privilege permissions (don't let users have Admin access)
    - Security policy controls
    - Configuration management controls
    - IAM controls (admin password vaulting, MFA, etc.)
    - Training for technical teams, leadership, and standard users
- Installation

- Attacker – Develop methods to install the payload. This includes backdoors and persistence methods on targeted systems under both privileged and non-privileged access conditions. Implement methods to cover evidence of installation by using appropriate hiding techniques.
- Defender – Develop detection and countermeasure capabilities for malware installation methods. These include deploying some or all of the following as appropriate:
  - Endpoint agents
  - Centralized logging aggregation, correlation, and analysis/SIEM
  - Resource hardening (all types)
  - Least privilege permissions (don't let users have Admin access)
  - Security policy controls
  - Configuration management controls
  - IAM controls (admin password vaulting, MFA, etc.)
  - Training for technical teams, leadership, and standard users

- Command & Control (C2)
  - Attacker – Develop methods to maintain communication with compromised systems and avoid detection. This includes using redundant methods to ensure resiliency, reliability, and stealth.
  - Defender – Develop detection and countermeasure capabilities for attackers and malware C2 methods. These include deploying appropriate network, endpoint, and logging security controls, devices, and agents. SSL/TLS decryption is a must. Admin and security personnel training is also an essential countermeasure.

- Actions on Objectives
  - Attacker – Develop methods to gather information, harvest credentials, elevate privileges, create privileged accounts, spread laterally, and deploy malicious payloads across the organization. Attackers may also act on other objectives using a dynamic network of compromised systems, avoiding detection through stealthy communication.
  - Defender – Develop detection and countermeasure capabilities for lateral movement and exfiltration methods. These must include internal movement between systems, in addition to ingress/egress traffic. Methods include deploying appropriate network, endpoint, and logging security controls. These will leverage network monitoring devices and endpoint agents. Having a baseline for what is normal within the defender's environment is also critical for comparison against anomalous activity that is detected. Admin and security personnel training is an essential countermeasure.

Knowledge of the Current Solutions Space

Team members must maintain awareness of the current security technologies, investigation methods, and countermeasures that can be brought to bear. The Incident Commander and team members need to be able to utilize or recommend relevant tools to best detect, investigate, contain, mitigate, and/or remediate threats. In addition to being able to utilize whatever security and investigative capabilities a customer already has in use, sometimes solutions need to be rapidly deployed in order to detect and/or respond to security threats.

This is easier to do as a professional services provider or value-added reseller (VAR), as these entities would have a wide variety of access to nearly any vendor. With access to helpful vendor sales or business development teams and the right negotiation tactics, this access could provide the ability to utilize a full spectrum of tools to best accommodate the respective needs of customer environments.

The sampling of various tools can also be accomplished in an in-house situation through a constant stream of product evaluations or demos. However, this takes significant time and dedication, which can become extremely onerous. In order to begin to understand the tools' capabilities, time must be spent on proof of value (PoV) evaluations and bake-offs against other products to understand the strengths and weaknesses of each.

Trade shows, particularly RSA, are a good place to preview and sample the entire landscape of security tools in their sanitized demo environments and/or in PowerPoint previews. However, it is hard to get a real sense of their true capabilities, as anything experienced from marketing fluff in a controlled environment will highlight strengths and avoid revealing any gaps. It is the author's opinion that anything vendors demonstrate via a PowerPoint presentation should be avoided. This is usually a clear indication that the product has too many flaws or errors to demo live, and it should probably be avoided at all costs.

Moreover, it is impossible at trade shows to get a true understanding of scale and, more importantly, the capabilities and efficacy of the various solutions at scale. Most solutions being demoed will hopefully work on a scale of one, which makes them demo-able at a trade show. However, when they are tested on a scale of thousands, tens of thousands, or hundreds of thousands, it is possible to get a true sense of their efficacy (or lack thereof) in the real world, solving real problems.

As such, it is important to understand which solutions work and which don't and identify the specific problems that will be encountered at scale within various environments and evidence universes. Additionally, no single solution solves every problem, and the combination of solutions that can work together to address the needs at the scale of the particular environment and evidence universe being investigated needs to be considered. This requires a broad and deep understanding of the environment, evidence universe, and the solution space. Ultimately, understanding what products work best for which situations comes down to having seen the respective products succeed of rail at scale in real-world implementations.

Knowledge of Evolving Laws and Regulations
Updates to laws and regulatory requirements come out frequently, and they are often conflicting and hard to navigate. The application and enforcement of such typically drive the

scope deeper and broader with each release. This influences information security and incident response/management requirements. Laws, statutes, ordinances, and their respective interpretation in court may also change the nature of how information security controls are applied and how incident response/management is conducted. Specifically, it typically influences the process, goals, and objectives when performing such.

Sometimes, the interpretation of existing regulatory compliance requirements is modified by special guidance that comes out or by the interpretation of existing laws in court. These circumstances effectively create new requirements out of existing language. This is in part because the regulation must evolve with advancements in technology and/or the use, transmission, and storage of the data. This extends the coverage of the previously established regulatory requirements into the new ways in which the subject matter is evolving or which could create risks to consumers.

For all these reasons and more, the Incident Commander must remain up to date on all relevant laws and regulations affecting their industry and respective considerations. This will enable him/her to lead and assist legal and compliance team members and leadership in interpreting security requirements under the context of relevant laws and regulations.

Appropriate Training and Certifications

Team members must take adequate cybersecurity training and certifications respective to their focus and preferably be as educated as reasonably possible across the cybersecurity, computer forensics, network forensics, and incident response landscapes. While certifications are not a true measure of knowledge or aptitude, they are very meaningful to regulators, auditors, and courts of law – particularly as an expert witness. As such, it is important to ensure that the Incident Commander and response team members are properly trained and certified, if for no other reason than how they will be perceived by others. Yes, perception matters!

If not for having adequate training and certifications, it is entirely possible that the team will perform a solid investigation following all the best practices yet have their efforts dismissed for lack of qualifications. Shrewd legal teams can cast doubt on perfectly executed work using ad-hominem attacks on responders or forensic team members who don't have industry-standard training and certification. So, to establish credibility, encourage adequate training and certification.

Traveling Consultant/Responder Requirements

If you are building a professional services team, there are extra considerations over and above an in-house team. Not only do they need the right equipment and training, but there are also some significant personal considerations that they need to be prepared for.

Go-Bag

Responders should always have a go-bag at the ready. It should include a week's worth of clothes, toiletries, necessary accessories, and travel-required documents (such as a passport for international travel). The responder should keep the go-bag and investigative toolkit in the trunk of their car in a state ready for deployment at all times.

The reason for this is that the responder could get a call at any time and need to run to the airport and hop on the next plane to destinations unknown. Oftentimes, there is no time to return home to pack. Make sure to include at least the following items, as they will be appropriate in any environment:

- 2 suits or 2 sport coats and 2 pairs of slacks
- 5 button-down shirts
- Matching belt and pants
- 2 ties
- 5 socks
- 5 undergarments
- Work-out clothes and shoes
- Toiletries, sewing kit, and lint roller

Don't forget your workout clothes! They are essential for reducing stress and maintaining sanity! Also, if you travel a lot, you will need to be dedicated to getting enough exercise.

Multiple Large Limit Credit Card(s)

Incident response/management consulting travel is expensive, usually frequent, and sometimes engagements are back-to-back. An average week of consulting travel costs about $2500 per week if going to a single location. Sometimes, it can cost more or even a lot more. Costs increase significantly if travel to multiple locations is required. This is the case if traveling to certain high-cost areas, like San Francisco, New York, or other expensive locations.

An average hotel in most places in the United States costs somewhere between $150 and $250 per night. However, a cheap hotel in Manhattan is over $600 per night. Moreover, just about everything else in Manhattan, San Francisco, and other upscale locations are more expensive as well, such as flights, food, transportation, etc.

A responder will need to be able to cover travel costs for at least a month and probably longer, as it may take a while to be paid back. Additionally, there are other incidental costs incurred for IR/IM consulting, such as shipping costs, evidence drives, or other random hardware or software costs that need to be considered as well.

It is not uncommon for a responder to spend upwards of $200k or more per year in aggregated expenses, all of which they will typically need to cover using their own credit card(s). As such, if a responder needs to maintain the ability to charge two months' worth of expenses, then a credit limit of about $35k would be required on one or more cards, not including personal expenses that the responder also charges. Therefore, including personal charges estimated at $15k, a responder may need about $50k in credit capacity for all use cases, sometimes more.

Another issue that happens with credit cards and travel is that sometimes card charges that are encountered during travel to multiple cities in a short period of time trip card fraud red flags, which can cause the responder's card(s) to be disabled. This creates the need for multiple high-limit credit cards to avoid a lapse in payment capacity if it is not possible to call the bank due to travel complications.

Travel Rewards/Points Programs

There are significant benefits in having status in rewards programs beyond monetary benefits, which can be significant in and of themselves. These include advantages such as priority booking and reservation guarantees. These will provide between 24 to 48-hour booking requirements for guaranteed admittance that permits the responder to get into the desired hotel, even if it is fully booked.

Accommodating travel changes is also very important. Circumstances change, and responders may need to travel sooner or later than originally expected. Sometimes, changes may only be permissible to top-tier rewards program members. Moreover, change fees can be very expensive, especially in aggregate.

Direct monetary benefits can be very significant, considering the numbers involved. Some representative examples are in order. If the cardholder possesses a 2% cash-back card or up to 5% travel rewards card and charges $200k in travel per year, the direct cash benefit could be between $4000 and $10,000, depending on the situation. And, this is just the beginning.

Hotel points and travel miles programs result in free family vacations. It is not unrealistic to get 2 - 3 weeks of hotel and airfare covered per year from consulting travel. This helps make up for time spent away and garner support from family members.

Free first-class upgrades are helpful, as it is so much more comfortable and relaxing to travel in first class rather than by coach class. This also enables the responder to have more room in order to work while on the airplane and make travel-time billable (such as preparation or reporting). Working from coach class is almost impermissible.

→ **As a side note, if the responders/consultant is working on any kind of casework involving sensitive, confidential, or restricted information, their laptop MUST be protected with a privacy screen!** ←

Free room upgrades can enable the responder to obtain a much more comfortable room for travel. This usually includes a more sizable workspace for working in the room. It may also result in a suite upgrade, which is particularly nice as a workspace for a team or outside of work during family vacations.

Free rental car upgrades are convenient and make things more comfortable, as well as reduce costs if there is a need to pay for a larger vehicle on a recurring basis. The benefit-holder can usually book an Intermediate-class car but receive a full-size or premium vehicle for the same price. This may be required for transporting the forensic team, luggage, and equipment. It is not uncommon for teams to need to bring a significant amount of equipment onsite, depending on the situation.

Spouse and Family Support

More important than anything, the Incident Commander responders need to have an understanding and patient spouse and support from the rest of the family. It simply does not work without this, and the importance of such cannot be overstated.

The responder is likely to be gone frequently and for long periods of time. This may happen at a moment's notice, regardless of plans with family and friends. Responder will miss many weekends, birthdays, anniversaries, holidays, events, children's school activities or achievements, music/dance recitals, and almost anything else that may be important to family members.

Spouses will need to be able to maintain the house, finances, and all family affairs in the absence of the responder. Mutual trust of spouses in all matters is critical. Codependent relationships will not last, and each of the spouses will need to be strong, independent, and capable of being on their own or managing the family and home for extended periods of time.

Hardware, Software, Services, and Tooling

The response team needs to have very robust, dedicated hardware, systems, devices, and software to support cybersecurity, incident response, and forensic workflows throughout the various phases of the investigation. While there are a large number of open-source or free projects that provide some interesting functionalities, they are all very limited in scope, scale, or functionality. Ultimately, enterprise-level software solutions and big-iron hardware or similar virtual/cloud services must be obtained to provide the necessary functionality in scalable solutions support for these workflows across operational environments.

Physical Lab and Portable Hardware

Having a physical forensic lab is a must for any company of notable size and any professional services provider offering related services. Once a company grows to between 500 and 1000 employees, there will be enough work to keep a small team and lab busy. The lab should be located in a secure, physically isolated environment with very limited physical or remote access, as appropriate for the circumstances, and access controls should be configured according to best practices.

The hardware required to support computer forensic and incident response investigations is typically highly specialized, server-class hardware having large amounts of memory, processing power, and storage. The amount of capacity required in all resource areas increases over time to match the needs of the resources being investigated, which also increases over time. These requirements are consistent whether the hardware is stationary in the lab or portable to support onsite or remote investigations. More specifically, it is important to have forensic hardware that can be quickly deployed at any time to support responders doing onsite evidence acquisitions, mobile investigations, or response activities.

For either fixed or mobile forensic hardware, the investigators need to have hardware enabling them to connect to all drive and mobile device types to ensure they can acquire evidence in a forensically sound manner. These devices tend to have high failure rates, so their forensic kits should have significant redundancy for each type of connector and/or write blocker. Ensure that the lab and the portable forensic kits for each team member are fully stocked and have plenty of extras.

Portable Investigation Kits

The Incident Commander should work with responders to ensure they have and maintain an investigative toolkit that is fully stocked, organized, and ready for rapid deployment at all times. Responders should never borrow from their toolkit or leave it in a partially stocked state. Doing such could leave it incomplete for the next deployment. It should be kept with the responder's go-bag, which should also be available at all times. In this way, the responder is always ready to go if/when the call arrives. Remember, when that call arrives, there is typically no time to do anything but grab and go. Anything else may take too long.

A fully stocked investigative toolkit with the following bullet-pointed contents would enable onsite responders to quickly collect a large amount of evidence in a forensically sound manner. Note that the quantity of drives listed might not contain enough storage space to facilitate capturing forensic images of large quantities of evidence. The storage capacities are increasing all across the evidence universe: endpoints (workstations and servers), virtual machines, data stores, etc. The investigators may have to purchase additional evidence collection drives and/or collect original evidence drives, depending upon the situation. A critical requirement is that the size of the portable forensic toolkit must meet carry-on size criteria for airlines. This simplifies travel and avoids the loss or theft of crucial resources:

- Pelican 1510 case

- 2 Forensic laptops with required software licensing and keys
- 2 Network taps with required cables
- Portable Wi-Fi devices
- 4 – 4TB USB 3.0 hard drives – wiped/encrypted
- 2 – 1 TB USB 3.0 flash drive
- 2 – 2.5/3.5 hard drive dual docking bay
- 2 – Write blocker kits for each drive type
- 2 – Mobile device connectors for each in-scope mobile phone type
- Anti-static and evidence bags
- Labeler with extra labels
- Chain of custody forms

Virtual Hardware

Whereas physical hardware ultimately has scalability issues and can, at most, reside in one place, virtual hardware can be infinitely scalable and accessible by response personnel from all locations. This can be especially useful if multiple people need to upload evidence and share in the investigative processes. It is not uncommon for onsite investigators to get assistance from remote team members. As with the physical forensic lab resources, the virtual lab hardware must be extremely secure, according to best practices. Having virtual lab forensic resources does not negate the need for physical hardware and connectors or write blockers, but once the evidence has been collected, it can be uploaded and processed in virtual hardware.

Analysis Software

The response team needs to have access to all of the software and licensing to support any resources or data types they are likely to encounter in the evidence universe. Typical focus areas are computer forensics, network forensics, and mobile forensics, but there are many nuanced sub-types within those categories. Moreover, new operating systems, file systems, storage types, and smart devices are developed on a continual basis, and investigative software must be updated frequently to remain relevant.

Analysis systems should ideally be configured in an identical manner and deployed from a clean image prior to each investigation. The investigative software included should provide evidence collection and analysis capabilities across all technology areas (network, endpoint, and logs) and support each system, OS, device, and artifact type that is a target of the investigation. Whether provided on-prem or via cloud services, incident response, and forensic teams need to have the following analysis capabilities:

Enterprise Forensic Acquisition and Remote Analysis

Consultant paradigm:

If the response team is acting as consultants who are performing investigations at a customer site, the customer may already have enterprise forensic software deployed. If they do, and it was previously deployed to the investigation targets, it will save time to use their existing capabilities. This will expedite all forensic workflows, such as live analysis, volatile data collection, memory collection, remote full or partial disk imaging, and forms of data collection. All of the data can be collected using the customer's capabilities and then brought back to the lab systems via evidence files for deep-dive analysis.

If the customer does not possess these capabilities, the response team will need to provide the forensic agent installer that is keyed to the investigative machine(s). All investigative machines should have their forensic agents keyed the same so as to permit swapping or use of multiple systems without reconfiguration. The consultants can employ as many investigative systems as necessary to simultaneously collect and analyze data from customer endpoints. As an additional side note, the endpoint agent installer should be provided to the customer to install as soon as the contract is signed.

In-house paradigm:
If the response team is an in-house investigative team, they should have the agents pre-deployed at all locations and on all systems (workstations and servers). This will ensure rapid ability to respond and obtain broad access to affected resources. The investigative agents must be part of the standard system build, regardless of the operating system type or system use case.

The last thing the response team can afford during urgent response activity is to have delays introduced by the need to perform agent deployment that will enable the endpoint portion of the investigation to move forward. Performing agent deployment to affected systems following a breach 1) takes time and 2) could alert attackers to the investigative team's awareness of the incident. There is no such thing as "just-in-time" delivery when it comes to deploying forensic agents to endpoints.

Volatile Metadata Timeline & Retrospection Analysis
The same logic and reasoning for enterprise forensic agents apply to endpoint detection and response (EDR) agents, provided they are separate agents and toolsets. The sooner the agents are installed, the more effective the response team can be. Cloud-based EDR agents have a significant number of advantages over other models.

For starters, cloud-based EDR can provide the response team with almost immediate visibility into the activity on systems of interest. Consultants can view the activity and begin response actions remotely or even while en route. As such, they can identify attacker activity and contain it before greater damage is done.

Moreover, being as the cloud-based EDR can be installed across all systems in the environment and report back to a centralized cloud environment, differential comparisons can be made across the systems to identify anomalies. This comparative function provides the ability for investigators to perform least-prevalent detection across all endpoints, whether inside or outside the security perimeter. This helps responders quickly identify suspicious or malicious applications based on the deviation from normal and can shorten detection time for malicious applications by orders of magnitude. This type of analysis cannot feasibly be performed in any EDR model other than the centralized cloud EDR.

Conversely, EDR agents that scan endpoints and collect targeted data can, at most, collect the pre-configured data for the endpoints that are scanned. If the content is not selected for collection or if the endpoints are unavailable inside the security perimeter, then the data will not be collected. There is very little capability to perform anomaly detection, least-prevalence detection, or threat detection and investigate endpoints outside the security perimeter unless the EDR agents report to a centralized cloud location.

Further, EDR agents deployed to all systems (whether inside or outside the security perimeter) enable volatile metadata analysis, timeline analysis, and retrospection. These analysis methods have superseded the analysis capabilities of standard enterprise forensic agents, which are much slower and less capable. The ability to reach out across all endpoints to identify IOCs, malicious script activity, suspicious content from threat feeds, system/activity anomalies, or least-prevalent binaries is typically the fastest way to identify malicious applications, infected machines, compromised user accounts, and at-risk data.

Stand-alone volatile data analysis tools are also helpful for capturing and analyzing volatile metadata and RAM dumps. They are equally capable of identifying malicious activity, malware samples, artifacts, and IOCs. However, they take significant time and effort to utilize and are not scalable in an enterprise environment or for remote systems.

Malware Analysis and Reverse Engineering

When malware samples are discovered, it is important to have a secure, isolated environment to perform analysis of them. This usually requires different virtual machines for various operating system types and configurations to ensure malware operates as intended according to the targeted platform. This is important to obtain an understanding of how the malware would install and function on the affected system/configuration types.

Malware analysis actions typically include behavioral analysis, static analysis, disassembly, cryptography, and other steps for reverse engineering. Analysis actions may require several different software packages to facilitate workflows and analysis methodologies for all the use cases.

Some workflows can be automated, like behavioral analysis. However, many malware analysis actions, like static analysis, require deep-dive, manual workflows requiring experts. Both of these workflows should be performed in isolated, non-internet-connected environments to prevent outbound communication and leakage. This provides a better control environment and will reduce reliance on online sources that may introduce risk and create an unsafe situation for analyzing malware samples.

Log Aggregation and Analysis/SIEM

The response team will need to analyze a wide variety of logs from numerous sources during the investigation. Log sources typically include all types of:

- Network devices – Firewalls, WAF, Wi-Fi, routers, load balancers, UAM, UBA, UEBA, etc.
- Security infrastructure – WAFs, IDS, IPS, antivirus, antimalware
- Varieties of systems – Windows, Mac, Linux, and Unix variants
- Management services – Directory services infrastructure, DNS, DHCP, IAM, etc.
- Applications of all kinds – Web, database, commercial, custom, etc.

Log parsing and analysis utilities need to be able to interpret, decode, convert, and align log types from disparate sources. This will prepare them to be searched holistically and facilitate events being displayed along a unified timeline. Log parsing and analysis often require more than one tool to consume data from all log sources. It may also require custom parsing scripts to be configured if no out-of-the-box solutions are available.

If a full SIEM solution is needed, it will not scale to an investigative laptop and will need whatever hardware is required to support the quantity of data sources. However, small-scale, limited SIEM solutions are very helpful for processing logs during an investigation.

Network Traffic Capture/Analysis

Unless endpoint agents capture network traffic, other endpoint artifacts and logs usually cannot definitively identify what happened over the network. At most, they will show metadata, metrics, residual artifacts left on the system, and alerts resulting from network traffic. However, no substantive content will be available.

Captured network traffic is a key piece of evidence that can either prove or disprove what happened during an incident like no other artifact type can. Think of it as a video recording of what happened on the network, and anything transferred across it might be visible if recorded. Network traffic contents can be the most definitive proof of whether sensitive, regulated data left the organization.

If notification or reporting of the data loss is required, a clear view of what happened on the network may be required. It could explicitly show what content was exfiltrated and avoid the need to over-report. Conversely, it can provide a solid basis for defending that data was not exfiltrated.

Inherent in network traffic analysis is the ability to collect, decode, decrypt, and/or interpret the data in the traffic. This requires a lot of skill and a little luck, especially when dealing with encrypted traffic and obtaining keys. Long story short, the odds are good that the attackers were lazy and did a really bad job. However, it can still be very time-consuming if performed manually. It is best automated through technological capabilities.

Aggregated Timeline Analysis

In order to understand the full picture of what transpired during an incident, it is necessary to align content from all relevant log sources and system artifacts into a single, unified timeline. For example, to understand how a web server data breach occurs, one would need to look at any log source or artifact type that can help tell the story.

Identifying potential evidence sources involves tracing the path of the attack to enumerate all relevant logs across all sources along the way. This will help develop an understanding of the way the attack affects compromised computers and applications, as well as enumerate all likely artifacts. For a fully compromised web server, these sources would include at least network traffic, firewall logs, IDS/IPS logs, web-service logs, web application logs, database logs, operating system logs (various types), file system artifacts, registry artifacts, and memory artifacts.

Each of these has a combination of disparate and overlapping data types, with the overlapping data types having different names for the fields. A tool performing aggregated timeline analysis needs to normalize and align the events from the different log types into a single view and represent all of the salient content in a discernable way.

Vulnerability Assessment

Every investigation needs a starting point. If it is expected that an incident may be related to an external attack, and there are no good indicators of the entry point, the vulnerability assessment may provide one. This is typically not necessary, but sometimes it is needed and helpful in driving mitigation and remediation efforts.

Vulnerabilities using authenticated scans can quickly identify all of the unpatched applications and security misconfigurations a lot quicker and more thoroughly than a forensic process ever will. However, if systems are compromised and have malware or backdoors installed, it is possible that authenticated scans will leak credentials. This is a risk, but ultimately, it might not make a difference if the credentials have already been harvested. In any case, authenticated scans of potentially compromised systems are a bad idea.

Additionally, there are typically more system vulnerabilities that exist than are the focus of a breach investigation. If systems are behind on security patching, usually more than one significant vulnerability exists. In order to keep the attackers out, it is necessary to close all of the doors and windows. Attackers will always find a way in, so long as gaps exist.

A word of caution is in order. Identification of specific security gaps will enumerate how the systems could have been breached. However, they will not reveal specifically how they were breached. Regardless, they at least provide a starting point for artifact collection, forensic analysis, vulnerability mitigation, and remediation activities that must occur.

Removable Media Forensic Acquisition

Remote collection and analysis tools are great for scalability. However, sometimes they aren't feasible because of complicating circumstances. Examples include issues whereby some systems or environments may be air-gapped, may not be network-connected, may not be able to take an enterprise forensic agent, or may have stability issues preventing the proper function of installed tools. As such, it is essential to always have a backup plan that will facilitate local collections for all platforms within the scope of the investigation. Make sure to have all necessary tools on USB3 removable media in order to collect the necessary evidence artifacts from all systems in the evidence universe.

A word of caution is in order, however. Infected systems can use removable media as a lateral movement vector, and there is the potential to spread malware to otherwise uninfected systems. Ideally, removable media devices should have the ability to be write-protected, particularly on insert and removal, which is when most malicious activity happens.

Cloud Services

There are a variety of cloud services that are essential to an Incident Commander and response teams. The following are some notable examples.

- Endpoint Detection and Response (EDR) – EDR is an essential tool for both in-house and professional services teams. As mentioned in other chapters, the advent of EDR technologies is probably the biggest game changer for incident response and investigations in the past several decades. These tools can provide real-time monitoring, response, and evidence collection of key endpoint artifacts and the rapid ability to retrospectively analyze what transpired on a compromised system. It speeds up the analysis process by several orders of magnitude and often negates the need to perform full-fledged forensic analysis. What formerly took days or weeks can be accomplished in minutes.

  The broader EDR tools are deployed, the better the resources are automatically protected with blocking controls for malicious sites or applications and/or provide investigators a rapid view into what occurs if attacks are successful. Not only is it easy to identify what systems were affected, but the investigators can quickly identify the method of intrusion, attacker activity performed, malware involved, accounts compromised, and data exfiltrated (or at risk) in less time than it takes to read the sports page in a local paper.

  The use cases for in-house teams using EDR and professional services consulting divisions deploying it to customer environments are similar, but the licensing needs are very different. In either case, the teams need to be able to deploy it to the entire scope of systems to get the greatest visibility and control. The main difference between the two scenarios is that professional services teams need to be able to deploy agents into separate customer environments in a multi-tenant situation and keep all tenants, searches, and data completely separate and distinct.

- Malware sandbox – Most incident response investigations invariably turn up binaries, scripts, emails, and/or possibly malicious websites that need to be analyzed to determine if they are malicious or not and to ascertain their capabilities, signatures, and possible relationship to threat actors. The best place to do this is a paid cloud-services malware sandbox that provides a secure, private, and confidential environment in which to analyze possible malware samples. It is critical that the samples are not uploaded to a publicly accessible malware analysis site but rather to an environment dedicated to the response team. If malware samples are uploaded to a public repository, such as Virus Total, they become available to all customers and searchable by anyone on the Internet. So, in an Advanced Persistent Threat (APT) situation where a dedicated adversary has gained access to a victim site and is using a unique piece of malware to maintain access, they will typically search continually for hashes of those unique malware samples on public databases, like Virus Total. If an investigative team member uploads a sample of that malware to a public site, it will almost immediately disclose that their presence has been discovered, and the attackers will quickly change tactics and probably go silent. This will complicate the investigation dramatically. So, long story short, use a paid service that keeps all samples confidential.

- Threat intelligence – Having multiple online services to obtain current and actionable threat intelligence is absolutely essential. They can be instrumental in identifying key blocking controls for malicious IOCs that may prevent breaches (by blocking malicious files, domains, or IP addresses before they become a problem) or be used to block other IOCs related to a threat actor during an ongoing attack. These feeds can also be incorporated into security controls, such as network security devices, endpoint security controls, and SIEMs. This will create the opportunity to provide enrichment for the detection and blocking of known threats.

- Domain research – Free domain research tools are not particularly good. A paid service providing an extensive history for domains and IP addresses and a pivoting ability to identify the rest of the attacker's infrastructure is absolutely critical. Just like threat intelligence, this type of service can enable responders to fully identify and even get ahead of attack campaigns by proactively implementing blocking controls for currently unused attacker infrastructure that may be part of future stages.

- Secure file transfer – It is common to send or receive very large files consisting of evidence from various sources, such as forensic drive images, device images, network traffic captures, log files, database files, or malware samples. These services must be able to temporarily receive, store, and/or send terabytes of information in a secure manner.

10 PRE-ENGAGEMENT & INCIDENT ONBOARDING

Value Proposition

To ensure the success of the incident management and response team during incident response engagements, proper preparation steps should be followed to ensure customers are properly onboarded and environments are documented. Ideally, preparation starts prior to an incident and is updated with all notable changes: 1) When a new environment is created, 2) When an incident response/management retainer or other agreement is initiated (in a consulting paradigm), 3) When a new subsidiary is being acquired, or 4) When a new division or department is being created (in an internal paradigm).

The Incident Commander (or the assisting project manager should) begin to develop an environment profile that can be used to expedite the incident response and management processes and ensure responders are familiar with the environment(s) they are working in. This typically becomes harder the more federated an organization becomes.

As changes are made to the respective environment(s), the entity profile(s) should reflect these changes. These updates should be part of a mature, cyclical process entities use to ensure rapid response and recovery of the entity environment(s) is feasible.

If not, preparation and fact-gathering must start immediately at the time of incident notification and the onset of the engagement. This is much harder than it sounds, and the challenges cannot be overstated, considering all of the resources that would normally be engaged to answer environment-related questions are fully engaged in response activity.

As such, it is critical to collect salient information about the customer environment ahead of time (rather than at the outset of the investigation), providing the specifics of people, processes, and technology within the customer's environment. The more comprehensive and accurate it is, the better it enables the incident response processes that will follow.

If it is not possible to gather it ahead of time, it should be collected as early in the engagement as possible. This should preferably happen before responders are sent onsite. This will enable the Incident Commander and response team to be prepared to provide guidance as soon as possible, rather than have to learn on the fly.

Landscape

In order to prepare for and perform incident response or management, it is necessary to build a customer profile. This begins with defining the overall customer landscape. The necessary data that must be gathered to do this will vary significantly by customer.

Following is a baseline dataset outline consisting of three primary categories (Demographics, Critical Infrastructure, and Threat Landscape), which have broad applicability across most customer environments. This outline should be fleshed out, modified, augmented, or simplified as appropriate:

Demographics
- Size
  - # of personnel – This includes all types of human resources, such as full-time, part-time, temporary workers, contractors, interns, volunteers, etc.
  - # of systems – This includes all computing endpoints of all types, such as physical or virtual workstations, servers, containers, etc., that are in their environment, whether managed or unmanaged.
  - # of locations – This includes any locations with computing infrastructure or a network connection.
  - # of data centers – This includes any self-managed, shared, or hosted data center environments.
  - # of Internet points of presence – Includes any location providing Internet access to one or more locations.
  - Annual revenue – An approximate number is sufficient, which is used to help with scale and budgeting the appropriateness of solutions.
- Location(s)
  - Cities/states/countries – Enumerate the location, type, and purpose of all entity sites, offices, etc., including all major, minor, satellite, and other

locations and the quantity of personnel and systems at each site.

- o Administrative/IT locations – Specifically identify locations that are allocated as administrative and/or Information Technology locations.
- o Data centers – Identify the location of all data centers and specifics regarding the customer capabilities and services within that data center.
- o Network types – Enumerate the types of network environments that the customer utilizes and the segmentation methods employed. Network diagrams are very helpful for this purpose.
- o Network points of presence (PoPs), bandwidth, and connection types – Identify ISPs, throughput, and the physical connection type provisioned.
- o Cloud environments – Enumerate all public, private, and/or hybrid cloud environments utilized and the respective interconnections between them.
- o Hosted environments – Enumerate all web or other resource hosting services that are utilized and the respective interconnections between them.
- o External connections – Identify all persistent remote connections to external environments and infrastructure, whether managed by the customer or an outside party.

- Line of business
  - o Key products/services – Focus on those that provide the greatest revenue and/or have the most valuable intellectual property.
  - o Industry vertical(s) – Enumerate each key vertical, and there can be more than one for each of the products or services they are involved in.
  - o Large customers – Identify key customers that drive the greatest amount of revenue and/or who have contracts that drive special requirements.

- Regulatory impact – Enumerate all applicable regulatory bodies, including federal, state, industry, or payment type.

Critical Infrastructure

- Key resource types – For each of the following, identify the types of resources and approximate quantities of devices involved.
  - o Physical servers
  - o Physical workstations
  - o Virtual host servers
  - o Virtual systems
  - o Virtual applications
  - o Externally hosted cloud infrastructure
  - o Managed mobile devices
  - o SIEMs and log monitoring infrastructure

- Key application/service types – Enumerate the information technology and evidence universe that the response team may need to investigate.
  - o Customer Resource Management (CRM)

- o Enterprise Resource Planning (ERP)
- o File storage
- o Email and messaging
- o Directory services
- o Identity and Access Management
- o Databases
- o Proprietary applications
- Security devices/capabilities
  - o Firewalls and other network security infrastructure
  - o Endpoint security infrastructure
  - o Data security infrastructure
  - o Application security infrastructure
  - o Account management and activity monitoring infrastructure
  - o SIEM and Log monitoring infrastructure
- Key vendors, partners, or affiliates – Enumerate external entities that drive regulatory, security, compliance, or audit requirements
- Crown jewels – Key assets and intellectual property within customer environment(s) and resources

Threat Landscape

- Attackers – Identify attack sources, countries, groups, or other entities known to pose a risk.
- Attack motivations – Identify what attackers are after within the customer environment.
- Tools, tactics, and procedures (TTPs) – Enumerate TTPs for known/likely attackers, including attack vectors, exploit methods, and related toolsets.
- Known malware types – Enumerate known/likely malicious applications and artifacts used by known attack groups

IR/IM Capabilities

From a high level, a customer's response capabilities can be broken down into "People, processes, and technology." However, it obviously goes a lot deeper than that. Identification of IM capabilities should enumerate key elements of these three critical areas. They should be documented ahead of time and provided prior to or at the beginning of response activity to guide the process:

- People – A contact list of all key technical personnel, SMEs, key department heads, approvers, network/system/application owners, legal representatives, compliance team members, and anyone else needed to assist with incident response and management.
- Process – Full access to all security, response, business continuity, and disaster recovery plans, programs, playbooks, workflows, and relevant diagrams.

- Technology – A comprehensive listing and related diagrams for the visibility, monitoring, response, blocking, and prevention capabilities across the entire environment. This should include IAM, network, endpoint, and SIEM (or other log collection and monitoring) capabilities across all locations, resources, network connections, crown jewels, sensitive data, and/or accounts.

PART 2 – THREAT RESPONSE

11 ANTI-FORENSICS & DETECTION EVASION

What is Anti-Forensics & Detection Evasion?

Over the last few decades, there has been a continual, evolving effort with malware to use novel techniques to remain undetected. The methods have changed significantly over time, based on the available functions of operating systems and the detection methods of security tools. Some key concepts in evasion include hiding in plain sight through imitation, living off the land (using available functions), or having advanced binaries that inject functions to manipulate the operating system behavior to prevent the malware files from being detected.

Legitimate Process Replacement & Imitation

Process replacement and imitation is pretty much the oldest trick in the book when it comes to malicious applications, but it is still in use today. This involves hiding malicious executables in plain sight by making them appear to be legitimate applications.

This is commonly done using the same name as a legitimate system binary but running it from a different directory or changing the name slightly and running it from the same directory. There are 12 processes frequently targeted for this, often called the "Dirty Dozen":

- csrss.exe
- explorer.exe
- lsaiso.exe
- lsass.exe
- RuntimeBroker.exe
- services.exe
- smss.exe
- svchost.exe
- System
- taskhostw.exe
- wininit.exe
- winlogon.exe

The key to identifying malicious instances of what appear to be benign system applications is to understand the normal state. This includes understanding the following:

- The path they should be running from
- The parent process that is supposed to call them
- The quantity of application instances that should be running simultaneously
- The expected command-line options
- The expected behavior

Any deviations from the normal state are clear indicators of the need for an investigation. In some cases, one can jump immediately from identification to conviction, as there are no benign deviations from the norm.

A correlating factor that can help identify process imitation is that it is often accompanied by Timestomping. This is explained in more detail later, but it involves the manipulation of file times to make the masquerading executable look as if it were installed at the same time as adjacent executables in the same directory. The following are some examples of hiding in plain sight.

Svchost.exe

A great place to hide malware has always been svchost.exe. There are always a lot of them running simultaneously, and they commonly handle network communication. This makes them the perfect executable to imitate in order to hide malware activity. The following image shows svchost.exe running from the wrong path and having the wrong flags.

Name	PID	Status	User name	CPU	Memory (p...	Command line
svchost.exe	15320	Running	Colby	00	576 K	C:\Users\Colby\AppData\Local\Microsoft\Network\svchost.exe
svchost.exe	21616	Running	SYSTEM	00	1,324 K	C:\WINDOWS\system32\svchost.exe -k netsvcs -p -s wlidsvc
svchost.exe	9684	Running	SYSTEM	00	1,284 K	C:\WINDOWS\system32\svchost.exe -k SDRSVC
svchost.exe	18128	Running	SYSTEM	00	2,192 K	
svchost.exe	720	Running	SYSTEM	00	504 K	c:\windows\system32\svchost.exe -k dcomlaunch -p -s PlugPlay
svchost.exe	1028	Running	SYSTEM	00	14,028 K	C:\WINDOWS\system32\svchost.exe -k DcomLaunch -p
svchost.exe	1136	Running	NETWORK...	00	9,392 K	c:\windows\system32\svchost.exe -k rpcss -p
svchost.exe	1188	Running	SYSTEM	00	2,120 K	c:\windows\system32\svchost.exe -k dcomlaunch -p -s LSM
svchost.exe	1432	Running	SYSTEM	00	1,272 K	c:\windows\system32\svchost.exe -k localsystemnetworkrestricted -...
svchost.exe	1440	Running	LOCAL SE...	00	1,300 K	c:\windows\system32\svchost.exe -k localservicenetworkrestricted -...
svchost.exe	1520	Running	LOCAL SE...	00	13,236 K	c:\windows\system32\svchost.exe -k localservicenetworkrestricted -...
svchost.exe	1640	Running	LOCAL SE...	00	7,240 K	c:\windows\system32\svchost.exe -k localservice -p -s nsi
svchost.exe	1716	Running	LOCAL SE...	00	1,784 K	C:\WINDOWS\system32\svchost.exe -k LocalService -p
svchost.exe	1752	Running	LOCAL SE...	00	1,344 K	c:\windows\system32\svchost.exe -k localservicenetworkrestricted -...
svchost.exe	1872	Running	NETWORK...	00	3,608 K	c:\windows\system32\svchost.exe -k networkservice -p -s NlaSvc
svchost.exe	1880	Running	SYSTEM	00	5,640 K	c:\windows\system32\svchost.exe -k netsvcs -p -s Schedule
svchost.exe	1984	Running	LOCAL SE...	00	2,856 K	c:\windows\system32\svchost.exe -k localservice -p -s netprofm

Applications having the same name as a legitimate system application or utility running from anywhere under the AppData directory are highly suspect. The AppData directory is writable and executable by normal, non-privileged users and restricted accounts (like that of web browsers), so it is the perfect place to drop malware from compromised sites.

This is very typical of malicious activity and is an immediate red flag. Note also that svchost.exe is being run without arguments, which is never seen. Svchost.exe is always seen with the "-k" flag followed by other arguments. As such, any instance of it running without expected flags is also a key indicator and red flag.

The following image depicts a commonly encountered svchost.exe process name misspelling that is used to hide in plain sight. It has been disguised by using all uppercase letters for the process name and accompanied by a number "0" replacing the letter "O."

Just to be clear, svchost.exe ≠ SVCH0ST.EXE. It can be hard to see at first glance, and sometimes process names, especially since sometimes process names do appear capitalized. Note that this imitation of svchost.exe has the correct arguments. So, just because it has the right flags does not make it legit.

Name	PID	Status	User name	CPU	Memory (p...	Command line	
svchost.exe	8792	Running	SYSTEM	00	1,060 K	c:\windows\system32\svchost.exe -k localsystemnetworkrestricted -...	st.exe
svchost.exe	9120	Running	SYSTEM	00	1,924 K	c:\windows\system32\svchost.exe -k netsvcs -p -s Appinfo	vc
svchost.exe	9388	Running	SYSTEM	00	3,456 K	c:\windows\system32\svchost.exe -k localsystemnetworkrestricted -...	
svchost.exe	9820	Running	LOCAL SE...	00	3,568 K	c:\windows\system32\svchost.exe -k localservice -p -s CDPSvc	
svchost.exe	12740	Running	Colby	00	4,716 K	c:\windows\system32\svchost.exe -k unistacksvcgroup	
svchost.exe	13108	Running	SYSTEM	00	2,696 K	c:\windows\system32\svchost.exe -k netsvcs -p -s lfsvc	ugPlay
svchost.exe	15380	Running	LOCAL SE...	00	1,976 K	c:\windows\system32\svchost.exe -k localservicenetworkrestricted -...	
svchost.exe	16368	Running	LOCAL SE...	00	1,540 K	c:\windows\system32\svchost.exe -k localservice -p -s bthserv	
svchost.exe	3636	Running	LOCAL SE...	00	1,048 K	c:\windows\system32\svchost.exe -k localservicenetworkrestricted -...	M
svchost.exe	11436	Running	LOCAL SE...	00	892 K	c:\windows\system32\svchost.exe -k localservice -p -s BthAvctpSvc	estricted -...
svchost.exe	2008	Running	SYSTEM	00	2,000 K	c:\windows\system32\svchost.exe -k localsystemnetworkrestricted -...	estricted -...
svchost.exe	20336	Running	Colby	00	1,256 K	c:\windows\system32\svchost.exe -k printworkflow -s PrintWorkflo...	estricted -...
svchost.exe	15472	Running	SYSTEM	00	2,060 K	c:\windows\system32\svchost.exe -k localsystemnetworkrestricted -...	
svchost.exe	15392	Running	NETWORK...	00	2,940 K	C:\WINDOWS\System32\svchost.exe -k NetworkService -p -s DoSvc	
svchost.exe	15088	Running	LOCAL SE...	00	1,176 K	c:\windows\system32\svchost.exe -k localservicenetworkrestricted -...	estricted -...
svchost.exe	3544	Running	LOCAL SE...	00	1,036 K	C:\WINDOWS\System32\svchost.exe -k LocalServiceNetworkRestrict...	NlaSvc
svchost.exe	16468	Running	SYSTEM	00	4,824 K	c:\windows\system32\svchost.exe -k netsvcs -p -s BITS	
svchost.exe	20472	Running	SYSTEM	00	996 K	C:\WINDOWS\system32\svchost.exe -k appmodel -p -s camsvc	le
svchost.exe	17336	Running	SYSTEM	00	2,896 K	C:\WINDOWS\system32\svchost.exe -k netsvcs -p -s wlidsvc	profm
SVCH0ST.EXE	21288	Running	Colby	00	532 K	C:\Windows\System32\SVCH0ST.EXE -k netsvcs -p wildsvc	

Also contributing to this problem are the number ones (1), capital "I," and lowercase "l," which all look very similar. Depending upon the font, they might look identical and can be used to convincingly substitute system apps with convenient misspellings. Svchost.exe, iexplorer.exe, explorer.exe, lsass.exe, winninit.exe, lsm.exe, services.exe, and other system processes spelled with an "o," "i," or "l" are easily affected by this, especially by toggling upper-case and lower-case letters as convenient.

Where the misspelled apps are in the same directory as the app for which they are masquerading or other system apps that they try to blend in with, timestomping is commonly also used to make their existence appear legitimate. Timestomping is generally used to make the imitation files have a similar created date/time as the default system files in the same directory.

Lsass.exe

If responders know what they are looking for, the following images containing process metadata really stand out. There are many things wrong with what is depicted in these images, but it is permitted to happen by Windows, anti-virus, and anti-malware software by default.

Path	= lssas.exe
User Name	= \ Colby
PID/Parent PID	= 3888 / 20972
Started by	= cmd.exe

Path	= lsass.exe
User Name	=
PID/Parent PID	= 96 / 940
Started by	= wininit.exe

Name	PID	Status	User name	Image path name
lsass.exe	21872	Running	Colby	C:\$RECYCLE.BIN\lsass.exe
lsass.exe	96	Running	SYSTEM	C:\Windows\System32\lsass.exe

Command line	Description
c:\$RECYCLE.BIN\lsass.exe	Windows Command Processor
	Local Security Authority Process

The issues related to lsass.exe are as follows:

- Wrong parent process – The parent process should always be wininit.exe
- Wrong user – The user should always be Local System
- Wrong # of processes – There should only be one instance
- Wrong icon – It should have the system process icon
- Wrong description – It should say Local Security Authority Process
- Running from $RECYCLE.BIN – This should require no explanation

Dirty Dozen Quick-Reference Table

The following table shows a quick reference for all of the dirty dozen processes, which are most likely to be impersonated or manipulated. See Appendix A for a larger version.

Process	Parent Process	Local User	Start Time	# of instances	Image Path
csrss.exe	smss.exe	Local System	w/in seconds of boot	2 or more	%SystemRoot%\System32\csrss.exe
explorer.exe	userinit.exe	Logged-on user(s)	1st instance w/ logon	1+ per user	%SystemRoot%\explorer.exe
lsaiso.exe	wininit.exe	Local System	w/in seconds of boot	0 to 1	%SystemRoot%\System32\lsaiso.exe
lsass.exe	wininit.exe	Local System	w/in seconds of boot	1	%SystemRoot%\System32\lsass.exe
RuntimeBroker.exe	svchost.exe	Logged-on user(s)	varies	1+ per user	%SystemRoot%\System32\RuntimeBroker.exe
services.exe	wininit.exe	Local System	w/in seconds of boot	1	%SystemRoot%\System32\services.exe
smss.exe	System	Local System	w/in seconds of boot for master instance at at time of each session	1 for master instance and 1 child per session	%SystemRoot%\System32\smss.exe
svchost.exe	services.exe	varies	varies	multiple	%SystemRoot%\System32\svchost.exe
System	N/A	Local System	at boot	1	
taskhostw.exe	svchost.exe	varies	varies	1+	%SystemRoot%\System32\taskhostw.exe
wininit.exe	smss.exe	Local System	w/in seconds of boot	1	%SystemRoot%\System32\wininit.exe
winlogon.exe	smss.exe	Local System	w/in seconds of boot for master instance at at time of each session	1+	%SystemRoot%\System32\winlogon.exe

What is particularly helpful about this table is that it enumerates most of the valid values for the key metadata common in tools like Task Manager/Process Explorer. Using this table significantly helps identify malicious processes trying to impersonate system processes. Note that not every value is important for all processes, but this combination of details will help identify if any of these processes have been impersonated. Each one of these factors should be carefully scrutinized.

Injected Processes & Libraries

A frequently used method of modern malware to avoid detection is to inject malicious code into legitimate processes or libraries that then function in a way desired by malware authors. These injected functions fundamentally change the way the affected processes operate.

In this way, application functionality is rewritten, function calls are intercepted or rerouted, and processes or libraries behave in the way malware authors intend. This usually involves capturing user content and hiding it from user/system/security visibility.

Zeus is a good example of a particularly nasty, advanced malware using injection as a hiding method. Due to the source code being released in 2011, it subsequently became a code base for future malware code developers to work from. While it was originally released as a sophisticated banking trojan with advanced features, it went viral after its source code was published, and many subsequent malware families can trace their origins back to it.

User-mode rootkits typically function in this capacity and hide from detection by injecting themselves into Explorer.exe and other Windows native or security-related processes. This prevents malware-related processes, libraries, data files, connections, and/or other related artifacts from being detected, deleted, and/or blocked.

Injected code is so effective and successful at evasion because it is a standard Windows operation to inject code from processes or libraries into other processes or libraries. Identifying that injected code exists does not mean that it is malicious. More analysis is required to determine if the injection created suspicious or malicious capabilities and/or functions.

Options for DLL Injection

In order to function through injection, malware needs to place malicious code in the address space of another process. This can be done in multiple ways, and all of them can be identified through memory analysis.

The easiest technique to manipulate application functions for attacker purposes is to inject a dynamical link library (DLL) file into the other processes while they are running. They will simply accept hooks, functions, code, or whatever is offered. There are two common DLL injection techniques and lots of variants. This section will briefly cover the two most common methods from a high level:
1. The SetWindowsHookEx() function
2. A combination of CreateRemoteThread() and LoadLibrary() functions

This content runs deep, and a full, lab-oriented discussion of exactly how this works is beyond the scope of incident management and the Incident Commander role. It goes more into the technical aspects of incident response and/or reverse engineering.

DLL Injection with SetWindowsHookEx()

Attackers can use the SetWindowsHookEx() hooking mechanism to inject DLLs into a remote process:

1. The attacking process first has to load the DLL into its own memory space using the LoadLibrary() function.
2. The attacking process then retrieves the address of the filter function in the remote process using the GetProcAddress() function, followed by the GetWindowThreadProcessID() function to determine the ID of the target thread.
3. When the filter function in the hook filter receives the message sent to the application, it executes it.
4. Next, the attacking process calls the SetWindowsHookEx() function to install the filter function and set a hook in the hook chain of the remote process.
5. When doing so, the attacking process specifies the DLL and function that will act as the filter function.
6. Then, a message has to be sent to the victim process to invoke it.
7. Primary methods to send the message or otherwise invoke the process include:
   A. Intentional with the attacking process sending a message (e.g., using the BroadcastSystemMessage() function to reach out and call it) or
   B. Passive with the attacking process waiting for an external message to be generated (e.g., a key press, USB install, network connection. or other pre-defined criteria chosen by the attack).
8. Once a message has been sent to the victim process, Windows loads the malicious DLL into the victim process's address space.
9. The message is then passed to the malicious filter function, which executes the attacker's code.

This is a really long-winded way of saying 1) it looks for a process to modify, 2) it modifies the targeted process with hooks to intercept the data, and 3) it defines criteria or triggers to execute, intercept, and/or modify functionality.

DLL Injection with CreateRemoteThread()

Alternatively, a combination of CreateRemoteThread() and LoadLibrary() functions can be used to facilitate DLL injection, as follows:

1. OpenProcess() – Open the remote or target process
   o First, the remote process (AKA victim process) must be opened so that it can be modified
   o Malware will typically use the OpenProcess() function call
2. VirtualAllocEx() – Allocates space in the target process for the hooks or payload
   o The end goal is to call LoadLibrary() in the victim process

- The argument that LoadLibrary() takes is a string name of a DLL
- This means the memory must be allocated in the remote process to hold the string
- Malware will typically use the VirtualAllocEx function call

3. WriteProcessMemory() – Writes the DLL name to be injected into the remote process
   - Once the memory in the remote process has been allocated, the name of the DLL must be written to that location in memory
   - Since this memory is in another process, the WriteProcessMemory() function call is typically used

4. GetModuleHandle() – Locate the library addresses using a variety of steps that involved using the GetModuleHandle() function to access kerner32dll to identify the location of the LoadLibrary() function
   - The first step to locate the LoadLibrary() function is accessing kernel32dll with the GetModuleHandle() function
   - To locate LoadLibrary(), the code must first locate the address of the DLL that contains LoadLibrary(), such as kernel32dll
   - To locate kernel32dll, a specimen will typically use the GetModuleHandle() function
   - Once the name of the DLL is written to the remote process, the address of the LoadLibrary() function (in the remote process) must be located.
   - LoadLibrary() is located in the kernel32dll file
   - Due to the way Windows loads processes into memory, kernel32dll is always at the same address on the same machine
   - When LoadLibrary() is located in the current process, you will know the address of LoadLibrary() in the remote process

5. GetProcAddress() – The next step to locate the LoadLibrary() function is to use the GetProcAddress() to locate the address inside of kernel32dll
   - Once the kernel32dll file has been located in memory, a specimen will typically then call GetProcAddress to locate the address of the LoadLibrary() function within the kernel32dll file

6. CreateRemoteThread() – Once the LoadLibrary() function address has been obtained, the remote thread can then be created
   - CreateRemoteThread() will function for any application, not just graphical ones
   - One restriction is that it only works on NT/XP based system, not Windows 95/98/ME

7. LoadLibrary("evil.dll") – The target of the thread is the evil library
   - LoadLibraryA will be run in the newly created thread
   - LoadLibraryA will load the malicious DLL into the remote address space

Hidden Processes & Artifacts

Some malware utilizes various methods to hide its artifacts from detection. These could include processes, files, registry components, network connections, or other forensic artifacts that the malware author wants to hide from users and security/investigative applications.

This is performed in a variety of ways, depending upon the protection ring involved and the depth of the operating system and respective hardware access the malicious application is capable of modifying. Overall, artifact hiding is typically accomplished through memory manipulation in one or more ways:

- Unlinking/modifying process tables
- Function call interception or redirection
- Process or DLL injection
- Driver installation

The various methods are usually broken down into user-mode or kernel-mode rootkits. However, you can also have hardware rootkits, which can include memory rootkits, BIOS rootkits, CPU rootkits, or other even more specific variants. Technically, all of the hardware rootkits are really a subset of kernel-mode rootkits, which have the capability to compromise the kernel itself. Regarding all of the respective methods, there are risks and benefits to each.

User-Mode Rootkits

User-mode rootkits function at OS protection ring 3. They utilize a variety of methods that all involve intercepting calls between applications, libraries, APIs, and the kernel. This is done in order to manipulate the input or output of those calls when communicating to the same or other applications, libraries, or APIs. Most often, this is performed through DLL and API injection (AKA hooking).

For DLL and API injection, it entails the hooking of specific applications or general-use library functions (such as ntdll.dll), which in turn connect to the Windows kernel. There are many functions and methods to inject/hook DLLs or processes, and a deep dive into that topic is beyond the scope of this course.

However, by way of explanation from a high level, the process generally involves:
- Identifying the location to set the hook and/or inject code

- Setting permissions to read/write
- Allocating space in process/DLL memory
- Making changes to memory (hooks, executable code, etc.)
- Obtaining the file handle
- Executing the code

There are a lot of variations on this, and the process is highly technical. The Injected Processes and Libraries section explains the most common variations.

Kernel-mode Rootkits

Kernel-mode rootkits function by modifications of tables in memory (such as seen with Direct Kernel Object Manipulation (DKOM)) or by altering the code in the kernel itself. These capabilities are usually initiated through the installation of drivers that patch kernel functions, by altering kernel files, or by installing on the hardware/firmware in one or more innovative ways. The latter method allows malware to get underneath the operating system completely and is the hardest to detect.

In Windows, the Kernel files are NTLDR & NToskrnl.exe. However, making modifications to them usually results in a blue screen of death (BSOD), as they fail the kernel file validation check. It is challenging to go this route, and there are many other, more viable methods.

The previously mentioned hardware methods are generally installed in one or more of the following areas. However, they are much rarer to find. They are typically the work of nation-state actors, sometimes require manipulation or implementation during the manufacturing process, and are not generally commoditized. More specifically, the most covert variants are made for specific hardware and/or firmware versions or ranges of versions. Each of the following will be covered in more detail in future sections:

- BIOS-based
- CPU-based
- Device-based
- Hypervisor-based
- Disk-based

User and Kernel-mode Rootkit Usage Decline

Another key subject to discuss is that the use of user-mode and kernel-mode rootkit methods are fraught with danger. They were increasingly common between 2003 and 2012, but they started to fall out of favor for several key reasons.

For starters, they have the potential to destabilize the operating system due to the complexities of application and library integration and interoperability. If system destabilization occurs, it increases the risk that the system might be reported to IT helpdesk personnel and that it might be re-imaged to resolve the unknown problem and restore functionality. Alternatively, it also increases the risk of detection and investigation by responders who might identify the malicious activity and discover the attacker's toolsets. In either case, it prevents attackers and malware from achieving their goals.

Also, Windows operating systems, starting with Vista (released in 2006), began to require signed code for kernel-mode drivers. This complicates the process of creating binary, executable rootkits, especially if they require drivers. However, Vista was not widely adopted, and it prolonged the use of rootkits until Windows 7 became widely deployed a couple of years after its release in 2009.

In addition to stability concerns, the act of hiding the malware can also make it easier to find if investigators or applications are aware of hiding techniques. In fact, by performing direct memory interrogation, process table comparison, and/or differential comparison of data returned by operating system APIs vs. the data carved out of memory, it is possible to identify hidden artifacts. Specifically, hidden processes, files, registry components, and network connections can be easily automated to identify these anomalies. A wide variety of tools were developed that used memory and file system anomaly comparison methods that turned traditional user and kernel rootkit hiding methods against themselves.

Interestingly, at the same time, Microsoft made it more difficult for binary rootkits. They introduced powerful scripting capabilities in PowerShell with Server 2008 and Windows 7. When advanced local scripting capabilities are combined with the constant stream of vulnerabilities and powerful attack vector capabilities that are built into web scripting languages, such as JavaScript, the malware industry began to focus on living off the land. Because of this, both user and kernel-mode rootkits were unnecessary, introduced greater risk, and became much less common. As such, by enhancing scripting capabilities, operating system vendors (not just Microsoft) enabled the switch from binary to script-based malware.

Hollowed Processes

Hiding malicious activity using hollowed processes is similar to injected processes and libraries. However, instead of injecting malicious code and functions into otherwise legitimate application memory space for which their primary functions still remain (but function in an altered state), the memory content and functionality within hollowed processes have been effectively removed and replaced by a completely different application.

This is a particularly good hiding strategy, as although the hollowed process has become a malicious application in memory, the original metadata and binary file on the file system remain the same as prior to exploitation. Analysis of any of the disk-based artifacts would determine that the file(s) of the affected process(es)' are benign, legitimate applications. As such, the hollowed processes might be erroneously validated as legitimate and subsequently ignored.

This type of threat evades the typical, white-listed hash-analysis method of forensic examination, which utilizes gold image baselines, NIST NSRL hash sets, or other known good hash sets for comparison purposes. If the files on the compromised system are contained in the known good hash sets or baselines, they are considered valid and are typically excluded from further analysis.

Hollowed Processes Step-by-Step Explanation

1. The attacking process starts a legitimate, benign target process in a suspended state. This causes the executable section of the target process to load in the memory. To identify the target process's addresses in memory, the following two tasks are performed:
    o The PEB (Process Environment Block) identifies the full path to the legitimate process.
    o The PEB's ImageBaseAddress points to the address where the legitimate process executable is loaded.
2. The attacking process obtains the malicious code (usually executable) to inject into the target process, which can come from the resource section of the malware process or from a separate file.
3. The attacking process identifies the base address of the target process so that it can unmap the executable section of the legitimate process by reading the ImageBaseAddress from the PEB.
4. The attacking process deallocates the executable section of the legitimate process.
5. The attacking process allocates memory space in the target process with read, write, and execute permissions, typically at the same address location where the executable was previously loaded.
6. The attacking process writes the PE Header/sections of the executable into the previously allocated memory.
7. The attacking process modifies the start address of the suspended thread to the address of the entry point of the injected executable.
8. The attacking process resumes the suspended thread, and the target process begins executing malicious code.

Hollowed Processes Detection:

The best way to identify that the hollowed processes were exploited and have malicious code running in memory is through monitoring API calls or direct memory interrogation and analysis. Examples of API calls that unmap process memory and should be investigated are:

- ZwUnmapViewOfSection and NtUnmapViewOfSection directly unmap process memory.
- WriteProcessMemory can be used to modify memory within another process.

These days, there are a variety of tools that are helpful for this. Depending on how well the attackers have covered their tracks, there can be quite a few anomalies that stand out.

1) Identification that a process was started in the suspended state – this is rare and should be investigated. If identified, it is very unlikely that this is benign.

2) The existence of the full binary file in memory, including the MZ header – This is a dead giveaway of process hollowing and is one of the key signatures identified in memory analysis tools, such as Volatility's Malfind.

3) Virtual Address Descriptors (VADs) table protection set to PAGE EXECUTE READWRITE – This indicates that memory can be written to and then executed.

4) Memory protection flags are not set to VirtualProtextEx – This indicates that the protections are disabled.

5) Application memory size discrepancies when compared to the same legitimate process memory – While it is true that process memory can and does vary in size, this is worth looking into. However, there could be benign reasons for this.

Fileless Malware

Fileless malware is not a new concept, and there are examples of it in the 20th century. However, it entered the 21st century in 2001 with a bang when Code Red began spreading across the Internet. It was later followed in 2003 by SQL Slammer. Both of these are examples of memory-resident malware, which made the concept of fileless malware well-known among security professionals.

Since then, fileless malware has been through repeated cycles of evolution and advancement corresponding to the capabilities of modern operating systems and applications. These include the ability for fileless malware to leverage scripting languages, macros, registry configurations, remote execution/management, and APIs. They have also been shaped by advancements in security controls. The changes in fileless malware concepts include a variety of methods pursuant to the end goal of eliminating the binary, executable malware files from being stored on the file system of the compromised host, thus reducing the likelihood of detection or blocking.

By eliminating the use of a malicious executable, it greatly reduces the likelihood of detection, tracing, and blocking by security controls. It also complicates the process of reverse engineering malware functions. Because of this, most successful crimeware exploit kits and related malware use fileless capabilities. In fact, there is constant innovation in this space that far outstrips the advancement in security capabilities that can detect and/or block it.

For the purpose of clarity, the term fileless malware is usually somewhat of a misnomer in that it is not accurate to say there are no files associated with the malware. There is always a file or set of instructions of some sort, but the malicious activity occurs without leaving a file as a forensically discoverable artifact on the affected host.

The way fileless attacks are carried out is similar to the manual attack processes performed by hands-on attackers. They run a series of commands or perform a set of steps in a serial manner to obtain and maintain access to a system. The primary differentiator is that fileless malware automates what is otherwise a manual process and extends its effect through broader and more rapid distribution.

In many cases, malware files or artifacts only exist at the time of exploitation and disappear immediately afterward. They will either alter the system in a persistent or non-persistent manner. With non-persistent malware, a reboot will restore the function of the system to a known good state. With persistent malware, the malicious functions return every time the system is started, logged in to by users, or other trigger mechanisms.

Usually, the malware that compromised the system implements a persistence mechanism that is disguised locally in plain sight. It will be hidden somewhere that will not leave behind an easily discoverable forensic artifact.

Innovative methods have been developed, adapted, and/or enhanced to create local persistence mechanisms for fileless malware. There is an interesting variety of places malware authors have identified to place malicious code without leaving an independent forensic artifact residing on the file system.

Some older examples include inserting code into macros, functions, or metadata portions of other legitimate files or within slack space, including file slack, partition slack, disk slack space, or even on computer hardware. These methods can and often are still used today, particularly malicious macros.

Some notable modern examples include placing the entirety of the malware in registry key or value entries (often more than one with pointers to the next). Alternatively, and which is becoming increasingly common, persistent, custom WMI subscriptions and classes are created by attackers and/or malware, which are fully functional programs that utilize available system functions.

In most cases, there is usually an element of "living off the land" by malicious applications. This means that it utilizes the native capabilities of the system and its various functions, APIs, processes, libraries, WMI, or other capabilities. This includes making changes to the way legitimate system processes start or function through the injection of malicious code or libraries, often encoded within Registry Run keys and scripts.

Oftentimes, the malicious file, script, and/or application used in fileless attacks are stored remotely. In such cases, the affected system is externally acted upon to trigger the remote execution of this script using either a manual or automated process. Alternatively, an application, script, or trigger on the affected system reaches out to the remote script or file and runs the malicious code remotely.

For remote persistence mechanisms, the affected system has usually suffered compromise or malicious changes to system configurations or legitimate applications. Malicious changes often include modification to the registry entries that affect system boot, user login, or the application launch processes that download remote content from external systems (such as a C2 server) and load malicious code each time the system starts, the user logs in, the system or application is started, or a document is opened.

Triggers can be inserted virtually anywhere. Other options include scheduled tasks, application links/shortcuts, or anywhere a shim can be inserted to add additional instructions or call other code or commands that can load first. Office-type documents are an extremely common example of this, as there are all kinds of functions, macros, or other capabilities to insert code or make calls to remote sites.

If the ability of the affected system or application to contact the C2 server is blocked and the affected system is rebooted, it will start without the malicious changes. However, the C2 connection attempt would be visible in network traffic captures and logs and can aid in the detection, blocking, and other investigative processes.

There are numerous examples of fileless malware that have made the headlines over the years, some of which are still commonly detected and pose a threat as of 2024. Note that the projects are not static but are maintained for a time and sometimes taken over by later groups that modify the original code base and customize it for their specific purposes. Moreover, it is not uncommon for earlier malware to be rebranded with slight modifications and become the basis for an entirely new malware family.

A particularly notable example of fileless malware is Poweliks, which was introduced in 2014. Based on known trends, it seems to have kicked off the latest wave of really advanced fileless malware variants that have made the scene. Poweliks was interesting, as it makes the Run subkey call to rundll32.exe (a legitimate Windows system file used to load DLLs) and passes in several parameters. Once that happens, the malware can pretty much do anything the attackers desire. These malicious parameters include JavaScript code that loads Poweliks into memory and executes it.

Shortly after Poweliks, Angler also introduced fileless infection methods, and almost everything since has used it as a primary method. As always, malicious code is highly adaptive and evolves quickly. When innovative and effective infection methods hit the streets, it is not long before other maintained crimeware exploit kits are using them.

Scripted Malware

```
powershell -nop -w hidden -encodedcommand
JABzAD0ATgB1AHcALQBPAGIAagB1AGMAdAAgAEkATwAuAE0AZQBtAG8AcgB5AFMAdAByAGUAYQBtACgALABbAEMAbwBuAHYAZQByAHQAXQA6ADoARgByAGSAaABgABPAGPAAgABLGPAPBBGAPBDPAGPB
AbgBUAHkAWgBaADUARQAxAFUAOABBAFgAZgBQBAFcAWQBDAGQASQBzAGBAQQBqAGEATgBpAEcAZgAzAHYANQA4AAEcAZABjADcACwAyAGQAbAA3AAE4J
gAWABrAFcAVABpAGQAVABnAGQAdgBQAHMUgB2AEEAZgBLAHQATgB3AQBCAE9ATwBRACsAaQB9ADMAMAMQB6AGUAUQBzAGEAYwBLADkAMABjAE
EMAUAA3AGUAYwBMAHoAVgBsAHkAAQQA4AGgAQgBEADAAOABPAFcAOQBKAEUAUAUBNAGgAUwB1AGMGMAbQA2ADQARAB3AHcASgB0OAGYAYQBPAG0AwA8A
AGUAWABqADYAVwBWAHkAWAH1kAWAB4AEUAQgBsAHUAVwBNAGoAAcgBTAFkAagBoAAHYAZwBSAGMMATgAwADkAVAABzcABAAwAHcAMQBFAFMAdwBFAEoAAZQBkJ
UAEIAZgBwAAEoAYgBwwAAGYwAcwB2AFYAAaQB2AHIANgA3AHMMAMAB3AADgAcgBAHoAAaABSAFgAAgB3B3AHgARAAA1AGcAUQA3AFIAMABjAEYAZABXAXAEcAbwB
BHADCcAaQAvAHEAMQBUADQAcQBfAFMMaAwArAGgAagBSAHgAU1wBzAG44AZgBnAGMATwB0OAGUAUABOAHgAUgB3B3AE0OAQBQB5AGYAdgBQBQAADUAQwBMMAEoACGJ
QBmAAEoAVwwBrADYAU1gB5AGkAQwwA5AAE8ABcACQBmACBARgB5ADIAdgBXAAGG0OARwB4AFYAODAAbhAEsAdAArADAAcgBqAHEEAWwAA5AEYAegA4AGUASWwBXAFcARI
TgAzAAEUATgBPAAEoAbBgBJAAFAQgAAOQBkQBkAAGCARQABDADQAbwwBwBwBE4AUAABBAAAFYAMwArAHAHIAQwwBiAAHUASABmAHkAdQQAyADcAdWwA8AHgAMQBrAAGsANWwB5AAEgAA
AawBYAE4AdQQBGAFMAawwBkAAEcAaQQAA0AEUAUAUgBZAAHIAegBRAHUAZQQA2AHggARQBYAAFkAegg04AAGIAAQABqQBmADKkAbABoAA1QAaAaQBtADcJ
```

Scripted malware or malicious scripts have been involved in attacks since the very beginning and evolved to automate and extend the manual attack process. They are fast, efficient, and effective. They run the same every time and continue to fall under the security radar even after all these years.

The increase of sophistication in scripting languages, as well as the enhanced ability of various applications to use scripts and macros has enabled attackers to use various script types to perform malicious activity that was previously only possible using executables. Moreover, with the increased requirement by operating systems for signed executables and the multitude of benefits of using scripts, malicious scripts (usually of more than one type) have become the preferred malware platform. In addition to the covert nature of scripts and lack of detectability, if they are written in the appropriate language and inserted into a compatible document type, they enjoy cross-platform compatibility.

Scripted Malware Execution Methods

There are a variety of command interpreters and script execution utilities shown in the table below that are native to Windows that attackers often exploit to gather system information, establish communications, download secondary scripts, and exploit the operating system or applications. Note that it is common for malicious applications leveraging scripts to use multiple script types and command interpreters during the various phases of the attack.

Bitsadmin	Bitsadmin.exe is a command-line tool used to create, download, and/or upload jobs and to monitor their individual status and progress.
Cmd	Cmd.exe is a native command interpreter in Windows, which is considered a legacy utility that has mostly been eclipsed by PowerShell. However, it is still used by admins, attackers, utilities, and malware.
Cscript	Cscript.exe is a non-interactive scripting mode used to run Windows Scripting Host (WSH) script types (.asp, .bat, .htms, .js, .vbs, .wsf, .wsh).
Mshta	Mshta.exe is a native Windows utility designed to execute Microsoft HTML Application (HTA) files., including Windows Script Host code (VBScript and JScript) that are embedded within HTML in a network proxy-aware fashion.
Msiexec	Msiexec.exe is a default Windows process that is triggered whenever an MSI or MSP is executed. It is used to install, modify, or uninstall MSI and MSP packages.

Powershell	PowerShell.exe is a task-based command-line shell and scripting language built on the .NET framework that is used to control and automate system administration tasks.
Regsvr32	Regsvr32.exe registers dynamic-link libraries (.dll) files as command components in the registry.
Rundll32	Rundll32.exe loads and/or runs 32-bit dynamic-link libraries (.dll) files.
Msbuild	The Microsoft Build Engine (Msbuild.exe) is a platform for building applications and provides an XML schema for a project file to control how the build platform processes and builds software packages.
Winrs	Winrs.exe is the Windows remote Management enabling administrators to manage and execute programs remotely.
Wmic	Wmic.exe is an interactive command shell used to get and display WMI information.
Wscript	Wscript.exe is an interactive scripting mode for executing WSH script types (.asp, .bat, .htms, .js, .vbs, .wsf, .wsh).
Wsl	Wsl.exe (Windows Subsystem for Linux) is a feature of Windows that allows users to run a Linux environment without the need for a separate virtual machine or dual booting.

Scripted Malware Metrics

According to combined metrics sources from 2023, executables still constitute a large portion of malware at ~34% of samples observed. However, that means 66% of current malware file types use a combination of other formats, most of which involve malicious scripts (such as JavaScript, VBScript, Powershell, etc.) or user-created documents (such as MS Office files, Adobe PDF, etc.). Moreover, none of these malware formats are mutually exclusive. A single malware sample may contain elements from one, more, or all of the common formats.

The above-listed script types are the primary attack vectors. However, they usually contain secondary script types. They may contain combinations of script types listed above or PowerShell, native scripting commands, binary data, or shellcode. Considering that any script type can contain any other script type, there aren't any limitations besides creativity.

Not surprisingly, .js is at the top of the list. However, it is seldom used alone. It is usually an entry point to piggyback other malicious activity on top of. It is not uncommon to find .js files that contain embedded and/or encoded PowerShell, .vbs, native scripting commands, executable binary data, or assembly shellcode.

Moreover, .js is truly cross-platform and works on nearly every OS and browser type by default. Nothing more is required, and exploit scripts can be written to contain attack methods for any browser or OS they find themselves on. Malicious MS Office and PDF docs will work on systems with default security controls, which include most workstations and many servers.

JavaScript

An increase in using JavaScript as an attack vector was seen starting in 2016. One of the really handy capabilities of JavaScript is that it allows any code to run when a user visits a website. Malware delivered via infected JavaScript files doesn't need any user interaction. It is particularly dangerous because malicious JavaScript files are downloaded onto the PC and executed as soon as the user unknowingly browses an infected website without having to click on anything. This is typical of a drive-by attack.

Moreover, there is also a growing trend of coin miner JavaScript infections (both client-side and server-side), some of which are intentional. An alarming trend is growing where some unscrupulous companies provide a coin miner to all who visit their site. As if advertising and popups weren't bad enough, now we get coin miners while browsing these sites.

VBScript

VBScript is native to Microsoft Windows, has full capabilities to perform administrative-type functions, and can be as impactful as PowerShell. Because of its broad capabilities across the Windows operating systems and applications, VBScript has long been a key element of spam and phishing campaigns. It is a highly capable attack and installation vector within Windows environments.

In addition to local system impact, it can perform functions in Active Directory management or implementation of group policies. This opens the door to the creation and manipulation of user accounts, groups, organizational units, Group Policy Objects (GPOs), and other AD concepts.

PowerShell

PowerShell has become the underlying language used by Windows command snap-ins and, with the right permissions, can do virtually anything on Windows operating systems, built-in utilities, and various Microsoft applications. However, prior to PowerShell v5 (default on Windows 10, but available on Windows 7), PowerShell did not have many security controls or leave behind artifacts of its execution. The lack of logging results in a very low rate of detection and subsequent blocking capabilities on systems having early PowerShell that are compromised by attackers or malware.

Most targeted attack groups already use PowerShell in their attack lifecycle, and it has become a staple in commodity malware. Fileless attacks abusing PowerShell are increasing, considering its advanced functionality over all things Microsoft. PowerShell is a method of command execution from other script types and can execute payloads directly from memory, making it very stealthy.

In addition to its capabilities as a primary infection vector (once invoked by another script type – like JavaScript), it also has remote access and lateral movement capabilities under the context of the affected user. Additionally, by default, it uses encrypted traffic and can evade network detection mechanisms.

Moreover, scripting engines like PowerShell have the ability to access the Win32 API, allowing malicious scripts to "live off the land" and load anything they require. This includes libraries or executables necessary to perform desired malicious tasks and evade detection. In 2016, Symantec reported that of all of the PowerShell scripts analyzed through the Blue Coat sandbox, 95.4% were malicious.

Stealth and Evasion
Some of the stealth and evasion benefits include the following:
- Scripts are not usually required to be signed, and script signing is uncommon due to the complexity of the process and its impact on enterprise environments, applications, and administration.
- Scripts can be nested within other scripts or office documents and be composed of multiple scripting languages within a single script. They can also include embedded binaries or shellcode. This permits maximum flexibility and compatibility of exploits.
- Scripts are easily encoded or embedded within websites, emails, documents, or other artifacts. They can be automatically executed on website access or via various other mechanisms.
- Polymorphism of malicious scripts is trivial as new variants do not require a new code-signing certificate, unlike drivers or other restricted executables.
- Scripts, unfortunately, bypass most antivirus (AV) and antimalware (AM) detection capabilities that lack the ability to identify their execution and the malicious intent thereof. While AV/AM solutions may identify the execution of a script parser, like Cscript or Wscript, they typically do not trace the activity or flag malicious actions.
- Some script types run on various platforms (JavaScript being chief among them), and the scripts can be coded to interpret the browser/OS type and provide specific exploits that target them.
- Modern scripting languages contain anti-debugging features. These include layers of obfuscation, encryption methods, and defenses against alteration that may be introduced by reverse engineering functions, such as setting breakpoints.
- Many scripting languages can access the operating system, service, or application API features. They can have full read/write/execute capabilities under the context of the user account running the scripts or of the account(s) to which the script was able to escalate via some sort of privilege escalation capability.

Malicious WMI Subscriptions and Classes
Windows Management Instrumentation (WMI) is a native Windows management tool that allows administrators to perform a variety of actions. This includes gathering metrics, installing software/updates, or self-query the operating system. WMI has access to all Windows system resources that it divides into classes for different tasks. Examples include executing/deleting/copying files, changing reg values, starting services, initiating network connections, etc.

WMI is built into every modern version of Windows and is the primary method for the creation of agentless agents, which have become increasingly popular. More specifically, because of the powerful capabilities built into WMI, it is entirely possible to create entire programs that are constructed of custom, persistent WMI classes and Subscriptions created by PowerShell scripts.

This ability is used for both benign and malicious purposes. These inherent WMI features are a benefit to admins, as they allow them to perform tasks very quickly. However, they can just as easily become a nightmare when used for malicious operations. In the same way an administrator uses WMI for benign purposes, an attacker can use WMI to covertly and surreptitiously run malicious code across an entire enterprise of Windows systems. WMI provides persistence by auto-running programs stealthily on startup or based on specific triggers, such as logging on, key entries, network connections, etc.

One of the most innovative methods of fileless malware and evasion seen today is the ability of malicious actors to create entire, fully functional malicious programs through custom WMI classes on the Windows victim operating system. It is possible to create all aspects of a malicious application in this way.

This would leave very few forensic artifacts on the file system itself. It is virtually undetectable by modern automated analysis tools. The process of analyzing and validating WMI classes and subscriptions has all of the challenges of doing such for scripts. It is very challenging to identify the malicious intent and potential for harm.

This type of malicious code involving PowerShell and WMI can only be identified via a highly manual inspection and validation process. The critical steps include implementing advanced logging, performing memory analysis, conducting a manual review of classes/subscriptions, performing a very deep inspection of the System32\wbem\Repository directory, and dissecting its content for anomalies. These actions are commonly aided through the use of a PowerShell script to collect targeted content, but they can be successfully performed using any method that can interact with WMI.

To assist with the enumeration of WMI subscriptions, Microsoft has a free PowerShell Script available (Get-WMIEventSubscription.ps1). For WMI classes, the Get-CimClass PowerShell command is very useful.

Malicious WMI Example: PoshSpy

A good example of WMI malware in the wild is APT29's use of POSHSPY. PoshSpy was identified by Mandiant in 2015 as a secondary backdoor used by APT29, which could be engaged if APT29's primary backdoors were compromised.

PoshSpy utilizes a combination of PowerShell and WMI to "live off the land" and infect the victim system with a persistent backdoor that is nearly invisible, as it utilizes legitimate processes and libraries for all actions. In addition to the stealthiness of the install and persistence mechanisms, PoshSpy is also very covert in its communications. It uses infrequent beaconing, traffic obfuscation, extensive encryption, and geographically local, legitimate websites for command and control (C2) to make identification of its network activity difficult to spot.

Hardware-Based Malware

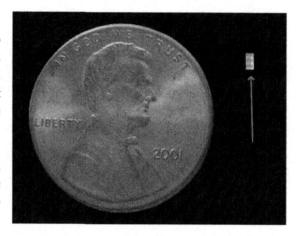

Hardware-based malware is fairly rare to encounter, but it has a long history. It is highly specialized for the targeted technology, and it is more likely than not used for nation-state activity and espionage purposes.

There are many examples of it in the wild, but the scope of such is very narrow. It is one of those types of technologies that is too complex and customized to be very scalable.

While it is true that there are some vulnerabilities that affect an entire platform or series of hardware, chipsets, or other components, usually the scope is much narrower. It is more likely that each version/variant of each type of hardware with accompanying firmware may require custom coding for the malware or backdoor to function successfully. Hardware-based malware is essential malicious firmware, which is highly specific to the hardware itself.

Anyone who has ever had to swap out the controller on a hard drive has very likely been through this pain. The hardware/firmware combination must be exactly right, or they will not function properly or at all. It will be little more than a brick with an integrated circuit attached to it.

Any hardware with a chipset could be vulnerable to hardware-based malware. The following is a list of examples of hardware-based malware seen in proof-of-concept and/or in the wild. These rootkits permit malware code to hide covertly in hardware where it could exist undetected by conventional methods. This section will provide a high-level overview of the following list one by one:

- BIOS-based
- CPU-based
- Device-based

- USB-based
- Hypervisor-based
- Disk-based

Antivirus and antimalware tools typically do not have access or methodology to scan hardware, as the hardware typically can only be accessed from Ring 0. Unfortunately, AV typically sits at Ring 3 and has limited access down to Ring 1. Therefore, it has no access to Ring 0. However, some AV solutions have a reboot and scan function to inspect deeper levels.

BIOS-Based

The concept of flashing the BIOS firmware with malicious update code that loads before the OS and has the ability to control the OS and hardware has been around for a long time. There is known proof of concept code going back until at least 1998, and new examples come out and become publicly known at least every 1-2 years. There are undoubtedly more that have not been disclosed.

The following image shows the timeline of many of the known BIOS rootkit examples, both proof-of-concept and found in the wild. For what it is worth, the fact that you can even put a good percentage of them on a chart for a graphic and point at them shows that this is obviously not the preferred method of backdoor implementation, and the use is very limited.

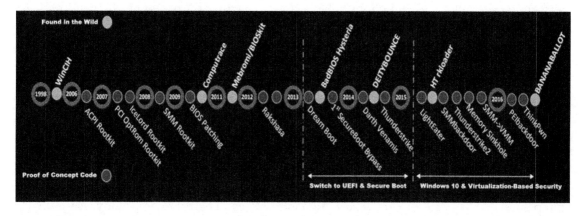

CPU-Based

An early, widespread example of a CPU backdoor was baked into the Via C3 family of x86-compatible CPUs. These were deployed in the early 2000s for a wide variety of purposes, all of which were vulnerable to this engineered vulnerability. They include use cases such as industrial automation, point-of-sale systems, ATMs, healthcare hardware, and some desktop and laptop PCs. Each contained a hidden but easily accessible 'backdoor' that could enable full root access or "God mode" for an attacker with awareness of their existence and access to the affected systems.

The security researcher who discovered it, Christopher Domas, dubbed the backdoor in the co-processor "The Rosenbridge." It is more deeply embedded than any known coprocessor, having access not only to all of the CPU's memory but also to its register file and execution pipeline. The backdoor is a small, non-x86 core embedded alongside the main x86 core in the CPU. It was either enabled by default or could be enabled with non-privileged access. The embedded core can be fed commands wrapped in specially formatted x86 instructions that the core executes, which bypass all memory protections and privilege checks.

It is notable that, unlike many other backdoors, it is possible to find manufacturer documentation and information on this one detailing how it works. This means that it is not extremely secret, but it is still a hardware backdoor. However, this is just one example. Many other examples of CPU backdoors and methods were developed or identified, including:

- Malicious microcode
- Modern coprocessors in both Intel and AMD CPUs:
    - Management Engine (ME)
    - Active Management Technology (AMT)
    - AMD Platform security processor (PSP)

Chip/Chipset-Based

Integrated circuits are absolutely ubiquitous, and the quantity manufactured numbers easily into the trillions. Each integrated circuit has numerous microchips in various varieties, performing a multitude of functions. These chips are either purpose-built by vendors for a specific purpose or commodity chips that are common across many vendors or devices.

They could be manufactured anywhere. However, the compromised chips/chipsets most often come from China, Taiwan, Malaysia, or other countries. Alternatively, hardened chips/chipsets are usually made in the United States or their native country and are typically used for hardened military purposes within the native country of manufacture.

Examples are frequently identified where the design of the chips has been modified to provide backdoors, vulnerabilities, "god-mode" passwords, or other weaknesses. The blame for all forms of these backdoors varies, but it is usually attributed to nation-states or companies that operate at the behest of nation-states. There are too many examples of compromised chips and chipsets to cover in any detail. Some notable examples include:

- Supermicro motherboards – The Chinese PLA developed microchips as small as a sharpened pencil lead and inserted them into Supermicro motherboards that were distributed all across the world and used in every business sector. This includes Amazon, Facebook, and Apple. The malicious chips were connected to the Board Management Controller (BMC), provided backdoor access to every piece of hardware on the system, including memory, and modified the way the OS functioned.
- Trusted Platform Module (TPM) Chip – The TPM chip that protects BitLocker encryption keys has long been reported to be vulnerable to backdoor decryption and access by covert government entities and law-enforcement agencies. In fact, per the Snowden documents, this access was boasted by researchers at the CIA conference in 2010 and reported again by the German government in 2013.

- 2012 – A secret nanoscale "backdoor" was found to be etched into the silicon of a supposedly secure programmable chip (ProASIC3 (PA3)). It could give attackers access to classified US weapons systems, networking, nuclear power plants, power distribution, aerospace, aviation, public transport, and automotive products.

USB-Based

Malicious code designed to utilize USB as an infection and transport method is extremely common. This has long been a staple for malicious activity, including infecting any computer. They can even be used for compromising air-gapped networks, passing command and control, keyboard emulation, snarfing files, compromising smartphones, and electrically frying the affected system. Notable USB-based malware examples include the following:

Year	Method / Name	Year	Method / Name
2003	Hacksaw file dump to USB	2014	DNS override from USB mal firmware
2005	Autorun exploits	2014	Keyboard emulation by USB mal firmware
2005	USB buffer overflow attack	2014	Hidden partition patch
2008	USB Cold boot	2014	Password protection bypass
2010	Rubber Ducky	2014	Virtual machine break-out
2010	PHUKD/URFUKED	2014	Boot sector virus
2010	Smartphone-based HID attacks	2014	See You: disable Mac webcam LED
2010	.Ink Stuxnet/Fanny USB flash drive exploit	2014	USB backdoor to airgapped networks
2010	Hiding data on USB mass storage	2014	Device firmware upgrade
2011	Unintended USB channels	2015	Turnipschool (Cottonmouth-1)
2011	Unauthorized malicious driver update	2015	USB wireless USB dongle attacks
2012	RIT attack via USB mass storage	2016	USB Thief
2014	USBdriveby	2016	USBee attack
2014	EvilduIno	2016	USB Killer
2014	Defailt gatewy override	2018	Attacks on smartphones over USB-C

Hypervisor-Based

Modern CPUs have hypervisor support, providing an isolated environment for malware to operate undetected. Malware that virtualizes the victim operating system and effectively gets underneath it is relatively rare, but it does exist in the wild and can be very hard to detect. It is quite often a tool of nation-states, cyber espionage, and other sophisticated attacks.

It works by changing the boot record to start the malware bootloader first, which launches the malware, which then launches the operating system. By doing this, it loads the malware in such a way that it resides between the hardware and the operating system, acting as a virtual machine host that imitates the interfaces between the hardware and the operating system to avoid detection and gain access to all hardware interactions. Essentially, the malware and attackers can see everything that is happening in the now virtualized victim OS, but if done right, the victim OS has no awareness of the malware that has usurped its control of the hardware. Moreover, the security agents or other security controls on the virtualized host would have no visibility into the malware environment to detect if anything was amiss.

The main way to detect these types of malware families would involve identifying the anomalies that exist by nature of being in a virtualized environment. Many forms of malware are VM-aware. There are a plethora of detection techniques for this, which is easy as commercial VMs have a lot of tells. However, in this case, victim OSs and security controls need to be covert and VM-aware to make sure they are still contained in a secure environment.

A different twist on the hypervisor-based malware concept is that CPU hypervisor support can also be used to spin off child VMs for malware purposes. These miniature environments are also isolated from inspection and detection of malicious activity, as they are not accessible by host-based security controls.

Disk-Based

Boot Sector or Bootloader rootkits (AKA bootkits) are backdoors that have been around since the beginning and enable malware to start before the operating system and get underneath it. The first known instance of a bootkit is the Brian virus, discovered in 1986. It was designed to infect MS-DOS systems.

They do this by modifying the boot record to point to the bootkit that launches and then starts the operating system afterward. Bootkits start just prior to the operating system by infecting the master boot record (MBR) or the volume boot record (VBR).

Being as they attach themselves to the boot record, the rootkit won't appear within the standard file system view. As a result, antivirus and anti-malware software will seldom detect malware files. However, booting from external media and scanning hard drives may identify it.

Disk-based forensic analysis will also identify it. However, it will require walking the file system artifacts, bootloader, pointers, etc., to fully understand the chain of events. This is a fairly deep-dive process to fully enumerate.

Device-Based

Examples of device-based backdoors have been found on the controllers of hard drives, network cards, network switches, routers, firewalls, and many other hardware types. In a sting between 2005 and 2008, the FBI and ICE seized over 74,000 counterfeit Cisco network devices that were either in transit to or installed in the United States. They were discovered within key corporate entities of all types, critical supply chain companies, and within military and other government entities. These devices were found to have allowed backdoor access that circumvented traditional security controls.

The devices (which were manufactured in the Shenzhen province in China) were very high-quality fakes and extremely hard to detect from real devices. Unless the devices and their packaging were compared side-by-side, they were almost indistinguishable. What is worse is that they also had a high failure rate. Sometimes, they overheat, catch on fire, and expose victims not only to unauthorized access but also to the risk of physical harm.

While it might be expected to receive counterfeit equipment sold by some random fly-by-night companies on eBay, this was not necessarily the case. Many were sold by Cisco Silver and Gold partners through standard channels.

Timestomping/Forensic Manipulation

In order to hide in plain sight, malware often uses various anti-forensic techniques to manipulate the file system and avoid detection. One of the most common methods is Timestomping, which changes the Modified, Accessed, Created, and Last Written timestamps on the affected file systems.

Timestomping is often found in conjunction with legitimate process replacement and/or imitation tactics. The combination of these hiding-in-plain-sight techniques makes the binaries blend in when performing timeline analysis and initial verification. Malware will usually place malicious files in system directories and change the times of the malware to be similar to that of adjacent files in the same directory. This creates the impression that the malware files have been there a long time, and they will frequently be missed when performing a standard timeline analysis.

One of the first things most investigators do when performing timeline analysis is to sort files by the various timestamps to identify files that were Modified, Created, or Last Written around the time of compromise or afterward. Of particular interest are Portable Executable (PE) file types (.acm, .ax, .cpl, .dll, .drv, .efi, .exe, .mui, .ocx, .scr, .sys, .tsp) and scripts (usually Windows Script Host (WSH), PowerShell, VBA, or HTA file types). However, other file types may also be notable as malicious tool components or other artifacts of exploitation.

Timestomping Detection

The methods for Timestomping vary across different file system types, as do the detection methods. The concepts are basically the same, but the way of doing it across various file system types may be somewhat different. Ultimately, identification is possible through deep-dive analysis and anomaly detection. A challenge with timestomping detection methods is that individually they are prone to false positives. However, when combined, they can tell a much more compelling story.

From a high level, the timestamp anomaly detection methods typically involve analysis and comparison of 1) all file timestamps, 2) nanosecond portions of timestamps, and 3) the file system catalog record numbers. Moreover, it is crucial to perform validation that all of the analysis methods come to the same conclusion. Timestomping detection requires a preponderance of the evidence for affirmative detection, and the techniques are different depending on the operating system and file system. Each of these will only be covered briefly in this section:

- File times are analyzed to identify mismatches in both visible and hidden timestamps. This is easiest in Windows as there are duplicate sets of timestamps within the $STANDARD_INFORMATION attributes vs. the $FILE_NAME attributes. Long story short, the timestamps within the $STANDARD_INFORMATION attributes are the timestamps you see in a directory listing or the normally viewable file metadata from Explorer.exe and forensic tools. These are modified through timestomping, but those of the $FILE_NAME attributes are not. However, this method has a lot of false positives, as there are legitimate reasons for this situation to exist. Benign explanations typically involve the extraction from an archive, such as .zip, .rar, .cab, .tar, .tgz, or almost any other archive file type.

- The full-length timestamps down to nanoseconds of suspected files must be analyzed. As luck would have it, NTFS represents time as the quantity of 100 nanosecond intervals since 1601-1-1. However, timestomping only writes values down to the microsecond portion of the timestamps, and it zeroes out the 100-nanosecond portion. As such, there is only a 10% chance that the nanosecond portion of a timestamp will be zero in the normal course of file system activity.

- The $MFT record number or inode number for suspected files should be analyzed to verify they are similar to that of other files written to the file system at that time. It is common for timestomped files to have a much higher record or inode number. The $MFT record numbers of timestomped files will be more closely aligned with files created on the data of compromise (or other date of malware installation) than system files written at the date of OS installation. It is also possible that older record or inode numbers are reused following the deletion of some other file and reallocation of the record number. However, it is unlikely.

While each of these anomalies could be the result of normal activity, it is very unlikely all of them could happen simultaneously for the same file(s). It would be even more unlikely that the files in question with matching timestomping indicators would be associated with suspicious or malicious activity unless they were actually involved in it.

Polymorphic Malware

These days, a very high percentage of malware that responders run across in the wild has an automated ability to change itself and its respective artifacts from system to system or within new environments. The more unique the malware becomes, the harder it is to find it with IOCs or other conventional methods that require a distinct list of everything bad. Without a blacklist of known malicious hashes, it results in the reliance on heuristics. This has always been a significant weakness and chink in the armor for antivirus/antimalware tools.

If hash values, filenames, install paths, file sizes, registry entries, communication ports, IP addresses, domain names, and DNS servers change with each instance of the malware, it can complicate detection by both automated and manual analysis methods. This is due to the focus being on what is defined using these values and the ease of changing them dynamically. If investigators are looking for known metadata they expect to see, they will not find it using any common forensic indicators.

This is true for both malicious binaries and for scripts, which are even more tricky. It is easier to be polymorphic in scripts, as nobody is expecting them to be signed. Most antimalware antivirus solutions are incredibly weak in their ability to discern between benign and malicious scripts and their respective functions. Unless there is a hash of a known bad script, it is unlikely to be detected. With the common practice of modifying scripts through random polymorphic activity, known hashes are not even a possibility.

Detecting Polymorphic Malware

Polymorphism of all forensic attributes provides a method to circumvent detection by antivirus and antimalware, but it creates uniqueness in the process. The more malware tries to become unique, the more it stands out if investigators and their tools are looking for it.

Emphasis on: → IF THEY ARE LOOKING FOR IT ←

Identification of uniqueness works especially well in large environments where there should be many examples of most types of software and network traffic. More specifically, if investigators are able to look across all systems and traffic in the environment and identify processes, libraries, drivers, and/or network traffic connections that are "least-prevalent," the polymorphic malware and connection methods boldly stand out and can be easily identified. The simple fact that they are unique makes them worthy of investigation.

Uniqueness or least-prevalence in a corporate environment that is based on standard workstation images for various departments is a notable find and a key starting place that can expedite an investigation. But, it is not always malicious. It is not uncommon to find least-prevalent binaries on developer systems and custom software used by the customer. Any legitimate, unique binaries should be whitelisted when found in order to eliminate distracting noise and expedite the investigative process.

A significant challenge that information technology and security professionals face is that most organizations don't have an understanding of what is normal within their environment. This is true for both endpoint configuration and network traffic.

Analysis seeking to identify polymorphic malware utilizing any method of analysis is significantly augmented by baselining the normal state of the environment, systems, applications, services, network connections, ingress/egress activity, and network flows. By understanding what is the normal baseline state of the environment and quickly determining what is least prevalent, responders can act rapidly and decisively against polymorphic threats. These two strategies should always be combined for an effective response.

Tunneling, Proxies, And Covert Channels

Just like malware hides its artifacts on the host, it can also conceal its C2 communications and exfiltration activity using a large variety of methods. Any protocol can be tunneled within any other protocol. As such, it is a wide-open playing field. However, some protocols or methods are faster and more efficient, while others are stealthier and more covert. So, there is some trade-off, depending upon the use case.

Notwithstanding the fact that any type of protocol can be chunked up and stuffed inside any other, just because you can doesn't mean you should. Some protocols and combinations thereof work more efficiently and effectively than others. The goal of covert tunneling is typically to avoid immediate detection, not to prevent identification via deep-dive protocol analysis. Therefore, the tunneling method doesn't need to be very covert, just covert enough.

Fast Data Transfer/Low Stealth

The most common tunneling techniques currently seen utilize HTTP(S) and DNS, as they are typically open, comparatively fast, and usually evade detection. HTTP(S) is usually the favored protocol, as it includes SSL/TLS and typically evades detection from IPS and DLP.

For fast and reliable methods, the tunneling protocols used to create covert channels usually occur within the data portion of the packets, and it simply creates an encrypted channel using an SSL/TLS certificate. This is as simple as using an SSL/TLS VPN through an anonymous proxy on a foreign host. In most cases, there is a need for it to be more exotic than that.

It is basically just HTTPS relaying through a remote server to an intended destination. Nothing is actually being manipulated, and the protocol is operating in the intended way. The traffic just blends in with other HTTPS traffic, except it might be identified by one or more of several key indicators. These include:
1. Traffic is sent to a known covert proxy destination.
2. A high volume of data being transferred.

3. The nature of the content being transferred triggers alerts if SSL/TLS decryption is implemented to decrypt the traffic, or the traffic is sent in plain-text format and matches signatures or heuristics.

In this case, the tunneling is functionally synonymous with proxying. It is a very common method of performing covert communication, which can hide C2 traffic and data exfiltration. There are many free or paid proxy varieties to choose from, some of which are more covert than others and offer a wide variety of countries and states/providences to proxy through. Another differentiating factor of the various proxy solutions available is that they may be limited based on throughput speed and/or aggregate data volume.

TOR is popular for a variety of malicious purposes, including hacking, malware C2 communication, exfiltration, etc. However, its popularity has led to it being identified and blocked by default using next-generation network security devices that are commonly found within large organizations. This reduces its efficacy for attackers, malware, and C2 purposes. Moreover, TOR traffic detection/blocking rules are becoming more common on less expensive firewalls and can be identified with open-source traffic signatures and IPS software. Blocking TOR, however, is like plugging one hole in a sieve, as it makes no difference outside of blocking that single covert communication method. An infinite quantity of others are still available.

A simple Google search of "anonymous proxy servers" will yield pages and pages of free proxies that can anonymize network traffic activity and provide full VPN services from practically any region or country desired. This enables attackers to mask the origins of their traffic and make it appear to originate from or be destined to wherever desired. This can be especially convenient if routed through countries that do not assist in hacking investigations or attribution.

Other common methods of proxying that can appear benign at first glance are that attackers may utilize 1) a series of compromised computers domestically or 2) dynamically created AWS, Azure, or other cloud instances to redirect traffic through a series of hops that typically lead out of the country and beyond the ability to investigate.

Moreover, the use of AWS, Azure, and other cloud infrastructure for malicious purposes has become another staple of botnets and cybercrime. This is due to the ease of automated provisioning, the immediate flexibility of the environment, and the unrecoverable nature of deleting non-persistent virtual machines. Long story short, it is possible for malware to automatically create an exfiltration path, transfer stolen data, and then delete the infrastructure, leaving no trace of evidence behind. It is the recipe for the perfect digital crime.

However, the extremely basic network hiding techniques discussed thus far are just the beginning. Using anonymous proxies is nothing more than carefully routing traffic through desired locations over inherently secure protocols and hoping responders don't notice.

It is important to remember, however, that the tunneling traffic can function at deeper levels of covertness. Depending upon the environment, attacker needs, and responder detection/blocking capabilities, the traffic may or may not actually be formatted according to the true protocol. As an example, HTTP(S) or DNS ports could be used to push a stream of raw data to target destinations. Sending data within the constraints of the specific protocol will result in fewer red flags, but it may also slow down the ability to transfer content.

As such, the attacker/malware may use any open port and flood data through it without using the actual protocol that is typically associated with that port. A specific example would be to use a tool like Netcat to open a network socket and send data over any standard protocol that is open through a firewall. Typical examples include HTTPS/TCP 443, DNS/UDP 53, and/or any other open outbound protocols.

This is ideal if the goal is to send data to a remote host as fast as the network will allow. This method will be very fast, but it is incredibly visible. It will be easily detected if the right monitoring and detection/alerting use cases are in place for outbound data volume or if next-generation firewalls have protocol anomaly detection rules in place.

DNS is usually chosen if UDP 53 is open outbound and the affected company has SSL/TLS decryption capabilities implemented. Quite often, UDP 53 is not inspected by network security controls. Out in the field, it is not uncommon to encounter UDP 53 (DNS) C2 and exfiltration during investigations. It has been a tactic used across numerous high-profile incidents that have made the headlines.

Slow Data Transfer/High Stealth

Some of the more covert methods avoid the use of the packet data fields or flooding data over a port and, instead, cleverly hide data within various packet header fields. However, they can often only transfer 1 or 2 bytes at a time and are painfully slow – meaning absolutely glacial! They are only fit to transfer a very small amount of data. As such, the slower, covert methods are usually viable for C2 communication, but exfiltration is painful and may or may not be successful, depending upon file size (must be small) and network conditions.

ICMP and SYN tunneling are used for extreme stealth reasons, but there is a significant overhead associated with it. The benefit is that, like HTTP(S) and DNS, they are also seldom blocked, and they do not show up as easily re-constructible sessions. On the network, ICMP may appear like a continuous ping (or even a ping flood) of a remote site or a combination of remote sites in a round-robin manner. Additionally, there are numerous other covert methods that can be employed with this covert C2 and limited exfiltration mechanism.

SYN tunneling is even more covert in that it would appear to be a combination of connection attempts that are never established, as they don't complete the 3-way TCP handshake. 1 or 2 bytes of data are just stuffed into the SYN request that is received by the external C2 server, which then sends a reset after each.

In the case of both ICMP and SYN tunnels, the activity is seldom flagged by network security devices. The downside to these methods is that they are both very slow, considering there is a much smaller amount of data that can be sent in each packet. As such, it takes a very long time to exfiltrate a significant amount of content, and it may not even be possible. It is really only feasible to transfer C2 and very small files.

In addition to the slowness, there are also significant issues of unreliability. To begin with, the protocols are not stateful, and they have no session management. If a packet is lost in transit, it will not be detected on the receiving end. It will just result in missing content or file corruption, depending upon the file type.

Recently, a new twist has developed in proxying C2 and exfiltration traffic that involves utilizing webmail services for C2 and exfiltration. Gcat creates an encrypted proxy using Gmail, which is usually open in most environments. This avoids the issues experienced with making proxied network connections to covert, malicious hosts that may wind up on a blacklist or be identified in a variety of ways as suspicious activity.

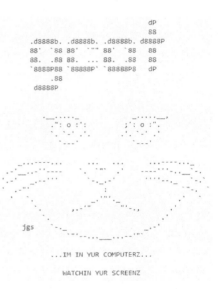

Gcat has the capabilities to log into a webmail service, send/receive data to/from the malware operator, and retrieve instructions in the same manner. It offers all of the capabilities of a proxy but through the Gmail front-end. This method of C2 and exfiltration would appear as normal webmail traffic from the workstation's user and is fully encrypted. Unless the environment utilizes SSL/TLS decryption and inspection, they would be blind to this communication method.

Detecting Covert Traffic

The attacker's selection of an appropriate network communication method is driven by knowledge of the network and what is permissible. Once an attacker gains an understanding of the traffic types that are allowed outbound from an organization, they can devise a method to get data out. There is almost no end to the variety of methods they can choose from to do this, and they won't typically be any more complicated than necessary.

As such, it is important to limit permitted outbound protocols (especially DNS) and keep firewall rulesets as tight as reasonably possible. Security controls obviously need to permit traffic to facilitate legitimate business needs. However, it must also detect and prevent unauthorized activity, and it must provide an audit trail to inspect when new covert communication methods are successful.

For all of the reasons mentioned in describing tunneling, proxying, and other covert channel types, it is very important to use next-generation network devices with key features enabled for covert activity detection and blocking. This includes performing protocol inspection and validation capabilities of firewalls and IDS/IPS devices to identify and block tunneling traffic.

Required security controls include 1) restricting permissible outbound protocols, 2) utilizing SSL/TLS network traffic decryption, and 3) enabling protocol analysis and validation capabilities. This will significantly reduce the risk of protocol manipulation, tunneling, and exfiltration. These capabilities, however, are nascent at best and still require manual configuration and inspection.

DNS Manipulation (DGA And Fast-Flux)

DNS is the phonebook or directory listing of the Internet. The ability to manipulate it is the ability to control where systems connect to and to mask malicious network activity through obscurity. DNS is the first and sometimes the only point of reference for identity on the Internet. Circumventing DNS identity controls removes a large degree of inherent trust. Granted, identity is also established by PKI certificates, but those are not implemented for every protocol, nor are they applicable to DNS evasion methods for malware, C2, and exfiltration.

Many security controls are based on the trust of answers returned in response to DNS queries, as well as DNS reputation services that are used for validation and blocking by reputation. Clever tricks to manipulate DNS for malicious purposes have become a standard practice for manual hackers and malware authors to implement hijacking and detection evasion techniques. A couple of notable examples are Domain Generation Algorithm (DGA) and Fast-Flux.

DNS Manipulation (DGA)

A notable example is the Domain Generation Algorithm (DGA), which is widely used for legitimate purposes and content caching. Akamai is a highly popular cached content provider and legitimate use of DGA. A network analyst would be hard-pressed to examine a packet capture and not see Akamai traffic. DGA has been used increasingly for years to facilitate malicious purposes and is an adaptive method to circumvent network blocking controls for known malicious sites.

Locky ransomware was an early, high-volume example of DGA use for ransomware purposes. However, it is not unique, and DGA is also common in other advanced malware, ransomware, and crimeware applications and suites – yes, there is an app for that. Locky's use of DGA involves creating a large quantity (between 100s and 10,000s) of domains with names created by an algorithm based on a crypto seed. The DGA generated domain names are generally one-time use and enable C2 and exfiltration traffic to bypass detections of known malicious sites.

Being as they are created in huge volumes and not typically used more than once (if at all), they cannot be effectively blacklisted. Moreover, only a small percentage of domains are used at a time and point to valid C2 servers. The malware makes connection attempts until it finds one that resolves.

All of this complicates the detection and blocking processes as they would require the algorithm and crypto seed used by the malware or employ some other mechanism to accurately guess the domain name variants. Some characteristics regarding the malicious DGA domains that are easy to identify are as follows:
1) It was very recently created.
2) It is seldom categorized.
3) It has no reputation associated with them.
4) The IP address is not associated with Akamai or other legitimate caching services.
5) The domain name and IP address usually point to some sort of cloud architecture.

More specifically, the attacker systems, services, or proxies are generally hosted within Infrastructure as a Service (IaaS)/Platform as a Service (PaaS) cloud infrastructure. The usual choices are Amazon Web Services (AWS) or Microsoft Azure, but other similar environments may be used. Systems in these environments can be automatically created quickly, changed on the fly, and securely deleted without the ability to recover systems or data. Data that passes through temporary/non-persistent cloud environments presents an extreme forensic challenge. It is effectively non-recoverable, and logs will be minimal.

DNS Manipulation (Fast-Flux)

Fast-Flux (both single and double) is a relatively new DNS trick that utilizes compromised hosts in a round-robin series for proxying malicious traffic to attacker infrastructure. Each time the domain name is resolved, it points to a different system in the attacker's infrastructure of compromised hosts.

Single Fast-Flux (or Single-Flux) involves using the compromised infrastructure just for proxying the traffic through the compromised host to the attacker's infrastructure. The DNS servers are normal, uncompromised systems performing a standard function. The rotating malicious infrastructure is extremely difficult to detect or block and extends the life of the malware campaign by delaying the blocking and detection of the respective infrastructure.

Double Fast-Flux (or Double-Flux) is similar to Single-Flux, but it adds Flux capabilities for the DNS servers as well. This makes the malicious activity even more difficult to identify and block, as all visible systems change with each communication initiated.

12 RESPONSE ACTIONS: ARCHITECTURAL REQUIREMENTS

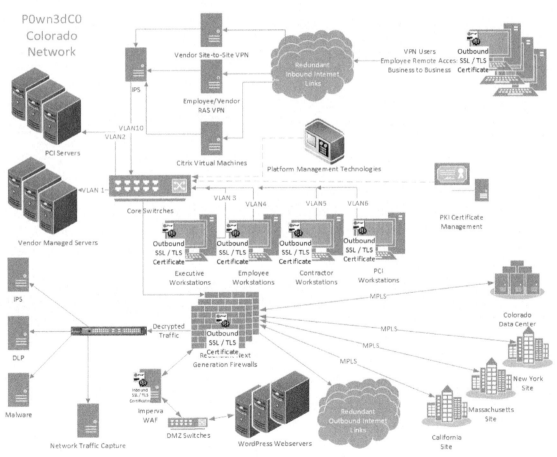

This section contains prescriptive guidance for architecting environments to optimize detection, response, and blocking of suspicious or malicious activity, whether from malicious actors or applications. Success in incident management and the ability to detect and respond to malicious activity requires a comprehensive security architecture and design process from the ground up.

It must include consideration for detection and response capabilities within each person, process, and technology to provide maximum coverage across all environments, resources, users, data, and use cases. Success in analysis is a rigorous step-by-step process to be reasonably safe. It happens by following all the steps, not automagically through automated tools or routine, static workflows.

Modern attack methods are highly adaptive and covert by design. They require a comprehensive and even more adaptive process to successfully identify and respond to threats.

Automated Detection and Blocking

To complicate matters, most environments are full of blind spots in each of the key technology areas: 1) Account activity, 2) network activity, 3) endpoint activity, and 4) log collection, correlation, and analysis.

Even if tools are 100% deployed and visibility is everywhere, no tool identifies everything. Moreover, automated security methods can provide a false sense of security and require an effective manual validation process. In summary, visibility gaps in key technology areas combined with sloppy security processes enable unauthorized activity and persistence to continue undetected and unabated.

While known threats and automated detections have gaps, it would be silly not to use them for the value they provide. If resources are being targeted by known threats, security monitoring, detection, and blocking controls should be in place to identify and stop them at all levels. These include account management, network traffic monitoring, endpoint monitoring, SIEM, etc. Moreover, automated correlation and analysis is oftentimes the only scalable way to make use of integrated threat feeds and identify threats across large data sets.

All infrastructure, networks, systems, devices, services, applications, data, user accounts, and access methods should be provided access monitoring, identification, alerting, and blocking for known threat use cases and suspicious behavior indicators. Disparate data sources should have logs and alerts synced and correlated between them as much as possible to provide an incident timeline that does not need to be converted or manipulated to be interpreted.

Keep in mind that the security provided automatically by default using security tools is minimal at best. To be perfectly candid, it is basically just a starting place. Automated detections typically identify a part of a thread of malicious activity, and it is up to the responders to pull on the thread and identify all related activity, artifacts, and impact. Unfortunately, there is no such thing as an automated find-all-evidence button.

Sadly, the presence of automated detection capabilities is generally the baseline required for most regulatory requirements. For organizations that simply seek to accomplish the minimum requirements and stop there, their security program remains minimally effective.

While the detections provided by baseline automated security capabilities are far from perfect, it would be embarrassing and indefensible to ignore them and be compromised by easily identified, well-known threats. Activity that should be monitored with automated tools for suspicious or malicious activity is as follows:

- Network connections to/from high-risk areas from/to unauthorized locations
- Process attributes and behavior
- User behavior and resource access activity
- File and data access activity
- Email activity, links, attachments, and other artifacts
- Notable events based on business use cases, high-severity alerts, and volumetric activity
- Suspicious scripts
- Dangerous applications
- Threat feed integrated alerts (preferably multiple feeds)

Considerations for Network Monitoring

For critical networks, resources, accounts, and data within the organization, it is essential to implement enhanced monitoring and detection to identify and elevate high-priority events for faster response. This must occur in multiple vantage points, preferably at each touchpoint with the critical resources. It must also occur at key choke points and within high-risk/value areas.

Implementing visibility and providing means to interrupt threats to critical resources in as many locations as possible will minimize the potential for attacks to be successful. It will also minimize subsequent exposure risk, malicious activity, and organizational risk. The following sections contain key considerations for doing this:

Key network connections and remote access methods

Each of the following are network connection types or methods that need to be considered for enhanced monitoring, depending upon the sensitivity of the data they contain or the access they enable. Each of these will be covered in more detail through this section:

- Ingress/Egress – All traffic going in and out
- Inter-site – All traffic between company sites
- Intra-site for sensitive locations or networks – All traffic within a specific network segment or site
- DMZ – All systems directly accessible from the Internet or within the DMZ
- Client VPN/RAS – All remote access methods to internal networks
- B2B VPNs/Extranets – All partner/vendor accessible or integrated networks
- Cloud – All virtualized environments

Ingress/Egress Traffic

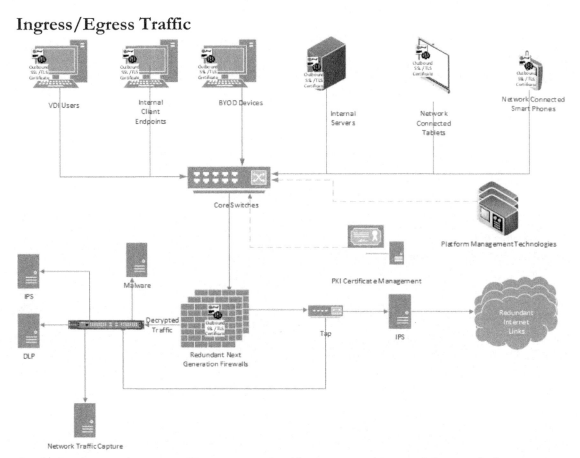

Analyzing ingress/egress traffic may reveal evidence at any phase of the attack that traverses the network. This includes phases such as infiltration, exploitation, exfiltration, and C2. Collecting and analyzing network traffic is best facilitated with next-gen firewalls or IPS devices. It also requires SSL/TLS decryption and deep packet inspection to identify protocol anomalies, tunneling methods, and malicious traffic to be detected.

However, notwithstanding the potential value for detecting and analyzing attacks, network-based methods have become increasingly less effective with the broad implementation of network traffic encryption. This involves not only the encryption provided by SSL/TLS certificates on compromised (but legitimate) sites but also includes that utilized by malicious actors in their respective crimeware tools and exploit kits. Moreover, with the advent of so many covert communication methods and the ubiquity of network traffic encryption, the efficacy of network detection, response, blocking, and prevention is highly problematic.

As such, SSL/TLS decryption is no longer optional but is required. Otherwise, the detection rate becomes extremely low, and the ability to detect and respond to malicious activity over a network will be significantly diminished. Even with decryption, network detection is still a challenge, and it lacks the efficacy it once provided. This is due to a combination of protocol manipulation, undecipherable encoding, and/or encrypted communication that cannot be decrypted by traditional SSL/TLS decryption MITM methods for deep packet inspection.

Beyond encryption employed by attackers and malware to hide traffic and contents, much more evasive techniques are also utilized and must be considered in security architecture plans. Protocol manipulation, DGA, and covert tunneling for C2 and exfiltration traffic are becoming very common and are automated by crimeware suites. The myriad of private VPN and anonymous proxy services further complicates the situation and necessitates a well-planned detection and response strategy.

The fastest way to identify these anomalous traffic types is through automated deep packet inspection that can flag specific anomalies for manual analysis. Identification should take place from multiple perspectives. Examples include that which is based on deviations from expected benign activity and reconstructing activity or traffic to reveal the intent of the attacker and the content transferred. Without deep-packet inspection, there are outwardly observable, anecdotal metadata indicators that are also useful but not always conclusive.

As bad as this sounds, the situation is actually much more challenging than can be easily described. Identifying abnormal network traffic can be hard enough in and of itself. It must captured, translated into a readable format, parsed, and then either compared with deviations from expected traffic, heuristics, and/or matched with malicious signatures/patterns for known bad. Moreover, all of these signatures need to be maintained and kept up to date.

But, that is just the start. Understanding the implications of the traffic requires significant investigation, decryption, decoding, and other deep-dive skills, tools, and methodologies that facilitate them. It can be very expensive and time-consuming. In order to be successful at such, the response team must also have capabilities for strong scripting and malware reverse engineering in order to reconstruct and carve out data exfiltrated through tunneling.

Considering the linear perspective of the steps involved, each must be successful. If the content is not fully collected in transit, decrypted, reassembled, decoded, and then parsed, it will ultimately not be readable. The end result is only usable if each step along the way is successful.

Usually, it fails right off the bat, with responders being unable to collect or decrypt the traffic. However, unencrypted traffic that is only partially collected or isn't sufficiently decoded is almost as difficult to perform as cracking encryption. This is particularly true if it is fragmented across numerous traffic streams or is session-less in nature.

ICMP or SYN tunneling is a good example of traffic that is typically not encrypted and could theoretically be reconstructed if fully captured. However, it is very difficult to reconstruct, as there is no standard format for doing such, and the method is inherently unreliable.

It sends a very small amount of data in a stateless manner. As such, each packet must be collected, and the covert data section must be carved out and recombined across all of the packets involved in the activity. This will take much more than automated collection and analysis methods. It generally requires a lot of luck during traffic collection and necessitates manual scripting skills to decode and reconstruct the relevant bits and bytes from the captured packets.

Inter-Site Traffic

Analyzing internal traffic between disparate sites or network segments will show the attack spreading (AKA lateral movement) across the WAN. Inter-site detection and blocking controls are much easier than intra-site controls, which will be discussed next. Visibility, analysis, and response to inter-site traffic require advanced edge firewall technology to be implemented at the boundaries of each site, even if the boundary connections are all essentially internal (such as connected via MPLS or VPN).

All the same concerns and challenges for ingress/egress connections apply, except it is actually worse. Decryption between systems becomes more difficult, as SSL/TLS decryption is not tenable or even relevant for internal traffic in most use cases. Malicious Inter- or Intra-site traffic is more likely to use protocols for internal network services rather than HTTPS.

It may not be necessary anyway, as developers are often lax about the security of internal websites/applications, assuming all access is legitimate and benign. It is not surprising to find internal sites/applications containing sensitive, confidential, or restricted content that don't implement MFA, use encryption, or perform input validation.

Notwithstanding the target-rich environment that vulnerable internal websites and applications might present, in terms of scale, it is not the primary attack vector. Large-scale lateral movement activity (such as the rapid spread of malware, ransomware, wiperware, etc.) usually happens over sensitive, internal protocols using credentials or exploits for vulnerable services. It is typically performed over sensitive protocols that facilitate SMB, RPC, RDP, Active Directory, Kerberos, or high-value and often vulnerable internal network communications.

Further, inter-site/intra-site network monitoring, detection, and blocking controls are often the only way to identify lateral movement unless security controls are installed or built into the system, site, and/or application. The ability to detect and block malicious traffic between sites or network segments allows responders to isolate malicious activity to a single site and network segment and prevent it from spreading to others. However, it does nothing to detect malicious activity or provide security within the particular site or network segment (AKA intra-site).

Intra-Site Traffic

For sensitive locations, networks, systems, or devices (such as those having regulated content), it may be necessary to inspect traffic within a specific network segment or site. Identifying malicious intra-site communication typically involves monitoring traffic on one or more SPAN ports on local switches that connect to an Intrusion Prevention System (IPS) and/or a User Activity Monitoring (UAM) solution.

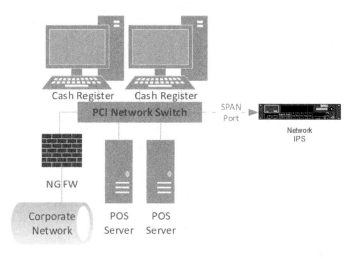

This is where the immense volume of network traffic involved and the capacity of the technology required becomes completely unscalable. Active monitoring or blocking of network security threats at this level is usually untenable. Monitoring of intra-site traffic is usually only permissible on highly sensitive network segments, such as server VLANS, payment VLANS, or other types of highly regulated or extremely business-sensitive network segments.

While monitoring and detection at this level become expensive, blocking becomes even more difficult, as it is not possible to be performed inline. All monitoring is done out-of-band, and automated blocking is limited to the efficacy of sending RST packets to terminate malicious traffic sessions.

While this does sometimes work, and manufacturers will usually claim to have the problem solved, using RSTs to end malicious activity is often unreliable. It may or may not succeed, and your mileage will vary. Long story short, the attacker's malicious tools or malware (at both ends of communication) can easily be configured to ignore the RST packets, and there is nothing to physically prevent the activity from continuing. In this case, the network security device is nothing more than a referee that can be easily ignored.

Reliable blocking of intra-site traffic would need to happen at the endpoint or switch level, disconnecting systems either physically or virtually by disabling network interfaces, blocking ports, or simply unplugging the affected system(s). This is possible via endpoint agents performing host isolation or network other controls initiating dynamic segmentation via ingress and/or egress ACLs on switch ports.

DMZ Traffic

All systems directly accessible from the Internet or within the DMZ should be monitored, inspected, and appropriately investigated. It should not be optional or simply considered a cybersecurity value-add.

Every network packet within the DMZ should be captured, analyzed, and saved for a reasonable time (at least 30 days, preferably more) to permit deep-dive retrospective analysis over time. This will permit the identification of previously exploited threats that were unknown and undetectable at the time.

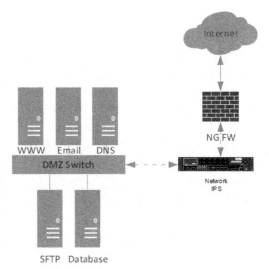

Intra-DMZ, internal network, or Server VLAN access from the DMZ should be restricted and monitored as much as possible to prevent DMZ hosts from being compromised and jumping to other systems that are accessible over sensitive ports not available directly from the Internet. In many environments, DMZs are completely flat, and too much DMZ → Internal traffic is allowed and not monitored. If attackers compromise a system within the DMZ, it is usually a good bet they can move laterally within the DMZ or internally without too much problem.

If DMZ connections are narrowly defined and permitted, it is easier to detect and respond to failed connection attempts and blocked ports than it is to detect malicious activity interlaced with benign activity for which there are not clearly definable alerts. Just like with a honeynet, if connection attempts are made from compromised systems within the DMZ to other systems or ports that are not accessible from the DMZ, it is an immediate red flag that needs to be escalated and investigated.

Client VPN/RAS Traffic

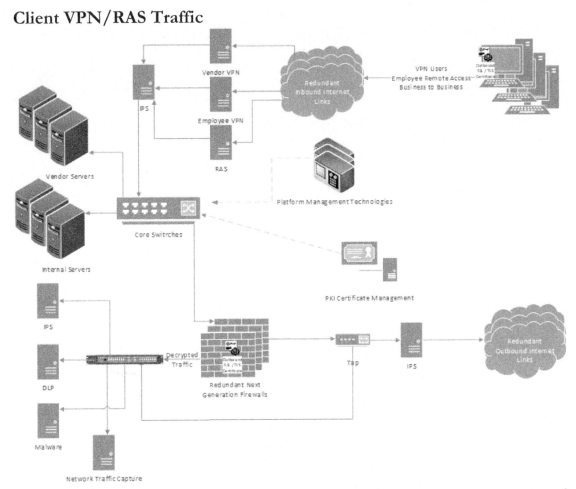

All remote access methods to internal networks or integrated environments, such as cloud infrastructure, must be monitored and inspected for malicious activity. This includes remote network access methods, such as a Client VPN, RAS, and/or other methods, which require the deployment of enhanced monitoring capabilities.

In addition to activity from attackers using stolen credentials or malicious insiders doing prohibited activities remotely, it is a primary conduit for exposure from inadvertently compromised systems. More specifically, off-network systems from roaming or work-from-home users are much higher risk than those that stay inside of the corporate network. There is a much stronger potential for externally located systems that connect intermittently via VPN to be less protected by security controls and behind on security updates.

Remote access capabilities enable potentially compromised systems to obtain access to on-network resources after rolling around in the mud and being exposed to all manner of potentially malicious activity. This is very high risk and could allow attackers and malware access to sensitive systems via the compromised roaming laptops. It is unfortunately common for systems to be compromised off-network and bring malware infections in through remote access that results in the spread of malware, ransomware, and the exfiltration of sensitive information.

It is key for all remote access activities to be restricted (even from employees) and monitored as much as possible. The access and traffic should be treated similarly to how a DMZ should be handled, as noted in the DMZ traffic section. Known malicious traffic, access to prohibited systems and ports, and volumetric connection activity that is indicative of scanning and a potential compromise should be seen as highly suspicious and quickly investigated.

Considering all Client VPN/RAS connections should be only permitted via successful MFA access, alerts should be configured to flag connection attempts that are 1) not authorized by MFA, 2) situations where the request comes from unexpected locations, and 3) locations significantly different than the MFA authorization on mobile devices. These could reveal potentially compromised credentials and unauthorized remote access.

B2B VPNs/Extranets

All partner/vendor-accessible or integrated networks are at least as dangerous as VPN/RAS access, which was covered in the previous section. All the same considerations for Client VPNs/RAS apply to B2B vendor/partner VPN access and extranets. However, the situation is even more dangerous.

Many well-known breach scenarios involve careless vendors having access to otherwise secure environments. These types of situations have resulted in security breaches impacting the attack target, its customers, and its employees. A company can have very strong network and endpoint security controls, only to be compromised by a vendor with limited security capabilities and poor security practices within their own environment. If the vendor has a full-time connection or is capable of connecting to the customer environment, they become an entry point to the customer environment. Their vulnerabilities and security problems become the customer's vulnerabilities and security problems.

Obviously, B2B VPN connections are a necessary evil used to allow vendors or partners access to provide services and administer systems. Unfortunately, it is generally much less restrictive than it should be. B2B/vendor remote access should be tightly restricted, similar to DMZ access, and specifically limited to only that which is needed (systems, ports, protocols, etc.). Just like with other remote access, configuring rules to identify access attempts to unauthorized resources, ports, protocols, or volumetric activity should be flagged and quickly investigated to identify the potential for malicious access attempts.

Additionally, special care must also be taken to ensure that vendor/partner accounts having remote access are still currently employed with the respective vendor/partner. It is possible that these users have separated from their former company, and their continued access could pose a risk/threat, particularly if they left the external entity under hostile circumstances. As such, the vendor management team should take care to audit vendor/partner accounts at least quarterly, and access from disabled accounts should be flagged and investigated for malicious intent.

Cloud

Network traffic to, from, or within all integrated or stand-alone virtualized environments must have adequate monitoring, inspection, and blocking controls. All the same considerations for remote access environments carry over to the cloud, but now the hardware is in someone else's control. Remember the old adage, "There really is no such thing as a cloud environment. It's just someone else's computer."

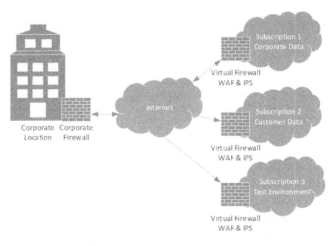

Each cloud environment should be treated like a separate DMZ environment and be specific to a use case – corporate, customer, testing, etc. All of the traffic, access, and activity to, from, or within the cloud environment must be strictly controlled and monitored. Identified anomalies must be identified, alerted on, escalated, and investigated.

These environments must be tightly restricted and specifically limited to only that which is needed (systems, ports, protocols, etc.). Just like with other DMZs and remote access environments, malicious activity should be flagged and quickly investigated to identify the potential for malicious intent. All the same general use cases apply, e.g., identify access to unauthorized resources, ports, protocols, or volumetric activity.

It is always best to define normal activity and restrict permissible actions to a known good state. This not only prevents the unauthorized or malicious activity from occurring. It also makes it easier to identify. All activity monitoring from visibility sources must be tied in with the corporate SIEM for the best alerting and quickest eyes-on-glass analysis.

Another consideration is that modern cloud concepts have moved past full-featured VMs and into stripped-down containers. As such, security capabilities often come from the application, network, or hypervisor rather than endpoint controls. This changes the paradigm for detection and response primary identification methods and may create a gap unless properly architected. However, any fully functional VMs should employ all applicable endpoint agents and security controls to identify malicious activity. These should be built into their standard images.

Identifying Critical Resources

For critical environments, resources, users, and data within an organization, it is essential to implement enhanced detection methods to identify and elevate high-priority events. These pertain to high-risk use cases (both security and business-related) and facilitate a faster response. This will minimize the exposure and organizational risk, as well as the subsequent activity required to respond. Being as it is not possible to have enhanced detections or elevated alerts on every system type, this section will identify the highest-risk resource types and use cases.

These key system types all have essentially the same need for monitoring and security controls. However, they may be implemented in different ways by disparate toolsets, depending upon the platform and security use cases. Implementation considerations include a combination of the platform, application, and service to determine the specific agent-based and/or network-based controls. Configurations also vary by security use cases being served.

It is usually best to implement both network and endpoint controls in a belt and suspenders approach to security and detection capabilities. This is particularly true for systems (like laptops) that go off-network and are not protected by traditional network security controls.

Long story short, it is almost impossible to get agents deployed on every endpoint. Even if it were possible, some endpoints are not within the security perimeter and may not report to control and logging infrastructure.

Moreover, the state of security within the network perimeter is not necessarily safe. There are almost never any network security controls for east-west (internal) traffic, particularly within the same subnet. As such, endpoint controls are used to protect trusted systems from compromise by other trusted systems. The most urgent focus for implementing security controls should include the following considerations, which may have significant overlap:

Business Critical Servers, Services, and Applications

This includes any resources that are required to maintain business operations and support key functionality. These types of resources are best enumerated through interviews and tracing the process flow for every business-critical operation and supporting function. The objective is to identify the underlying infrastructure and key details (networks, systems, services, applications, accounts, and data). This requires a combined process of discussion with 1) business owners/users and 2) key subject matter experts. This will help identify the business processes and interfaces that are used, which will then inform a technical review of the supporting infrastructure that supports the data flows.

Systems with Regulated Content

This includes any resources that transmit/receive, process, and/or store any form of PHI, PCI, PII, SOX, or other regulated data types. Depending upon the regulation type, this may be extended to any systems that provide services to, support, or otherwise can connect with systems involved in regulated data. The more that regulated resource types are integrated with or accessible from other non-regulated resources on the network, the more difficult and extensive this process becomes. This means that if they are comingled with (as opposed to segmented from) other servers,  workstations, and devices on the corporate network, it becomes harder to protect them due to broader accessibility.

Payment Processing Systems

This is essentially a subset of "systems with regulated content" and includes any resources (workstations, servers, or devices) involved in transmitting/receiving, processing, or storing financial information. From the perspective of PCI resources, it focuses on those payment processing systems used for credit card processing and all resources that support or can access the same. However, there are other types of payment systems that should be considered, such as those that facilitate ACH transactions or involve other payment methods. Any resources involved in payments of any kind are obviously prime targets.

Executive and Administrator Workstations

Execs and admins are high-value targets for a variety of reasons. Compromising their systems provides attackers and malware with access to sensitive resources. Not only are there accounts and systems high-profile targets, but these types of users are statistically more likely to click on phishing emails. Executives are often fooled by what appear to be business problems that need to be addressed but are actually whaling attacks. Admins often tend to over-use administrative accounts for common uses, such as Internet browsing, and their credentials become compromised. Either that or admins accidentally infect their systems while investigating suspicious activity.

Network, Directory Services, and Security Infrastructure

This includes all of the supporting network devices, directory services systems, account management systems, and security infrastructure in all their varieties. These resources are more or less transparent to the user experience and can have a profound security impact. These resources are the framework and glue that holds everything together or could facilitate covert backdoor access. Implementing security capabilities for network services infrastructure includes the need to protect and monitor potential suspicious activity related to network devices, DNS servers, DHCP servers, Active Directory servers, Enterprise Directory servers, NTP servers, etc. Malicious modifications to these types of systems can jeopardize the inherent trust in the network environment. They change the behavior in fundamental and dangerous ways that can result in the interception of traffic, hijacking of accounts, and theft of data.

The network security infrastructure is usually an integral part of the network infrastructure, such as next-generation firewalls, WAFs, security modules contained in network load balancers, IDS/IPS devices, or capabilities in other network devices, etc. Whether it is a security module installed on a network device or an independent device in and of itself, access to it must be secured and restricted as much as possible.

The same is true for endpoint security controls and the respective servers, services, or interfaces that administer them. Any compromise of these capabilities can result in the full compromise of the environment due to the level of access the agents provide.

Storage Repositories and Backup Servers

The storage and backup infrastructure are another set of very high-value targets that must be protected at all costs. Exploit kits, crimeware suites, and ransomware/wiperware modules are increasingly targeting these types of systems.

Having good backups is the key to protecting against the permanent loss of data from storage repositories. High-level threat types include any type of unauthorized change, encryption, or deletion. Having good backups means that destructive malware has less impact than it otherwise would because the data can be recovered.

An important and obvious caveat to mention is that backups are only as good as the ability to restore them. Sadly, untimely upgrades, lost keys/passwords, personnel changes, backup corruption, or other issues can result in the inability to restore data from backups.

Assuming that backups are good, this is not to say that there is no impact if ransomware-encrypted data is recovered from backups. Even if it can be recovered from backups, there may still be HIPAA impact if PHI is involved, and other regulatory requirements may also require reporting. However, at least the customer will not have to pay the attacker exorbitant ransom to get it back.

If the attackers or malware can wipe out or encrypt the storage repositories and the backups of the same, they could potentially force companies to pay to recover their data. This is the golden ticket for attackers. Protecting these types of systems is paramount to preserving business operations, intellectual property, and regulatory requirements.

Critical Virtual Machines, Containers, and Cloud Infrastructure

This is the same as all the critical system types previously mentioned. However, it also includes the portion of them that are located in the cloud. These are sometimes forgotten or not well integrated into the overall security and monitoring program. Cloud-based network and endpoint security controls have similar concepts and security functionalities. In some environments, cloud security controls have the same vendors as their on-prem counterparts.

However, there are also cloud-specific security capabilities for uniquely cloud concepts. These include virtual machines, hypervisors, containers, dockers, etc. Oftentimes, there can be greater efficiencies using cloud-based alternative concepts. These can take advantage of economies of scale and centralized visibility that could be applied to all virtual objects in a resource group rather than implemented individually on each virtual resource.

Moreover, some virtual objects, like containers, are not fully functional operating systems. They contain just enough functionality for an application/service to function and no more.

As such, no agent-based technology can run on them. The only controls that may be available are the following, from a very high level. Depending upon the technology, these types of security monitoring, detection, and/or blocking controls may or may not exist:
1) Those applied at the network level
2) Those available on the hypervisor level
3) Those that can be integrated into the container or docker object

Endpoint Detection, Response, Collection, and Analysis

Just like there are critical resources that must be protected, there are critical protections that must be in place to protect them and provide confidentiality, integrity, availability, and incident response capabilities for in-scope resources. The following is a list of activity monitoring, alerting, and blocking capabilities that should be implemented to protect critical systems (if not all systems). There should be as much deployment and coverage as possible, or there will be critical holes in detection and response capabilities. This will help quickly identify, respond to, block, or prevent malicious activity.

Endpoint Detection and Response (EDR)

The biggest game changer for incident response and investigations in the past several decades is the advent of EDR technologies. These tools can provide real-time monitoring, response, and evidence collection of key endpoint artifacts and the rapid ability to retrospectively analyze what transpired on a compromised system. It speeds up the analysis process by several orders of magnitude and often negates the need to perform full-fledged forensic analysis. What formerly took days or weeks can be accomplished in minutes.

The broader that the EDR tools are deployed, the better the resources are automatically protected with blocking controls for malicious sites or applications and/or provide investigators a rapid view into what happened if attacks are successful. Not only is it easy to identify what systems were affected, but the investigators can quickly identify the method of intrusion, attacker activity performed, malware involved, accounts compromised, and data exfiltrated (or at risk) in less time than it takes to read the sports page in a local paper.

Even better than EDR is EDR + integrated with other investigative resources. For best results, use EDR solutions combined with network traffic analysis/blocking solutions and all relevant log data aggregated into a SIEM for automated correlation, analysis, alerting, and retrospective history. This enables the entire story to be told from all views (endpoint activity, network activity, account activity, and log correlation) within a historical timeframe. This provides a window (storage permitting) for investigators to look back historically to determine if attacks occurred, the attack path, and potential impact.

Internet Access and Artifacts

Internet access to malicious sites is obviously the primary attack vector to compromise endpoints, which have become the primary target of attackers. The myriad of browser plugins, vulnerable endpoint applications integrated with browsers, and having direct Internet access leads to a very large attack surface. When this is combined with the extreme difficulty in the timely patching of endpoint applications and browser plugins, it creates a strong likelihood of exploitation.

Because of this, the inside is the new outside. The Internet is full of overtly malicious sites, compromised legitimate sites, and waterhole attacks that automatically compromise vulnerable endpoints. All access to the Internet must be monitored, tracked, and validated as much as possible. Moreover, malware artifacts should be analyzed to identify methods used to bypass security controls and compromise endpoint applications and operating systems.

This is particularly important in the modern fileless malware environment that typically lives off the land and utilizes various scripts, native command interpreters, WMI classes, and memory-resident capabilities. Protection, detection, and response are best performed through a combination of firewall/proxy, network traffic, EDR, and endpoint forensic technologies.

Email Activity, Links, Attachments, and Other Artifacts

Malicious emails are essentially an extension of hostile Internet activity. They contain bundled attack vectors (or pointers to them) within a discrete package (the email). All email access should be tightly restricted, monitored, and controlled to identify and prevent malicious attachments, links, spoofing methods, and other malicious activity from occurring.

All attachments, links, images, and other embedded objects should be automatically analyzed to identify malicious potential. Links should always be rewritten and clicking proxied through the email security solution to identify end-user access (clicking) and simplify the investigative process. It will enable quick identification of users who clicked on malicious links and the machines they clicked on. This will also provide the potential to block clicks from other users to the same malicious sites.

This is particularly helpful for systems located outside the security perimeter. Otherwise, there might not be a method to identify whether their users clicked on the malicious link or not. Knowing such will enable responders to take action to prevent compromised systems and accounts from infecting or obtaining malicious access to the corporate environment, either on-prem or remotely.

Process/Application Behavior

Modern EDR capabilities provide the ability to monitor, validate, and provide retrospection for processes and applications. This enables responders to validate that processes are acting within normal bounds and not maliciously. This is usually done through a variety of methods:
1) Profiling normal behavior
2) Flagging deviations therefrom
3) Identifying malicious activity based on a chain of events

A simple example of this would be as follows:
1) An uncategorized application starts an instance of svchost.exe.
2) It initiates a connection with a known attacker C2 site.
3) The uncategorized application can now be categorized as malicious due to the network activity.

Alerts pertaining to this type of activity should be quickly investigated to rapidly halt malicious activity. Moreover, the retrospective functionality and activity linking of many EDR solutions make for quick identification of root cause (s), which otherwise might take much longer.

User Behavior Monitoring

A combined approach of evaluating User Activity Monitoring (UAM), User Behavior Analytics (UBA), User and Entity Behavior Analytics (UEBA), Data Loss Prevention (DLP), access logs, and firewall logs is required to obtain a reasonable idea of what internal or external malicious entities are doing. To facilitate such, business logic, privacy, and security rules should be developed, integrated, or otherwise implemented to identify suspicious, prohibited, or malicious activity.

Repository/Share/File Activity

A combined approach of evaluating User Activity Monitoring (UAM), User Behavior Analytics (UBA), User and Entity Behavior Analytics (UEBA), Data Loss Prevention (DLP), Identify and Access Monitoring (IAM) solutions, and access activity logs, is required to track user actions and potentially malicious activity by the user or by malicious applications acting under the user's context. Business, privacy, and security-related rules need to be created based on data sources, data classifications, and user activity.

Configuration Changes and File Integrity Monitoring

Through the use of endpoint software that performs configuration management and file integrity monitoring, it is possible to identify unauthorized activity by unauthorized entities or malware making potentially malicious changes. Configuration changes are frequently made by malware binaries, malicious scripts, or attackers. Being able to identify them in an automated manner can speed up initial detection and simplify root-cause analysis. It may also enable the responders to prevent the same type of malicious activity from occurring on other vulnerable systems in the environment.

Site/Web Application/Database Activity

All external-facing and sensitive internal websites and corresponding databases should be monitored and validated via WAFs and database activity monitoring software. These systems are ideal for identifying unusual, suspicious, and/or malicious activity as they learn the objects they are monitoring and identify deviations from normal. Known malicious activity that appears successful should be immediately investigated.

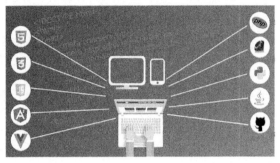

Notable Events Based on Business Use Cases

Every organization should make custom rules in their SIEM(s) that identify violations of business rules/policy or risks to the entity, its employees, customers, data, and intellectual property. These need to be customized for each organization according to their respective needs across people, processes, and technology.

Volumetric Activity

Some malicious activity does not appear overt. It may only be detected by identifying an excessive number of connections or activity to a service or protocol. As such, all Internet-facing, business-sensitive, and administration applications, services, and access methods should implement rules to identify excessive volumetric activity. This type of activity could be related to DoS, DDoS, scanning activity, file harvesting, mass file writes, or other malicious actions that happen in excessive quantities. This will typically require a combination of implementing controls on border network devices and also at the Internet Service Provider (ISP) level.

Threat Feed Integrated High Severity Alerts

Multiple threat feeds should be integrated into the detection and blocking capabilities within all IAM, network, endpoint, and SIEM tools to identify emergent threats as quickly as possible. No single organization can have the breadth of reach and exposure necessary to obtain the required insight on evolving threats that would enable them to stay ahead of them. As such, threat intelligence should be crowd-sourced as much as possible. The intelligence from crowdsourcing should be integrated with detection and blocking technologies at all levels.

13 RESPONSE ACTIONS: MALICIOUS ACTIVITY USE CASES

This section discusses high-value malicious activity use cases and the respective evidence sources, indicators, and response activity that must follow. The goal is to ensure the stage is set to conduct a successful investigation. This includes capturing key evidence artifacts from relevant data sources to be analyzed in order to ensure a thorough and decisive investigation.

Initial IOCs/Artifacts

Initial artifacts typically found in the alerts can come from any source. The usual sources include network security devices, endpoint monitoring technologies, or analysis and correlation rules within a SIEM. All of this technology can be significantly augmented using multiple threat feeds, alert integrations between technologies, and correlation rulesets between them. Linking them together in this way leverages the detection capabilities found in one technology for use across others that could also benefit from it. Detections, notifications, indicators, and artifacts often include the following components.

Network Addresses/Ports/Protocols

Automated alerts and IOCs usually contain lists of IP addresses, domain names, FQDNs, URLs, and the respective ports and protocols they use. This socket information could be related to any part of the attack lifecycle or activity type. Network device detection ability is enhanced through next-generation firewalls implementing SSL/TLS decryption and application awareness. This will identify script and application activity, as well as the hand-off to 3rd party inspection tools. Key indicators commonly found in suspicious or malicious network traffic include:

- Exploitation – The initial compromise
- Malware download – Downloading either primary or secondary malware tools
- Exfiltration – Transferring stolen content outside the victim organization
- Known malicious signatures – Pre-determined IOCs, YARA rules, hashes, etc.

- Known malicious site connections – Any known malicious external host/site
- Unusual foreign connections – Any ingress/egress traffic from suspicious countries
- C2 connections – Outbound connections to hosts associated with malware command and control (C2)
- Protocol anomalies – Any protocol manipulation used to hide traffic and/or facilitate covert communications
- Tunneling traffic – Any protocol encapsulation and/or encryption method used to hide traffic from detection and blocking capabilities
- Connection time or duration anomalies – Any uncharacteristic connections that are off-hours, last too long, or are otherwise suspicious
- DGA detection – Any use of domain generation algorithms other than known, legitimate sources
- Newly registered domain connections – Any newly created domains that could be used to facilitate nefarious purposes
- Suspicious connections to domains that have just changed ownership – Malicious purpose and re-use of previously legitimate domains

Memory

Alerts may contain suspicious memory artifacts that render systems or applications in scope. If the attacker is using fileless threats over encrypted network connections to perform attack activity, it is possible that the only indicators that may be found are in memory. These include the identification of key objects and malicious activity indicators, such as the following.

- Malicious hosts – Domain names, hostnames, IP addresses, etc.
- Encryption keys – Memory is usually the easiest way to obtain them in a usable state
- Golden tickets – Forged Ticket Granting Tickets (TGTs) are only found in the client computer's memory
- Silver tickets– Forged Ticket Granting Service (TGS) service tickets (STs) are only found in the client computer's memory
- Skeleton keys – Manipulation of the LSA process on a domain controller(s) to implement a secondary password for all accounts
- Credentials – Usernames and passwords
- Commands and communication – Any executed commands, command history from logged-in sessions, or communication artifacts, which often include commands
- Data streams and exfiltration traffic – Samples of files or other artifacts sent across the network that remain in whole or in part within memory
- Function calls – Related to malware and respective objects
- Calls to file system or registry objects – Identify all files, artifacts, compromised processes, functions, or other objects that malware interacts with
- Process injection – Carve out injected components, hooks, functions, calls, etc.
- Process hollowing – Carve out the entire malicious binary
- Malicious scripts – Show decoded/decrypted contents of formerly encoded, obfuscated,

or encrypted scripts

- Other fileless memory-based anomalies – Generally consist of memory-resident malware components, which are typically scripts, binaries, or other artifacts loaded into memory.

Commands/Script Activity

Automated alerts can identify malicious client-side, server-side, or network activity at any type of command interface. It requires the right visibility tools and monitoring logic capable of recovering command history. This can be anything from system command-line interfaces, API or instrumentation query interfaces, script interpreters, or database commands. Commands and scripted actions are high-value threat activities and should be monitored for malicious intent. They can be key to identifying fileless malware activity, which might not otherwise be detected.

WMI

Alerts may include references to malicious WMI classes or backdoors that can be persistent, asynchronous, and/or fileless in nature. Windows enables the creation of fully functional fileless applications using WMI, including custom WMI classes and subscriptions. As with anything, this feature can be used for benign or malevolent intent. While these should be considered immediately in-scope when found, this is another nascent space that is hard to detect and easy to circumvent detections.

Logs

If logs are configured to record and preserve the right activity, they can be critical for quickly identifying unauthorized or malicious activity from the vantage point of the log source. However, by default, logs typically do not capture all of the information needed to inform incident response investigations.

Moreover, the efficacy of logs is a balance between the verbosity of activity tracked and the capacity of storage and searchability. Being as log storage capacity is finite, if too much data is captured, it will reduce the length of the window of live storage below the minimum online retention period. Also, storing log data that is not helpful during an investigation is effectively just noise that takes up storage space, incurs unnecessary expense, and complicates the search and review process. It is possible to DDoS the responders and the overall investigation by burying them in too many logs, thus preventing the detection of real IOCs.

Alternatively, not capturing the right events needed for an investigation will effectively result in the logs being blind to the required information and useless to the response activity. For best results and to reduce the likelihood of tampering, logs must be sent to a central location within a SIEM for collection, correlation, searching, alerting, and archival. Having all critical logs in a central location enables powerful rules to be created that may identify, correlate, and trigger automated events for malicious activity.

IOCs & YARA Rules

Automated alerts and IOCs typically contain a listing of involved IOCs. They typically consist of specific files, processes, services, and registry entries involved in the detection or commonly associated with the particular malware variant.

Obviously, these need to be considered in-scope and searched across other systems in the environment. This may expand the scope of the investigation if related artifacts are found elsewhere.

However, the data in the alerts is just a starting place. Usually, there are additional or different files, processes, services, and/or registry entries involved. This is particularly true with modern polymorphic and/or scripted malware, which commonly modifies many aspects of itself from system to system to avoid detection. This polymorphism can be used against itself by leveraging cloud-based EDR capabilities. These solutions have the ability to identify unique processes, drivers, or targeted file types. In a standardized corporate environment where systems are based on role-based images, the configurations and files should be consistent, or at least non-unique across the organization. As an example, a unique process on a suspect system is highly suspicious, and it should be considered within the scope of the investigation.

Sometimes, artifacts or indicators are identified in groups, such as IOCs and/or YARA rules. These are basically any definable network, system, or log artifact in all their varieties, colors, and flavors. However, if polymorphic malware is involved, then patterns of behavior and expressions or parameters that describe the behavior become the indicators.

Oftentimes, there are attacker toolkits residing on disk. These are likely to identify dual-purpose/potentially unwanted programs (PUPs), like security testing tools, pen-testing tools, administration tools, password reset tools, network sniffing/MiTM tools, or covert communication/tunneling tools. All of these types of tools may have legitimate uses on the system and could potentially be used by admins as well as attackers.

Targeted Files, Registry Locations, or other Artifacts

Additional details contained in alerts that can be used to create malicious activity use cases include the details of accounts, system configurations, file system artifacts, or application artifacts, as discussed in this section. Most of these artifacts are under the purview of EDR or anti-malware detection capabilities.

Each threat type and affected operating system or application has a certain limited subset of related artifacts that are key to identifying malicious activity and establishing root cause(s), exploit method(s), and impact. These vary by circumstance and expedite the detection and containment of malicious activities if properly considered and configured.

Some common examples of targeted forensic artifacts that can be used for malicious activity use cases include the following. These will manifest differently on each operating system type:

- Account/group/role configuration – Identify unauthorized accounts, group memberships, and/or other changes made by the attackers to elevate privileges or create backdoor accounts.
- File system catalog ($MFT, FAT, Inode table, etc.) – Capture the entire file system catalog to obtain a listing of files, folders, metadata, and deleted content.
- Recently created/written binaries and scripts – Create a file system timeline to identify changes from attacker activity and malware installation. This includes the enumeration of all recently created or written binaries and scripts to inform targeted collections.
- Deleted file history – Identify any files/folders that were deleted either from the directory catalog, Recycle bin, and/or folder records.
- Targeted MRU history – View recent activity across desired MRU locations to identify the most recently used sites, files, applications, searches, mapped drives, printers, etc.
- Program execution configuration settings – Identify tampering of application execution, such as shimming the execution of other programs or scripts first or specifying custom parameters that change the functions at execution.
- Prefetch files – Enumerate all prefetch files to identify application execution history, suspicious/malicious files executed, and the respective prefetch settings for malicious files: C:\Windows\Prefetch.
- Internet browser history – Enumerate websites visited, scripts executed, and files downloaded or opened.
- Network settings – Enumerate all network interfaces and settings to identify any unauthorized interfaces or configurations that could be used for surreptitious access.
- Temporary/AppData file locations – Enumerate non-privileged user-writable locations and identify any files, binaries, or scripts downloaded to temp, AppData, or other public subdirectory locations and perform targeted collections.
- WMI or other fileless application configuration – Identify fileless programs added to the system, such as custom WMI classes utilized by Windows, typically located in the default location: C:\Windows\System32\wbem.
- Auto-runs and services configuration – Enumerate any programs or services that run on startup or login, which may identify malicious applications.
- Scheduled tasks – Enumerate all scheduled or recurring tasks, which may identify malicious applications, scripts, or functions.
- Targeted event logs – Collect key event logs from the system and/or applications, such as Security logs.

- Link files – Capture link files to enumerate recently accessed files, programs, removable drives, or shares to provide quick evidence of previous activity.
- USB device history – Enumerate all removable devices inserted into the system and their respective details about the devices and the users that inserted them. Default locations include the following registry keys:
  - SYSTEM/CurrentControlSet/Enum/USBSTOR
  - SYSTEM/MountedDevices
  - NTUSER.DAT/Software/Microsoft/Windows/CurrentVersion/Explorer/MountPoints2
  - SYSTEM/CurrentControlSet/Enum/USB

Out of this targeted collection and analysis activity, malware and/or malicious script samples may be identified and made available for deeper-dive analysis. These will help identify the attacker IOCs and TTPs.

Malicious Activity Use Cases

This section contains a high-level listing of common malicious activity use cases that monitoring and response teams must have the ability to detect and respond to. This response should preferably be performed in an automated or semi-automated manner. These are key indicators of malicious activity that occur at various stages of the attack lifecycle. This section will cover each of these use cases individually.

- *Elevated account anomalies*
- *Shared accounts*
- *Service accounts logging in interactively*
- *Account compromise or password-guessing attempts*
- *Successful logon from a Disabled Account*
- *Login attempts from hostile countries or malicious hosts*
- *Multiple logons with impossible travel*
- *Repeated detections from the same host or account*
- *Honeynet detections*
- *Malicious cloud access*
- *Injection activity*
- *Phishing activity*
- *Business email compromises*
- *Insecure data storage*
- *Private VPN or Anonymizer Activity Detected*
- *Insecure, sensitive data transfer*
- *Rapid data leakage*
- *Slow, extended data leakage*
- *Malware activity*
- *Suspicious application activity*
- *High-volume file read/write activity*
- *Log tampering*
- *Threat feed detections*

Elevated Account Anomalies

There are many types of elevated account anomalies. These typically include anything having to do with the following, which could be malicious, benign, or just a bad idea.

- Internet browsing from a privileged account
- Suspicious account creation/modification
- Unauthorized software installs
- Suspicious script execution

- Workstation to workstation login
- Suspicious permission changes
- Large quantity file access or changes
- Any activity that violates policy statements

Elevated account misuse will be of particular interest when establishing the scope and identifying the impact of an incident. Each notable type of elevated account or access misuse requires malicious activity use cases designed to detect the respective threats. The use cases will utilize one or more detection methods from the respective evidence sources that may result in alerts individually or correlated to provide more enhanced detection.

- Evidence Sources – Most of this data will be stored in the following locations
    - Local operating system or application logs
    - Directory services (Active Directory, Enterprise Directory, vaulting, etc.)
    - Aggregated within the SIEM
    - Endpoint Detection and Response (EDR)
    - User Activity Monitoring (UAM)
    - User Behavior Analytics (UBA)
    - User and Entity Behavior Analytics (UEBA)
- Data collection requirements: Collect evidence starting ~1 month prior to the onset of suspicious/malicious activity and up to the current date/time (or date/time of containment). This will establish a baseline of normal activity and capture any unauthorized actions or anomalies. Be careful, as the malicious activity may have started sooner than originally known.

Shared Accounts

From both security and compliance perspectives, shared accounts are always a bad idea. They raise a variety of concerns. In addition to questions about being able to establish non-repudiation for the purposes of regulatory compliance, they also enable attacker activity to go undetected. It is highly possible that malicious activity performed under shared accounts may be perceived as legitimate.

If multiple admins use the same shared admin account, they may dismiss suspicious/malicious activity as admin tasks being performed by another authorized user of the admin account. It becomes very difficult to identify who did what. If attackers have compromised the shared accounts, distinctly identifying their activity may not be possible.

However, if every administrator has their own distinct account tied back to them that only they use, identifying unauthorized activity becomes a lot easier. To improve the chances of identifying unauthorized and malicious admin activity, there should be a routine administrator activity review process whereby privileged accountholders validate their activity.

Regarding automated use cases, the identification of accounts that appear to be shared (particularly if they are not supposed to be) may identify compromised credentials used by attackers or malware. If accounts are not shared, but the same account is used simultaneously from different systems or locations via remote access from different sources or from other automated indicators, the credentials of that account may be compromised and should be investigated and remediated.

If the accounts and credentials are tied to other alerts or potentially compromised and otherwise in-scope systems, the shared activity should be considered suspicious until ruled out through the investigative process. All systems and data accessible by these accounts may have been compromised or at least could be considered at-risk.

- Evidence Sources: Finding employees, attackers, and malware using the same account requires a broad view across numerous types of evidence sources within the environment. It involves correlation and analysis from all authentication traffic using a central SIEM. Rules must be created to identify the instances where one account logs in as another or performs a "RunAs" function to use the context of another account. Rules must be created for all corresponding events on systems and applications in scope. It also involves identifying "land-speed" violations involving successful logon attempts from distances too far away from each other in too short of a time period. The activity may also be related to malware that has compromised the system, in which case the malware use case requirements should be followed:
  - Systems
  - Devices
  - Applications
  - Services
  - Remote access capabilities
  - Multi-factor authentication methods
  - Local operating system or application logs
  - Directory services (Active Directory, Enterprise Directory, vaulting, etc.)
  - Aggregated within the SIEM
  - Endpoint Detection and Response (EDR)
  - User Activity Monitoring (UAM)
  - User Behavior Analytics (UBA)
  - User and Entity Behavior Analytics (UEBA)
- Data collection requirements: Collect evidence starting ~1 month prior to the onset of suspicious/malicious activity and up to the current date/time (or date/time of containment). This will establish a baseline of normal activity and capture any unauthorized actions or anomalies.

Service Accounts Logging in Interactively

Service accounts are dangerous in that they are essentially shared, privileged accounts. Preferably, they are created to serve a particular function. Unfortunately, they are often used more broadly for mixed purposes on systems and applications.

In most cases, the passwords don't usually change, and there is usually no MFA or password vaulting in place. This is a recipe for an ongoing, long-term security threat if the credentials are compromised. Moreover, the more broadly the same service account is used, the wider the potential scope of impact for the security breach.

For this reason, the permissions of service accounts should be as narrowly contained as possible and should be limited to a specific function. This will isolate the scope of impact if the accounts become compromised.

Moreover, they should not be granted permission to logon interactively. A service account should just be utilized to authorize access for a single non-interactive service. If they are restricted in this way, it makes it easy to identify suspicious or malicious activity associated with them.

If proper service account restrictions are in place, any service accounts found to be functioning outside of defined parameters would be considered a red flag. Typical malicious indicators include any violation of the security controls or monitoring use cases that should be implemented for service accounts and/or associations with known malicious activity:

- Logging in interactively – Any interactive activity
- Functioning outside of its intended scope – Anything outside the scope documented in change control records
- Associated with in-scope systems/applications – Use may indicate a compromised service account being used by attackers or malware.

Identification of these events may also indicate bad IT processes, which are rather common. In many environments, admins use shared service accounts as a method of getting around restrictions against shared admin accounts. Without proper restrictions, they are effectively the same thing.

This is more common than it should be and is a perfect vector that enables attackers to move throughout the organization when service accounts become compromised. If the same service accounts are used across many systems or applications, the combination of compromised credentials and interactive logons enables attackers to move freely across the environment simply by logging in. No other exploits or malware are required. To prevent this type of attack, service accounts should be as tightly restricted as possible, and alerts should be defined for prohibited activity.

- Evidence Sources – Most of this data will be stored in the following locations
    - Local operating system or application logs
    - Directory services (Active Directory, Enterprise Directory, vaulting, etc.)
    - Aggregated within the SIEM
    - Endpoint Detection and Response (EDR)
    - User Activity Monitoring (UAM)
    - User Behavior Analytics (UBA)
    - User and Entity Behavior Analytics (UEBA)
- Data collection requirements: Collect evidence starting ~1 month prior to the onset of suspicious/malicious activity and up to the current date/time (or date/time of containment). This will establish a baseline of normal activity and capture any unauthorized actions or anomalies.

Account Compromise or Password Guessing Attempts

Any systems that are determined to be the source of account compromise (whether user, administrator, services, applications, or another account type) should be considered as in scope for deep-dive forensic analysis. All activity and the systems/applications they logged into must be investigated. It is entirely likely that one of these compromised accounts is patient zero, depending upon the timeline of events. Most likely malicious activity and methods of compromise include:

- Password guessing (brute force, password sprays, password dumping, or other methods)
- Pass-the-hash
- MFA bypass, circumvention, or insecure failover
- Session hijacking
- Token theft
- Other less common authentication circumvention attempts

This type of activity could come from a malicious inside actor inappropriately using company systems to escalate his/her privileges and gain elevated access to accounts, systems, applications, and/or data. This is typically performed using automated software tools, but it could also be performed using scripts or semi-automated or manual methods.

The activity is even more likely to come from a malware infection or exploit kit that has compromised a system and is attempting to move laterally. Detection of this type of activity on an internal system typically starts at a later stage in the attack lifecycle. This is because the intrusion or infection has bypassed security controls, made a beachhead on the system, and is attempting to increase its foothold to other systems.

Whether from a malicious actor or application, the activity may look the same from the receiving endpoint or from a network inspection point of view. The observable evidence would show a remote host connecting to another host using a network socket (source IP address, source port, destination IP address, destination port). In either case, the actor or application may use the context of the logged-in user, other stolen credentials, brute-force methods, bypass methods, or fail-over attempts that are permissible on the target types.

Rulesets must be developed to identify this type of activity across all authentication mechanisms and interfaces. Preferably, the actions taken should automatically lock the user out for a period of time following a reasonable number of failed attempts. An alert should also be triggered on the respective lock-out activity. The activity may also be related to malware that has compromised the system, in which case the malware use case requirements should be followed.

- Evidence Sources – Most of this data will be stored in the following locations:
    - Local operating system or application logs
    - Directory services (Active Directory, Enterprise Directory, vaulting, etc.)
    - Aggregated within the SIEM
    - Endpoint Detection and Response (EDR)
    - User Activity Monitoring (UAM)
    - User Behavior Analytics (UBA)
    - User and Entity Behavior Analytics (UEBA)
    - Web Application Firewalls (WAFs)
    - Next-gen firewalls
    - Database logging
- Data collection requirements: Collect evidence starting ~1 month prior to the onset of suspicious/malicious activity and up to the current date/time (or date/time of containment). This will establish a baseline of normal activity and capture any unauthorized actions or anomalies.

Successful logon from a Disabled Account

For various business purposes, many environments disable unused accounts rather than delete them. Oftentimes, the practice is related to seasonal employees or contractors that come and go and come again. For these use cases, it makes sense to keep the accounts provisioned and toggle between active and disabled rather than create them anew each time. So, the account state may change many times between active and disabled over the life of the relationship with the user. In this way, roles and permissions do not need to be reassigned to the account, and granting access to the same intended resources is as easy as re-enabling the account.

A challenge, especially in large environments, can be monitoring and maintaining the intended state of accounts and identifying accounts that are not in the correct state. Moreover, identifying logons and activity from accounts intended to be disabled is an additional process requiring perfect knowledge of the intended account activity state. There is a tremendous amount of record-keeping and organization involved in this endeavor that is required in order to facilitate detection and alerting activity.

Attackers can use this to their advantage by re-enabling disabled accounts and using the formerly disabled accounts to avoid detection. There are minimal logs incurred in doing so, and it is usually a safe bet that nobody will notice.

Alternatively, the creation of a new account and assigning it elevated permissions (such as Domain Admin) results in a lot of logs. This throws a lot more red flags and results in the increased potential of an investigation by auditors or responders. Simply put, it is a lot louder than simply re-enabling an existing account that already has elevated privileges.

In large environments, this type of activity is very likely to go undetected, even if there is some sort of account review process. If admins audit the quantity or names of accounts that exist, it will appear as if nothing changed. Yesterday's list would be the same as today's list, with nothing new added.

Validation of the intended account state is an additional manual review process unless integrated into an HR system and built into automated detections. Automated validation of accounts and their respective state (active/disabled) against intended accounts and state should be an automated use case. However, the ability to detect this requires rock-solid account management and change-tracking processes. As stated, this is a challenge in most large organizations, where extensive quantities of contractors, vendors, seasonal workers, or other temporary accounts exist that require frequent state changes and recurring account management. Per the author's experience, this has very seldom been observed in the wild.

Any unauthorized change in state or successful logons from accounts known to be suspended is highly suspicious. It is a common method used by attackers to avoid detection of backdoor accounts, as reactivating disabled privileged accounts (such as built-in admin accounts) having elevated access is simultaneously highly effective and covert. These accounts should definitely be considered within the scope of the investigation. The activity may also be related to malware that has compromised the system, in which case the malware use case requirements should be followed.

- Evidence Sources – Most of this data will be stored in the following locations
    - Local operating system or application logs

- o Directory services (Active Directory, Enterprise Directory, vaulting, etc.)
- o Aggregated within the SIEM
- o Endpoint Detection and Response (EDR)
- o User Activity Monitoring (UAM)
- o User Behavior Analytics (UBA)
- o User and Entity Behavior Analytics (UEBA)
- Data collection requirements: Collect evidence starting ~1 month prior to the onset of suspicious/malicious activity and up to the current date/time (or date/time of containment). This will establish a baseline of normal activity and capture any unauthorized actions or anomalies.

Login Attempts from Hostile Countries or other Malicious Hosts

Login attempts from hostile countries have always been a security issue. However, it is of elevated risk and impact with the recent increase in credential phishing and Business Email Compromise (BEC) activity that has plagued the Internet.

Most of the malicious activity originates from hostile countries known for cybercrime, where law enforcement is unhelpful with investigations for incidents affecting western countries. As such, any authentication, sensitive data access, or privileged user access from known hostile countries should be closely scrutinized and alerted upon. Sensitive activity from any country that the customer is not affiliated with and for which that activity should not be extant should be added to the alerting ruleset.

Massive troves consisting of many billions of stolen credentials are circulating the dark web and could potentially affect anyone with a digital presence. These stolen credentials are typically collected and tried against the known accounts associated with the user.

Considering people tend to reuse, synchronize, or just slightly modify passwords, the stolen credentials are often more useful than just the known 3-tuple site1/username1/password1. Attackers will typically cycle through lists of known passwords and common modifiers (appending or replacing letters with numbers or special characters) for all accounts associated with a targeted list of users in the form of a password spray attack. Considering it is more than likely possible the affected users utilize the same passwords or password base in multiple locations, it is more than likely to yield results.

- Evidence Sources: The sources will vary by resource type, but authentication attempts are typically found in local operating system logs, application logs, cloud access logs, directory services (Active Directory, Enterprise Directory, PAM, or another type), and/or aggregated within the SIEM, depending upon the configuration and malicious activity correlation rules or threat feed integrations. They may also be found in webserver logs, WAFs, next-gen firewalls, and potentially in database logging.

- Data collection requirements: Collect evidence starting ~1 month prior to the onset of suspicious/malicious activity and up to the current date/time (or date/time of containment). This will establish a baseline of activity and capture any unauthorized actions or anomalies. If email accounts are compromised in BEC incidents, the entire history of mailboxes relating to compromised accounts (whether internal or external) must be searched to identify the potential compromise of sensitive, regulated data that may be reportable.

Multiple Logons with Impossible Travel

An alternate method of detecting unauthorized logons using valid, compromised credentials is to geolocate the respective logon locations by either the IP addresses(es) of the computer(s) involved and/or the location(s) or the mobile device(s) granting MFA access to identify impossible situations that cannot be legitimate. Under normal circumstances, it is unlikely that a valid user would logon to the  company VPN using a workstation in Nigeria and have the MFA access for the same logon granted from a mobile device in California. Similarly, it is very unlikely that a user would access corporate cloud-based resources from Colorado and then from China in the same hour. The travel times are simply impossible, and one or both of the connections are likely malicious.

It is possible that there may be valid explanations for it, such as 1) the user traveled and left their MFA-granting mobile device at home and received assistance from their spouse at home, or 2) they were using a proxy that routed traffic through a different country. However, the traffic is highly indicative of malicious activity, and it should be contained and investigated before it is permitted to continue. More often than not, the activity is malicious and a sign that the affected user's credentials have been compromised and need to be reset and the account activity reviewed.

At this point, one might ask, in relation to MFA, why a user would grant unexpected MFA access requests. The answer is that it happens all the time. They may be logged in and think they need to grant MFA to remain logged in or think it is just one of their applications needing to renew its session, and MFA is required for their current access. MFA provides a certain amount of added security, but it also introduces confusion for non-technical users, who may have a propensity to grant unsolicited requests. **Note:** there are ways to improve the odds, such as configuring MFA requests to list the application for which they are granting access.

Impossible travel activity is highly indicative of successful credential phishing followed by unauthorized access to Internet-facing resources and/or cloud-based Business Email Compromise (BEC). As with most hacking attempts, much of the malicious activity happens in hostile countries known for cybercrime, where law enforcement is unhelpful with investigations of incidents in western countries. They essentially have free reign to do whatever they want with impunity, so long as they pay those who grant them this privilege.

A side note on this is that foreign attackers can use remote proxies to make their traffic appear that it is coming from the United States or any other country they desire. If they determine that they are being detected and blocked using this method, they could quickly redirect traffic through a proxy to make it appear they are in the US.

The use cases or analysis strategies need to compensate for this by tightening the impossible travel rules to be within neighboring states, under ~500 miles, or another similar thought process to reduce both false positives and false negative detections.

- Evidence Sources – Most of this data will be stored in the following locations:
    - Local operating system or application logs
    - Directory services (Active Directory, Enterprise Directory, etc.)
    - Aggregated within the SIEM
    - Endpoint Detection and Response (EDR)
    - User Activity Monitoring (UAM)
    - User Behavior Analytics (UBA)
    - User and Entity Behavior Analytics (UEBA)
    - Web server and application logs
    - Web Application Firewalls (WAFs)
    - Next-gen firewalls
    - Database logging
    - Virtual Private Network (VPN)/remote access solutions
    - Cloud-based email and storage repositories
- Data collection requirements: Collect evidence starting ~1 month prior to the onset of suspicious/malicious activity and up to the current date/time (or date/time of containment) in order to establish a baseline of activity and capture any unauthorized actions or anomalies. If email accounts are compromised in BEC incidents, the entire history of mailboxes relating to compromised accounts (whether internal or external) must be searched to identify the potential compromise of sensitive, regulated data that may be reportable.

Repeated Detections from Internal or External Hosts and/or Users

Recurring alerts involving the same hosts or accounts (whether internal or external) that have been identified as the source of repeated suspicious or malicious activity are strong indicators that something deeper and undetected is going on. Usually, where there is smoke, there is fire, even if detection devices are only catching a whiff of it every now and then. The usual indicators include access attempts to networks, systems, accounts, or data. Individual detections might be easily dismissed. Patterns of unauthorized activity of any and all types must be detected and investigated.

In the case where there are malicious insiders, the actors may be poking, prodding, and trying to escalate their privileges to obtain access to unauthorized systems, applications, and data. Every once in a while, security controls detect their activity, giving rise to repeat detections.

These individuals might not have any suspicious or malicious tools on their systems. Moreover, the activity may be explained away as accidental (Oops! Did I do that?!?!), even though they remain a human threat. From a visibility perspective, this activity often looks like a string of failures, followed by successful access, followed later by a large amount of data access or download.

In the case of malicious external actors, this usually takes the form of prodding for weaknesses until they find one, and then they go silent. This can take many forms, like vulnerability scanning, exploit testing, password sprays, or brute-force attempts. Essentially, anything the customer is susceptible to will be attempted.

They usually try very hard for a period of time and then stop, either because they were unsuccessful or because they got in at some level and didn't want to draw any additional attention to themselves. Only good visibility, detection, and correlation capabilities will enable the security and response teams to identify which use case happened and determine the state of security within the environment.

However, detected suspicious/malicious activity might not necessarily be the direct cause of a malicious actor. Oftentimes, automated threats are partially detected and addressed through automated means. Unfortunately, the remaining components may enable the exploit kit to re-infect the system.

Common occurrences of this exist where an exploit kit is undetected on a system, but some of its modules it uses may be detected when extracted and used. Those specific modules are alerted upon, but a full scan of the system does not identify the deeper threat persistence mechanisms related to the undetected exploit kit.

It is very common for covert malware to remain hidden within customer environments for extended periods of time. This is essentially the APT attacker model and marketplace where attackers gain and maintain perpetual persistence within as many desirable environments as possible. This access is used for the attacker's own purposes or to provide for-pay access to 3rd parties. Think of it as a bad-guy shopping mall where all of the stores are compromised environments, and the products are their respective systems, devices, applications, accounts, and data.

As such, repeated detections from specific hosts or accounts should be considered in-scope for the response activity until ruled out through the investigative process. Repeated suspicious or malicious activity could be a strong indicator of something significantly worse lying under the surface.

- Evidence Sources – Most of this data will be stored in the following locations:
    - Local operating system or application logs
    - Directory services (Active Directory, Enterprise Directory, vaulting, etc.)
    - Aggregated within the SIEM
    - Endpoint Detection and Response (EDR)
    - User Activity Monitoring (UAM)
    - User Behavior Analytics (UBA)
    - User and Entity Behavior Analytics (UEBA)
    - Web server and application logs
    - Web Application Firewalls (WAFs)
    - Next-gen firewalls
    - Database logging
    - Virtual Private Network (VPN)/remote access solutions
    - Cloud-based email and storage repositories
- Data collection requirements: Collect evidence starting ~3 months prior to the onset of suspicious/malicious activity and up to the current date/time (or date/time of containment). This will establish a baseline of activity and capture any unauthorized actions or anomalies. Identify all systems communicating with repeat offenders and pivot to collect evidence related to them.

Honeynet Detections

Any hosts and/or accounts involved in connections to a honeypot should be considered highly suspicious and possibly compromised. However, automated security scanners typically create a lot of false positives for this type of event unless the honeypots are excluded from the scans. Additionally, authenticated scans from legitimate scanners to honeypot systems create an interesting problem in that passwords become exposed to the honeypot. If the honeypot operators are not supposed to know those passwords (typically, they should not), then the exposed passwords need to be reset.

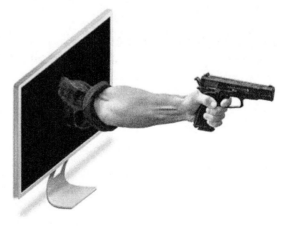

Further, if the honeypot can see them, credential harvesting tools and malware on other systems can as well. If an endpoint is compromised and malicious applications are monitoring network connections and authentications, it can intercept credentials or hashes from authenticated scans. It could then use them to escalate privileges and perform lateral movement across other systems. It is entirely possible that malware isolated to a single system could intercept domain admin credentials from an authenticated scan and spread throughout the entire domain.

- Evidence Sources – Most of this data will be stored in the following locations
    - Honeynet environment logs
    - Internal firewalls
    - Local operating system or application logs
    - Directory services (Active Directory, Enterprise Directory, etc.)
    - Aggregated within the SIEM
    - Endpoint Detection and Response (EDR)
    - User Activity Monitoring (UAM)
    - User Behavior Analytics (UBA)
    - User and Entity Behavior Analytics (UEBA)
- Data collection requirements: Collect evidence starting ~1 month prior to the onset of suspicious/malicious activity and up to the current date/time (or date/time of containment) in order to establish a baseline of activity and capture any unauthorized actions or anomalies.

Malicious Cloud Access

Cloud services (such as AWS, Azure, or others) have become an essential part of attacker infrastructure. As such, access to foreign, newly provisioned, or otherwise unknown cloud infrastructure is often highly suspect and may be considered in the scope of the response activity.

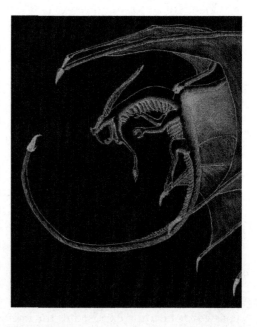

Moreover, the service has moved well beyond attackers using persistent malicious virtual machines contained in the cloud. There is now a mature capability of automatically spinning up non-persistent systems in the cloud that act as temporary proxies to downstream attacker infrastructure, providing support for Malware as a Service (MaaS) capabilities.

MaaS offers all manner of automated host compromise and management functions using malicious cloud infrastructure. Using this dynamic, non-persistent functionality, any stage of the attack lifecycle can now be facilitated by cloud services using dynamic IP addresses and hostnames. This infrastructure evades detection, as it has no reputation to trigger on. As such, the alerting potential may be limited to the identification of potentially malicious activity on new IP addresses and domains having no reputation and possibly located in foreign countries.

- Evidence Sources – Most of this data will be stored in the following locations:
    - Cloud-based email and storage repositories
    - Cloud Access Security Broker (CASB)
    - Data Loss Prevention (DLP)
    - Directory services (Active Directory, Enterprise Directory, PAM, or other type)
    - Aggregated within the SIEM
    - Cloud-based Web Application Firewalls (WAFs)
- Data collection requirements: Collect evidence starting ~1 month prior to the onset of suspicious/malicious activity and up to the current date/time (or date/time of containment). This will establish a baseline of activity and capture any unauthorized actions or anomalies.

Injection Activity

Any place there is an interface that can accept data, there is an opportunity to perform some sort of malicious injection activity in whatever methods and formats are appropriate. This can happen internally or externally. It effectively means that any method of passing data could be manipulated. Common methods include:

- APIs
- CLIs
- WMI
- Database interfaces
- Dynamic web content interfaces
- Authentication interfaces

All of these interfaces may be used to pass commands, control the affected systems, gain unauthorized access, steal data, or perform whatever else the attackers dream up. In order to identify this activity, each interface needs a method of securing the respective interfaces and detecting suspicious or malicious activity. Any such host or user attempting to perform injection activity is almost certainly suspect and should be considered within the scope of the investigation unless that activity is related to a security scanner.

- Evidence Sources – Most of this data will be stored in the following locations:
    - Data Loss Prevention (DLP)
    - Directory services (Active Directory, Enterprise Directory, etc.)
    - Aggregated within the SIEM
    - Endpoint Detection and Response (EDR)
    - User Activity Monitoring (UAM)

- o User Behavior Analytics (UBA)
- o User and Entity Behavior Analytics (UEBA)
- o Web server and application logs
- o Web Application Firewalls (WAFs)
- o Cloud-based Web Application Firewalls (WAFs)
- o Next-gen firewalls
- o Database logging
- o Virtual Private Network (VPN)/remote access solutions
- o Cloud-based email and storage repositories
- Data collection requirements: Collect evidence relating to the suspicious activity and the respective systems or malicious actors involved in it and all suspicious/malicious activity up to the current date/time (or date/time of containment) and identify any unauthorized, suspicious, or malicious activity.

Phishing Activity

Everyone with email gets phished, but those who have clicked on malicious links, opened attachments, or entered credentials are at extreme risk of system and/or account compromise. Any users identified to have been affected by phishing activity will likely be considered in the scope of the investigation, particularly if the phishing activity can be tied back to a credential compromise, malicious download, or known attacker exploit and C2 infrastructure.

Users who click on suspicious links or open malicious attachments are a significant threat to the organization and its respective resources and data. Moreover, any data stored on the systems, shares, email, or other resources accessible from the affected system or using the exposed user credentials may also be considered compromised and potentially reportable. The more one digs into this rabbit hole, the worse it typically gets. Accounts and systems usually have a lot more access to sensitive information than is typically known.

An even more malicious and significant finding would be if the user was successfully phished and then initiated phishing attacks on others. This is a strong indicator that not only was the user compromised and is in scope, but all those who received phishing emails from the user need to be investigated and in scope as well. This compounds the investigative universe by placing all the data stored in the successfully phished users' scope of influence at-risk. This includes all accessible systems, applications, email accounts, shared accounts/groups/boxes, network shares, and Internet-accessible shared resources. Each of these resources is at least considered to be in the scope of evaluation to determine the risk of compromise and the associated impact.

- Evidence Sources: Phishing activity is best identified with email security gateways and URL rewriting capabilities. However, once clicked on, strong EDR and anti-malware capabilities are most capable of identifying malware-related activity both on and off the corporate network and traditional security perimeter. Detection is augmented by network visibility controls, such as next-gen firewalls, IPS, SIEM correlation rules looking for defined thresholds outside of normal activity, and threat feed integrations. The activity may also be related to malware that has compromised the system, in which case the malware use case requirements should be followed.

- Data collection requirements: Collect evidence starting ~1 month prior to the onset of suspicious/malicious activity and up to the current date/time (or date/time of containment) in order to establish a baseline of activity and capture any unauthorized actions or anomalies. If email accounts are compromised in BEC incidents, the entire history of mailboxes relating to compromised accounts (whether internal or external) must be searched to identify the potential compromise of sensitive, regulated data that may be reportable.

Business Email Compromise (BEC)

A BEC is a form of fraud that involves the compromise of an email system and using the email thread history to social engineer trusted parties for the attacker's benefit. It is a particularly successful attack method, as the attackers most often use the compromised email system to perform the communications. In 2022, the FBI reported it logged more than 21,000 BEC complaints, which amounted to more than $2.7 billion in losses.

The attacks usually manifest as attempts from malicious parties using compromised vendor email systems to get trusted parties in customer companies to make changes to payment methods and thus intercept monies owed or other malicious actions. However, there are many variations on this theme, and they can be either external or internal communications. Some examples include stealing intellectual property, tricking victims into installing malware, stealing victim credentials, getting admins to reset credentials to ones known by the attackers, requesting payroll departments to change direct deposit accounts to those used by attackers, etc. There are an unlimited number of uses, but they usually either result in the attackers gaining more access or stealing money, intellectual property, or other data.

It is a type of attack that is particularly hard to automatically detect or defend against, considering the use of otherwise benign email systems. For all intents and purposes, emails often look just like legitimate communications. The best ones change as little as possible to keep from being detected by victims.

The attackers may alter a few items in the email to re-route verbal communications to the attacker's phone number. Email communications will still go to the compromised user's inbox, but the responses are typically forwarded and then deleted using automated email rules to avoid detection by the actual user.

However, the attacks may also occur as stolen email histories that continue the conversations on look-alike domains or as spoofed emails. These variants are easier to detect but also often go unnoticed. Phishing rulesets are often successful at identifying them, depending on the circumstances.

For all of the BEC variants, the best defense is user training and a secure process for validating sensitive requests that come in over email. These include contacting parties at known, trusted phone numbers of record (not those in email signatures) and requiring secondary validation methods, such as ID-proofing, answering identity validation questions, requiring authentication and MFA, etc.

Insecure Sensitive Data Storage

Hosts or storage locations found to be storing insecure, sensitive data may potentially be involved in the scope of a security incident. However, they are much more likely to be in the scope of a compliance incident/investigation, depending upon the nature and reason for the storage. The data could be from either of two misuse cases:

1) Malicious insiders, external attackers, or malware collecting and storing up data to exfiltrate
2) Benign activity from an authorized user operating in an insecure manner, either intentionally or accidentally

The identification and determination of such is highly contextual. In either case, the insecure data storage should be investigated to determine its source and nature, as both impetus options need to be addressed.

For the sake of prioritization, depending upon the location where the sensitive data is stored, it may indicate a stronger likelihood of malicious activity vs. irresponsible benign activity. If the data is in the "Documents" folder on a workstation, it is more reasonably justifiable as simply a user's bad idea than if it is stored on a user's personal cloud account or concealed within a malware-created AppData sub-directory.

- Evidence Sources: Insecure, sensitive data storage is usually identified by DLP systems (network, host, or cloud-based) or EDR capabilities.
- Data collection requirements: Collect all user-created documents, command or application history logs, browser history files, link files, and MRU locations.

Private VPN, Anonymizer, or other Tunneling Activity Detected

Any hosts found to be using one or more of the vast myriads of private VPNs, anonymous proxies, or other tunneling methods may or may not be ruled within the scope of response activity, depending upon the nature of the use. While it is true that malware, crimeware, and the various forms of exploit kits have covert communication and exfiltration capabilities, many privacy-focused browsers use these same methods as well.

Almost any function that malware performs could have a legitimate, intended function, and false positives are highly possible. Malware authors don't need to develop their own methods and technologies if they can simply repurpose established capabilities for their own purposes. Using otherwise legitimate applications and functions is more covert anyway.

Additionally, when privacy browsers are used in a corporate environment, their use is seldom benign. They typically are utilized to circumvent corporate security controls, for whatever reasons, which are mostly prohibited or malicious:

- Inappropriate use
- Data theft/corporate espionage
- Accessing prohibited/blocked sites
- Personal privacy

Moreover, by purposefully circumventing corporate security controls (protocol inspection, IPS, firewall controls, DLP, etc.), the user of these privacy browsers has also nullified the associated security protections. There is a reason certain types of sites are blocked, such as porn sites. Free porn sites often come with free malware that freely installs on the affected system and compromises the operating system, accounts, and data. This is a significant risk that needs to be investigated, at least as a compliance incident, but possibly as a security incident.

Even worse, if it is found that malware or attackers are the cause of the activity, then no benign purpose could be assumed or hoped for. The activity is likely C2 or exfiltration, and the affected systems, accounts, and data are definitely in scope.

- Evidence Sources: The most thorough way to identify covert network activity is using the host-based activity analysis methods provided by EDR, anti-malware, and DLP capabilities. This will ensure that it is identified both inside and outside the security perimeter. Other options include network traffic captures, next-generation firewalls/IPS devices, and SIEM correlation rulesets that are capable of protocol analysis. The activity may also be related to malware that has compromised the system, in which case the malware use case requirements should be followed.

- Data collection requirements: Collect evidence starting ~1 month prior to the onset of suspicious/malicious activity and up to the current date/time (or date/time of containment) in order to establish a baseline of activity and capture any unauthorized actions or anomalies.

Insecure Sensitive Data Transfer

Hosts found to be sending sensitive data outbound may potentially be involved within the scope of a security incident. However, they are more likely to be in the scope of a compliance incident, depending upon the nature of the traffic. The traffic could be from attackers or malware exfiltrating the data or from the user sending the data out in an insecure manner, either intentionally or accidentally.

The identification and determination of such is highly contextual. In either case, the insecure data transfer should be investigated to determine its source and nature. Any potential impetus needs to be addressed.

For the sake of prioritization, depending upon the location the sensitive data was transferred to, it may indicate a stronger likelihood of malicious activity vs. irresponsible benign activity. If the data is transferred to an OFAC-listed country, some other country that is known for cybercrime, or a foreign cloud location, it is more likely to be malicious than benign.

Any insecure data transfer should be investigated, but some observed transfers should be given a much higher priority.

- Evidence Sources: Sensitive data leakage is usually identified by one or more of the following sources, which could be located on the host or network. Depending upon the rulesets, data sent may trigger rules on specific detection tools or within the centralized SIEM. A SIEM might find this type of activity indirectly using correlation rules relating to the volume of traffic, quantity of connections, external host, or other rulesets.
  - o EDR capabilities
  - o Host or network DLP systems
  - o Next-gen firewalls and IPS devices
  - o Network traffic captures
- Data collection requirements: Collect evidence starting ~1 month prior to the onset of

suspicious/malicious activity and up to the current date/time (or date/time of containment). This will establish a baseline of activity and capture any unauthorized actions or anomalies.

Rapid Data Leakage

When malware designed for cybercrime or espionage infects a system, it will often begin to exfiltrate targeted data types. These typically affected content such as user-created files, database content, or other data types having marketable information. Exfiltration usually happens rapidly and will result in a significant data spike unless there is some sort of throttling. However, exfiltration methods and data speeds on crimeware suites/exploit kits are typically configurable.

These may be implemented in order to be covert. Sometimes, the goal is to get as much data out of the environment as quickly as possible, and the malware operators don't try to hide their activity. At other times, they try to hide their activity and exfiltrate data slowly over a long period of time. If their intent is to maintain covert persistence and milk the environment for as long as possible, they are more likely to use low and slow exfiltration methods in an attempt to be covert.

Further, many organizations do not effectively monitor for data exfiltration, and there is no reason to throttle it. In many cases, malware operators have free reign of organizations and their systems, accounts, and data once they get a foothold inside of the organization. It is not uncommon to find malware infections in organizations that have existed for many years and remain undetected. If the C2 infrastructure remains in place, the malware can be sending out data the entire time.

Minimal steps employed to avoid detection during rapid data leakage typically involve using common, secure ports/protocols (such as HTTPS, SFTP, or others) and sending data to a seemingly benign destination. Unless SSL/TLS decryption has been implemented, the rapid exfiltration will only be numerically quantifiable.

Contributing to the problem, SSL/TLS decryption is still not widely deployed in most organizations. Even if it is installed and enabled, it is usually somewhat neutered. The neutering usually involves preventing the decryption of traffic to sites handling regulated information. These are usually those that are categorized as financial, healthcare, payment, banking, or others with regulated content.

The neutering of decryption capabilities introduces additional areas for blind spots and unfettered exfiltration. If attackers want to prevent traffic to their exfiltration site from being decrypted, they compromise and hijack or establish a site that is categorized as financial, healthcare, or other regulated content.

The advent of cloud services, such as AWS, Azure, and others, has also made a safe home for attackers and malware to perform rapid data leakage with plausible cover. The IP addresses in cloud environments are often highly dynamic, thus negating the value of IP reputation and blocking.

As such, if a significant amount of data is going to a cloud destination, it might be mistaken as legitimate because the customer utilizes cloud solutions or integrates with companies or solutions that do. Very often, destinations in cloud environments are deemed benign until proven otherwise and are often excluded from detection and blocking rules. This is usually based on the fear of impacting business processes.

Reasonable outbound data transfer baselines should be established for the organization respective to destinations, as appropriate. For example, next-generation firewalls should be configured to identify and alert when > 500MB (or some present amount) of data is sent to unauthorized locations.

Various size thresholds may be set for various destinations or traffic types. Further, some destinations or traffic types may have higher or lower limits. Some destinations (like designated company cloud service locations) may be exempted and have no preset limit at all.

- Evidence Sources: Rapid data leakage is usually identified by one or more of the following sources, which could be located on the host or network. Depending upon the rulesets, data sent may trigger rules on specific detection tools or within the centralized SIEM. A SIEM might find this type of activity indirectly using correlation rules relating to the volume of traffic, quantity of connections, external host, or other rulesets:
  - o EDR capabilities
  - o Host or network DLP systems
  - o Next-gen firewalls and IPS devices
  - o Network traffic captures
- Data collection requirements: Collect evidence starting ~1 month prior to the onset of suspicious/malicious activity and up to the current date/time (or date/time of containment) in order to establish a baseline of activity and capture any unauthorized actions or anomalies.

Slow, Extended Data Leakage

Not all exfiltration activity happens quickly. Some activities attempt to be covert by sending small amounts of data over a long period of time. Oftentimes, this activity will use tunneling methods over session-less (stateless) protocols or incomplete TCP handshake attempts. This network traffic is hard to detect without the right people, processes, and technology in place. Attempting to detect this type of activity will drastically expand the scope of analysis. Finding evidence of such will further expand the investigation and incident response activity. Long story short, there is a lot of work involved in identifying, collecting, reconstructing, and decoding this traffic in order to make it available for analysis.

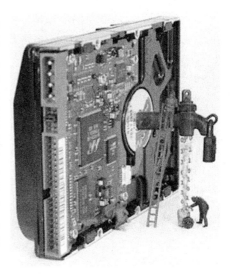

This type of low and slow communication or exfiltration activity happens when environments have fairly strong automated detection and blocking controls, and the attackers need to fly beneath the radar to avoid detection. Common occurrences for this are ICMP, SYN, or DNS tunneling. All of these methods are generally undetected, but they can be painfully slow. However, it is possible to exfiltrate a sizable quantity of data in numerous small dumps slowly over a long period of time, most of which will not even be logged. Following is additional high-level information about the three most common low and slow covert tunneling methods:

- ICMP Tunneling – Extended, voluminous ICMP traffic from internal to external hosts
- SYN Tunneling – A continual pattern of failed SYN requests where internal hosts send a SYN, and the external host responds with an RST
- DNS Tunneling – Continual traffic to external DNS servers or queries for the same domain name

In order to identify and alert on this type of activity, network devices must specifically be configured to look for extended traffic activity to or from the same hosts over a long period of time (for example, > than 12 hours). This could indicate tunneled content wherein each packet contains a small amount of data, which is assembled and reconstructed on the receiving end. While this activity could use stateful protocols, more often than not, the protocols are stateless. The following are additional details for the examples mentioned:

- Evidence Sources: Slow, extended data leakage is usually identified by one or more of the following sources, which could be located on the host or network. Depending upon the rulesets, data sent may trigger rules on specific detection tools or within the centralized SIEM. A SIEM might find this type of activity indirectly using correlation rules relating to the volume of traffic, quantity of connections, external host, or other rulesets.
  - o EDR capabilities
  - o Host or network DLP systems

- o Next-gen firewalls and IPS devices
- o Network traffic captures
- Data collection requirements: Collect evidence starting ~1 month prior to the onset of suspicious/malicious activity and up to the current date/time (or date/time of containment). This will establish a baseline of activity and capture any unauthorized actions or anomalies.

Malware Activity

Any network activity traced back to known malware is obviously suspect, and all hosts, accounts, and data involved are within the scope of the investigation. This could include a very broad variety of event types. Depending upon the method of detection, it may have a high likelihood of being a false positive or negative.

A significant challenge in identifying malware is that the more specific the identification method is (which eliminates false positives), the less likely it is to identify new malware variants (which increases the likelihood of false negatives). Conversely, the more adaptable and flexible the detection method is, the more new malware variants it may find, but the more false positives it will encounter.

For example, traditional, exact hash-matching methods (such as MD5 or SHA hash matching) are used by antivirus and will conclusively identify known malicious threats. There are few false positives, except when benign files are mistakenly included in the hash set – yes, this happens!

However, when even the smallest thing changes, the malware sample all of a sudden becomes unrecognizable and eludes detection. This can be done using a simple packing utility, like UPX, or dozens of others that are freely available. The act of packing malware is ubiquitous and essentially a standard operating procedure for attackers. However, it is also used for benign purposes by legitimate software creators.

It is also done by using random filler bytes or bits inside of binaries or scripts. These can be arbitrarily changed without altering the intended functions. In addition to altering the hash value, the filler bytes also change the size of the respective file, which can vary significantly.

The advent of polymorphic malware made antivirus almost completely irrelevant. Polymorphic scripts made detection even more difficult. In the cases of both polymorphic binaries and scripts, everything outwardly observable about malware can change, which makes them unidentifiable by traditional automated means.

This is the primary reason for the demise of antivirus as a viable security control. The over-reliance on exact hash-matching and lack of other effective detection methods (such as heuristics) is a deal-killer. Moreover, it created a space for the next-generation anti-malware tools that are making their way into the market.

Next-gen anti-malware tools take a different approach and use a combination of heuristic analysis to identify malicious activity paired with an algorithm to identify deviation from known good behavior. They also integrate data from threat feeds and crowdsourced intelligence. This provides significant detection enhancement for malicious threats and expedites the process of blocking threat campaigns.

However, this method has a tendency toward false positives and flagging legitimate, benign processes exhibiting the potential for malicious capabilities. This most commonly happens with dual-purpose, admin-type applications that are utilized by admins as well as attackers or malware in exploit kits.

Additionally, rare applications, such as those found in custom-developed or niche use cases may be flagged as malware and unnecessarily blocked. These are usually found on developer systems. This is best addressed by validating, whitelisting, and/or signing uncommon applications and importing the certificate.

However, the evolution of malware from file-based to fileless (including scripted, WMI-based, memory-based, registry-based, kernel-based, hypervisor-based, disk-based, CPU-based, chipset-based, other hardware/device-based, or covert methods or sub-methods) has created a vast landscape of places that malware can hide and security tools need to inspect and act upon. In many cases, there is absolutely no automated method to directly identify malware. It may be possible to identify the activity of the malware using a combination of endpoint and network monitoring capabilities having sufficient visibility and behavioral or protocol analysis capabilities.

The surest way to identify polymorphic malware activity in any of its forms is to have a solid baseline of known good, benign activity and to identify suspicious or malicious activity as anything that deviates from that baseline. Unfortunately, this creates a significantly heavy lift on the front end to develop the correlation rulesets necessary to define the known good activity and alert on that which is notably beyond the realm of such. This will vary significantly across environments and will involve a combination of automated and manual activity.

- Evidence Sources: Polymorphic malware activity is best identified with strong EDR and anti-malware capabilities that can identify malware-related activity both on and off the corporate network and traditional security perimeter. Detection is augmented by network visibility controls, such as next-gen firewalls, IPS, SIEM correlation rules looking for defined thresholds outside of normal activity, and threat feed integrations. If endpoint and network behavioral monitoring/alerting controls are not in place, targeted or full disk acquisitions must be performed in addition to the collection of network traffic captures.

- Data collection requirements: Review retrospective endpoint/network monitoring interfaces for 24 hours prior to the onset of suspicious/malicious activity and up to the current date/time (or date/time of containment). This will establish a baseline of activity and capture any unauthorized actions or anomalies. For deeper dive forensic activity, collect and search targeted files, registry locations, memory, pagefile, and other artifacts as required (if a full disk acquisition is not performed). Search evidence 24 hours prior to the deletion/clearing activity and up to the current date/time (or date/time of containment) in order to establish a baseline of activity, identify user/application/script activity and authentication from any sources, and capture any unauthorized actions or anomalies.

Suspicious Application Activity

Modern malware authors have become smart enough to learn how to use legitimate system applications and functions to do their dirty work. This is called "living off the land." With the power and full-featured capabilities of resources freely available on the system, it is no longer necessary to create custom-compiled malware to perform malicious activity.

All that is necessary to gain complete control of a system is to develop PowerShell scripts, VB scripts, macros, or use other scripting methods that utilize available resources to perform attacker or malware activity. On Windows, this is typically performed by calling the native Windows functions and processes using a variety of direct or scripted methods, such as calling default WMI classes, creating custom WMI subscriptions, or using any method available from installed command interpreters.

The attackers can do nearly anything they desire without the need to do custom binary development. All of the functionality is natively available. The attackers just need to put together a script and use it.

The primary indication of attackers living off the land is that applications may be observed behaving in unexpected ways or having abnormal circumstances. Indicators of such include the following:

- Processes with abnormal quantities of occurrences
- Non-standard parent-child relationships
- Communications with unexpected processes
- Unusual network or Internet connections
- Association with unexpected files
- Unusual process start-times
- Unexpected file paths

Depending upon which of the above is observed and the processes involved, it may not be enough to immediately convict the respective processes as manipulated or the systems they reside on as compromised. However, if any of the above indicators are observed, it certainly warrants a deeper dive investigation. Applications found to be operating in non-standard ways may be considered in the scope of investigation, particularly if associated with other in-scope hosts, accounts, data, or activity.

However, this is a nascent space at best, and it is full of false positives and false negatives. For best results, identifying suspicious activity requires legitimate and intended activity to be well-defined. In this way, anomalies will stand out. As such, each application needs to be profiled and have the key attributes identified and analyzed. These include:
1) Intended parent process
2) Expected process children
3) Expected account/owner
4) Quantity of processes
5) Expected process path
6) Time of execution
7) Expected process interconnections and libraries

This level of profiling doesn't usually exist. It is not native to Windows nor identified by default by most automated tools. However, it could be developed using a combination of endpoint agents, advanced endpoint monitoring/logging, and SIEM tools.

- Evidence Sources: Suspicious application activity is best identified with strong EDR and anti-malware capabilities that provide retrospective analysis and understanding of the normal functional behavior of applications. These solutions can identify malware-related activity both on and off the corporate network and traditional security perimeter. Detection is augmented by advanced activity logging functions (like Sysmon) and sending all data to a SIEM for analysis with correlation rules looking for defined thresholds outside of normal activity.
- Data collection requirements: Review retrospective endpoint/network monitoring interfaces for 24 hours prior to the onset of suspicious/malicious activity and up to the current date/time (or date/time of containment). This will establish a baseline of activity and capture any unauthorized actions or anomalies. For deeper dive forensic activity, collect and search targeted files, registry locations, memory, pagefile, and other artifacts as required (if a full disk acquisition is not performed). Search evidence 24 hours prior to the deletion/clearing activity and up to the current date/time (or date/time of containment) in order to establish a baseline of activity, identify user/application/script activity and authentication from any sources, and capture any unauthorized actions or anomalies.

High-Volume File Read/Write Activity

Crimeware suites, exploit kits, and their respective modules that perform sensitive data harvesting, ransomware, wiperware, and/or other malicious file modification activity all have one thing in common. In performing this activity, they all utilize extremely high volume read/write functions that parse and/or maliciously alter large quantities of files on local file systems, network shares, and/or other repository types.

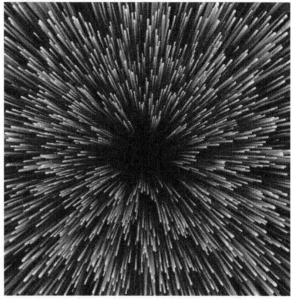

This type of activity is identifiable utilizing endpoint DLP, EDR, and/or anti-malware tools that are configured to monitor for such actions. Identifying this type of activity early may be the key to stopping ransomware or other file manipulation attacks before they do too much damage. File manipulation attacks have always been popular, and the trend is not declining. It is critical that exclusions be put in place for security applications that legitimately perform similar activities. Otherwise, they will fight each other and likely render each other ineffective, and the system they are installed on will be vulnerable.

However, this is another nascent space, and it has the potential for both false positives and false negatives. Making this use case successful will require significant research and customization based on the tools, configurations, and capabilities that are extant in the customer environment.

- Evidence Sources: This activity is best identified with strong endpoint DLP, EDR, and anti-malware capabilities. These tools provide retrospective analysis, profile the normal functional behavior of applications, and identify malware-related activity both on and off the corporate network and traditional security perimeter. Detection is augmented through the use of a SIEM and relevant activity correlation rules.

- Data collection requirements: Review retrospective endpoint/network monitoring interfaces for 24 hours prior to the onset of suspicious/malicious activity and up to the current date/time (or date/time of containment). This will establish a baseline of activity and capture any unauthorized actions or anomalies. For deeper dive forensic activity, collect and search targeted files, registry locations, memory, pagefile, and other artifacts as required (if a full disk acquisition is not performed). Search evidence 24 hours prior to the deletion/clearing activity and up to the current date/time (or date/time of containment) in order to establish a baseline of activity, identify user/application/script activity and authentication from any sources, and capture any unauthorized actions or anomalies.

Log Tampering

Any host found to have demonstrated activity consistent with log tempering (such as clearing or selective deletion) is likely compromised by malware or attackers. It may be considered either a security incident or a compliance incident, and it may be within the scope of the response activity.

Log deletion (whether selective or complete) is seldom an authorized activity unless the size of the log files or databases compromises the stability of the system. In such a case, log size may need to be pruned to free up resources. Such legitimate log alteration activity should be properly recorded via change control. This will help avoid alarm later when the log deletion is discovered.

Other reasons for log deletion are very likely malicious activity performed by unauthorized individuals or applications designed to hide the actions they performed. And, while it is true that privileged users can delete logs to hide their activity, log deletion events themselves are typically logged. As such, this is a trigger to identify unauthorized deletion activity, as well as a starting point for investigation.

- Evidence Sources: Evidence of log clearing or deletion can usually be found within the logs themselves, either from an entry stating such or a significant gap in time. SIEMs may also capture and store this information, depending upon the configuration. Evidence may also be found in unallocated space on the file system, in log databases (depending upon the structure), and in the system memory or pagefile.
- Data collection requirements: Collect all log files, search unallocated space for relevant keywords/expressions, and collect memory/pagefile. Search evidence 24 hours prior to the deletion/clearing activity and up to the current date/time (or date/time of containment) in order to establish a baseline of activity, identify user activity and authentication from other sources, and capture any unauthorized actions or anomalies.

Threat Feed Detections

The old adage that "it takes a village" has some merit in the world of cybersecurity and incident response. When new waves of threats are developed, chances are somebody else saw something like it first. The attack campaigns often ripple through industry verticals and become modified as necessary for each new victim, target type, and/or industry.

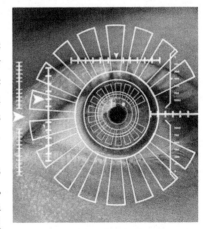

It is a frequent occurrence to see large swaths of industries hit, such as healthcare, insurance, banking, retail, government contractors, government entities, etc. When one campaign is finished, the attack method gets tweaked to suit the next campaign or target type.

The pattern of attack across similar swaths of companies is helpful in that there is actionable intelligence to be gathered and used by others in similar circumstances, such as having the same types of targeted systems. If this information is crowd-sourced and available through threat feeds, it can be integrated into its monitoring and response technologies. This will simplify the detection and response processes and shorten the attack lifecycle. The typical security tools compatible with threat feed integrations include:

- EDR and HIPS capabilities
- Network monitoring capabilities
- IAM and MFA capabilities
- SIEM activity correlation rules

Threat feed detections may be helpful in more quickly identifying malicious activity, which may expand the scope. However, your mileage will vary depending on the threat feed source, IOCs provided, and the dynamic nature of the threats. If the threats are highly polymorphic and distinct between each organization, there will be minimal actionable intelligence. If there are standard endpoint artifacts (files, registry keys, processes, etc.) or network indicators (domain names, IP addresses, etc.), then the threat feeds will provide high-value, actionable information.

- Evidence Sources: Threat feeds can be integrated into many next-generation firewalls, IPS agents/devices, EDR platforms, anti-malware platforms, and SIEMs to enhance detection capabilities.

Data collection requirements: Collect evidence starting ~1 month prior to the onset of suspicious/malicious activity and up to the current date/time (or date/time of containment) in order to establish a baseline of activity and capture any unauthorized actions or anomalies.

Risk-Based Alerting (RBAs)

RBAs are a key feature included in modern SIEMs that are a profound force multiplier when it comes to prioritization of detection and response capabilities. With risk-based alerting (RBA), sets of individual suspicious or malicious use cases or rule sets can be combined to create alerts on suspicious patterns of activity rather than on single risk events. Some events are not necessarily malicious enough to trigger a response by themselves, but in context with other events for a specific system or user along a timeline, they can be strong indicators of overtly malicious activity.

This is a significant game-changer, considering the individual events are often both too voluminous and inconsequential to respond to by themselves. RBAs can enable responders to zero in on the specific events that need to be investigated for further response. While it does not completely eliminate false positives in incident response, it is a giant leap forward that significantly reduces them and enables response teams to focus on the most important alerts based on cumulative risk scores.

14 RESPONSE ACTIONS: VALIDATION AND FIRST STEPS

This section provides guidance for detecting, reporting, and validating an incident. It enumerates the steps and considerations involved in obtaining incident notification details, validating an incident, and kicking off the evidence-gathering/investigation processes. The goal of this phase of an incident is to ensure the right focus and resources are brought to bear in response to an alert, notification, or escalation.

Incident Notification and Details Gathering

Upon notification of an incident, the Incident Commander and other assigned response personnel should gather all salient information. This includes the required information respective to their environment, the current incident or threat activity, and the resources involved to begin building an incident response profile.

The contents of the incident response profile vary by engagement but generally contain the following high-level items. These will help drive investigating a real incident or eliminating the event as a false positive:

Detection Method

Usually, threats are detected or reported from one of the following sources:

1) Automated alerts
2) Threat hunting activity
3) User reported
4) Externally reported

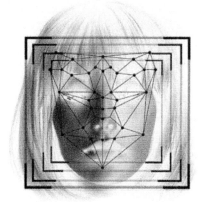

Depending upon the detection method and source involved, the associated detection, response, priority, and processes may vary wildly. For the purposes of discussion, detection sources/methods will be divided between inside and outside sources, as follows.

Inside Sources

Insider detection and reporting methods are as follows, which are ordered from best to worst in the ways of detecting threats. It is ideal to detect and resolve threats before they become a problem. This usually involves automated detections for blocked attempts to access protected resources or otherwise perform malicious activity. Less desirable is for the security or response teams to find it through manual threat hunting. However, even worse is for end-users to find and report it. This means that the attack got through all layers of security undetected and remained for a period of time before the users found it:

- Automated detection – These are typically system-generated alerts or hits on manual correlation rules from security technologies, such as network security, endpoint security, SIEMs, and threat feed integrations. The efficacy of these hits is as good as the signatures, IOCs, heuristics, or rules that created them. Your mileage may vary. Overall, they are likely to have both false negatives and false positives.

- Manual detection – These are usually hits on threat-hunting activity by security team members. These are generally the highest accuracy hits as the content is (or should be) custom-crafted, tested, and validated by the threat hunter. Therefore, the false positive and negative rate is typically low if the threat hunters follow a rigorous process. Once again, your mileage may vary. If threat hunters are just duplicating what is identified on a threat feed or threat site, as opposed to doing manual research and testing, this activity will essentially only be as good as the threat feed and may as well just be integrated and automated.

- Hacking and malware identifications can be anecdotal and inaccurate based on the user experience unless ransomware is involved. However, the identification of inappropriately shared, stored, or transferred information is usually very accurate. Ideally, any type of detection by end-users should be accompanied by screenshots and as much descriptive information as possible. However, the information they gather and share should be done in such a way as to avoid compromising their endpoint or incurring further legal and regulatory liability.

External Sources

If reported by or known to an outside entity, the best plan for dealing with them is to gather the information that they have to offer. However, do not over-engage them in the incident response processes. Information flow involving outsiders should ideally be a one-way street (inbound only). An exception would be for partners/vendors that are involved in joint incident response activity. With them, IOCs and salient findings need to be shared to facilitate the response activity, but information should still be filtered.

More specifically, be careful not to overshare anything that could introduce additional confidentiality concerns. Any findings or artifacts should be securely transferred using encrypted transfer methods to avoid creating a greater compliance incident on top of a security incident. Moreover, if reported by or known to an outside entity, there are additional risks and action items. A limited public disclosure has effectively already occurred, and there are few controls over what outside entities say. Media notifications and complications are much more likely in this scenario. Typical external sources include the following entity types:

- Law enforcement – This usually only happens if the situation is very significant or related to another case for which they need info from the customer environment. However, law enforcement typically won't provide the response team or others at the customer site with much substantive information. If it is more of a public service, they will say something like: You might want to investigate the system at IP address x.x.x.x and then provide nothing else. If they do provide this information, take it seriously. There is very likely a real threat there. However, if they want to get actively involved in the case, they are likely to take over, and their goals very likely will not align with the customer's goals. It is highly probable that they will want to permit malicious activity to continue for an extended period of time in order to obtain further intelligence about it. This will almost always result in a compromising situation for the customer, who typically just wants to clean up their environment and return to business as usual.

- Partners/vendors – This is probably the friendliest group of outsiders who will contact the customer regarding an incident. However, if the customer hears about an incident from them, the service they provide is likely the source of it, and the systems or data involved may be at risk. This is usually the beginning of a lot of work. It is critical to obtain IOCs and malware samples that can be used to drive detections in your own environment. It is also essential to explore whether partners/vendors have adequate in-house response capabilities or if it should be recommended/required that they retain a trusted third-party firm to assist.

- Customers/clients/patients – If the end customer complains about a security incident, there is very likely a problem, either real or perceived. At the very least, the customer faces some reputational risk. If the customer voices the problem to a media outlet, there is at least a public disclosure and probably an exaggeration of information surrounding the incident in the media before the entity is ready for media attention. Information, screenshots, and other available artifacts should be gathered from the customers. However, when gathering information, it is essential not to ask them to do anything that will further jeopardize the confidentiality, integrity, or availability of their systems or data or that of individuals whose data was exposed.

- Security researchers – If a security researcher escalates a vulnerability or security incident, there is definitely a problem to deal with, whether real or perceived. At the very best, they will likely try to extort the victim for a finder's fee, and at worst, they will publish an article about it or put it on their blog or podcast. In either case, there is a situation to deal with. The most innovative and effective approach the author has found to deal with security researchers who continue to probe the external environment and report issues is to put them under a short-term contract and make them sign an NDA. Either way, it is typically a bad situation. It is a catch-22. If the affected company "feeds" them, the researchers will come back for more. If the affected company doesn't feed them, the researchers will likely write negative articles or blog posts or find more public ways to monetize their findings, regardless of the real security significance of the findings. It can turn into a no-win, hostage-type situation.

Symptoms

It is particularly important to identify all of the known symptoms of a reported event or security incident in order to help validate it and begin root cause analysis. Symptoms gathered should include details about its behavior, artifacts, logs, and impact on affected networks, endpoints, and the users' experience.

Attack Vector

This may or may not be known at the early stages of a response. But, if it is, immediate steps need to be taken to mitigate the threat. These may include patching vulnerabilities, configuration changes, and/or implementing compensating controls if mitigation is not possible. In any case, the attack vector needs to be identified as quickly as possible to secure the system or environment and protect it from further exploitation.

Exploit Method

Just like the attack vector, the exploit method should be identified as quickly as possible to prevent additional exposure. Moreover, the exploit method might apply to other attack vectors and usually needs to be identified and secured separately to prevent it from being a continued risk. This is usually where compensating controls come into play.

Known Artifacts, IOCs, and YARA Rules

These need to be identified quickly and used to enumerate related threats in other locations and to implement containment controls with related security controls in any location. These are basically any definable network, system, or log artifact. However, if polymorphic malware is involved, then patterns of behavior and expressions or parameters that describe the behavior become the indicators.

However, if polymorphic malware is involved, then patterns of behavior and expressions or parameters that describe the behavior become the indicators. E.g., the malware generates a file with an alphanumeric name from 8-10 characters long located in an AppData subdirectory that also has an alphanumeric name from 10-15 characters long.

Initial Scope

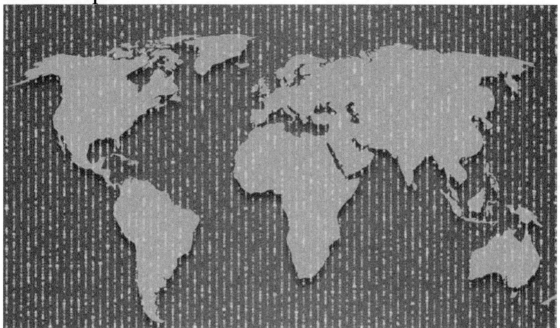

The initial scope usually includes locations, networks, systems, applications, accounts, data, etc. It is essential for performing early analysis and implementing initial containment measures to prevent the activity from spreading. The initial scope will be used as the basis for limiting or blocking additional exposure or exfiltration and reducing the overall risk. The quicker the scope is defined, the faster the containment measures go in place, the smaller the incident can be kept, and the less risk there is to the organization.

Building the Profile

Based on the details provided in the notification compared with the information known about the affected system, it is possible to make a quick assessment regarding the impact on the affected resources and determine if the actions were suspicious or completely irrelevant and could in no way compromise the system. E.g., an automated scan was detected that was searching for any vulnerability, but it was not performing any form of exploitation. In such a situation, the impact would be null.

Alternatively, if the activity targeted a known, existing vulnerability on a critical system containing restricted, regulated data and successfully gained root access, the impact would be very high. In aggregate, preparing this information and enabling subsequent analysis as early as possible will help ensure responders can hit the ground running. Moreover, it will minimize the need for additional research, which just slows down the response process.

The more research that is required at the beginning of the investigation, the longer the actual response onset is delayed. Depending upon the information required to begin, it could take hours, days, or even weeks to obtain. Delays could mean the difference between 5 systems affected or the threat spreading to 5000 systems (or worse).

Incident Validation

Prior to beginning the incident response activity, the team needs to validate if there really was an incident. It is very common for customers or end-users to suspect a security incident has occurred when, in fact, they just have a network, operating system, application, or other configuration issue.

Any time there is a disruption or negative impact on a service or some sort of misunderstood technical anomaly, it could be perceived to be the result of a security incident. It is important not to jump immediately into incident response mode and the various related workflows when anomalous problems are reported.

Automatically assuming that reported events are real incidents could result in the team spinning unnecessary resources and wasting a significant amount of time and/or money in well over half of the reported events. Rather, begin by trying to identify if there is a non-malicious technical issue that could explain the situation. If not, then escalate the issue.

Very commonly, there are many non-malicious causes for events, as follows:
- Application errors
- Resource/sharing conflicts
- Browser plug-in crashes
- Endpoint slowness
- Network slowness
- Misconfigured security controls
- System updates
- Overly broad incident detection signatures
- Other unexpected error messages that raise suspicions

These types of events or detections create alarm amongst users and administrators who are becoming increasingly suspicious of hacking and malware. It will save a tremendous amount of time if false incidents can be avoided through proper troubleshooting prior to escalating an incident. This will also help preserve the team's reputation by not crying wolf on false incidents, which erode faith, support, and responsiveness from the stakeholders.

Incident Validation Questions

To reduce the likelihood of investigating false incidents, begin by asking probing questions with a critical approach intended to identify possible non-incident-related causes and explanations. The following are some sample questions and intended deliverables that could be used to obtain answers and artifacts that will substantiate or dismiss an event as a possible security incident. For the record, these are just a starting place to drive discussion, and obtaining answers or deliverables will undoubtedly drive additional questions:

Question/Request	Objective/Deliverable
Why does the customer suspect an attack?	Obtain a record of observances that led to their suspicions.
What kind of suspicious behavior has been observed, and why does it stand out?	Obtain a narrative on why the customer or admin believes the activity is suspicious and how it differs from the normal state.
Gather preliminary details and artifacts.	Collect and research screenshots, events/alerts, and related artifacts that led to their conclusion.
Identify suspected incident scope and timeline based on detection and known details.	Determine how long the event and potential incident may have been occurring and begin to identify where evidence artifacts that can better establish or refute the existence of an incident may exist.
Identify and collect corroborating metrics or evidence artifacts that can confirm or refute initial suspicions and the existence of a real incident.	Identify metrics, statistics, logs, configuration files, event/incident-related files, malware samples, scripts, registry entries, or other artifacts.
Is the customer possibly mistaken or making unfounded assumptions?	Review all initially gathered information, perform research on collected artifacts, and make a determination on whether the incident is valid or a false positive.
Identify alternate explanations for the observed suspicious activity.	Enumerate potential non-security-incident sources, such as network anomalies, endpoint issues, application conflicts/errors, etc.

15 ONSITE & ONBOARDING INSTRUCTIONS

Initial Instructions

It should be very clear at this point that incident response and incident management require much more than just technical skills. Soft skills, such as strong communication and organizational behavior are critical to the success of the engagement. These skills need to be immediately demonstrated at the beginning of an investigation and upon arriving onsite. The Incident Commander and responders need to look and act the part. As the saying goes, you only have one chance to make a first impression. Make it a good one!

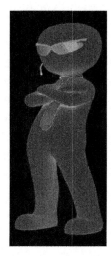

The following are the etiquette and operational instructions for incident response and management personnel to be used upon the commencement of an engagement and/or arriving onsite. This will ensure smooth initial contact and information gathering. It is important for responders to do all of the following as appropriate for the investigation.

Appearance

To begin with, appearances matter. The Incident Commander and responders should dress business casual with clean, pressed clothing, particularly on the first day, and gauge the customer culture to determine appropriate attire. Always be at least as well dressed as the customer personnel or take a small step up, but don't overdo it. This means dressing nicely, but not too nicely. For an extreme juxtaposition, a team of response personnel in tuxedos will not fit in with a bunch of surfers wearing shorts at a company with a casual culture.

Timeliness

Timeliness definitely matters. Responders should arrive 5 to 10 minutes early, as rested as possible. They should bring all of the required tools and be prepared to address the customer's response needs in a professional manner. If large quantities of tools are optionally needed, it is acceptable to leave some tools in the locked trunk of the vehicle.

If meetings are conducted remotely using a conference call or collaboration software (Teams, Zoom, Webex, GoToMeeting, etc.), being on time is completely fine. However, joining conference calls a couple of minutes early can enable people to have some informal conversations and get to know other participants in a more friendly setting. Relationship-building is critical!

Introductions

Incident response/management is as much of a people game as it is a technical game. The Incident Commander and response team must meet and greet all essential parties and try to remember everyone's names. Knowing people's names will help develop a relationship and begin establishing trust that will assist with obtaining access to environments, systems, and data required for the investigation. Collecting business cards from key parties and writing appropriate notes on the back of the business card can help.

When doing this remotely using collaboration software, make sure to take screenshots of meeting attendees, take notes on the names of individuals, and familiarize yourself with their avatars or images if they share their cameras. For remote introductions, all the same recommendations apply, but keeping track of who everyone is and what they do is a lot easier. Remember to take good notes and quickly learn names, roles, and relationships.

Secure Work Area

Establish a secure work and discussion area. It is critical to have an appropriately sized secure area to facilitate discussions between the response team and extended teams that may be involved. For on-site meetings, preferably reserve an appropriately sized conference room with multiple whiteboards or at least one large one.

Collaboration software with digital conference rooms and conference bridges having screen-sharing capabilities to facilitate discussions with remote parties must also be available. In lieu of a physical whiteboard, the Incident Commander sharing his/her screen and showing key content will suffice, and it makes it quicker to share content.

However, screen sharing is much more limited in space, and not as much can be shown in a single view. A notable function that is hard to display is task management and the respective details (assignees, status, dependencies, etc.). Detailed lists will have to be shared, and then items will be reviewed during status calls or working sessions.

A digital augment that can assist with this is to utilize an incident management system having a site dedicated to each incident with appropriate views applicable to the users. It should contain relevant content authorized for the specific users or groups who will access it. This solution is ideal from a security perspective, as it can be locked down and explicitly authorized. Having an incident/case management system is ideal for managing all of the respective tasks, responsibilities, details, and artifacts of an incident.

Kickoff Meeting

Regardless of the tracking method(s) chosen, organize and conduct an onsite kick-off meeting and begin gathering information critical to the investigation. Make sure that the required stakeholders and leadership personnel are involved in order to provide support for the response endeavors. This is the best opportunity to set the necessary tone and provide initial direction for the investigation, gain support, and organize the initial activity.

During the initial meeting, the Incident Commander should work with the extended team to develop the communication plan, identify key contacts, determine the cadence for providing status updates, and develop the strategy to establish and maintain communications that are protected by legal privilege. The initial meeting should include all personnel owning, authorizing, or making changes to affected environments and resources.

Additionally, make sure to identify regulatory compliance and external reporting requirements that will drive the evidence-gathering, handling, investigative, communication, and reporting processes. Companies and organizations must always comply with customer data breaches and other regulatory notification requirements.

Response personnel should become familiar with all business needs, regulatory requirements, and timelines impacting a customer from the outset of the response endeavor. In this way, team members can lead compliance discussions or at least not appear uninformed or make mistakes on communication and reporting needs.

It is also critical to identify actions that have already been performed prior to the response team being engaged. This includes all system changes, investigation activity, containment actions, mitigation efforts, and/or remediation actions performed by the customer, their personnel, and/or contractors.

Finally, it is critical to understand the environment and enumerate the investigative/evidence universe in which the response activity will be conducted. This is where the whiteboard comes in particularly handy.

Whiteboarding – Infrastructure

One of the most powerful tools for incident management is a conference room full of whiteboards. This is the best way to get all members of the response team and stakeholders to visualize the incident and required response activity. It involves visually laying out all of the key environments, resources, attack methods, investigative tasks, and task owners. It is the best way to get everyone to understand the problems and solutions in the same way and all nod their heads at the same time. The same can be done with screen sharing and/or digital whiteboard technology if it is being performed remotely. Regardless of location, when fleshing out and capturing the investigative/evidence universe, the following are some key considerations that need to be enumerated and documented from the outset.

Network Architecture
The first thing that needs to be enumerated is the network architecture for the scope of the evidence universe. This can be as big or as small as it needs to be for the scope of the investigation. It may include all sites, data centers, cloud environments, and key network segments, or it may be isolated to a single environment for which the response is focused (such as the DMZ). Whatever the scope, draw the basic network architecture showing all relevant locations, connections, integrations, and key infrastructure.

Ingress/Egress Methods
Identify ingress/egress points of presence (PoPs), remote access methods (VPNs, MPLS, etc.), vendor/partner integrations, and their respective bandwidth and connection types. This will be important for identifying all ways in and out of the network and to determine the need for the deployment of monitoring capabilities at key choke points. Sometimes, emergency technology deployments need to be made as a result of an incident to facilitate response activity.

It is common to find unmonitored ingress/egress methods, particularly involving wireless networks or those that involve employee, department, subsidiary, vendor, partner, and SOHO remote access methods. Each and every way in and out of the network could be a method used by attackers and malware to communicate, exfiltrate, and maintain C2. As such, they must all be monitored and controlled.

Security Controls and Key Data Sources
Just as with network and system infrastructure, the security controls and key data sources need to be identified, capabilities enumerated, contacts identified, and tasks assigned. These types of controls typically include any resources that can monitor, inspect, alert, block, or otherwise halt or prevent malicious activity involving networks, systems, applications, or accounts. These systems may need to be analyzed individually or integrated and correlated through a SIEM to facilitate advanced detection use cases involving data from disparate devices.

Critical Infrastructure and Crown Jewels
In order to understand what a target of interest could be and thus identify what needs to be protected, all relevant critical infrastructure and organizational crown jewels within the scope of the response and investigation need to be enumerated. As with other resources, this will be as broad or narrowly focused as appropriate for the response activity. These types of resources typically involve systems, applications, users, and data that involve intellectual property and/or business operations.

Attack Targets and Compromised Infrastructure
Identify any resource(s) that have been targeted or compromised by attackers or malware and the respective impact of the compromise. This will include the functional, security, and/or

regulatory impact on systems, applications, data, and accounts. Identifying this information will drive investigative, containment, and restoration tasks and assignments. This will also help begin the discussion regarding change controls and approvals for resources that need to be contained, remediated, or restored.

Attack Vectors

Identify possible attack vectors and threats to the organization. If not already known, this will involve enumerating all of the most likely attack vectors that resulted in the successful intrusion. Depending upon the stage of detection, this is sometimes obvious, but not always. If incidents are identified during later stages, the response team will have to work backward to find the initial point of intrusion, for which there may be many options. Enumerate each known or potential attack vector on the whiteboard and identify data sources, owners, and action items required to investigate.

Whiteboarding – Incident Management

Using the physical or digital whiteboard is the perfect place to visualize the respective incident management plan/workflow (from the appropriate playbook) in the form of a flowchart and/or series of steps. It will be used to enumerate applicable steps, identify goals or milestones, document deliverables, identify required resources, and enumerate required information. There are a lot of moving parts, and tracking them in this way is helpful to ensure the response team has received everything required to be successful.

A section of the whiteboard should be used to develop an incident timeline and document all activity. Identify all threat indicators, exploit milestones, notable indicators, compromised systems (or groups of systems), observed malicious activity, unauthorized account activity, and data that could have been affected or exfiltrated.

Document exploited attack vectors, exploit methods, and a full list of incident root causes for the various stages of the attack. Identify vulnerabilities that could have led to the compromise and explore possible containment, mitigation, and/or remediation steps. These could include immediate stop gaps or long-term solutions.

As this information is identified, the whiteboard is a key tool for the project management aspect of incident management-related activity and high-level task tracking. It provides a method to enumerate critical actions/tasks, prerequisites, resource assignments, track statuses, and make it visible to the entire extended response team and stakeholders. This is very helpful as it enables everyone to hold everyone else accountable for task completion. Moreover, it can assist with obtaining additional resources to complete pending tasks and prerequisites.

The content captured on the whiteboard will be a succinct subset of what is captured by the Incident Commander in the case notes. Moreover, for logistical and space-related reasons, the whiteboard will likely only be able to include outstanding tasks. Completed tasks will likely need to be removed as space will be required for newly identified tasks or other content. The full list of tasks and their respective end state and other details should be captured by the Incident Commander and/or assigned resources for later review and reporting.

Regardless of the breadth or depth of content captured on the whiteboard, capturing all of this content independently/redundantly in incident notes is critical. The whiteboard should never be the only location where key information is captured, as it can be changed by anyone and removed at any time. Taking copious incident case notes is critical for capturing the details of the investigation and for subsequent uses. It is possible they may be required in court.

Another notable incident management use of the whiteboard is to capture identified deficiencies, gaps, and related lessons learned. These should include considerations for people, processes, and technology. They will be used for containment, compensating controls, and/or initial remediation actions. These will also inform the various types of status updates and subsequent incident and remediation reports.

Using the whiteboard as a method to flesh out the deficiencies and recommendations is ideal as it makes the discussion public amongst the extended response team and stakeholders. This will assist in soliciting solutions from SMEs and identifying potential shortfalls. It also gives people time to think about it, even if subconsciously, and put together a well-thought-out plan that is likely to be accepted and supported.

Backdoor Identification

One of the first orders of business in most security breaches is to identify any indications of malware and backdoors left behind. Without identifying and eliminating any and all such threats, any response activity performed will only be temporary, as the attackers will use their backdoors to return after the engagement is over. Either that or responders will be in a constant battle for ownership of the customer environment(s).

Moreover, just because one backdoor method was found, it does not mean that it was the only one. There are usually layers of backdoors, including applications, scripts, scheduled tasks, accounts, etc. This helps ensure that if one or more are found, others still exist to enable the attackers to regain access to the affected systems or environments.

Searching for backdoors left behind is performed at all 4 of the key technology areas, including 1) account/access management, 2) network traffic analysis, 3) endpoint activity and anomaly analysis, and 4) SIEM/log correlation integrated with multiple threat feeds. Depending upon the nature of the threat and whether it is part of an APT infection or just run-of-the-mill malware, it may be necessary to monitor known backdoor activity to identify all of its methods and locations prior to attempting to remove it.

It is critical to identify all characteristics of attackers and malware. These include attacker servers, domain names, DNS servers, ports/protocols, exploit methods, binaries, scripts, persistence mechanisms, registry keys/values, files, accounts, groups, OUs, and other relevant artifacts. Proper monitoring and tracking will help ensure that when the responders act to remove it, it is successfully removed all at once.

External Communications Restrictions

Protecting communication is critical. The Incident Commander should remind everyone involved not to discuss the customer's case with anyone outside of the investigation and the circle of trust.

The phrase "Loose lips sink ships" is definitely applicable to the communications strategy surrounding an incident. All communication should be restricted to "need to know" and not openly discussed, even with internal parties.

Non-authorized customer personnel should also be notified not to discuss any events surrounding an incident with anyone under any circumstances. If ever asked by a member of the media or untrusted outsider, the investigative team should be instructed to avoid conversation or simply say "no comment."

Customer insiders should be advised to do the same or provided with a short, pre-approved statement drafted by the legal and public relations departments containing no substantive information. This pre-approved statement is helpful to have as it can be used for customer employees' family and friends who may press for information and which the employee may feel obligated to at least say something.

All outbound communications should be managed and directed by the customer's legal, compliance, or media relations team, as appropriate. From whom public announcements are made differs from company to company, but most often, it is a collaboration between public relations representatives, attorneys, and/or senior executives.

If customers ask for guidance in communication with the public and media, response personnel should advise that it is best to say as little as possible until all the facts are known and then only say what is prudent. This will ensure that outbound communications do not jeopardize the investigation or any type of legal proceedings that may be ongoing by law enforcement.

16 RESPONSE ACTIONS: COMMUNICATION AND DOCUMENTATION

Critical Items to Document

During an incident, there are numerous details to discuss/record, and it seemingly never ends. It just gets disrupted by the next incident that comes along, which then takes priority. The full response process, findings, lessons learned, and post-incident activity need to be documented.

Good documentation feeds the full-lifecycle incident management processes and ensures that the customer environment improves with each incident. It will also facilitate answering legal or audit questions or concerns that may arise resulting from an incident.

Following is a high-level list of critical items to capture, communicate, and document along the way for effective incident management. Remember, unless it is documented, you don't get any credit for it, and it may be used against you. Each of these topics will be covered in more detail throughout this chapter:

- Incident notification details – Capture all of the detection information and reasons the event/incident was identified and escalated.
- Incident timeline – Collect all key events, notable observations, and milestones. The timeline needs to start early and be maintained all along the way, or data will be lost.

- Impact Identification – Identify all resources (networks, systems, applications, data, users, customers, regulatory, etc.) and objects of all kinds that were impacted by the incident.
- Affected resource vulnerabilities – Diligently capture all details of affected systems or devices and the related vulnerabilities that led to the exposure.
- Stakeholder contacts and escalation – Identify the resource owners, admins, and contacts for objects affected by the event/incident.
- Compliance and Legal teams – Identify legal personnel, communication requirements, and legal/compliance rules and objectives.
- Action items, owners, and status – Capture all objectives, action items, tasks, subtasks, prerequisite tasks, owners, and escalation personnel and track the details and changes through completion or other final states.
- Containment and mitigation – Enumerate methods used to halt malicious activity, such as the containment actions utilized to block access or the mitigation actions implemented to prevent new compromises.
- Root cause – Affirmatively identify the root cause, which will inform definitive remediation tasks to be established, which will prevent a similar incident. It will also enable regulators to decide on whether the entity has appropriate controls in place.
- Investigation findings – Establish and document the actual findings of the investigation and related impact, which will ultimately be the biggest headline in an incident.
- Deficiencies and recommendations – Identify and document a list of deficiencies in people, processes, and/or technology that led to the compromise or negatively impacted the response activity.
- Recovery and restoration – Perform a review of the recovery and service restoration processes and the capabilities or gaps identified therein.
- Remediation – Identify the deficiencies, recommendations, and lessons learned that need to be distilled into remediation items. Some can be accomplished in the short term, but many will need to be developed into long-term project plans that require proper budgeting and funding, as well as be managed as multi-year projects. All of this requires detailed, documented, and supporting examples from past incidents to establish the need.

Incident Notification Details

The Incident Commander should capture and retain all incident notification and escalation content to detail the facts surrounding the threat detection and reasons for escalation. Long story short, every action, artifact, communication, and finding in an incident should be reviewed and evaluated for lessons learned. There is almost always room for improvement.

There may also be a subsequent audit or legal action that needs to review all details related to an incident. The notification and context of such is usually the start date for regulatory timelines. The better documented the incident is, the easier the audit or discovery process will be, and the better the ultimate result of the review.

The contents of the incident notification details will vary by detection but generally contain the following high-level items. When aggregated, these will inform metrics and drive changes in people, processes, and technology:

- Detection method – This is usually from automated alerts, threat-hunting activity, user-reported observations, or externally reported events. If reported by or known to an outside entity, there are additional risks and action items. Media notifications and complications are much more likely in this scenario. Identifying and documenting this is important, as it will set the tone for communications and whether public relations/media, compliance, and legal teams need to start right away with working on external communications. It will also assist in documenting the efficacy of automated detection tools.

- Symptoms – It is particularly important to identify all of the known symptoms of a reported event or security incident in order to review later and validate with fresh eyes. This will validate that the right choices were made, as well as findings to feed the lessons learned process. Symptoms gathered should include details about its behavior, artifacts, and impact on networks, endpoints, and logs, as well as the user experience.

- Attack vector – It is very important to document and provide metrics on attack vectors (AKA vulnerabilities) in order to focus the patching, mitigation, configuration, and/or compensating control efforts. Unless you track and can provide metrics on attack vectors for incidents, it is not possible to answer basic questions with empirical data, such as: "What vulnerabilities are responsible for the most incidents?"

- Exploit method – Just like the attack vectors, the exploit methods should be tracked for similar reasons. Exploits compromise vulnerabilities via attack vectors, and the exploit methods typically need to be addressed separately using the same or different tools, depending upon the situation.

- Known artifacts, IOCs, and YARA rules – All known signatures used to identify and/or block attacks should be documented and archived for later review, audit, and lessons learned.

- Initial scope – Documenting the initially detected scope (locations, networks, systems, applications, etc.) is helpful for evaluating the efficacy of visibility tools once the full scope of the incident is known. If there is a significant gap between what was initially detected vs. what was subsequently discovered to have existed once the incident is fully investigated, this should go into the lessons learned and continuous improvement process to enhance detection capabilities.

In aggregate, capturing and documenting the incident notification details will pay big dividends in the lessons learned and continuous improvement processes. Care should be taken to identify deficiencies and recommendations in people, processes, and technology. With respect to technology, attention should be given to all visibility areas, including account management, network, endpoint, and logs/SIEM.

Incident Timeline

Date (UTC)	Time (UTC)	Activity	Actor	Internal System	External System	Data Source / Control	Comment
2019-08-11	18:58:11	User visits compromised website	Dave Smith (user)	LVWS295843	p0wn3dsit3.com	Firewall	not detected
2019-08-11	18:58:25	Malicious Java/PowerShell script downloaded	Dave Smith (user)	LVWS295843	malicious-site.com	Firewall	not detected
2019-08-11	18:59:16	Malware callback detected on endpoint	Dave Smith (user)	LVWS295843	malicious-site.com	Firewall	Initial detection
2019-08-11	19:23:07	Event reviewed by SOC and escalated	Jack Frost (SOC)				Event escalation
2019-08-11	19:43:11	Capture volatile data	Dave Rambo (CERT)	LVWS295843		EDR	Initial data collection
2019-08-11	20:05:49	Implement endpoint isolation	Dave Rambo (CERT)	LVWS295843		EDR	Containment
2019-08-11	20:55:17	Capture logical disk image (key artifacts)	Dave Rambo (CERT)	LVWS295843		Endpoint Forensic Agent	Full evidence collection
2019-08-11	21:05:51	Authorize LVWS295843 for reimaging by IT	Dave Rambo (CERT)	LVWS295843			Sal Smith took possession
2019-08-12	14:27:41	Forensic analysis completed	Arny Swartz (CERT)	LVWS295843			No PCI/PHI/PII data
2019-08-13	10:33:08	Forensic report completed	Arny Swartz (CERT)	LVWS295843			Report completed
2019-08-13	11:08:44	Evidence archived/ticket closed	Arny Swartz (CERT)	LVWS295843			Ticket completed

The incident timeline needs to start early and be maintained all along the way, or the associated activities and data will be lost. It is not that hard if an individual is assigned to assist the Incident Commander by taking notes and tracking the notable events and milestones on the incident timeline.

Moreover, considering the high volume of information flow during significant incidents, a dedicated resource should be used to track notable details. This resource should be assigned to capture and track all response-related activities. This includes observations, developments, findings, activities, action items, assignments, and statuses. All of these will need to be distilled into an incident timeline with references to related artifacts and details.

The example in the table above shows a simplified set of data elements that are not intended to be comprehensive. The contents may need to be adjusted to capture details respective to relevant data sources or actions, depending upon the circumstances.

In order for the timeline to make sense, all data sources should utilize synchronized NTP servers to avoid time drift, and all entries should be displayed in UTC to show a true sequence of events. These two requirements are essential, or the timeline becomes meaningless and unusable. Trying to synchronize logs from multiple sources misaligned by time drift is chaos.

The span of the timeline in the example is highly simplified to succinctly show key milestones during the investigation. In a real incident, there will likely be many more steps along the way. This example clearly and cleanly shows the start and endpoints with key milestones for this type of investigation.

Impact

Just about anything and everything can be affected during an incident. It is critical to properly identify the full scope of an incident and track the related resources and artifacts. This will help to ensure they are properly identified, contained, mitigated, remediated, recovered, and/or reported. Each affected resource will need to be investigated, returned to a known good state, and have findings documented and reported. Any and all of these impacted data sources and objects may or may not be essential to the reporting process, depending upon the respective findings and regulatory impact.

Typical resource types and objects that were impacted by a security incident include the following list. For each of those found to be affected, the investigative team must document the related malicious activity, security gaps, contents, accounts, and recommended security controls:

- Networks – Track the flows of malicious activity between or within interconnected network segments.
- Remote access methods – There are a variety of remote access methods that attackers can use to gain or maintain access to compromised systems or devices. These include corporate client VPNs, private host-based VPNs, B2B VPNs, peer-to-peer software, etc. Each of these will drive different containment, mitigation, and remediation tasks.
- Systems – For affected systems, it is critical to identify and document all network activity, vulnerabilities, affected applications, affected user accounts, and data stored on them. They should be considered compromised and handled accordingly.
- Devices – Impacted devices can be some of the harder resources to investigate and document, considering many of them may be proprietary, vendor-managed, or unmanaged. Quite often, vendor-managed and unmanaged mean the same thing. Devices are very likely "vendor unmanaged." Notwithstanding that, if devices and security gaps are not identified, documented, and remediated, they could potentially remain extant threats to the environment. Moreover, compromised devices indicate a maintenance issue that is likely broader than the scope of the incident and which needs to be addressed in a more holistic manner. This usually requires business and management-level changes via contracts, process changes, or device management technology.

- Applications – Just like affected systems can lead to the compromise of applications and their data, the same is true in reverse. Any vulnerable applications can result in the compromise of the host system and its stored data. As such, all of the same activity and documentation requirements would apply. For affected applications, the investigative team needs to identify and document all network activity, vulnerabilities, affected systems, affected user accounts, and data stored on them, as they should be considered compromised as well and handled accordingly.
- Repositories – Each type of affected data repository (local file systems, file shares, email stores, databases, etc.) involved in an incident or on a system involved in an incident (whether consisting of structured or unstructured data) needs to be reviewed, and the findings should be documented following a security breach or the identification of malware. Any or all of the respective data may have been exposed. The primary driver for this is regulatory compliance impact and the potential need to report. However, there may also be business drivers or intellectual property concerns that drive an investigation.
- Data – All data involved in an incident, located on a system involved in an incident, or within an application involved in an incident needs to be reviewed, and the findings documented following a security breach or the identification of malware. Any or all of the respective data may have been exposed. The primary driver for this is regulatory compliance impact and the potential need to report. However, there may also be business drivers or intellectual property concerns that drive an investigation.
- Users – All user accounts involved in malicious activity and those on compromised systems or applications must be identified. For each, all activity must be enumerated, suspicious activity identified, impact identified, and accounts disabled or passwords reset. MFA and/or OTP controls must also be evaluated and implemented.
- Customers – All customers impacted by a security incident and the respective users, data, and actions taken need to be identified and documented for remediation, after-action, and reporting activities.
- Vendors – All vendors impacted by a security incident and the respective connection methods, applications, systems, users, data, and actions taken need to be identified and documented for remediation, after-action, and reporting activities.

Affected Resource Vulnerabilities

Diligently capture all vulnerability-related details for affected resources, such as systems, devices, applications, etc., and identify the attack vector that led to the exposure. Common vulnerabilities and affected resource details that need to be captured include the following items and anything else that is relevant to the data source:
- System/device version(s) and patch level(s)
- Application version(s) and patch(es)
- Pre-incident and post-incident vulnerability scans and penetration tests
- CVE #s and criticality
- Recommended patches
- Recommended security configurations and/or compensating controls

The following table, based on data provided by The National Institute of Standards and Technology (NIST) National Vulnerability Database (NVD), shows the published vulnerability trends that have been reported between 1988 and 2023. Note the steady and steep progression over time, showing an increase in vulnerabilities. This type of information needs to be identified and documented, as it will drive subsequent mitigation and remediation activity.

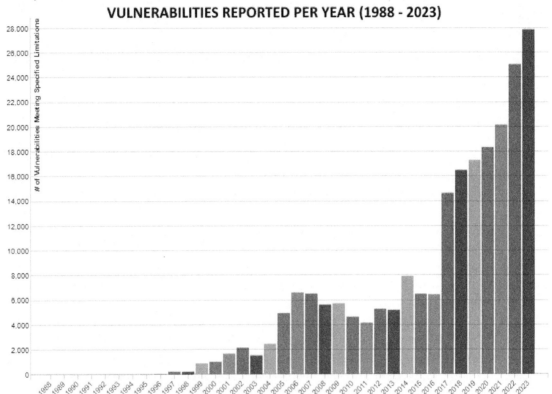

Stakeholder Contacts and Escalation

Undoubtedly, one of the most important and difficult actions in an incident can be identifying the resource owners, admins, and contacts. If this is not known ahead of time, it can be the hardest and most frustrating part of an incident. Carefully documenting this info as it is identified will be critical through the various stages of the incident management lifecycle.

It is required to identify and document at least the following contacts and stakeholders as quickly as possible during the response process. They will be required to assist with actions performed against affected resources. Key contacts to identify and document throughout the process are:

- Business owners – Owners will need to be consulted and usually obtain their approval before any type of changes can be made (including post-breach incident containment), depending upon the details in the Incident Response Plan.
- Department heads – Department heads need to be advised, as taking systems offline could impact business processes, customer services, revenue, etc. Additionally, even if there is no service disruption, there is likely to be financial impact that will need to be approved.
- Change approvers – It will be critical to have the specific change approvers for resources documented, who may or may not be the same as business owners, department heads, system/application owners, or others. These entities will need to be communicated with throughout the response process and be provided with visibility to reports.
- System owners/admins – It is important to involve system owners/admins, as they will be able to answer questions regarding how the system works, what the legitimate system capabilities/functions are, what data is stored on the system, identify what artifacts may need to be examined, identify unauthorized changes, and be able to assist in the system restoration, hardening, and recovery processes.
- Application owners and development personnel – Application owners/developers will be able to best answer application deep-dive questions regarding the capabilities and functions of affected applications and assist with determining data elements, files, configurations, and other artifacts that need to be examined. They are also key to the restoration, hardening, and recovery processes.
- IT support personnel – IT support is usually of most value when trying to take possession of or make changes to systems and devices. These include unplugging the system, locking it in an IT closet with an appropriate label, and holding it for examination. These individuals or the original custodians are typically the start of a chain of custody.
- Network personnel – The regional/local network team is important to document as they will be able to implement and remove network containment measures as well as define what is permissible or typical for network traffic to/from affected resources. Using network containment methods is typically the fastest way to contain threats.
- Vendor relationship owners – Many organizations have relationship owners who manage or laisse contacts with vendors and through which all contact must flow. It is critical to identify and document these individuals as they can simplify the process of navigating the vendor environment and identify vendor account managers, support team contacts, and the history of the resources.
- Vendor support team – Viable vendor contacts can be one of the most difficult types of contacts to maintain. However, it is critical to have them documented and updated, as they will be consulted throughout the incident management process. This is due to the fact that they typically understand their systems/applications/devices better than onsite support teams and will often need to assist with updates or configuration changes.

Compliance and Legal Teams

Everyone knows that it is a good idea to consult an attorney when they have legal trouble, but IT and security teams are notorious for not recognizing they are in legal trouble. Laws and regulations vary by country and state. Investigative activity that is completely benign and appropriate in one location can result in fines or jail time in another. It is essential to involve knowledgeable attorneys who understand the subject matter and respective laws and regulations in order to set expectations and keep the teams and company out of trouble.

Adding an attorney at the end of an email thread is the oldest trick in the book, and it doesn't work. You can't just bolt on legal privilege at the end and hope all of the previous activity and communications are protected.

Care should be taken from the outset of response activity to take all reasonable steps to protect communications through legal privilege and reports through attorney work-product. For best results and protection, all communications and activity should be guided by an attorney from the outset.

Long story short, if response activity is not guided by an attorney and if attorneys are not included in communications, legal privilege is not assured. Therefore, all communications, assessments, reports, or other work-products may be discoverable. One of the best ways to prevent communications from becoming discoverable is to communicate them verbally. To state it very clearly, don't put anything in writing that you don't want to risk being discovered and produced at a later date.

Keys to Preserving Legal Privilege (Consult Your Attorney)

- Involve attorney(s) at the beginning and ensure they make an initial statement that "The activity is protected under legal privilege and all actions will be guided by the attorney(s)."
- All findings must be communicated orally first.
- Only attorney-approved content is permitted in the reports (including drafts and final versions of reports, attestations, investigative findings, etc.).
- Documents must bear the appropriate legend to protect legal privilege on at least the first page of the documents.
- Attorneys must receive the drafts and final reports from internal and external teams and then authorize them for further dissemination.
- Attorneys must direct the distribution of reports, findings, and other documents.

Common Legal Privilege Legends (Consult Your Attorney)

- Communications
  - Privileged and Confidential
  - Attorney Client Privilege
  - Attorney Client Communications
- Reports/Work-Product
  - Privileged and Confidential – Attorney Work-Product
  - Privileged and Confidential – Prepared at the Direction of Council

Action Items, Owners, and Status

Incident response and/or management nearly always involves a significant amount of project management, often under high pressure or even hostile circumstances. Larger incidents are more like extreme program management. Moreover, full-lifecycle incident management is perpetual program management that continually spins off new projects, each having action items, owners, and individual completion status.

Incidents create scores of action items and subtasks or prerequisite tasks. Each of these tasks need to be assigned one or more owners, sponsors, approvers, and other required entities. All of the respective actions/tasks must be tracked to completion or other final state. Not every task results in a positive conclusion. Failed or blocked tasks usually result in alternate tasks using a different method to accomplish the desired result.

All of the resulting tasks could become the subject of an audit or other after-action activity. The ability to produce documentation proving adequate corrective activity following an incident is critical in defending against audits and lawsuits and avoiding compliance pitfalls and fines. Strong documentation of completed post-incident tasks to apply lessons learned is key to proving an effective incident management program.

Containment and Mitigation

Some of the first questions that get asked during or after an incident are about the methods used to halt malicious activity. These include containment methods to stop ongoing activity or mitigation to prevent new compromises. This information (including change management thereof) must be captured in detail. It will need to be included in the incident timeline and the after-action reporting. Further, this will be used to address key questions in an audit or lawsuit. Common actions that need to be captured include the following topics.

Containment Controls and Locations

- System and policy configurations and hardening – Local security policy is becoming increasingly complex and replete with advanced capabilities for system firewall controls, application controls, account safeguards, and numerous other security restriction capabilities.
- Application configurations and hardening – Applications are becoming increasingly advanced in security configuration capabilities that can be configured out of the box to halt malicious activities, including firewall rules, certificate authentication, account safeguards, and other restriction capabilities.
- Network security devices/software – Network controls (firewalls, WAFs, proxies, IPSs, etc.) are always the go-to when it comes to blocking malicious ingress/egress activity quickly from any protected source.
- Endpoint security agents – The advancements in endpoint security tools, particularly EDR capabilities, have provided amazing abilities to detect and block malicious activity from endpoints, regardless of their location. This is particularly helpful for remote/traveling systems.

Mitigation Methods

- Patches and updates – Security patches and updates are always the go-to for proactively preventing malicious activity and stopping it before it starts or preventing additional exploitation. Telemetry and validation of patching activity should be diligently captured.
- Configuration changes – Sometimes security patches are not the answer, but configuration settings need to change, such as hardening systems beyond default configurations. The implementation of these changes needs to be recorded, validated, and documented.
- Compensating controls – Sometimes, there is no direct method (like security patches or configuration changes) to mitigate the risk to systems, and compensating controls need to be put in place. While these are often temporary stopgaps, they may also become permanent mitigation controls and must be captured and documented.

Root Cause

The root cause of an incident is possibly the most important item to be identified and captured during an incident. The nature of it typically drives culpability discussions and influences the outcome of lawsuits and audits, as well as the determination to impose fines or restrictions.

Large, impactful incidents caused by easily preventable root causes stemming from well-known vulnerabilities that should have been patched long ago are a recipe for disaster. It opens the affected company up to all manner of lawsuits, fines, restrictions, and government oversight.

On the other hand, a novel attack against an unknown attack vector using an undetectable exploit method would be seen much differently. The affected company may get a pass, as well as public sympathy.

Moreover, affirmatively identifying the root cause of an incident will inform mitigation and remediation activity to prevent a similar incident. It will also enable auditors/regulators to make a determination on whether the entity had appropriate security controls in place at the time of the incident.

If the incident's root cause is not identified and appropriately resolved, there is a high probability of reoccurrence. Further, the recurrence of the same incident exploiting the same vulnerability is very hard to rationalize. It leads to increased culpability and additional business risk due to bad security practices, which could be interpreted as regulatory non-compliance.

Oftentimes, identifying and documenting the root cause (s) will make the affected organization look bad. However, not putting in the effort to identify it will make the organization look even worse. It shows that in addition to the security control issues that caused a breach, there are process and other maturity issues that are sure to result in another one.

Investigation Findings

The actual investigation findings, type of data affected, and quantitative impact will ultimately be the biggest headline in an incident. These include the number of affected customers, systems, records, etc. Headlines and data breach reports are full of these metrics, which are stack-ranked by descending order of magnitude and splashed across the Internet. Moreover, the type of data and quantity of records impacted are the most discussed data elements and the biggest drivers for regulatory impact, fines, and lawsuits.

However, there is a lot more data than that, which ultimately needs to be included in the investigation findings for the documentation to be complete. Each of the sections listed in the template are key artifacts that need to be communicated, captured, and documented, if applicable. Some of the sections will not apply to a given incident, depending on the situation.

Deficiencies and Recommendations

No response is adequate or complete without documenting a list of deficiencies and recommendations pertaining to gaps in people, processes, and/or technology that led to the compromise. The recommendations should also include both short- and long-term suggestions to accommodate business needs and financial constraints.

Oftentimes, short-term recommendations will consist of compensating controls to address security concerns using existing technology reconfigured in different ways to address deficiencies temporarily until the intended solution can be put in place. They are intended to address the worst of the threat(s), provide at least minimal acceptable resource functionality, and are hopefully good enough to keep everything moving in a state that is at least secure enough.

While it is true that sometimes short-term solutions are adequate to become long-term solutions, this is not usually the case. Typically, short-term solutions are sub-optimal and are just intended to be a mitigating stopgap until a more formal solution can be developed. However, if there is no viable long-term option, or the full, long-term solution is not permissible for whatever reason (financial, political, etc.), then imperfect short-term solutions might become long-term solutions anyway.

Long-term solutions are intended to be more comprehensive and facilitate all applicable use cases and requirements. They typically require significant effort and mature processes for requirements gathering, business-needs planning, cybersecurity architecture, budgeting, etc. In large environments, this becomes highly complex and very complicated. Long-term solutions will require enumeration of all in-scope resources and the business, integration, compliance, and security requirements for the same.

The deficiencies and recommendations are effectively just a starting place for this type of discussion. The incident may have identified a small part of a much larger problem that needs to be fully enumerated and addressed as part of a comprehensive, long-term, holistic solution implemented to address a much broader threat.

The template shown in this section will enumerate facts to drive discussion for both the short and long-term solutions. However, they are most directly applicable to short-term solutions as long-term solutions will potentially expand far beyond the scope of what was identified during an incident response investigation.

The template will typically expand out like an accordion when all of the deficiencies, recommendations, action items, and prerequisites are blown out to document each of the potential changes to people, processes, and technology. If these items are not captured or acted upon, they are likely to repeat and increase the legal and regulatory risk to the organization.

Deficiency and Recommendations Summary

1. Date detected?
2. Date resolution required by?
3. Detection Source: User reported / Security Tool / Threat Intel
4. Person Reporting: Employee Name (or outsider)
5. Deficiency Summary: Brief summary of problem
6. Recommendation Summary: Brief summary of recommended solution or course of action
7. Deficiency Remediation Details:
   7.1. Scope:
      7.1.1. Environments
      7.1.2. Networks
      7.1.3. Systems/Devices
      7.1.4. Accounts
   7.2. Urgency:
      7.2.1. Risk: High / Medium / Low
      7.2.2. Priority: High / Medium / Low
      7.2.3. Business Value: Explanation
      7.2.4. Regulatory Impact: PCI / PHI / PII / SOX
      7.2.5. Actionability: Explanation
   7.3. Cost:
      7.3.1. Level of effort: Man hours
      7.3.2. Hardware costs: Current capacity + growth
      7.3.3. Software/Licensing/Subscription costs: Current capacity + growth
      7.3.4. Maintenance costs: Current capacity + growth
   7.4. Owner(s) / Sponsor(s): List of owners and roles
   7.5. Action Item(s): List of actions and details to be defined for each action
      7.5.1. Description
      7.5.2. Status
      7.5.3. Prerequisite(s)
      7.5.4. Assignee(s)
      7.5.5. Individual Steps/Components – if appropriate

Recovery

```
Ooops, your important files are encrypted.

━━━━━━━━━━━━━━━━━━━━━━━━━━━━━━━━━━━━━━━━━━━━━━━━━━━━━━━

If you see this text, then your files are no longer accessible, because they
have been encrypted. Perhaps you are busy looking for a way to recover your
files, but don't waste your time. Nobody can recover your files without our
decryption service.

We guarantee that you can recover all your files safely and easily. All you
need to do is submit the payment and purchase the decryption key.

Please follow the instructions:

1. Send $300 worth of Bitcoin to following address:

   1Mz7153HMuxXTuR2R1t78mGSdzaAtNbBWX


2. Send your Bitcoin wallet ID and personal installation key to e-mail
   wowsmith123456@posteo.net. Your personal installation key:


If you already purchased your key, please enter it below.
Key: _
```

After an incident is contained and the deficiencies are documented, the incident management process is not yet complete. While it is true that some organizations may end the process there, it is far from complete, and there is still a lot left on the table to review.

Full-lifecycle incident management also includes oversight and review of the recovery and service restoration processes and the identification of the capabilities or gaps identified therein. As an example, there is nothing quite like a pervasive incident involving a ransomware or wiperware worm to test a company's ability to recover systems/data and restore services.

Many organizations develop their BC/DR capabilities based on natural disasters, power outages, single or maybe multiple system failures, or other fairly isolated and contained circumstances. Moreover, network or cloud backup solutions have made significant progress in replacing physical media backups (due to the automated simplicity of the process). Further, many organizations have no offline backups on physical media whatsoever.

As an extreme but plausible example, any organization would struggle with highly successful ransomware or wiperware that made significant penetration into their systems. However, if the malware takes out the network backup servers or the network backups themselves, it could become an unrecoverable incident due to gaps in the business continuity and disaster recovery (BC/DR) plans.

New vulnerabilities permitting new exploits utilized by new malware or existing exploit kits come out all the time. They could affect any or all types of systems, devices, services, or applications. Any business-critical resource should have an adequate BC/DR plan to address foreseeable incident types, especially destructive malware incidents. This includes coverage for online/network/cloud backup systems themselves. There should always be an offline backup and storage capability for live backups to ensure that compromising the live system/service does not result in a loss of backup data.

Remediation

The last mile of the full-lifecycle incident management process, which brings the reactive activity back to the proactive processes, is remediation. The deficiencies, recommendations, and lessons learned all need to be distilled into remediation items, which become proactive tasks to improve the organization's security posture.

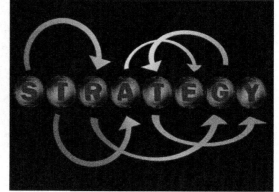

Remember, incidents that recur based on known vulnerabilities become an increased risk as the organization knew about them and did not fix them. This is somewhere between difficult and impossible to successfully defend against during audits, regulatory investigations, and lawsuits. The risk is only reduced when the known security gaps are fixed.

As part of the program or project planning, some of the tasks to fix these gaps can be completed in the short term, but many will need to be developed into long-term project plans that need to be funded and managed as multi-year projects. All of this requires detailed planning and supporting content, such as specific examples from past incidents establishing the need for security engineering support to create optimal solutions.

Program and/or project managers should be assigned to ensure that the proper resources are brought to bear to engineer/architect solutions, formally document plans, assign resources, and track action items through completion. Management of remediation activity should never be the realm of the incident management team.

Remediation is essentially a proactive activity resulting from either reactive or proactive drivers. More specifically, remediation tasks can be the result of a security incident (reactive) or assessment/audit findings (proactive). As such, the solutions need to be considered in light of the larger context of all concerns involved.

Remediation should be a holistic activity to accommodate all of the related drivers, use cases, and requirements. This type of scope requires a dedicated team with a proactive focus to address all needs rather than a reactive team that is trying to "solve problems on the fly."

17 RESPONSE ACTIONS: SCOPE AND IMPACT

This chapter will go over the various considerations to best identify and scope the respective impact of an incident, which will expedite and streamline the process of incident response activity. Quickly identifying the scope and impact of an incident is the first major step that enables its success. Without proper definition, it will either be under-investigated or likely unresolved. Alternatively, it may be over-investigated and take too long, possibly enabling it to expand in the process.

Details Gathering

Upon notification of an incident, the Incident Commander and other assigned response personnel should gather the required information to begin determining the scope, impact, and respective prioritization. This includes salient information respective to their environment, the current incident or threat activity, and the resources involved.

The initial scope includes all locations, networks, systems, devices, applications, accounts, and/or data involved in any of the related activities on either end of network traffic. The initial details and respective scope vary by detection but generally contain the following high-level items. This content will help drive the investigation forward:

- Alert content: Source, symptoms, attack vector, exploit method
- Affected resources: systems, devices, applications, users, data
- Connections and communication activity: Ingress, egress, C2, exfiltration, lateral movement
- Initial artifacts (typically found in the alerts, especially network malware analysis tools): files, scripts, processes, registry, memory, WMI

All of this activity is collected and used to establish a starting point for the investigation and to use as search criteria to find other possibly affected systems that may expand the scope of the investigation. Having all of this data prepared from the outset will help ensure responders can hit the ground running and minimize the need for additional research, which slows down response and enables attackers and malware. We will go into each of these items in more detail.

Alert Content

Alert content is highly varied, depending on the source and alert type. The alerts should be configured to provide maximum information for correlation with threat intel feeds, asset databases, and other content providing relevant information. This will help identify the scope, impact, and prioritization:

Alert Source

When collecting evidence from alerts, regardless of source, make sure to include all systems involved in the malicious activity detected. This includes those activities that are external to the organization. The team will need to pivot off of all of the systems and artifacts found to identify the true scope, which will lead to the determination of the impact and respective priority of the security event. The usual locations for alerts are as follows:

- IAM/Directory services – Identify malicious, suspicious, or unauthorized activity from any infrastructure controlling single or multi-factor authentication and/or authorization of accounts, resources, and data on systems, devices, applications, services, and shares.

- Network – The most common and effective network alert sources are next-gen firewalls, WAF, IPS, network malware detection, and UAM. Each of these sources will have their own respective accuracy and value, which may be more or less accurate, depending upon the circumstances. SSL/TLS decryption is one of the most important factors in the efficacy of network-based inspection and detection, which is on a steep downward trend overall.

- Endpoint – Traditional endpoint security tools (such as antivirus and the associated firewall capabilities) provide fewer and less accurate results., and basically only tell you if there is a known malicious binary or site. However, the new generation of EDR and continuous monitoring tools are more capable of telling a compelling story. This includes answering questions regarding scope, impact, and prioritization. Specifically, it is possible to run a single query to identify "what processes on what systems are communicating with known malicious sites."

- SIEM – log aggregation sources correlated with threat feeds and multiple high-value tools can be amazingly helpful and informative if configured properly to capture and correlate information. It is ideal if alerts from any source can be correlated with asset, contact, system, and application sensitivity information within asset/inventory databases. The value in this is that if this content is pre-populated, it could enable alerts to include data enrichment identifying specific details regarding a threat, affected resources, and respective details. E.g., the EDR agent detected an "exploit kit" on workstation "WS-TK421" that is used for "customer credit card processing," has "PCI" impact, and is used by "Eddie Money" in "Accounts Receivable." The SIEM could also then be used to identify all systems communicating to the same malicious external site and produce alerts for all affected systems and users.

Affected Systems

Obviously, alerts usually contain affected systems, and it is key to investigate all systems mentioned in the alert. This includes both internal and external systems related to the alert and any other systems that those systems mentioned in the alert have communicated with. As responders pivot off of systems and look for related, suspicious connections, the scope will expand with each new connection identified.

Common problems encountered when identifying affected systems contained in alerts are the use of the following:
1) Virtual IP addresses (VIPs) – such as in DMZs and/or introduced by load balancers
2) Rapidly changing addresses with short lease times – such as on VPNs
3) Internal firewalling and/or NATing – Masks the identity of the actual system in the alert

Another key consideration is the placement of the security devices and the visibility of the true internal or external IP addresses for the in-scope system(s) displayed in the alert. Network detections are only actionable if the true IP address is included in the alert. Otherwise, the alerts are just noise. Sometimes they result in very loud noise!

Affected Users

The need to quickly identify the affected users cannot be understated. The alert should include this content, if possible, even if it leverages integration with an inventory or asset management system to pull the data and correlate it to the alert. However, if the name comes via a correlation query, the accuracy of the correlation will only be as good as the affected system-related information contained within the alert. If the affected system is inaccurately identified, the respective user correlated to it will be wrong as well. This could result in response activity being delayed while the affected users are identified.

Symptoms Identified

The behavior of a compromised system can help determine a lot about the nature of the threat and the potential security or business impact related to the threat. Some non-comprehensive examples include the following, which are neither mutually exclusive nor absolutely determinate:

- Slow network – Possible exfiltration, scanning, or worm-like activity
- Maxed-out CPU – Possible crypto-mining or other cryptographic activity
- Maxed-out disk I/O – Possible drive searching and content harvesting
- Maxed-out memory – Could be paired with any of the above or simply just be a memory leak in a benign application
- Anomalies seen on screen – Such as black screens that popped up and went away after visiting a website – probably a malicious script
- Files on systems or shares encrypted, renamed, extensions altered, and/or inaccessible – Probably ransomware or file share worm activity

Attack Vector and Exploit Method

Depending upon what is flagged in the alert from the network device (i.e., Firewall, WAF, IPS, etc.) or the endpoint agent monitoring network traffic, it should ideally contain information about the attack vector and related exploit method. The information is generally very high-level. However, it may sometimes contain snippets of traffic or even malware samples, depending upon the circumstances. Capturing this info is important for the following reasons:

- Detecting similar activity elsewhere and expanding the scope
- Understanding the threat potential based on the nature of the exploit
- Understanding the impact potential on affected systems, devices, and/or applications
- Informing containment and mitigation phases

Resources

Now, the fun begins! Using all of the data identified in the alert, the response team now begins determining everything that is potentially affected by the threat in a series of steps. It starts from a high level and then drills down deeper over time. With each step down this ladder, it becomes more difficult and resource-intensive to prove.

Unfortunately, due to the way rules, regulations, and laws are written, security and investigation best practices require the investigative team to assume everything on the affected system is compromised until proven otherwise. This is an uphill battle on an increasingly steep slope without the right visibility tools in place at each level (network, endpoint, IAM, SIEM, etc.) to assist in making affirmative determinations. Long story short, all the stars have to align to adequately substantiate that a compromise didn't happen. Proving a negative is very difficult and time-consuming. The basic flow is as follows:

Systems/Devices

A system or device is the first and easiest resource type to confirm that it has been affected by an attack. Due to alert naming conventions, the alerts usually name the affected resources. Even though alerts are not confirmed proof that a system or device has been compromised, they at least need to be refuted or validated and analyzed.

The affected resource and everything on it should at least be considered at risk from the threat and treated accordingly. It is reasonable to consider everything on that system or device to have been compromised by the threat, including the respective applications, services, accounts, and data on it. How it is treated will vary based on the threat and the nature of the affected resource.

This is where comprehensive asset attributes, configuration management, Data Loss Prevention (DLP), and access logging systems can be helpful. They can aid in the quick identification of sensitive data contained on systems or devices and enable the investigative team to understand the impact of resources being compromised.

Applications/Services

Sometimes, applications, services, files, or other resources hosted on a system are the source of a compromise due to security vulnerabilities in them. Sometimes, they are just collateral damage due to the system or application being compromised. As the saying goes: "Sometimes you're the windshield; sometimes you're the bug!" Either way, the end result is the same, and there is a mess to clean up.

It is extremely helpful to understand what accounts, data, access methods, logging, and security controls exist for applications and services that are at risk. This will facilitate determining if a particular threat would have been successful in compromising and accessing such and what the impact would be.

Accounts

Compromised accounts are not usually the first thing technical teams think about when assessing the scope of a threat based on the identification of a compromised system, device, application, or service. Attackers can usually count on this and use account credentials harvested from compromised systems to move laterally, exfiltrate data, and/or maintain persistence long after the initially compromised resource(s) has/have been remediated.

If any resource with accounts (user accounts, admin accounts, service accounts, etc.) has been compromised, it is reasonable to assume that the respective accounts may also have been compromised. As such, their activity needs to be closely analyzed using enhanced monitoring and validation tools until passwords can be reset and/or other controls can be implemented (MFA, password vaulting, OTP, etc.).

Data

Just as all applications and accounts should be considered potentially compromised without contravening evidence, the data should be considered the same. At this stage, it is unlikely to know the full impact of the data, but it should be noted what potential data types may be at risk and the respective regulatory or other ramifications, such as PCI, PHI, PII, SOX, intellectual property, etc. This will be sufficient for initial scoping, impact, and prioritization purposes.

Connections and Communication Activity

The first sign that something malicious is happening will probably be suspicious network activity. These are typically detected from a network or security device (next-gen firewalls, WAF, IPS, network malware detection, DLP, UBA, UEBA, and/or UAM), endpoint agent (such as EDR, DLP, HIPS, firewall, and/or anti-virus/anti-malware), or SIEM with rulesets configured to identify patterns of behavior.

As stated earlier, each of these sources will have its own respective level of accuracy and reliability. Each detection source may be more or less accurate, depending on the circumstances. Efficacy is affected by a wide range of variables.

SSL/TLS decryption is one of the most important factors in the efficacy of network-based detections, which are on a steep downward trend overall. However, the endpoint controls have evolved to pick up the slack and far surpass the capabilities that were ever available on a network level. Either way, the following are the typical activities detected that help determine the scope of an incident, which are listed in order of increasing difficulty to detect:

- Ingress – Any malicious inbound traffic
- Egress – Any malicious outbound traffic
- C2 – Any command-and-control activity, including the download of malware components
- Exfiltration – Any attempt to send stolen content out of the organization
- Lateral movement – Any attempt to spread laterally and compromise additional systems

Connections and Communication Activity Misuse Cases

In order to detect any of the previously mentioned suspicious or malicious network activity and determine the scope, the following types of misuse cases are typically employed. These are implemented at various monitoring levels:

- SIEM
- Signature-based monitoring tools
- Behavioral-based monitoring tools
- IAM-based detections
- Network monitoring devices
- Endpoint monitoring and retrospective analysis technologies

Obviously, some of the previously mentioned suspicious network activities may have completely benign explanations. However, each of them could also indicate malicious activity resulting in a compromise or secondary actions following that compromise:

- Elevated account anomalies – There are many types of elevated account anomalies. Elevated account misuse will be of particular interest when establishing the scope and identifying the impact of an incident. Anything having to do with the privileged account performing any of the following activities should be investigated and addressed:
    - o Internet browsing
    - o Unauthorized account creation
    - o Unauthorized software installs
    - o Unauthorized/suspicious script execution

- o Workstation to workstation login/communication
- o Insecure permission changes
- o Large quantity file access/changes
- o Anything that violates policy statements.
- Honeynet detections – Any hosts involved in connections to a honeypot should be considered highly suspicious and possibly compromised. However, automated security scanners typically create a lot of false positives for this rule.
- Injection activity – Any host attempting to perform malicious activity is almost certainly suspect unless that host is a security scanner.
- Insecure, sensitive data transfer – Hosts found to be sending sensitive data outbound may potentially be involved in the scope of a security incident. However, they are more likely to be in the scope of a compliance incident, depending upon the nature of the traffic. This means the traffic could be from attackers or malware exfiltrating the data or from the user sending the data out in an insecure manner, either intentionally or accidentally.
- Log tampering – Any host found to have demonstrated activity consistent with unauthorized log tempering (such as clearing or selective deletion) is potentially compromised and may be considered in the scope of a security or compliance incident and may be in the scope of response activity.
- Login attempts from hostile countries or other malicious hosts – logon attempts from hostile countries have always been a security issue but are of increasing risk and impact with the recent rise in credential phishing and Business Email Compromise (BEC) activity. Further, any logons from known malicious hosts render the detected systems, applications, services, and/or repositories within the scope of the investigation.
- Malicious cloud access – Cloud services (such as AWS, Azure, or others) have become an essential part of attacker infrastructure, and access to foreign, newly provisioned, or otherwise unknown cloud infrastructure is often highly suspect and may be considered in the scope of the response activity.
- Malware activity – Any network activity traced back to known malware is obviously suspect, and all hosts involved are in the scope of the investigation.
- Password compromise or guessing attempts – Any hosts that are determined to be the source of password compromise or guessing attempts (such as brute force, password sprays, password dumping, or other methods) should be considered as in scope of investigation and may also be the patient zero, depending upon the timeline of events.
- Phishing activity – Any users identified to have been affected by phishing activity, particularly if the phishing activity can be tied back to the known C2 infrastructure, will likely be considered in scope of investigation. A more malicious and conclusive subset of this would be if the user was phished and then initiated phishing emails to others. This is a strong indicator that the user was compromised and is in scope for additional investigation, thus placing all the data stored in the user's email account and any accounts or shared groups/boxes the user has access to at risk of impact.
- Private VPN, Anonymizer, or other Tunneling Activity Detected – Any hosts found to be using one or more of the vast myriads of private VPNs, anonymous proxies, or other

tunneling methods may or may not be ruled within the scope of response activity, depending upon the nature of the use. More specifically, if it is found that malware or attackers are the cause of the activity, then they are definitely in scope. However, the cause of the activity could just as likely be a user violating company policy and trying to avoid the detection of unauthorized web browsing or data transfer.

- Rapid data leakage – When malware designed for cybercrime or espionage infects a system, it will often begin to exfiltrate targeted data types, such as user-created files, database content, or other data types. This usually happens rapidly and will result in a data spike.

- Repeated activity from external host – Malicious external hosts with repeated, failed malicious access attempts to a system followed by successful access to that system would be considered in scope for response activity until ruled out through the investigative process.

- Shared accounts – Identification of accounts that appear to be shared may also identify compromised credentials used by attackers or malware. If the credentials are tied to a compromised or otherwise in-scope system, the shared activity should be considered suspicious until ruled out through the investigative process.

- Service accounts logging in interactively – Any service accounts found to be logging in interactively, which are tied to other in-scope systems, may indicate a compromised service account being used by attackers or malware. It may also indicate bad IT processes, which are rather common.

- Slow, extended data leakage – Not all exfiltration activity happens quickly. Some activities attempt to be covert by sending small amounts of data over a long period of time. Oftentimes, this activity will use tunneling methods using session-less protocols or incomplete TCP handshake attempts. This network traffic is hard to detect without the right people, processes, and technology in place. It will add significantly to the scope of an incident if found.

- Successful logon from a Disabled Account – Any successful logons from accounts known to be suspended are highly suspicious. A common method used by attackers to avoid detection of backdoor accounts is reactivating known accounts having privileged access. These accounts should definitely be considered in scope for investigation.

- Suspicious application activity – Applications found to be operating in non-standard ways may be considered in scope of investigation, particularly if associated with other in-scope hosts. However, this is a nascent space at best and is full of false positives and negatives. More specifically, identifying suspicious activity requires legitimate and intended activity to be well-defined. Unfortunately, defining and whitelisting benign application activity is highly manual, resource-intensive, and does not usually exist within the affected environment.

- Threat feed detections – Threat feed detections are helpful in identifying malicious activity, which may expand the scope. However, your mileage will vary depending on the threat feed source and IOCs provided. The efficacy can vary significantly.

Initial System IOCs/Artifacts

Initial artifacts typically found in the alerts (especially from network malware analysis tools) usually include a common set of indicators. Some have a greater quantity of visibility than others:

- Files/Processes/Registry – Automated alerts and IOCs typically contain a listing of involved files, processes, and registry entries that are associated with the detection or commonly associated with the particular malware variant.

Obviously, these need to be considered in the scope of investigation if identified and then searched across other systems in the environment. This may significantly expand the scope if other infected systems are identified.

However, the data in the alerts is just a starting place. Usually, there are additional or different files, processes, and/or registry entries involved. This is particularly true with modern polymorphic and/or scripted malware, which commonly modifies many aspects of itself from system to system to avoid detection.

This polymorphism can be used against itself using EDR capabilities that can identify unique processes, drivers, or targeted file types that should be consistent, or at least non-unique, across the organization. As an example, a unique process on a suspect system is highly suspicious and should be considered within the scope of the investigation.

- Memory – Alerts may contain common memory artifacts that render systems or applications in the scope of the investigation, including the identification of process injection, process hollowing, or other memory-based anomalies. Identifying this type of activity is a science in and of itself and is covered in greater depth in other sections.

But, if/when it is identified and verified, the affected systems are definitely in the scope of investigation, and the data contained in them should be considered at risk and likely exposed. Performing/exploiting such usually involves system/admin/root level permissions, and the system or device is likely fully compromised if the activity cannot be proven to be benign.

- WMI – Alerts may bear reference to malicious WMI classes, subscriptions, or associated backdoors. They can be persistent, asynchronous, and /or fileless in nature. Windows enables the creation of fully functional fileless applications using WMI, including custom WMI classes. As with anything, this feature can be used for benign or malevolent intent. While these should be considered immediately in the scope of investigation when found, this is another nascent space that is hard to detect and easy to circumvent detections.

Incident Artifact Preliminary Collection

Assuming that the validation questions indicate a possible security incident or cannot rule one out, it is time to begin collecting preliminary evidence to confirm the incident, further identify its scope, and ascertain the potential impact. The following are preliminary considerations and associated evidence artifacts to be collected:

Determine the Method of Compromise

Gather initial threat intel or IOCs related to the event/incident as contained in the alert. This will provide a starting place for collection, investigation, and root cause analysis. It will also enable response teams to begin to identify plausible containment and/or mitigation controls.

Identify Tools Available

Identify visibility, monitoring, response, and/or blocking capabilities that the customer has respective to the compromise and related activity. Depending upon the threat, some solutions work better than others, or perhaps not at all. The response team needs to identify all account management, network, endpoint, or log collection, parsing/searching, detection, and blocking capabilities that will be effective against the detected threat.

Ensure Evidence Collection

The Incident Commander must enable evidence preservation, ensure incident responders can act without additional delay, and provide rapid identification for containment of the spread of malicious applications and activity. Further, the Incident Commander and/or response personnel should instruct the customer to ensure that all preliminary evidence is collected, preserved, and validated. Also, ensure that the customer has an adequate retention period that will prevent evidence from being overwritten/deleted. Very often, logs and network traffic captures will overwrite themselves and are permanently lost. Preliminary evidence collection artifact locations include the following:

- Collect ingress/egress traffic from/to the Internet or sensitive environments – Sources include PCAP, NetFlow, WAF, Firewall, NIPS, HIPS, Proxy, VPN, DNS, etc.
- Collect internal artifacts from all in-scope systems affected by the incident – This includes volatile metadata, memory, registry artifacts, file system artifacts, logs, EDR retrospective data, etc.
- Collect available logs pertaining to the incident and affected resources – Sources include EDR, PCAP, NIPS, HIPS, Firewalls, Active Directory, DHCP, DNS, etc.
- Identify malware samples and perform analysis – Need to determine behavior, capabilities, IOCs, exploit methods, polymorphism, and mitigation techniques.

Identify and Obtain Malware or Related Artifact Samples

A note of caution regarding identifying, testing, or requesting malware samples from customers or security personnel →INSTRUCT THE CUSTOMER AND PRACTITIONERS TO **NOT UPLOAD** MALWARE SAMPLES TO PUBLICLY ACCESSIBLE MALWARE ANALYSIS TOOLS, SUCH AS VIRUSTOTAL, AS THIS COULD COMPROMISE THE INVESTIGATION.

Hashes of malware can be checked against public resources (like VirusTotal). However, no binaries or scripts should be uploaded as doing so could alert attackers of the customer's awareness of the security breach and malware samples.

Automated analysis can be performed within private, offline behavior analysis environments to limit the risk. Static analysis should also be performed offline. In both cases, analysis should be completed to identify IOCs and/or create Yara rules to provide content for searches across the environment.

Infrastructure Deep-dive

At this point in the preliminary investigation process, the Incident Commander and the response team have a preliminary understanding of the threat vectors and a basic understanding of the environment. As such, it is time to move into a deeper dive analysis of the customer environment and ascertain the evidence universe, begin performing triage, and prepare for containment measures. Critical focus areas include:

- Physical locations – Identify locations of all in-scope customer facilities and evaluate their current state, target value, vulnerability/susceptibility, business criticality, and severability if necessary.
- Network structure – Identify all connected and air-gapped networks that are in the scope of investigation and response activity.
    - Identify network topology (internal, external, DMZ), wireless, data centers, co-location facilities, cloud environments, connected partner networks, vendors or partners with network access, etc.
    - Identify the quantity of devices (servers and workstations) at each location.
    - Enumerate methods of remote access and security measures – such as a direct network connection, B2B VPN, client VPN, and access controls, such as with SFA, MFA, or OTP.
    - Enumerate ingress/egress points of presence (PoPs) – Identify the location, throughput, and connection type(s).
    - Obtain network diagrams for all locations.

- Workstations, servers, virtual machines, and containers – Identify operating systems, quantities, and system or application types, including:
    - Managed or unmanaged
    - Internal or remote/traveling
    - Physical systems, on-prem virtual machines, or cloud infrastructure.
- Account management capabilities – Identify IAM controls for at-risk accounts, whether on the domain, local system, service, or application.
- Sensitive data – Identify sensitive or regulated data, including PCI, PII, PHI, SOX, Intellectual property, and Critical infrastructure.

As applicable, create, update, and/or verify current asset inventory and contact/escalation lists. It is more than likely that resources will not be accurately documented, including their respective contacts.

Security Controls and Regulatory Deep-dive

Evaluate the security, investigation, logging/SIEM, and endpoint visibility and management technologies that can be used to assist with the investigation. These will need to be specifically evaluated based on the nature of the identified threat activity, scope, and affected resources or environments.

Identify and utilize network monitoring and packet capture capabilities for all in-scope locations. Enumerate all capacities and limitations. Visibility, collection, and retention capabilities are usually issues.

Identify and utilize endpoint detection and response (EDR) capabilities and coverage. This includes coverage across all endpoint types and locations. Efficacy against extant threat types and unsupported or unmanaged endpoints can be an issue. For systems without EDR, utilize script-based evidence collection across the network or local collection methods via USB. Local collection methods are obviously not scalable and need to be used only if absolutely necessary.

Identify and utilize log aggregation, SIEM capabilities, alert integrations, and correlation capabilities. This involves obtaining necessary log types for events that would, in full or in part, identify exploitation from threats. It is also critical to integrate SIEMs with multiple threat feeds for crowdsourcing intelligence and automated threat detection.

Identify and utilize methods of endpoint management that can gain visibility and deploy changes. These include configuration changes, patch management, and application installation. It may be necessary to deploy patches, endpoint agents/utilities, and policy configuration changes to deploy containment measures and/or otherwise mitigate threats.

Obtaining vulnerability scans and penetration test results will help identify the possible attack vectors, if not already known. These should include new and/or recently performed scans.

Identifying and reviewing current security, regulatory, and legal requirements, as well as security standards, policies, procedures, and playbooks, will help to ensure alignment with requirements. It may also identify teams, stakeholders, contact info, workflows, and other relevant information that is salient to the investigation.

After analyzing all extant threats, customer assets, and investigative solutions, the investigative team needs to work with the customer to identify and deploy investigative solutions to augment gaps in the customer's capabilities. Quickly deployable solutions that provide visibility and blocking controls include network IPS devices, EDR capabilities, and SIEM solutions with threat intel integration.

As applicable, create, update, or verify current asset inventory and contact/escalation lists. This must be done at each step along the way as new systems, attributes, or contacts are identified.

Incident Scope Refinement

Based on the initial analysis and findings, the scope will need to be adjusted. Scope refinement includes confirmation of all resources, accounts, and data likely involved.

This will enable proper triage and containment activity and enable reasonable estimates for investigative needs, capabilities, workflows, and resource requirements. Determining the criticality of the incident and the resources affected will help determine the severity of the incident, the prioritization of response, and the potential reporting activity.

Identifying what the customer has done prior to the arrival of the response team is critical. Enumerating anything they have done to investigate, block, and/or remediate the incident could enumerate details or findings that may have been missed in the original explanation. New details could update the incident start times and provide additional information for investigation and containment steps. The customer may have already identified and contained or eradicated earlier stages of an attack, which is essential information for determining the root cause(s) and establishing full containment/remediation.

Moreover, identifying if there were any recent or prior incidents and obtaining respective details will help establish a pattern of activity that can provide additional, possibly related information. There may have been a pattern of attacks occurring for a long time, and this latest event that was detected and escalated may just be a single manifestation of it.

Initial Containment or Isolation Measures

Based on the initially identified activity, it is possible to deploy preliminary containment controls at this phase for known indicators. These are most appropriate at the network, endpoint, and account management layers, as identified below.

These initial containment measures are a combination of blocking known threat activity and specific indicators from the incident. These typically must be implemented using existing controls that are configured for immediate assistance in stopping or preventing threats.

Network Controls
- Protecting vulnerable web applications with web application firewalls (WAFs)
- Using perimeter firewalls and/or network IPS devices to block IP addresses, domains, network ranges, CIDR blocks, TCP/UDP ports, and/or signature-based threats
- Utilize Next-generation firewall capabilities to block the following
    - Protocol anomalies – These include a whole host of indicators, such as some forms of tunneling or other methods of protocol misuse
    - Volumetric blocking – This includes blocking traffic transferred beyond an imposed cap of throughput and/or connections
    - Connection time or duration blocking – This can halt connections at unexpected times or those lasting longer than a predefined time period
    - DGA blocking – This will block domains created through Domain Generation Algorithms
    - Dynamic blocking from threat feeds or other integrations
- Disabling network switch ports for workstations and servers – This is typically the quickest and most definitive way to completely halt all threats related to an endpoint

Endpoint Controls

- Using host-based firewalls and IPS devices to block IP addresses, domains, network ranges, CIDR blocks, TCP/UDP ports, and/or signature-based threats
- Using host-based monitoring and EDR technologies capable of behavioral analysis, anomaly identification, and automated blocking of identified threats
- Source application traffic/activity blocking to halt any activity from known malicious processes
- Performing host isolation using endpoint agents, which has the advantage of blocking all network activity except that which is used for investigation by identified systems
- Antivirus/anti-malware configuration can be useful for eradicating known samples *WARNING – have very low expectations for the efficacy of containment activity for unknown, polymorphic, memory-resident, or script-based threats*

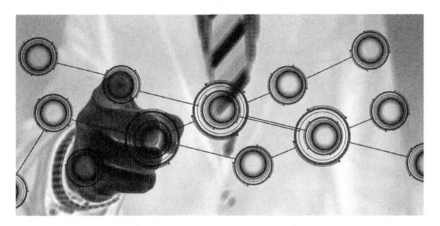

Account Controls

- Changing passwords – These should be administratively reset, not set to change at the next logon, for obvious reasons. This is critical because the attacker or malware that has the compromised credentials could just as easily change the password at the next logon.
- Disabling user accounts – This is preferable over deleting them, as it preserves them for investigation or re-enablement if found to be benign. Oftentimes, there are esoteric accounts that take time to validate their legitimacy.
- End active session(s) – It is critical to terminate unauthorized access for current sessions and force the reauthentication of user sessions following administrative password reset or account disablement.
- Disabling MFA tokens – Disable/invalidate any compromised tokens (physical or soft tokens).
- Terminate MFA session – Force the affected MFA sessions to reauthenticate to end MFA access that was surreptitiously gained, such as through social engineering or token theft.

18 RESPONSE ACTIONS: ENUMERATING ATTACKER INFRASTRUCTURE (PIVOTING)

This chapter discusses the methods used to identify any attacker infrastructure (hosts, IP addresses, domains, and DNS servers) that are in any way linked via DNS. When attackers strike, they almost never hit their target with everything they have right away, nor the best of what they have. Extended campaigns will eventually expose the target to additional infrastructure and more sophisticated threats. The way it is done, it might appear at face value to be a series of unrelated attacks from different domains, hostnames, IP addresses, cloud infrastructure, countries, etc.

However, it is possible to get ahead of the attackers by doing DNS pivoting for each new campaign the victim is hit with. The responders can enumerate the attacker's infrastructure if it is in any way connected. This is done by delving into DNS records to identify any associations between known systems or IP addresses with any other systems or IP addresses. This is performed iteratively until all DNS-linked attacker infrastructure is enumerated.

Pivoting – Information Origin Seed

After automated alerts identify malicious IP addresses and domains, the next step is to identify the rest of the attacker infrastructure from which additional malicious emails may come, links may point to, or malware may be downloaded from or communicate with. This will enable the response team to get ahead of the threat and hopefully prevent the next round of the campaign.

This is done by pivoting off of known domains and IP addresses to identify additional domains and IP addresses. This process may take numerous pivots to enumerate everything or until it becomes diluted by an IP from a mass-hosting site.

Hostname/IP address pivoting works as follows. The initial seed information from the alert or from the email headers may include hostnames and IP addresses from the sender's email server, malicious links, the illegitimate domain name the attacker is using, or those identified within malicious scripts or malware. Each of these IP addresses, domains, and their respective authoritative nameservers should be enumerated and placed in a table, as seen in the image below. Each new identification of a different domain, IP address, DNS server, or other unique artifact will result in a new line.

Domain	DDNS Provider	IP Address	IP First Seen	IP Last Seen	IP Address Owner	IP Country	IP Disposition	Suspicious Domains on IP
nameserver1.zapto.org	no-ip.com	59.188.8.49	2013-04-02 16:02:16	2013-04-24 06:29:55	HOSTASIA - Internet Access	HK	C2	
nameserver1.zapto.org	no-ip.com	8.8.8.8	2013-04-12 13:33:31	2013-07-18 07:07:19	[Google DNS]		Parking	
nameserver1.zapto.org	no-ip.com	127.0.0.1	2013-04-24 13:28:03	2015-12-29 05:26:22	[Local Host]		Parking	
nameserver1.zapto.org	no-ip.com	58.64.205.47	2013-05-06 05:27:28	2013-06-03 05:20:20	NWT iDC Data Service	HK	C2	
nameserver1.zapto.org	no-ip.com	59.188.8.53	2013-06-22 02:11:53	2013-08-01 13:36:19	HOSTASIA - Internet Access	HK	C2	homeweb.sytes.net mynews.sytes.net
nameserver1.zapto.org	no-ip.com	58.64.205.52	2013-08-01 13:38:41	2013-12-22 16:00:24	NWT iDC Data Service	HK	C2	homeweb.sytes.net hostweb.zapto.org
nameserver1.zapto.org	no-ip.com	58.158.177.102	2016-01-31 15:00:27	2016-02-02 03:25:17	ARTERIA Networks Corporation	JP	Sinkhole	

Pivoting – First Pivot

The first pivot off of the initial alert data only identifies two new C2 IP addresses (49.212.147.140 and 112.140.186.251) and one additional domain (aspweb.linkpc.net) that need to be blocked and researched in the next pivot. The rest of the IP addresses are just artifacts of parking the domain.

Domain	DDNS Provider	IP Address	IP First Seen	IP Last Seen	IP Address Owner	IP Country	IP Disposition	Suspicious Domains on IP
mynews.sytes.net	no-ip.com	49.212.147.140	2013-09-06 19:28:14	2013-09-06 19:28:20	SAKURA Internet Inc.	JP	C2	
mynews.sytes.net	no-ip.com	127.0.0.1	2013-11-22 01:40:14	2014-03-06 05:29:07	[Local Host]		Parking	
homeweb.sytes.net	no-ip.com	8.8.8.8	2013-04-12 14:34:46	2013-12-05 17:20:21	[Google DNS]		Parking	
homeweb.sytes.net	no-ip.com	58.158.177.102	2015-06-30 18:48:42	2016-02-02 03:25:17	ARTERIA Networks Corporation	JP	Sinkhole	
homeweb.sytes.net	no-ip.com	64.4.11.42	2013-03-02 08:46:38	2013-03-04 13:22:55	[Microsoft]		Parking	
homeweb.sytes.net	no-ip.com	65.55.27.220	2012-05-17 01:42:44	2012-05-17 06:32:38	[Microsoft]		Parking	
homeweb.sytes.net	no-ip.com	127.0.0.1	2013-02-10 21:52:06	2013-12-22 16:00:33	[Local Host]		Parking	
homeweb.sytes.net	no-ip.com	192.168.1.1	2013-02-18 17:24:09	2013-07-03 20:34:04	[Private Non-Routable]		Parking	
hostweb.zapto.org	no-ip.com	8.8.8.8	2013-08-01 06:26:13	2013-09-20 07:38:30	[Google DNS]		Parking	
hostweb.zapto.org	no-ip.com	65.55.27.220	2012-05-12 06:11:09	2012-05-17 01:35:14	[Microsoft]		Parking	
hostweb.zapto.org	no-ip.com	112.140.186.251	2012-05-17 02:08:03	2012-05-17 06:05:49	Sparkstation Pte Ltd	SG	C2	aspweb.linkpc.net
hostweb.zapto.org	no-ip.com	127.0.0.1	2012-03-25 11:56:21	2013-06-11 11:56:26	[Local Host]		Parking	
hostweb.zapto.org	no-ip.com	192.168.1.1	2013-04-07 08:28:45	2013-04-11 04:46:47	[Private Non-Routable]		Parking	

Pivoting – Second Pivot

The second pivot identifies one additional C2 IP address (112.213.126.90) that needs to be blocked, as well as 3 additional domains (dsx.aspweb.linkpc.net, homeweb.linkpc.net, piping.no-ip.org) that need to be blocked and researched in the next pivot.

Domain	DDNS Provider	IP Address	IP First Seen	IP Last Seen	IP Address Owner	IP Country	IP Disposition	Suspicious Domains on IP
aspweb.linkpc.net	dnsexit.com	127.0.0.1	2012-03-24 02:19:20	2012-06-02 05:44:31	[Local Host]		Parking	
aspweb.linkpc.net	dnsexit.com	112.213.126.90	2012-03-29 01:51:02	2012-03-29 02:21:50	Sun Network (Hong Kong) Limited	HK	C2	dsx.aspweb.linkpc.net homeweb.linkpc.net piping.no-ip.org

Pivoting – Third Pivot

The third pivot identifies 5 additional C2 IP addresses (77.235.134.114, 77.235.134.115, 141.138.182.14, 178.135.241.62, 210.56.58.224) that need to be blocked, as well as 2 additional domains (okok4o.zapto.org and koko4w.no-ip.org) that need to be blocked and researched in the next pivot.

Domain	DDNS Provider	IP Address	IP First Seen	IP Last Seen	IP Address Owner	IP Country	IP Disposition	Suspicious Domains on IP
dsx.aspweb.linkpc.net	dnsexit.com	127.0.0.1	2012-06-09 03:14:02	2012-10-17 19:58:50	[Local Host]		Parking	
homeweb.linkpc.net	dnsexit.com	65.55.184.16	2012-06-15 08:03:31	2012-06-15 09:18:08	[Microsoft]		Parking	
homeweb.linkpc.net	dnsexit.com	127.0.0.1	2012-06-15 11:29:48	2016-02-02 03:25:17	[Local Host]		Parking	
homeweb.linkpc.net	dnsexit.com	65.55.200.139	2012-06-20 09:58:02	2012-06-21 01:34:43	[Microsoft]		Parking	
piping.no-ip.org	no-ip.com	77.235.134.114	2013-04-03 02:04:43	2013-04-04 01:56:28	Broadbandplus	LB	C2	
piping.no-ip.org	no-ip.com	77.235.134.115	2013-04-04 23:12:26	2013-05-08 02:32:43	Broadbandplus	LB	C2	
piping.no-ip.org	no-ip.com	127.0.0.1	2013-01-05 15:20:23	2013-01-06 04:47:19	[Local Host]		Parking	
piping.no-ip.org	no-ip.com	141.138.182.14	2013-04-08 16:47:53	2013-04-08 16:52:05	Moscanet SAL(Wise)	LB	C2	
piping.no-ip.org	no-ip.com	178.135.241.62	2013-04-08 09:12:56	2013-04-08 15:46:38	OGERONET	LB	C2	
piping.no-ip.org	no-ip.com	198.199.78.132	2013-11-24 18:05:07	2016-01-13 17:12:56	Digital Ocean, Inc.	US	Sinkhole	
piping.no-ip.org	no-ip.com	210.56.58.224	2013-01-06 16:46:00	2013-02-04 19:20:09	Sun Network (Hong Kong) Limited	HK	C2	okok4o.zapto.org koko4w.no-ip.org

Pivoting – Final Results

The final results of all the pivots are shown here. Starting with 2 IP addresses and 3 domain names contained in the initial detection, through pivoting, we were able to identify a total of 11 domain names and 13 IP addresses spread across 4 countries and 9 ISPs. All of this is related to the attack infrastructure, and the domains and IP addresses identified should be blocked and alerted using firewalls, IPSs, email security tools, and EDR as appropriate. If alerts are identified for these domains or IPs, it could indicate the presence of malicious emails that were accessed, compromised endpoints, and/or malware in the environment.

This example is a fairly productive and clean example of pivoting and demonstrates how it can be useful in enumerating the attackers' external-facing infrastructure and using publicly available information to get ahead of attack activity during a response.

*Note: A key consideration when conducting pivoting is to identify domains that have a positive reputation that recently changed ownership and might be used by attackers to evade reputation services blocking controls.

*Warning: sometimes pivoting will identify a virtual hosting of numerous legitimate sites that might cause a business impact if the IP hosting the sites is blocked. This is often used by attackers to evade IP address blocking controls. In this situation, the specific malicious domain should be blocked.

Domain	DDNS Provider	IP Address	IP First Seen	IP Last Seen	IP Address Owner	IP Country
aspweb.linkpc.net	dnsexit.com	112.140.186.251	2012-03-21 08:20:29	2012-03-24 02:16:38	Sparkstation Pte Ltd	SG
aspweb.linkpc.net	dnsexit.com	112.213.126.90	2012-03-29 01:51:02	2012-03-29 02:21:50	Sun Network (Hong Kong) Limited	HK
dsx.aspweb.linkpc.net	dnsexit.com	112.213.126.90	2012-05-08 05:19:42	2012-06-07 14:16:13	Sun Network (Hong Kong) Limited	HK
homeweb.linkpc.net	dnsexit.com	112.213.126.90	2012-06-15 10:22:55	2012-07-15 14:50:41	Sun Network (Hong Kong) Limited	HK
homeweb.sytes.net	no-ip.com	59.188.8.53	2013-04-01 13:23:42	2013-04-24 12:44:54	HOSTASIA - Internet Access	HK
homeweb.sytes.net	no-ip.com	58.64.205.52	2013-05-17 13:26:23	2013-06-03 02:43:10	NWT iDC Data Service	HK
hostweb.zapto.org	no-ip.com	112.140.186.251	2012-05-17 02:08:03	2012-05-17 06:05:49	Sparkstation Pte Ltd	SG
hostweb.zapto.org	no-ip.com	58.64.205.52	2013-05-16 17:20:16	2013-05-16 21:33:40	NWT iDC Data Service	HK
koko4w.no-ip.org	no-ip.com	210.56.58.224	2013-01-07 20:07:59	2013-03-17 18:18:18	Sun Network (Hong Kong) Limited	HK
mynews.sytes.net	no-ip.com	49.212.147.140	2013-09-06 19:28:14	2013-09-06 19:28:20	SAKURA Internet Inc.	JP
mynews.sytes.net	no-ip.com	58.64.205.52	2013-11-15 22:20:12	2013-11-22 01:30:16	NWT iDC Data Service	HK
nameserver1.zapto.org	no-ip.com	59.188.8.49	2013-04-02 16:02:16	2013-04-24 06:29:55	HOSTASIA - Internet Access	HK
nameserver1.zapto.org	no-ip.com	58.64.205.47	2013-05-06 05:27:28	2013-06-03 05:20:20	NWT iDC Data Service	HK
nameserver1.zapto.org	no-ip.com	59.188.8.53	2013-06-22 02:11:53	2013-08-01 13:36:19	HOSTASIA - Internet Access	HK
nameserver1.zapto.org	no-ip.com	58.64.205.52	2013-08-01 13:38:41	2013-12-22 16:00:24	NWT iDC Data Service	HK
okok4o.zapto.org	no-ip.com	210.56.58.224	2013-01-14 16:20:35	2013-01-22 22:49:17	Sun Network (Hong Kong) Limited	HK
piping.no-ip.org	no-ip.com	112.213.126.90	2013-01-01 18:04:28	2013-01-05 07:02:59	Sun Network (Hong Kong) Limited	HK
piping.no-ip.org	no-ip.com	210.56.58.224	2013-01-06 16:46:00	2013-02-04 19:20:09	Sun Network (Hong Kong) Limited	HK
piping.no-ip.org	no-ip.com	77.235.134.114	2013-04-03 02:04:43	2013-04-04 01:56:28	Broadbandplus	LB
piping.no-ip.org	no-ip.com	77.235.134.115	2013-04-04 23:12:26	2013-05-08 02:32:43	Broadbandplus	LB
piping.no-ip.org	no-ip.com	178.135.241.62	2013-04-08 09:12:56	2013-04-08 15:46:38	OGERONET	LB
piping.no-ip.org	no-ip.com	141.138.182.14	2013-04-08 16:47:53	2013-04-08 16:52:05	Moscanet SAL (Wise)	LB

19 RESPONSE ACTIONS: TRIAGE, PRIORITIZATION, AND CONTAINMENT

This chapter will cover various options and thought processes for prioritizing incident response activity and the respective containment controls to be implemented. There are many considerations that go into triaging, prioritizing, and containing malicious activity. The actions necessary are highly specific to the customer environment, threat landscape, particular threat encountered, regulatory requirements, and business needs.

Prioritizing Response Efforts

Triaging and prioritizing response and containment efforts is a highly contextual judgment call that varies from one organization to another based on the interplay between a large number of complex factors. Most notably, these include the risk or impact of the threat, likely impact on business operations, customer impact, impacted data sensitivity, and regulatory concerns. Ultimately, everything has a priority, and some priorities are higher than others. The context of the threat and respective impact on each system, device, application, user, function, and/or data will inform the response priority and containment requirements. Obviously, some resources and threats have a higher priority than others, as it is not possible to do everything first.

For all containment efforts, there should be a simultaneous workstream of gathering volatile data that might otherwise be lost if the network connection is severed. If not, critical data may be lost, or malicious activity may be permitted to continue longer than necessary.

Sometimes, a choice must be made between evidence collection/preservation and rapid containment. This choice is highly contextual, but in general, the need to contain an active or rapidly spreading threat supersedes that of gathering host- or log-based evidence. Some types of evidence collection may take too long and place other systems, data, and/or individuals at risk. Oftentimes, all that there is time for is to capture volatile metadata and possibly memory.

Actively Spreading Malware Threats

First and foremost, priority needs to be given during incident response to rapidly spreading destructive threats. These typically involve worms, ransomware, wiperware, or other destructive, malicious activity that has the potential to bring down entire environments, compromise systems, and corrupt data.

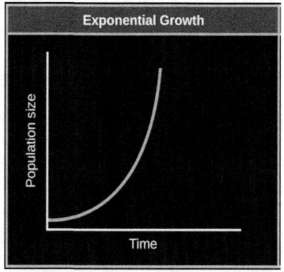

Containment activity involves isolating systems that are actively compromised and performing malicious activity, which may spread to other systems or negatively affect resources within the environment. This is the highest priority objective due to the potentially negative impact on every resource.

If critical systems and sensitive data are not already affected, they may be soon due to an actively spreading malware threat. Nothing is more important than stopping this.

An active, enabled threat on compromised hosts could quickly spread malware to other systems, including life-supporting/sustaining systems. As such, a very high priority and sense of urgency must be given to addressing systems with automated threats. So long as there is a self-replicating malware threat in the environment, the problem that the team is responding to is growing. If it gets too big, it may spiral out of control. It is entirely possible that worm-like activity could bring down all business-critical functions by exhausting system and/or network resources.

With rapidly spreading threats (for example, worms like WannaCry or NotPetya), there is a small window of time at the beginning of the intrusion where there are only a handful of hosts that are infected, and the threat can be stopped before it gets larger. Minutes later, that threat may have grown by orders of magnitude, and an entire environment could be compromised and need to be rebuilt from scratch. It is critical to stop self-replicating threats early, preferably at the bottom of the exponential curve.

Systems that Support Life

Any system or device that maintains life is clearly amongst the highest of priority during incident response and containment actions, if applicable. This is obviously a common consideration in healthcare environments, but others may apply as well. In such cases, it is possible that malware activity that compromises medical or infrastructure devices could potentially kill patients if not handled expediently.

However, as alluded to, healthcare is not the only consideration for systems keeping people alive or perhaps preventing their death. SCADA, military, nuclear, biological, chemical, refineries, manufacturing, or other environment types may have computer systems controlling life-enabling or disaster prevention infrastructure. A compromise of these systems may result in human casualties in catastrophic proportions. In the world of highly computerized control systems that we live in, a failure of industrial control systems could cause massive damage and death or worse.

It is also possible that the act of containing the malware and disconnecting the affected system could result in the loss of life. However unlikely, due to flawed systems and BC/DR designs, devices keeping individuals alive could fail to function as a result of the loss of connectivity and communications critical to their operations. These failures could cascade and result in mortal consequences. This could occur if their operation is reliant upon the communication stream, or the lack of such prevents urgent changes from being made that would cause an impairment to safety or prevent the loss of life.

As much as reasonable, playbooks for these types of systems/devices should be created ahead of time with pre-defined workflows and thresholds for threat-based containment actions. Allowing systems to stay online enables malicious threats to spread. However, taking the systems offline might cause an outage or inability to control essential functions. Compensating controls and partial containment measures provide a hybrid solution that restricts functionality to known good locations and prevents malicious access.

Threat-specific playbooks with detailed containment measures or compensation controls must be defined ahead of time for these systems/devices, which should be immediately addressed to enable the best course of action to prevent further compromise and enable them to be quickly contained and functionality restored with minimal negative impact or downtime.

Systems with Regulated Data

Next in line are systems or devices containing regulated data. Priority must be given to systems, devices, users, and data of a sensitive nature, such as those containing PHI, PCI, PII, SOX, or other regulated content.

This marks the transition from physical risk and keeping people alive or preventing the complete destruction of the digital environment from self-replicating malware and respective payloads to protecting the company against business and/or reputational risk. This and the next section may be a bit of a toss-up regarding their order of priority, but the regulatory risk should be perceived as higher as it is incredibly expensive in all respects.

While all systems, users, and data are important in one way or another, regulators and compliance entities will be holding the customer accountable for these system types and their respective data. Per the various data breach reports and statistics, the breach of regulated data, such as healthcare data, costs the most, with over $10M in combined breach costs on average, as of 2023. However, government fines for individual breaches of other regulated data types have gone a lot higher. Consider the following recent fines from various global regulatory agencies:

4) Didi Global – Fined $1.19B by the Chinese Cyberspace Administration in 2022
5) Amazon – Fined $877M by Luxembourg National Data Protection Commission (CNPD) in 2021
6) Equifax – Fined $575M by a combined lawsuit by multiple United States consumer protection agencies in 2019

In addition to the fines, the breaches themselves could result in a significant loss of value, reputation, revenue, or even the demise of the organization. As such, systems with regulated data should be sequestered to protect them from compromise or to stop malicious activity in progress. It is necessary to implement proactive containment measures to protect them from compromise during an ongoing threat. In the case of ransomware or wiperware, it would protect the customer not only from data loss but also the fines associated with the lack of availability of PHI data if HIPAA is a factor. As a reminder, HHS\OCR views ransomware-type activity as a reportable data breach, considering an unauthorized party obtained control of PHI data. This same logic can apply to wiperware or other malware variants that impact PHI data availability.

If not able to implement proactive containment controls, use reactive containment to stop data exfiltration and additional malicious activity. Keep in mind that every record that is not exfiltrated, deleted, or altered is a record the customer is not fined for. As such, timely and expedient implementation of containment controls is critical.

Critical Systems and Networks Supporting Business Operations

As stated, a close third are critical systems that support business operations. This also includes anything public-facing, or that enables the company to facilitate business transactions.

Some might argue that these system types should actually be second, or in some cases may actually be first, if the customer is in the healthcare sector. Clearly, these distinctions are contextual per organization, and there may be overlaps depending on the situation.

The reason systems that support critical business operations are lower in priority than previously discussed system types is due to the following key considerations:

1) They do not affect the health, life, or safety of customers or employees
2) They do not involve regulated data types
3) They only involve systems, networks, and/or communications for business operations that may need to be halted in order to protect systems of higher criticality.

These types of systems will usually be shut down regardless of the impact on business operations in order to reduce the regulatory and subsequent financial impact from fines, restrictions, and/or lawsuits. Companies are not typically fined by regulatory agencies if they suffer a malware attack and have to halt business operations in order to protect regulated customer data. However, companies will likely be fined for breaches of regulated data.

As such, shutting down networks or systems that facilitate business operations is a preventative measure to protect against worse threats. Interestingly, stopping new regulated data from coming in during a breach halts the increase in breached records or fines caused by the additional records. Obviously, these are all bad options. Unfortunately, during a security breach, the affected entities need to choose the least bad option of the choices available.

Ancillary Systems

Some systems are ancillary to business operations and other value, criticality, or impact considerations. Therefore, they fall to the bottom of the priority list of systems known to have been affected. These systems may be redundant, have other alternatives, or simply do not impede critical functions.

As long as there is no evidence that these systems don't pose an active threat, they should be handled after all other systems have been investigated first. While this may sound obvious, it often creates a political situation that must be dealt with during response and recovery activity. Leadership in some areas of the organization may prefer the use of the ancillary systems/services and apply pressure to expedite the investigation, validation, restoration, etc.

A clear definition of priority and the respective details pertaining to systems, services, content, and/or functions helps with successfully navigating political situations. It is harder to argue with a policy and procedures than it is to argue with a person. If people (including leaders) request that the response and restoration teams make exceptions, the team can point them to the formal exception process and step out of direct involvement.

Not Known to be Affected Systems

It may sound silly to mention this, but it is being stated for a reason. Systems that are not known to be affected should be prioritized last for any manual analysis.

This is worth mentioning as there will often be a push to verify that certain key systems not known to be involved in an incident are verified clean. This can be problematic as proving a negative can take a lot of time, and that time used is borrowed from other, higher-priority action items.

It is possible that the team may be spending precious time proving systems are not affected while the infection is spreading throughout the environment, which then compromises the same systems that were being validated. Long story short, making the wrong choices regarding the allocation of scarce resources during an investigation can permit it to spread unnecessarily.

Moreover, unaffected systems are addressed in various waves of automated analysis across the environment. This is performed while establishing the scope of an incident and identifying the existence of known IOCs or artifacts on systems.

However, manual verification tasks should be avoided until higher-priority systems and activities are first addressed. Every moment and step analyzing the wrong system is a step in the wrong direction that permits malicious activity to continue until it has been fully contained.

Inaccessible Systems

Some systems may be extremely urgent for response and restoration purposes, but for whatever reasons, there is no ability to analyze or act upon them. They may be externally managed, externally hosted, highly sensitive and unstable, or otherwise not accessible, immediately actionable, or untouchable by the response team.

These systems should be contained by isolating them from accessing other systems and the internal or external networks, as appropriate. If it is not possible to access, gather data, and/or investigate the systems themselves, build a wall around them and contain them in place until something can be done with them.

If possible, put network, endpoint, or other compensating controls in place to enable their legitimate function(s) without jeopardizing any resources, personnel, customers, or data. This may be done after careful evaluation, planning, and verification.

The key here is to enable legitimate activity without permitting anything malicious to occur. This is typically facilitated by only permitting specific hosts, ports, protocols, applications, and/or users to access and communicate to/from the affected system(s). Everything else must be summarily denied and logged.

Containment Measures

This section will discuss controls that may be utilized to implement containment measures for various use cases. These are not mutually exclusive, and they should be implemented as appropriate for each use case.

These controls are all informed based on initial detection and preliminary analysis activities. They typically must be implemented using existing capabilities that can be reconfigured for immediate assistance in stopping or preventing threats. Further, full containment may also require additional capabilities that are purchased, provisioned, and/or deployed by external responders hired to assist.

IAM Containment Measures

Depending upon the nature of the threat, a variety of IAM controls may be appropriate for lockout activity:

- Remote access restrictions – Lock down remote access to all environments:
    - o Terminate access to all corporate standard remote administration tools – These include those that are accessible via direct access, proxied access, or cloud-based access methods.
    - o Block user-installed remote access and administration tools – Blocking these requires first identifying tools and communication methods that the actor is using.
    - o Terminate access and existing sessions to corporate VPNs for all accounts that are compromised, controlled, or created by malicious actors.
    - o Validate and terminate rogue administrator, user, service, and application accounts – This includes local and domain accounts.
    - o Terminate compromised MFA tokens – Users may have multiple MFA tokens (such as physical or soft tokens used either for SSL or thick client VPNs) depending upon the method of access granted to the respective account types.
    - o Block private VPNs or network tunneling tools – Blocking these requires first identifying tools and communication methods that are in use.
    - o Block unauthorized cloud system/service access – This access is often the easiest to forget to block, particularly if authentication is not federated with corporate IAM systems.

- Accounts – Lock down all accounts considered at-risk or known compromised:
    - Lock or change passwords for administrator and user accounts (local or domain-wide) - Local accounts can be hard to chase down and need to be enumerated. This can be very hard to do at the time it is required. This should all be documented ahead of time.
    - Change passwords for service accounts (local or domain-wide), but only after careful planning and investigation. Doing this without enough research can cause an outage. As such, an intermediary step would be to make sure that the service accounts are not remotely accessible and cannot be logged into interactively.
    - Lock or change passwords for application accounts – Just like local and service accounts, these should be tracked in change management or IAM tools, as they can be very time-consuming to find at the time of investigation and lockout.
    - Terminate all MFA tokens associated with compromised accounts – Physical and virtual tokens need to be bricked so they no longer function on anything.
- Kerberos – Remove Kerberos persistence mechanisms.
    - Golden tickets – Reset all admin passwords, especially KRBTGT (2 times just over 10 hours apart), to invalidate any golden tickets/TGTs.
    - Silver tickets – Configure PAC validation to deny forged service tickets/TGSs.
    - Skeleton keys – Identify and remove any persistence mechanisms creating skeleton keys in domain controller memory.

Network Containment Measures

- Protect vulnerable web applications with web application firewalls (WAFs) – This can be the best way to stop most inbound malicious activity against vulnerable websites immediately. It can turn a vulnerable website with few to no security controls into a relatively secure site that has security controls that block common threats, at least temporarily. This will at least buy time and minimize business impact by enabling the existing, vulnerable site to function while a more secure site and web apps can be built.

- Using perimeter firewalls and/or network IPS devices to block IP addresses, domains, network ranges, CIDR blocks, TCP/UDP ports, and/or signature-based threats – This is a stop-gap security control that will block access from attackers until they figure out what the response team is doing. This control is easily circumvented by attackers through the use of proxies in countries or locations that are not blocked. If the attackers are determined, they will circumvent these controls and find another way in. However, it may buy the response team some time to implement additional controls to block future unauthorized access attempts.

- Utilize next-generation firewall capabilities to block the following suspicious activity:
  - Protocol anomalies – This includes a whole host of activity, including some forms of tunneling or other methods of protocol misuse to circumvent detection and blocking.
  - Volumetric blocking – This includes preventing the sending of data beyond an imposed threshold or cap.
  - Connection time or duration blocking – This will halt connections at unexpected times or those lasting longer than a predefined time period.
  - DGA blocking – Block domains created through Domain Generation Algorithms that do not correlate to a legitimate source.
  - Dynamic blocking from threat feeds and/or other integrations.
- Utilize cloud scrubbing services to sanitize inbound traffic and prevent hacking, malware, and volumetric attacks – This potentially blocks most of the malicious activity within the service provider's infrastructure.
- Utilize reputational services to prevent unauthorized, compromised, or defaced versions of websites/applications from being visible to customers – This places a cached, proxied layer between the client on the Internet and the web/application server that only permits authorized versions of content to be displayed by anyone visiting the domain/URL. However, it can be bypassed by going directly to the web/application server IP address.
- Disabling network switch ports for workstations and servers – This is typically the quickest and most definitive way to completely halt all threats related to an on-prem located endpoint (workstation, server, device, etc.).
- Block direct access to internal systems from remote access users/vendors/partners and require them to go through a jumpbox or virtualized infrastructure. Typical solutions include VDI or Citrix environments, with only permitted applications published and network access enabled. It is ideal if virtual environment access is set up as the primary access method during the onboarding of vendor relationships involving remote access. It is effectively a virtual device firewall that can significantly limit the risk of malicious activity from people or malicious processes. Moreover, it is rather tedious and cumbersome to try and bolt on during an incident response, as many steps are involved in the setup for all relationships that cannot simply be severed.

Endpoint Containment measures

- Using a host-based firewall and IPS devices to block IP addresses, domains, network ranges, CIDR blocks, TCP/UDP ports, and/or signature-based threats – This is a host-based network control that can provide selective containment controls enabling legitimate activity, but blocking malicious or undesired activity.
- Using host-based monitoring and EDR technologies capable of behavioral analysis and anomaly identification and blocking – This is a behavior-based method that can provide

selective containment controls enabling legitimate activity. But blocking malicious or undesired activity.

- Source application traffic/activity blocking – This is used to halt activity from known malicious processes. It is usually a method implemented through EDR and anti-malware tools. However, it may require some manual configuration if the malicious application is not known to the tool.
- Changing passwords on workstations and/or servers – This should be done as soon as reasonably possible, but it may drag on if admin or service accounts are involved.
- Disabling user accounts on workstations and/or servers – This should be done as soon as reasonably possible, but it may drag on if admin or service accounts are involved.
- Performing host isolation using endpoint agents – This has the advantage of blocking all network activity except that which is used for investigation by identified systems. This is typically performed with EDR, anti-malware, or policy configuration tools.
- Antivirus configuration can be useful, but have very low expectations – If a sample is available or a signature can be configured, AV may be useful in detecting the same infection elsewhere and stopping future examples of the same thing. Polymorphism usually negates the efficacy of this and can render black-listing tools ineffective.

Enhanced Detection of Critical Resources

As much as possible of the following activity monitoring, alerting, and blocking should be integrated with the threat feed. It should also be cross-integrated and correlated across the various investigative capabilities to leverage their respective detection and blocking IOCs with as many response technologies as reasonably capable. This will protect critical systems (if not all systems) by quickly identifying and/or automatically containing, blocking, or otherwise preventing malicious activity from occurring.

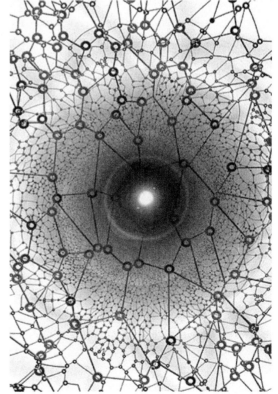

Specifically, multiple threat feeds should be integrated into detection and blocking capacities within all network, endpoint, and SIEM tools. This will more rapidly identify and respond to emergent threats. No single organization can have the breadth of reach and exposure necessary to obtain the required insight on evolving threats to enable the company to stay ahead of them. As such, threat intelligence should be crowd-sourced as much as possible, and intelligence from crowdsourcing should be integrated with detection and blocking technologies at all levels.

- Internet Access and Artifacts – Internet access to malicious sites is obviously the primary attack vector to compromise endpoints, which have become the primary target of attackers. The myriad of browser plugins and vulnerable endpoint applications integrated with browsers or having direct Internet access leads to a large attack surface, difficulty in timely patching, and a strong likelihood of exploitation. Because of this, the inside is the new outside, and the Internet is full of overtly malicious sites, compromised legitimate sites, and waterhole attacks that automatically compromise vulnerable endpoints. All access to the Internet must be monitored, tracked, and validated as much as possible. Malware artifacts should be analyzed to identify methods used to bypass security controls. This is particularly important in the modern fileless malware environment that utilizes various scripts, WMI classes, and memory-resident capabilities. This is best done through a combination of firewall/proxy, network traffic, EDR, and endpoint forensic technologies. All of these can utilize the latest threat intel to enhance detection, alerting, and containment capabilities.

- Email Activity, Links, Attachments, and Other Artifacts – Malicious emails are essentially an extension of malicious Internet activity and the bundling of selected attack vectors or pointers to them into a discrete package. All email access should be tightly restricted, monitored, and controlled to identify and prevent malicious attachments, links, spoofing methods, and other hostile activity. All attachments and links should be automatically analyzed to identify malicious intent. Links in emails should be rewritten, and clicks should be tracked (and/or blocked) to identify (or block) end-user access. This simplifies the investigative process and more quickly identifies accounts and systems at risk. Moreover, the ability to crowd-source phishing campaigns based on the most current threat intel can dramatically reduce the efficacy of such attacks.

- Process/Application Behavior – Modern EDR capabilities provide the ability to monitor, validate, and provide retrospection for processes and applications. This aids in the process of validating that they are acting within normal bounds and not behaving maliciously. This is usually done through a variety of methods, including profiling normal behavior and flagging deviations therefrom or from identifying malicious activity based on a chain of events. A simple example of this would be "an uncategorized application starts an instance of svchost.exe that initiates a connection with a known attacker C2 site. Therefore, the uncategorized application is malicious." Alerts pertaining to this type of activity should be quickly investigated to rapidly halt malicious activity. Moreover, the retrospective functionality and activity linking of many EDR solutions make for quick identification of root cause (s). This can be greatly expedited and simplified through the use of threat intel as other entities likely saw it first and can provide information on how to detect and proactively contain it.

- User Behavior Monitoring – By utilizing a combination of monitoring technologies capable of identifying user-related activity, it is possible to get a reasonable idea of user and account activity. This involves a variety of monitoring capabilities to be successful. Examples include:
  o User Activity Monitoring (UAM)
  o User Behavior Analytics (UBA)

- o User and Entity Behavior Analytics (UEBA)
- o Data Loss Prevention (DLP)
- o Identity and Access Management (IAM)
- o Access logs (for systems, services, applications, and data)
- o Firewall logs

Business logic, privacy, and security rules should be developed, integrated, or otherwise implemented to identify suspicious, prohibited, or malicious activity. Malware threats often appear as suspicious user activity, and solid threat intel can assist in the early detection of such activity.

- Repository/Share/File Activity – By utilizing a combination of user behavior monitoring tools, Data Loss Prevention (DLP), Identify and Access Monitoring (IAM) solutions, and access activity logs, it is possible to detect and track malicious actions. These may be actions perpetrated by attack groups or by malicious applications acting under the legitimate user's context, such as ransomware or wiperware. Keeping these detection signatures relevant is really only possible with automated methods like threat feed integration.

- Configuration Changes and File Integrity Monitoring – Through the use of endpoint software that performs configuration management and file integrity monitoring, it is possible to identify unauthorized activity by attackers or malware making potentially malicious changes. Configuration changes are made both by malicious binaries and scripts. Being able to identify them in an automated manner can speed up initial detection and simplify root-cause analysis. The detected activity can be correlated with threat feeds to identify malware families or variants potentially involved. These can be used to trigger alerts or containment actions accordingly.

- Website/Web Application/Database Activity – All external-facing and sensitive internal websites and corresponding databases should be monitored and validated via WAFs and database activity monitoring software. These systems are ideal for identifying unusual, suspicious, and/or malicious activity as they learn the objects they are monitoring and identify deviations from normal. Known malicious activity that appears successful should be immediately investigated. While it is true that these methods aim toward taking a behavioral whitelisting approach, it is also true that they are always doing a certain amount of learning and do not block activities they cannot convict. Specific, crowd-sourced knowledge regarding the malicious nature of the activity will expedite the conviction process.

- Volumetric Activity – Some malicious activity does not appear overt and can only be detected by identifying an excessive number of connections or activity to a service or protocol. As such, all Internet-facing infrastructure and access methods should implement rules to identify excessive volumetric activity that could be related to DoS, DDoS, scanning activity, or other malicious actions. Considering the evolving nature of volumetric attacks, threat feed integration is essential to identify the many new methods of DoS/DDoS or the known sources involved in ongoing campaigns.

External Communications Containment

The Incident Commander should remind everyone involved not to discuss the customer's case with anyone outside of the investigation and the circle of trust. This containment strategy revolves around performing human containment and limiting unnecessary and harmful communications.

The phrase "Loose lips sink ships" is definitely applicable to the communications strategy surrounding an incident. All communication should be restricted to "need to know" and not openly discussed, even with internal parties.

Moreover, not everyone on the response team needs to understand the full impact and all of the related findings. They should just be provided the information that they need to know for their jobs.

Also, be careful when discussing the details of the incident in public areas, like breakrooms. Curious people may be listening and repeating and/or amplifying what they overhear.

If customers ask for guidance in communication with the public and media, response personnel should advise that it is best to say as little as possible until all the facts are known and then only say what is prudent. This will ensure that outbound communications do not jeopardize the investigation or any type of legal proceedings that may be ongoing by law enforcement.

From whom public announcements are made differs from company to company, but most often, it is a collaboration between public relations representatives, attorneys, and/or senior executives. This group usually obtains technical input on the specific threats, impacts, and status from the Incident Commander or other response team personnel involved. Those not authorized to speak on the company's behalf are advised to say, "No Comment!" Alternatively, they may rehearse a short, pre-written statement approved by the legal and public relations departments. Non-authorized customer personnel should also be notified not to discuss any details pertaining to an incident with anyone under any circumstances.

20 RESPONSE ACTIONS: ARTIFACTS AND EVIDENCE COLLECTION

This chapter will go over the various options and considerations to best prioritize and perform artifacts and evidence collections. Prioritization is based on the customer environment, evidence sources, threat types, and legal and regulatory concerns. Not all evidence can or should be collected in the same way. There are specific considerations and adjustments that need to be made to ensure that evidence is captured appropriately in compliance with best practices and the rules of evidence. This will vary by evidence source and legal matter.

Initial IOCs/Artifacts

Every incident has a starting place/entry point. They usually begin with some type of indicator, whether identified by automated detection or manual analysis. The initial artifacts typically found in the alerts or analysis generally include the following components, some of which are a review of the Malicious Activity Use Cases identified earlier. These will be reviewed briefly with a focus on driving evidence collection rather than on incident use cases and detection:

Network Indicators

These involve one or more of the following: source or destination IP addresses, domain names, URLs, ports, or protocols that trigger security alerts from individual signatures or lists of IOCs. This type of information could be related to any part of the attack lifecycle, including exploitation, malware download, C2, exfiltration, etc. This information will drive evidence collection and analysis activity on either or both ends of the communication, as well as analysis of the traffic stream between the hosts involved in the activity.

Endpoint File System

These involve one or more of the following artifact types: files, scheduled tasks, executables, scripts, processes, services, log entries, registry keys, registry values, or any other endpoint-related artifact. Any or all of these artifacts can trigger security alerts and/or are contained within individual signatures or lists of IOCs involved in the detection or commonly associated with known malware variants or are identified using heuristics and deviation from normal behavior. These evidence artifacts need to be collected from affected systems and searched across other systems in the environment, which will expand the scope as relevant. However, the data in the alerts is just a starting place. Usually, there are additional artifacts involved, such as files, processes, services, and/or registry entries.

This is particularly true with modern polymorphic and/or scripted malware, which commonly modifies many aspects of itself from system to system in order to avoid detection. This polymorphism can be used against itself by utilizing EDR capabilities. EDR can identify unique processes, drivers, or targeted file types that should be consistent, or at least non-unique, across the organization. As an example, identifying a unique process on a suspect system within a large population of workstations is highly suspicious, and it should be considered a target of the investigation.

Moreover, EDR agents are the ideal tool for rapidly collecting file system evidence from endpoints, as they can be integrated with detections and automagically be triggered to pull the content at the time of detection. Endpoint forensic tools are also capable of collecting file system artifacts. However, the process is usually fully or mostly manual, even if enterprise forensic tools utilizing agents are involved.

Memory and Volatile Metadata Indicators

Alerts may contain common memory artifacts that render systems or applications within the scope of the investigation. Performing collection and analysis includes the identification of process injection, process hollowing, malicious scripts, or other fileless memory-based anomalies. If/when they are identified, the affected systems are also in scope of investigation, unless known false positives are involved.

The data contained on affected systems is considered at risk and likely exposed, considering the level of permissions required for a successful attack. The access level required to collect memory involves System or Admin level permissions. As such, the system(s) or device(s) involved are considered fully compromised if the activity cannot be proven to be benign.

Some indicators are more prone to false positives than others. Process hollowing is probably never a false positive. Alternatively, process injection very likely would be if that was the sole indicator. The latter happens all the time with a wide variety of software and utilities.

Collecting this evidence is the realm of EDR and endpoint forensic tools. As with the other endpoint-related use cases, EDR is preferred as it can be easily integrated and configured to pull content upon detection of an alert. Regardless of the tool used, it must be collected quickly in order to be preserved.

WMI Indicators
Alerts may reference malicious WMI classes, subscriptions, or backdoors. These can be persistent, asynchronous, and/or fileless in nature. Using WMI is an incredibly powerful and sneaky way to hide robust malware applications.

Modern Windows versions enable the creation of fully functional, fileless applications using WMI, including custom WMI classes. As with anything, this feature can be used for benign or malevolent intent. While these should be considered immediately within the scope of the investigation when found, this is another nascent space in the security realm that is hard to detect and easy to circumvent detections. They may go undetected.

Collecting WMI indicators involves capturing persistent WMI artifacts, as well as volatile artifacts that exist only in memory. As such, this requires an EDR tool capable of collecting file system artifacts and running PowerShell commands or WMI queries to pull the required content.

Collection Considerations
The following are considerations respective to evidence source types. Detections using any of these are significantly augmented if integrated with threat feeds to provide scalable identification of evolving threats. These should also be integrated between technology types to provide cross-platform detections and relevant artifact collection:

- SIEMs should collect all relevant logs from key devices, systems, and applications. All such content should be tied into a central SIEM and then aggregated, correlated, and archived for the retention requirements per regulatory requirements and business needs. If indicators, artifacts, or other evidence are found on the SIEM, it should be exported and archived off the SIEM for permanent storage or storage in alignment with evidence retention requirements.

- Network indicators are typically gathered from network malware analysis solutions, next-generation firewalls, and IPSs. Detection ability is augmented through implementing SSL/TLS decryption, deep protocol inspection, and application awareness to identify suspicious script or application activity.
- Endpoint indicators are typically gathered from endpoint security capabilities, such as anti-malware, endpoint forensic, and EDR (cloud-based or on-prem) solutions that come in various varieties. These are most powerful if they are able to compare all endpoints at once and correlate the respective activities to detect anomalies in artifacts or behavior across all of them.
- The data collection time frame is a key consideration, regardless of the data source. It is critical to establish a baseline of activity and collect data to determine the onset of malicious activity and identify any unauthorized actions or anomalies. It is made significantly easier through a review of retrospective endpoint and network monitoring capabilities and aggregated interfaces that enable the visualization of data across large data sets. Depending upon the threat type, the window required to establish a "normal" baseline prior to an incident may vary. However, activity from the beginning of the baseline window through either 1) the current date/time or 2) the date/time of containment should be captured, at minimum. Oftentimes, the window of evidence capture is extended for a reasonable time after the incident. This is done to validate that eradication was successfully completed and that there are no continuing indicators of malicious activity.

Prioritizing Evidence Collection

Prioritizing response, containment, and evidence collection efforts is a highly contextual judgment call that varies from one organization to another. Deviations are based on their business operations, customer impact, regulatory needs, and data sensitivity. For all response efforts, there should be simultaneous workstreams of containment and collecting evidence that might otherwise be lost if the network connection is severed while in the process of containing threats to minimize the impact.

If evidence is unavailable in the response process, it might not be possible to meet evidence requirements to prove the lack of compromise or limitations of impact.

○ **Later**
○ **Tomorrow**
○ **Today**
● **NOW**

A lack of evidence that something did not happen is not proof it did not occur. It is roughly equivalent to stipulating it may have happened, but the investigation was indeterminant. Thus, there may be a need to do an over-disclosure just to be on the safe side of regulatory requirements. It is a regulatory judgment call.

This is painful, as it would require the company to disclose the potential impact of a breach for which there is no evidence that it actually happened. There just isn't sufficient evidence to prove that it didn't happen or to limit the scope of disclosure based on empirical data observed from exfiltration activity. As such, the evidence is your friend either way.

Sometimes, a choice must be made between evidence collection/preservation and rapid containment. This choice is highly contextual, but in general, the need to contain an active or spreading threat supersedes that of gathering host or log-based evidence. This is caused by the fact that collecting evidence sometimes may take too long and place other systems, accounts, data, and/or individuals at risk. Oftentimes, all there is time for is to capture network traffic, volatile data, and perhaps memory. These evidence source types are the most volatile of evidence artifacts that will definitely be impacted by severing network connectivity.

However, memory has become increasingly large and can take too long to collect over the network. This leads to a second decision regarding dumping the memory locally for quick preservation, which might overwrite deleted data on the drive. The decision of whether to do this and where to dump the data will depend upon the circumstances. Determining factors that drive evidence collection and storage include network speed, available system storage, threat type, etc.

Other evidence artifacts (such as file system, registry, or other system or storage-related artifacts) can typically be collected following containment, with little to no risk of loss. While it is true that malware can be configured to wipe the system or remove artifacts if disconnected from the network, examples of malware this sophisticated are very rare, and if they exist, they are likely state-sponsored.

Order of Evidence Collection/Preservation

There are two main classes of evidence: 1) Live data and 2) Static data. Live data is active, dynamic artifacts and content that will be lost if not captured within a short period of time or immediately. This loss can occur due to the transient nature of live data and the fact that the activity and artifact(s) are not captured, collected, or stored.

It is commonly understood that memory, network traffic, or other dynamic content are live data, but logs can be considered such, as well. Depending upon the log storage and retention capabilities (or lack thereof), logs can potentially be just as volatile and could be considered either live or static data. They might overwrite within mere seconds and spoliated unless offloaded to a SIEM.

Logs that do not have adequate storage or are not offloaded onto a SIEM may overwrite themselves before they can be collected (if not immediately), and they leave no more trace than network traffic. As such, they are discussed under the "Live Data section of evidence collection and preservation.

Live Data

In order to prevent evidence loss or alteration, live data is best captured before containment. The act of performing containment blocks network connections and may kill processes related to malicious activity. This can result in the cascading loss of evidence for all associated volatile artifacts.

As such, continuous and/or automated collection of live data is helpful and sometimes essential in order to ensure live data is captured without slowing down incident containment processes. Following is the prioritized order in which live evidence should be collected to best preserve evidence and avoid loss or alteration of artifacts and content:

1. Network packet captures – The most volatile of all evidence is network traffic, which can be make-or-break information when determining the actual exposure. The best way to collect network traffic is to ensure that it is always collected and preserved for a period of time. This can be done in the form of a rolling collection that spans a pre-determined window of time that facilitates after-the-fact detection and analysis capabilities. It is not always possible to do this, however. At the very least, network traffic should be collected at the first detection of malicious activity at key target areas (ingress/egress, internal-to-internal, VPN/RAS, etc.). It should be collected for the entire incident timeframe and a reasonable period before and afterward to obtain a baseline and validate that malicious activity is no longer occurring.

2. Preserve all logs – Logs can shortcut the investigative process by revealing who did what and when. However, they are surprisingly volatile and may disappear quickly under default settings if not properly configured or captured, offloaded, and preserved. All security-relevant log types should be configured to forward logs to a central SIEM that can collect, aggregate, and correlate all of the logs from every source and enable storage and searching for the entire retention period. This will facilitate searching, use case development, and alerting in order to support information technology, security, or business process needs. Any log not being offloaded is at risk of being overwritten, manipulated, missed, or otherwise lost and ignored.

3. Volatile metadata – The term volatile metadata is used to describe information in memory related to processes, libraries, drivers, connections, live registry, and the respective details and interconnectivity, which changes from moment to moment. If enterprise forensic or EDR capabilities only have the ability to take snapshots for a moment in time, they should capture the volatile data at the time of alert in order to capture the most relevant information. Ideally, however, EDR capabilities should record volatile metadata activity and reconstruct all activity for review during the evidence retention period.

4. Full memory and page file – The full memory dump includes the metadata and the respective content stored in memory at the moment of collection, which is useful for finding decrypted or decoded information and hidden processes. This should be captured at the time of the alert as well as at subsequent trigger points as driven by unauthorized/malicious activity, such as C2, exfiltration, lateral movement, etc.

Note: This is the ideal place for containment if host isolation is available, which limits affected system connectivity to block network connections other than those permitted to or from investigative systems or other permitted security tools (E.g., EDR, DLP, enterprise forensics, vulnerability assessment, configuration management, policy enforcement, etc.).

Static Data

The convenient thing about static data is that it is unlikely to change as a result of containment. It can thus wait until after containment actions have been performed.

Having said that, however, for pragmatic reasons when performing an investigation, it is extremely helpful to have at least a targeted, minimal collection of file system artifacts to facilitate the investigation needs.

Volatile data will only answer so many questions, and each operating system and investigation type has a certain variety of file system artifacts that are needed to determine if and how a system has been compromised. If these are not collected prior to containment, the evidence collection process (which often consists of full-drive forensic imaging) can significantly lag and slow down the investigation. As with live data, these targeted file system artifacts can be automatically collected at the time of the alert using EDR tools with the right SIEM integration and evidence-collection policy.

5. Targeted files, registry locations, or other artifacts – Each operating system and specific threat type has corresponding system artifacts that are helpful to investigators in understanding what transpired. These vary by circumstance, but they could expedite the investigation if collected before the system is contained.

**Note: This is the ideal place for containment if host isolation is NOT available.*

6. Full file system artifacts/disk images – Making disk images and doing a full forensic collection is usually performed offline but can also be performed online if host isolation is enabled.
7. Databases, repositories, and structured data files – These are artifacts stored on the file

system or in various repositories, which need to be converted, imported, and parsed.

Evidence collection for live and static data will be covered in greater depth in the following sections. Each evidence source type will be addressed and discussed individually.

Network Packet Captures

Once network traffic is sent, it is gone unless there is a fragment of it in memory or it is being recorded via some type of network traffic recording system/device. The only artifacts that might remain would be firewall or IPS logs, primarily consisting of socket information and not data. Some companies store NetFlow information, which is not much better than metadata. It is essentially network traffic metadata + metrics.

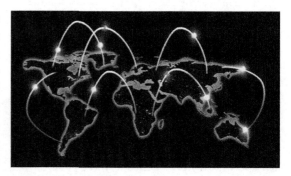

A rolling window of network ingress/egress traffic should be collected at all times and retained for a reasonable period of time, but this is less common than it should be. Many organizations only implement full packet captures for the purposes of troubleshooting or when an incident is in progress. However, they should ideally be captured and available for a year. This will provide the response team with a retrospective window to investigate and determine attacker activity, IOCs, and potential impact.

At the very least, when an incident is suspected, all ingress/egress traffic from all POPs should be collected and preserved until the incident is over. This could turn into many, many terabytes of PCAPs. Adequate considerations must be made to facilitate successful collection and storage from all locations, interface types, throughput speeds, and traffic volumes.

It is critical to collect the traffic from an un-NATed location and for outbound traffic SSL/TLS decryption to be implemented ahead of time. The best place to do this is on perimeter firewalls with inline SSL/TLS decryption and decrypted traffic-hand-off capabilities. This will facilitate decrypted traffic capture, native analysis, and expanded analysis.

If this does not happen, the traffic is mostly useless. It will consist primarily of encrypted data from unknown sources. Without decryption, all that will be discernable from it is the external socket information (IP Addresses and ports) and the volume of traffic sent or received.

A note about right-sizing and proper planning of traffic decryption is that it requires an appliance that has a capacity about 4x greater than the peak flow, as the act of decrypting SSL/TLS puts a heavy load on the system. For example, if the customer has 10GB ingress/egress pipes, they need a 40GB device to handle the load if full SSL/TLS decryption is enabled.

Also, note that implementing traffic decryption requires an endpoint management system to deploy the decryption certificate of the decryption device (used for man-in-the-middle). It will need to be installed in the certificate management storage location of all endpoints that will use the decryption service. If not, the clients affected by the decryption will receive an error, and the application or service may break.

Preserve All Logs

Logs are often surprisingly volatile. If they are left in default configuration within large organizations, they may only last for seconds before overwriting. Active Directory logs in large environments with default configurations are notorious for this.

This means that IT and Security teams need to make sure that all logs from any source are being preserved. This includes systems, devices, applications, services, databases, etc. The best thing about this task is that it can easily be farmed out to all of the respective subject matter experts (SMEs) with little to no impact on the responders' resources. Essentially, the responders can define and guide the SMEs, which separate and go their own ways to make the changes as necessary.

However, it usually must be clarified with the action owners that "all logs" means ALL LOGS, without exception. It is not completely possible to determine which logs will be needed from the outset of the response process to identify or clarify malicious activity. Usually, a combination of logs from disparate resources is required, depending upon the specific threats involved and the resources affected. It is much better to over-collect logs and not need them than to need them for an unforeseen aspect of a case and not have them available.

Moreover, it is not just enough to capture and retain logs. The logs themselves need to collect the right content. By default, in most cases, only certain failure events are logged, but success events are not.

As such, if an attacker tried to logon 100,000,000 times and failed, but the next attempt was successful, the logs would only show the 100M failed attempts. They would be blind to successful access. This makes it difficult to identify if attackers were actually successful or not in their attempts. A much deeper forensic analysis is required, but it does not guarantee results.

The ideal method for doing log collection and preservation is to push all logs to a central location that can correlate and facilitate queries across all data sources (such as a SIEM). The logs must be kept available for the entire retention period and capture the entire event window. It is ideal if all this is set up ahead of time, prior to the incident. It will broaden the window of searchability and enable the investigative team to gather log evidence prior to and during the time of exploitation across all relevant data sources.

Volatile Metadata

Name	PID	Status	User name	CPU	Memory (p...	Command line
svchost.exe	15320	Running	Colby	00	576 K	C:\Users\Colby\AppData\Local\Microsoft\Network\svchost.exe
svchost.exe	21616	Running	SYSTEM	00	1,324 K	C:\WINDOWS\system32\svchost.exe -k netsvcs -p -s wlidsvc
svchost.exe	9684	Running	SYSTEM	00	1,284 K	C:\WINDOWS\system32\svchost.exe -k SDRSVC
svchost.exe	18128	Running	SYSTEM	00	2,192 K	
svchost.exe	720	Running	SYSTEM	00	504 K	c:\windows\system32\svchost.exe -k dcomlaunch -p -s PlugPlay
svchost.exe	1028	Running	SYSTEM	00	14,028 K	C:\WINDOWS\system32\svchost.exe -k DcomLaunch -p
svchost.exe	1136	Running	NETWORK...	00	9,392 K	c:\windows\system32\svchost.exe -k rpcss -p
svchost.exe	1188	Running	SYSTEM	00	2,120 K	c:\windows\system32\svchost.exe -k dcomlaunch -p -s LSM
svchost.exe	1432	Running	SYSTEM	00	1,272 K	c:\windows\system32\svchost.exe -k localsystemnetworkrestricted -...
svchost.exe	1440	Running	LOCAL SE...	00	1,300 K	c:\windows\system32\svchost.exe -k localservicenetworkrestricted -...
svchost.exe	1520	Running	LOCAL SE...	00	13,236 K	c:\windows\system32\svchost.exe -k localservicenetworkrestricted -...
svchost.exe	1640	Running	LOCAL SE...	00	7,240 K	c:\windows\system32\svchost.exe -k localservice -p -s nsi
svchost.exe	1716	Running	LOCAL SE...	00	1,784 K	C:\WINDOWS\system32\svchost.exe -k LocalService -p
svchost.exe	1752	Running	LOCAL SE...	00	1,344 K	c:\windows\system32\svchost.exe -k localservicenetworkrestricted -...
svchost.exe	1872	Running	NETWORK...	00	3,608 K	c:\windows\system32\svchost.exe -k networkservice -p -s NlaSvc
svchost.exe	1880	Running	SYSTEM	00	5,640 K	c:\windows\system32\svchost.exe -k netsvcs -p -s Schedule
svchost.exe	1984	Running	LOCAL SE...	00	2,856 K	c:\windows\system32\svchost.exe -k localservice -p -s netprofm

For most incident response investigations on endpoints, volatile data is the primary evidence analyzed. It is fast, detail-rich, and contains most of the data needed for response-related analysis unless it has been manipulated by malware evasion techniques.

The term volatile metadata is used to describe either the point-in-time snapshot of information or the continuously collected timeline of metadata in memory. It will contain details related to processes, libraries, drivers, network connections, live registry keys/values, open files, and the respective details and interconnectivity, which changes from moment to moment. Volatile metadata is the quickest way to put together the story of what is happening at the time or during the window of collection. This can be used to definitively reveal specifically what transpired during the window of compromise and to understand the activity on a particular machine or between multiple machines.

While volatile metadata is good when collected at the time of an incident, there is still a lot of data lost unless it is continually collected. It is most valuable if it starts before an incident and captures all of the activity throughout the incident lifecycle. The only way to affirmatively identify what happened during an incident from exploit to exfiltration is to record the activity of every process, script, file read/write, registry read/write, WMI modification, and network connection and then display that data on a retrospective timeline. This will tell the story of what happened in short order and can be used to identify and/or block similar activity based on behavior and IOCs.

The network connections portion of the volatile metadata is particularly important and distinct as it will identify all network traffic. This also includes internal traffic of all possible types involving endpoints with EDR agents.

- Workstations to workstations
- Workstations to servers and repositories
- Servers to workstations

It will identify malicious traffic that could be spreading malware or making destructive changes (ransomware/wiperware) across workstations, servers, file shares, repositories, devices, etc. Continuous monitoring solutions that collect volatile metadata and create a retrospective timeline are often the only way to identify the activity and details involving lateral movement inside the organization.

Analyzing volatile metadata can be done orders of magnitude faster than using the conventional forensic analysis approach, especially since it does not have to wait until systems are contained and acquired. It has become the only way to keep up with emergent threats.

The downside of volatile metadata snapshots and retrospective timelines is that they can sometimes be manipulated using various memory tampering and hiding techniques. If relied upon solely, they can create a false understanding of the current state of activity if the hiding techniques are successful.

Moreover, volatile metadata completely lacks content and, therefore, also lacks context. This is another reason for collecting other evidence. This includes the support for continuously capturing volatile metadata to inform retrospective capabilities, as well as the collection and analysis of full memory dumps and full-disk acquisitions. Moreover, having continuously collected evidence avoids the potential for evidence loss created by containment activity.

Full Memory and Page File

Full memory captures, including the pagefile, are the big brother of volatile metadata. In addition to the metadata, it contains the respective content stored in memory at the moment of collection. This helps provide context to the metadata that can be used for prioritization.

For the sake of clarity, the memory dump provides pointers and arrays of data but very little substantive content. The pagefile contains the actual content and substantive data that is being pointed to. Therefore, it has additional content and context.

The full content of memory and pagefile is useful for finding decrypted or decoded information (such as encryption keys, passwords, scripts, chats, files, or other data) and is the best way to identify hidden processes or artifacts that are manipulated by malware. This may be the only place where certain types of data reside and could be found during an investigation in any reasonable period of time.

A good data/content example of this is encrypted chat communications that do not log conversations to disk and cannot be decrypted on the wire. The full text of the conversations and files transferred may be available to be carved out of memory with the correct parsing methodology.

A good malware example of memory being the only place to identify artifacts includes injected or hollowed processes and/or script-based activity that does not leave evidence on the file system. It also speeds up cryptography, credential harvesting, and decoding efforts by making them unnecessary. Everything is first decrypted or decoded in memory prior to use or execution. Rather than having to use exhaustive methods to decrypt or decode content or artifacts, it is available for the taking in its clear-text state in memory.

This may be a good time to pull malware samples out of memory, particularly if they are injected into other processes, libraries, or drivers. These samples should be provided to the malware analysis team (whether internal or contracted) for reverse engineering, identification of capabilities, and enumeration of IOCs.

Even if the investigator does not have a parser capable of harvesting the sought-after content or the knowledge of where to find it, these details can be worked out later. It is critical to capture this content prior to alterations to or containment of the system in order for it to provide maximum value. If it is collected post-containment, data related to active network connections and associated processes may be lost.

The challenge with collecting this evidence is that memory and the accompanying pagefile have become significantly larger in size, and it can take considerable time to collect. Typical systems encountered during investigations have between 4GB and 32GB of RAM for workstations, 16GB to 128GB RAM for servers, and some have vastly more. The respective pagefiles vary between 1.5x and 4x the size of RAM. This could mean a lot of data on current, high-capacity systems. There are two primary methods to collect this data, all of which have advantages and drawbacks that may influence the course of the investigation:

- If memory is collected over the wire to a forensic workstation, it is very slow. Depending upon network conditions and infrastructure, it could collect 4 and 16 GB per hour with all of the overhead involved, notwithstanding 100MB/S data transfer speeds on the wire. The upside to network collection is that it provides minimal impact on the endpoint and mitigates the risk of overwriting potential deleted evidence on the local drive.

- If memory is collected by creating an evidence file locally, it can be up to 5 times faster, depending upon storage media type and I/O speeds. However, there is a significant risk of overwriting deleted/unallocated evidence on the local file system.

Notwithstanding the large artifact sizes, memory only contains limited substantive data. It typically includes only recently accessed or proactively loaded information. At some point, file system artifacts are needed to flesh out the missing details and better inform the investigation.

Targeted Files, Registry Locations, or other Artifacts

Considering that limited data is stored in memory and a full-disk acquisition takes far too long, a common alternative is to gather the live evidence, as well as limited static evidence, required to establish the facts of an incident. This is a middle ground that collects minimal required evidence to provide the most likely content to facilitate an investigation without running an overt risk of handicapping it. It also avoids the risk of over-collecting content that can probably wait.

Each threat type and affected operating system or application has a certain limited subset of related artifacts that are key to establishing root cause(s), exploit method(s), and impact. These vary by circumstance but could expedite the investigation if collected before the system is contained.

Most of this data will remain unchanged post-containment unless there is some sort of logic that deletes artifacts when the network connection is severed. These types of malware functions exist, but they are not commonly seen and are more likely associated with nation-state activity than commoditized cyber threats. Some common, non-inclusive examples of targeted forensic artifacts include the following, which manifest differently on each operating system type:

Account/Group/Role Configuration

Enumerate all accounts, groups, and roles and their respective configurations on the system(s). Collect the SAM hive (WINDOWS\system32\config\SAM) and individual NTUser.dat files for each user profile (Documents and Settings\User Profile\NTUSER.DAT). The purpose of this is to allow the responders to identify unauthorized accounts, group memberships, and/or other changes made by the attackers to elevate privileges or create backdoor accounts.

File System Catalog ($MFT, FAT, Inode Table, etc.)

Capture the entire file system catalog to obtain a listing of files, folders, metadata, and a listing of deleted content. There will be a separate file system catalog for each disk partition. As such, all catalogs for each partition to be analyzed will need to be gathered.

File System Timeline (Recently Created, Written, or Deleted)

Create a file system timeline to identify changes from attacker activity and malware installation. This includes the enumeration of all recently created or written files, especially binaries, scripts, and/or malware-related artifacts.

These details will inform targeted collections. The analysis will utilize a combination of the file system catalog and folder entries, depending on the file system. In constructing this, it will also be key to identify any files/folders that were deleted either from the directory catalog, Recycle bin, and/or folder records.

Registry changes should also be enumerated and placed in the timeline. However, the date/time stamps are limited only to providing "Last Written" entries for Registry Keys. The individual values themselves have no timestamps, and there is no differentiation as to whether the key that was "Last Written" was created or modified. The creation or modification of the key itself or the creation, modification, or deletion of any value within the key will update the "Last Written" timestamp on the key.

Targeted MRU History

Enumerate recent activity across desired "most recently used" (MRU) locations. These may be used to identify the most recently used sites, files, applications, searches, mapped drives, printers, etc. There are a large variety of MRU locations that will need to be selected and targeted for collection, as appropriate. Following is a common, non-comprehensive list:

- LastVisitedMRU entry is created/updated when a new entry is added to the OpenSaveMRU key
  HKCU\Software\Microsoft\Windows\CurrentVersion\Explorer\ComDlg32\LastVisitedMRU

- Recent opened Programs/Files/URLs
  HKCU\Software\Microsoft\Windows\CurrentVersion\Explorer\ComDlg32\OpenSaveMRU

- Recent URLs
  HKCU\Software\Microsoft\Internet Explorer\TypedURLs

- List of files recently opened directly from Windows Explorer
  HKCU\Software\Microsoft\Windows\CurrentVersion\Explorer\RecentDocs

- List of entries executed using the Start>Run command
  HKCU\Software\Microsoft\Windows\CurrentVersion\Explorer\RunMRU
  HKCU\Software\Microsoft\Windows\CurrentVersion\Explorer\RecentDocs
  HKCU\Software\Microsoft\Windows\CurrentVersion\Explorer\ComDlg32\OpenSaveMRU

- Windows Search (has up to 4 subkeys)
  HKCU\Software\Microsoft\Search Assistant\ACMru
  Notable subkeys:
      5001: A list of terms used for the Internet Search Assistant
      5603: A list of terms used for the "Windows Files and Folders" search function
      5604: A list of terms used in the "Word or Phrase in a File" search function
5647: A list of terms used in the "Computers or People" search function

Clearing MRU History

Using the native Windows "Recent Opened Documents" Clear List feature that is accessible via the Control Panel → Taskbar and Start Menu, an attacker can remove the following registry keys and their respective subkeys:

    HKCU\Software\Microsoft\Windows\CurrentVersion\Explorer\RecentDocs
    HKCU\Software\Microsoft\Windows\CurrentVersion\Explorer\RunMRU
    HKCU\Software\Microsoft\Internet Explorer\TypedURLs
    HKCU\Software\Microsoft\Windows\CurrentVersion\Explorer\ComDlg32\OpenSaveMRU
    HKCU\Software\Microsoft\Windows\CurrentVersion\Explorer\ComDlg32\LastVisitedMRU
    HKCU\Software\Microsoft\Windows\CurrentVersion\Explorer\UserAssist

Program Execution and Compatibility Settings

Collect application compatibility settings and execution history. Identify any tampering with application debugging and execution settings.

This includes command-shell execution requirements, shimming the execution of other programs or scripts first, and/or specifying custom parameters that change the functions at execution.

- Debugging – Map to alternate debugger executable
  HKLM\SOFTWARE\Microsoft\Windows NT\CurrentVersion\Image File Execution Options

- File extensions – Instructions for executing files (.exe, .bat, .com):
  HKCR\exe\fileshell\opencommand
  HKEY_CLASSES_ROOT\batfile\shell\open\command
  HKEY_CLASSES_ROOT\comfile\shell\open\command

- Shimcache (AKA AppCompatCache) – Tracks process metadata and can identify unknown or deleted applications or modifications to the way applications function and potential malware persistence mechanisms.
  HKLM\SYSTEM\CurrentControlSet\Control\SessionManager\AppCompatCache\AppCompatCache

- Windows installer shims
  %WINDIR%\AppPatch\sysmain.sdb
  HKLM\Software\microsoft\windows nt\currentversion\appcompatflags\installedsdb

- Custom shims
  %WINDIR%\AppPatch\custom & %WINDIR%\AppPatch\AppPatch64\Custom
  HKLM\Software\Microsoft\Windows NT\CurrentVersion\AppCompatFlags\Custom

- Amchache – Records the recent processes executed and respective metadata
  C:\Windows\AppCompat\Programs\Amcache.hve

- Browser Helper Objects (BHO) – subkeys under BHO tell the IE browser to load designated DLLs
  HKLM\SOFTWARE\Microsoft\Windows\CurrentVersion\Explorer\Browser Helper Objects

- AppInit_DLLs - Lists the DLLs to be loaded by the User32.dll
  HKLM\SOFTWARE\Microsoft\Windows NT\CurrentVersion\Windows\AppInit_DLLs

Prefetch Files

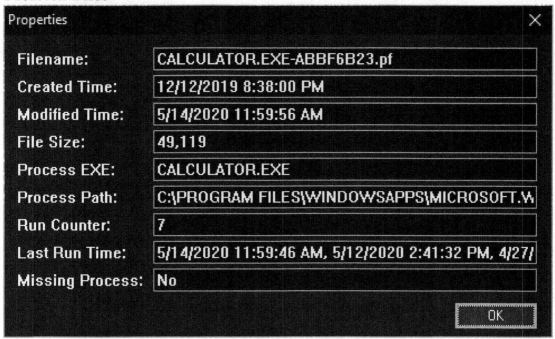

Enumerate all prefetch files to identify application execution history, suspicious/malicious files executed, and the respective prefetch settings for malicious files. These can provide an indication of the installation and execution history impact on the system. A full list of forensic artifacts that prefetch files provide is as follows:

- Executable Name
- Executable Path
- File MAC Times
- Hash
- File Size
- Prefetch File Version
- Run Count
- Last Run Time
- Previous 7 Run Times
- Volume information
- Full paths of files and directories used by the application

Prefetch File Location:
%SYSTEMROOT%\Prefetch → Typically: C:\Windows\Prefetch

Prefetch Settings:
HKLM\SYSTEM\CurrentControlSet\Control\Session Manager\Memory Management\PrefetchParameters

Internet Browser History

Collect browser history, databases, and download directories from all browsers and enumerate websites visited, scripts executed, bookmarks/favorites, and files downloaded or opened. Evidence from web browsers can provide information about what the user account or malware that is operating under the context of the user account accessed on the Internet and locally on the file system or network shares. Typical content (which varies by web browser) includes the following:

- History (Internet, local file system, and network shares)
- Cache content (text and images)
- Cookies
- Typed URLs
- Sessions
- Most visited sites and site visit counter
- Captured screenshots
- Financial information
- Form values (Searches, Autofill cached)
- Accounts & passwords (Autofill cached)
- Downloaded files (Downloads)
- Favorites/bookmarks

Network Settings

Enumerate all network interfaces, settings, and configured routes to identify any unauthorized interfaces or configurations that could be used to facilitate suspicious activity, network traffic manipulation, or surreptitious access. Following are some Windows examples of data to be collected:

- Ipconfig /all
- Route print
- All files in C:\Windows\System32\drivers\etc\

Temporary/AppData File Locations

Enumerate non-privileged user-writable locations and identify any files, binaries, or scripts downloaded to Temp, AppData, or other non-privileged writable and executable locations for each user profile or central to the operating system itself. Each operating system will have separate considerations and examples of these types of public subdirectory locations for which there will need to be targeted collections performed.

WMI or other Fileless Application Configuration

Identify fileless programs added to the system, such as custom WMI classes and/or subscriptions utilized by Windows.

- Collect persistent WMI class/subscription locations: C:\Windows\System32\wbem
- Enumerate/collect loaded classes/objects: Get-WmiObject –List

- Enumerate/collect permanent WMI event subscriptions:
  https://gallery.technet.microsoft.com/scriptcenter/List-all-WMI-Permanent-73e04ab4

Installed Apps, Autoruns, Services, DLLs, and Scheduled Tasks

Enumerate and collect information about any programs or services that run on startup or login, which may identify malicious or unauthorized applications. There are a variety of manual ways to do this, and some forensic tools have built-in capabilities, but the Sysinternals Autoruns tool is arguably one of the best maintained and freely available tools that can be used to pull the data. It works locally on live systems or on evidence files from systems.

- Installed programs listed in Control Panel>Add/Remove Programs
  HKLM\SOFTWARE\Microsoft\Windows\CurrentVersion\Uninstall

- Autorun – Run on every system startup
  HKLM\SOFTWARE\Microsoft\Windows\CurrentVersion\Run
  HKLM\Software\Microsoft\Windows\CurrentVersion\Policies\Explorer\Run

- RunOnce and RunOnceEx (only Win98/Me) – Run only once on next startup
  HKLM\Software\Microsoft\Windows\CurrentVersion\RunOnce
  HKLM\Software\Microsoft\Windows\CurrentVersion\RunOnceEx
  HKCU\Software\Microsoft\Windows\CurrentVersion\RunOnce
  HKCU\Software\Microsoft\Windows\CurrentVersion\RunOnceEx

- Command Processor Autorun – Executes each time cmd.exe is run
  HKLM\SOFTWARE\Microsoft\Command Processor
  HKCU\Software\Microsoft\Command Processor

- RunServices and RunServicesOnce
  HKLM\SOFTWARE\Microsoft\Windows\CurrentVersion\Run\Services
  HKCU\SOFTWARE\Microsoft\Windows\CurrentVersion\Run\Services
  HKLM\SOFTWARE\Microsoft\Windows\CurrentVersion\Run\ServicesOnce
  HKCU\SOFTWARE\Microsoft\Windows\CurrentVersion\Run\ServicesOnce

- Services – Service control information and executable path
  HKLM\SYSTEM\CurrentControlSet\Services
  HKLM\Software\Microsoft\Windows\CurrentVersion\Run\Services\Once
  HKLM\Software\Microsoft\Windows\CurrentVersion\Run\Services

- Winlogon – Executes scripts upon logon
  HKLM\SOFTWARE\Microsoft\Windows NT\CurrentVersion\Winlogon

- Winlogon Notify – Handles Secure Attention Sequence (SAS) (Ctrl+Alt+Del); can be edited to launch when SAS occurs
  HKLM\SOFTWARE\Microsoft\Windows NT\CurrentVersion\Winlogon\Notify

- Winlogon Shell – Winlogon pointer to launch Explorer.exe
  HKLM\SOFTWARE\Microsoft\Windows NT\CurrentVersion\Winlogon\Shell

- Startup Keys – Launches shortcuts, scripts, and executables during logon/reboot
  HKCU\Software\Microsoft\Windows\CurrentVersion\Explorer\User Shell Folders
  HKCU\Software\Microsoft\Windows\CurrentVersion\Explorer\Shell Folders
  HKLM\SOFTWARE\Microsoft\Windows\CurrentVersion\Explorer\Shell Folders
  HKLM\SOFTWARE\Microsoft\Windows\CurrentVersion\Explorer\User Shell Folders

- Boot Key – Points to the location under WinLogon
  HKLM\SOFTWARE\Microsoft\Windows NT\CurrentVersion\IniFileMapping\system.ini\boot

- Boot Execute Key – smss.exe calls configuration subsystems and opens or launches objects at the following locations
  HKLM\SYSTEM\CurrentControlSet\Control\hivelist
  HKLM\SYSTEM\CurrentControlSet \Control\Session Manager

- File Association – Used to specify the action when a certain type of file is opened
  HKEY_LOCAL_MACHINE\Software\Classes
  HKEY_CLASSES_ROOT

- DLL Search Order Hijacking – OS looks for DLLs in the following search order:
  Loaded in memory
  Listed in HKLM\SYSTEM\CurrentControlSet\Control\Session Manager\KnownDLLs
  The directory from where the application was launched
  System Directory (WindowsSystem32)
  Windows Directory
  Current Working Directory
  Directories defined in the PATH variable

- Shortcut Hijacking – Manipulate the shortcut icons "Target: attribute to launch the normal application, as well as force the download of malicious content from another site.

- Scheduled Tasks – Schedule the execution of malicious scripts or applications on a recurring basis:
  HKLM\SOFTWARE\Microsoft\Windows NT\CurrentVersion\Schedule\TaskCache\Tree

- Full List of Locations – Use Autoruns tool
  https://docs.microsoft.com/en-us/sysinternals/downloads/autoruns

Targeted Event Logs

Collect key event logs from systems, devices, and/or applications directly involved in or having visibility into security incidents. Ideally, these should be collected and correlated into a SIEM. But, it is rare that all log sources are. It is common to collect at least some of them from native log sources.

Link Files

Collect link (.lnk) files to support enumeration of recently accessed files, programs, removable drives, or shares, and that may provide quick evidence of previous activity. Link files are shortcut files that link to an application or file. They can be found anywhere on the file system and end with the .lnk extension. They contain the following information:

- The original path of the file
- MAC times of the linked file and the .lnk file, showing both access and source file information
- Volume and system information where the LNK file is stored.
    - Volume name
    - Serial number
    - NetBIOS name
    - MAC address of the host where the linked file is stored
- Network details for a network share or remote computer
- File size of a linked file

They are created when a user opens a local or remote file. They can be created manually by users or automatically by Windows.

They reveal access to files, documents, applications, etc. It is particularly notable if .lnk files are identified that point to artifacts that don't exist. This will identify artifacts potentially deleted by the attacker or malware.

USB, Mounted, and Mapped Device History

Enumerate all removable devices inserted into the system and their respective details. This can be found in the registry location:

- A list of mounted devices
  HKLM\SYSTEM\MountedDevices
  HKCU\Software\Microsoft\Windows\CurrentVersion\Explorer\MountPoints2\CPCVolume
- The history of mapped network drives
  HKCU\Software\Microsoft\Windows\CurrentVersion\Explorer\Map Network Drive MRU
  HKCU\Software\Microsoft\Windows\Current\VersionExplorer\MountPoints2
- USB Storage and external memory cards
  Registry location
    HKLM\SYSTEM\CurrentControlSet\Enum\USBSTOR
  PowerShell command
    Get-ItemProperty -Path HKLM:\SYSTEM\CurrentControlSet\Enum\USBSTOR** | Select *
  Logfiles also contain information about USB devices
    - %systemdrive%\Windows\setupapi.log – Windows XP/2000/2003
    - %systemdrive%\Windows\inf\setupAPI.*.log – Windows Vista/7/8/10

- setupAPI.dev.log – Device and driver installations
- setupAPI.app.log – Application installations
- Windows Pagefile
HKLM\SYSTEM\CurrentControlSet\Control\Session Manager\Memory Management

Out of this targeted collection and analysis, malware and/or script samples may be identified and made available for analysis. These samples should be provided to the malware analysis team (internal or contracted) for analysis to identify the capabilities and identify the IOCs.

Ideal Place for Containment

In a perfect world, this is the ideal place for containment. The team now has enough substantive evidence to investigate the attack, identify related activity, and implement containment without slowing the investigative process down.

The key is to be able to do this without slowing down the containment activity. Considering containment measures usually require approval, the preliminary evidence collection can be done if the process is well defined, visibility is available at all data sources, and well-trained/tested teams move quickly to collect the data.

It is strongly advised that adequate people, processes, and technology are employed to make the pre-containment evidence collection as invisible and seamless as possible. It is even better if the evidence collection is as automated as feasible. This is possible to do (but not necessarily easy) with proper correlation, configuration, and pre-defined triggers in and between visibility and investigative tools, such as firewalls, IPSs, EDR tools, SIEMs, threat feeds, etc.

Cloud-based network and EDR tools with activity recording and retrospection can automate most of it and potentially all of it. The success of this is highly dependent upon the circumstances and evidence artifacts desired. It is possible with the right technology and configuration of use cases, triggers, and automated actions that manual evidence collection may not be required at all.

Moreover, depending upon the nature and speed of the threat, all of the manual evidence collection steps may fly out the window, and urgent containment measures may need to be applied. In such cases, the only data that will be immediately available for investigation will be on devices that already store it, and any further evidence will come from post-containment activity, which will suffer a certain amount of data loss.

Full File System Artifacts/Disk Images

Depending upon the nature of the threat, this step may be optional. Incident response has been trending away from full-disk forensic investigations since remote, enterprise-wide volatile metadata and memory collection and analysis became possible around 2004. Since then, the practice of collecting disk images has become more selective over time, to the point that it is no longer the norm, based on the current threat landscape.

More specifically, if 10,000 systems were all infected with wiperware, there is little to nothing to investigate between the systems that are of interest. Investigations of this sort can usually be handled with a combination of volatile data analysis using EDR tools and network traffic monitoring tools that can see connections moving from system to system to identify the universe of affected systems. There is no need for a full disk image, and many other prior steps are no longer necessary.

On the other hand, if a server containing unencrypted PHI was breached with malware known to exfiltrate information, a full-disk acquisition absolutely must be performed in order to preserve the state of the system and data for further investigation. This acquisition and any other that may be turned over to law enforcement, subject to legal action, or involve regulatory compliance must be handled according to forensic best practices and should utilize chain of custody evidence tracking.

Evidence handling procedures and testimony activity must comply with the most recent updates to or interpretation of the Federal Rules for Civil Procedure and the Federal Rules of Evidence. Specifically, the following rules are the most notable:
- 1001-1008 (Best Evidence Rule)
- 902 (Evidence that is Self-Authenticating)
- 901 (Authenticating or Identifying Evidence)
- 802 (The Rule Against Hearsay)
- 702 (Testimony by Expert Witnesses)

Other rules relating to discovery and evidence production also apply, but they typically apply later in relation to subsequent legal action. These include Rules 26, 33, 34, 37, and 45.

Physical and Logical Disk Images

When performing evidence collection, the response team needs to determine the best method of performing full disk collections. Key considerations when performing evidence collection are as follows. Some of them are overlapping, nuanced, and highly contextual. The following are some comparisons and the respective benefits or disadvantages of each.

Online/Network-Based

Some systems need to have evidence collected without being taken offline. Online/network-based disk images may take longer to collect, depending upon network speeds. Following are some examples and explanations for common impetus:

- Full disk or partition encryption, where the decryption key is not readily available or where the system cannot be taken offline for whatever reason – This is often used if the encryption keys are not readily available.
- Covert investigations where it is undesirable to notify the user that he/she is being investigated – This can be done stealthily across the wire.
- Situations where the system is critical to operations and cannot be taken offline – This is often used on critical production systems to gather evidence until a replacement or recovery can be made.
- Taking the system offline may create some sort of damage due to disk or file system instability – This is often the case when systems have been online for years, and disks have become heavily fragmented or corrupted.
- Systems with striped RAID partitions – These need to be collected live, as the data spans across multiple disks, which cannot be easily reassembled if the disks are separated and the RAID is broken. If the responders are not careful and remove disks from a striped RAID array from the system and controller creating the stripe set, there is a potential that the data may be completely lost. At the very least, the responder will have a permutation problem in trying to reassemble the disks in the correct order and recreate the correct striping method. If the system with the RAID array is live, it will appear as a single physical disk with one or more partitions. It makes no difference at that point if the physical disk is collected or each of the respective logical disks are individually collected unless there are concerns about full-disk encryption (FDE).
- Mapped drives – These typically need to be collected online and are either captured using an EDR or enterprise forensic agent installed on the systems having the drives mapped. Alternatively, the associated UNC path is captured, and a logical image is collected directly from the fileserver either by logging into it locally or connecting to it from the forensic workstation. The history of mapped network drives is located in the flowing registry keys:
  HKCU\Software\Microsoft\Windows\CurrentVersion\Explorer\Map Network Drive MRU
  HKCU\Software\Microsoft\Windows\Current\VersionExplorer\MountPoints2

In all of these cases, forensic images are usually made while the system is live, without the user knowing of such. This will successfully capture data and minimize the risk of doing so.

Offline/Drives Removed

This type of collection is typically performed when forensic best practices are required. This is usually performed pertaining to any matter that involves a criminal case or where a civil case is likely to end up in court. This may also be the case where drive imaging is not a matter of urgency and is done as a matter of standard process (such as employee separation) or where disk-based evidence is not needed urgently. These are fairly common "standard workflow" use cases for forensic images taken from workstations in corporate environments. However, some notable caveats for these types of acquisition are as follows:

- Drive decryption cannot be an issue. The decryption key must be available to the responders, or the drive(s) were not encrypted in the first place.

- RAID striping considerations are not an issue. Considering servers are likely to have RAID arrays with striping, offline acquisitions with drives removed may or may not be pragmatic or feasible. If an acquisition on a server with a striped RAID array is part of a court case requiring forensic best practices and must be booted in order to get a good acquisition, this is not a deal killer. It just needs to be documented and explained as being forensically necessary to acquire the evidence. The standard of care for such cases is for forensic activity to be "minimally invasive." It is critical to document every step, identify the reasons for performing such, and enumerate any specific changes that were introduced by the acquisition process.

Physical vs. Logical

Making a choice of physical vs. logical collections when performing drive acquisitions is mainly a consideration of the amount of data that is required to be collected, combined with the ability to remove complications caused by FDE. There are benefits and disadvantages to performing either physical vs. logical acquisitions:

- Physical: If a physical acquisition of the full disk is performed, all partitions and everything stored in either allocated or unallocated space will be collected. If a physical acquisition of a logical partition is performed, all of the allocated and unallocated space will be collected, but the image will be isolated to the specific partition chosen. In either case, it will have acquired the physical disk or logical partition(s) in its encrypted state, as implemented by FDE software. This means the key will need to be entered into the forensic tool to decrypt the drive image and perform the analysis.

  - Logical: if a logical acquisition of a full disk or specific partition is acquired, it is effectively just a selection of folders, files, or other artifact types from the drive. At this point, FDE is transparent, and all content acquired will be collected in an unencrypted state unless some sort of file-based encryption has been implemented. This method of collection is desired in order to collect a defined subset of data that is required to perform the investigation and exclude everything else that is not of interest. This may greatly reduce the amount of data to be collected and reduce the acquisition time accordingly. Performing a logical acquisition of targeted objects is how the "Targeted Files, Registry Locations, or other Artifacts" step is accomplished.

Databases, Repositories, and Structured Data Files

This last category of evidence collection happens through a variety of different methods, depending on the data source. The workflows typically involve either of the following two options that can be used to cull email stores, storage repositories, file shares, databases, or structured data other sources for a subset of targeted file types, exact file matches, partial data matches, specific content, etc.

1. Secondary processing of full-disk images for targeted file types that can be pulled from the file system of the existing forensic images or the produced load files.

2. A new eDiscovery or enterprise forensic evidence collection utilizing connectors to pull the targeted content directly from a live evidence source. The connectors typically utilize native APIs that are parsed by the native or 3rd party connectors that crawl the data and return desired results. Option 2 permits more granular filtering and Boolean logic as it is effectively a live collection queried from structured data sources.

This type of forensic collection and analysis resides somewhere between forensic analysis and eDiscovery. It is absolutely the most boring thing that can be done during an incident response investigation, and it is often perceived as some sort of punishment by members of the IR team.

IR team members are almost never excited about performing eDiscovery tasks. Pragmatically, this portion of the collection and analysis is usually farmed out to members of the forensic and eDiscovery teams. It goes smoother this way, and resources can focus on their key strengths and side-step weaknesses or misuse of human resources and general discontent.

Each of the evidence drives associated with the respective content (if more than one) will have its own separate chain of custody forms, and all evidence handling should be conducted according to forensic best practices. This content is likely to be discoverable, and respective evidence and analysis methods/findings will need to be archived for the life of the retention period.

Evidence Upload and Analysis

The responders should have an Internet-accessible, secure file transfer service for the purposes of permitting customers or responders to securely upload requested content to a secure location for responders, lab technicians, or reverse engineers to download and review as soon as possible.

This system must be able to handle large file transfers and have tremendous storage capacity with separation between customers, cases, and their respective data that prevents cross-contamination, viewing, or alteration of content.

The system must utilize forensic hashing to verify evidence files and confirm they are transferred and stored in an uncorrupted state. It must be able to track the success or failure of uploads, downloads, and respective access.

This enables remote responders or those in transit to access and analyze customer information, artifacts, and evidence. With this access, they can remotely assist and/or hit the ground running, prepared with knowledge of the customer environment and respective situation. Enabled with this preparatory information, they can provide immediate investigative, containment, or remediation recommendations once arriving onsite. It also enables responders to make productive use of travel time if going onsite.

Tracking Evidence Collected

For evidence tracking, there is a significant quantity of details that need to be captured for each evidence item that is collected and/or analyzed. Not all of these will be applicable for every evidence item, and sometimes additional fields may need to be added, depending upon the circumstances:

- Chain of custody
- Location (address/building/office)
- Owner (company/person/custodian/account)
- Numbers (Evidence tracking/Model/Serial)
- Type (server/workstation/share/VM/application/container/repository/device)
- Hostname | UNC path
- IP Address
- MAC Address
- Description
- Operating system/application/service
- Management ownership
- Administration access

- Sensitivity/impact
- Regulatory compliance (PHI, PCI, PII, SOX, etc.)
- Business operations
- Customer services

There may also be a significant amount of variability for the type of content within each field, depending on the resource type. As an example, a server and a workstation have similar data fields, but they vary significantly from that of a network share or a medical device.

If there is a legal or regulatory impact on the systems or data involved, the chain of custody information should also be included. This should include all storage media and document appropriate hash values for each physical and logical drive image.

21 RESPONSE ACTIONS: POLYMORPHISM DETECTION

This chapter discusses the nuances of the very high percentage of malware variants that exist in the wild today that are highly polymorphic. They have the automated ability to change themselves and their respective artifacts from system to system or within new environments.

These methods typically thwart the endpoint and network technologies that otherwise would be used to detect and block them. This is true for both binary and script-based malware, with scripted malware now being by far the most common.

The more unique the malware becomes, the harder it is to find with IOCs or other conventional methods that require a distinct list of everything bad (blacklist of known-bad hashes). The lack of available blacklists containing known malicious hashes results in the need for advanced heuristics and anomaly detection functions. These have always been soft spots for antivirus and antimalware tools, which focus more on blacklists than heuristics and detecting malicious behavior.

If all forensic indicators change (such as hash values, filenames, install paths, file sizes, registry entries, communication ports, IP addresses, domain names, and DNS servers) with each new instance of the malware, it can significantly complicate detection by both automated and manual analysis methods. This is because the focus is on convicting applications by known malicious indicators rather than deviations from normal.

This is true both for malicious binaries and scripts, with scripts being the trickier of the two. Due to the fact that there is no such thing as known-expected behavior for random scripts that are downloaded from the Internet, there is nothing to compare behavior to.

Moreover, it is easier to be polymorphic in scripts, as they are typically not expected to be signed. Further, most antivirus/antimalware solutions are incredibly weak in their ability to discern between benign and malicious script functions. Most benign scripts are created for administrative purposes and performing system configuration functions. Malicious scripts may use the same functions for hostile activity.

Automated methods have difficulty discerning between the legitimate administrator and malicious actor functionality. Unless there is a hash of a known bad script, it is unlikely to be detected. With the common practice of modifying scripts through random polymorphic activity, known hashes are not even a possibility.

Detecting Polymorphic Malware

Current trends in malware often involve polymorphism and thwarting IOC-based detections that are implemented in so many threat feeds and subscriptions. Polymorphism of all known forensic attributes provides a method to circumvent detection by antivirus and antimalware, but it creates uniqueness in the process.

The more malware tries to become unique, the more it stands out if investigators and their tools are looking for it. Emphasis on: → IF THEY ARE LOOKING FOR IT ←

Identification of uniqueness works especially well in large environments where there should be many examples of most types of software and network traffic. More specifically, if investigators are able to look across all systems and traffic in the environment and identify processes, libraries, drivers, and/or network traffic connections that are "least-prevalent," the polymorphic malware and connection methods boldly stand out and can be easily identified.

Polymorphic Binaries

For a variety of reasons, effectively and efficiently detecting least-prevalence in binaries is much easier than it is in scripts. Binaries are part of the parent-child relationship, and their execution is automatically tracked by the ever-growing variety of EDR tools with retrospection and comparative capabilities.

Binary uniqueness and least prevalence in a corporate environment that has computers based on standard system images is a notable find and a key starting place that can expedite an investigation, but discoveries of such might not always be malicious. It is not uncommon to find unique, custom-created binaries on developer systems, as well as custom software used by the organization. Any legitimate, unique binaries should be whitelisted when found in order to eliminate distracting noise and expedite the investigative process.

Polymorphic Scripts

Detecting polymorphic scripts requires a highly organized approach involving a combination of requiring signed scripts and whitelisting of scripts based on content, source, or certificate – depending upon the security capabilities in place. Requiring script signing prior to execution breaks polymorphic techniques, as new script variants generated on the fly cannot easily be signed by a trusted authority. While it may be theoretically possible, it is highly implausible. Moreover, there is the added hurdle of ensuring that the signing authority is trusted by the systems to be compromised.

Anything polymorphically created will be least-prevalent and almost always unsigned. Endpoint agents and logging/alerting rules can be configured to block and alert on this. Implementing the right endpoint policy and agent-based controls to block and identify unsigned scripts is a notable security improvement, as this is the primary attack vector of modern malware.

Identifying Normal and Expected

A significant challenge that information technology and security professionals face is that most organizations don't have an understanding of what is normal within their environment. This is true for endpoint configuration, binaries, scripts, and network traffic.

Analysis seeking to identify polymorphic malware utilizing any method of analysis is significantly augmented by baselining the normal or known good state of the environment, systems, applications, services, scripts, network connections, ingress/egress activity, and network flows. By understanding the normal baseline state of the environment and quickly determining what is least prevalent, responders can respond quickly to polymorphic threats. These two strategies should always be combined for the most effective response.

Additionally, configuring system and endpoint policies to require signed code, such as processes, drivers, and scripts, is the key to proactively preventing malicious activity and enabling the detection of malicious code that attempts to run on the systems. However, depending on the size and complexity of the environment, this can become incredibly challenging to manage.

22 RESPONSE ACTIONS: ROOT CAUSE ANALYSIS

This chapter discusses the key considerations involved in performing successful incident root cause analysis. Numerous workstreams and subsequent activities hinge on affirmatively identifying the root cause of the compromise. It is a key pivot point for future activity.

Establishing the root cause for a successful attack during the forensic investigation is a critical data point that drives incident workstreams, post-incident processes, and pre-incident planning for future incidents. It will shape the response activity, inform mitigation and remediation steps, and be used as a trigger in regulatory or legal actions.

More specifically, it will indicate whether the customer had adequate security controls and also determine whether the incident detection and response capabilities were sufficient. If the security capabilities were not at least industry-standard and reasonable, attorneys and regulators might find something to sink their teeth into.

Identifying Root Cause

The definition of root cause analysis is highly contextual. However, for security incidents, it means: "Identifying the most basic cause that was responsible for the incident." This is most likely a security vulnerability or misconfiguration on systems, devices, applications, services, or accounts.

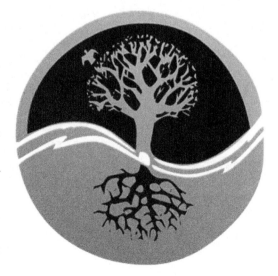

Because a security breach is usually the result of multiple individual security compromises, there may be multiple root causes with various attack vectors and exploit methods. There are also likely to be various contributing factors that either directly or indirectly aided in the success of the breach.

Just like a plane crash, every successful hacking incident is a result of layers of security failures from defense-in-depth that missed the mark at every stage or were non-existent, to begin with. At the very least, the technology must have failed at various stages.

By way of example, consider the following string of events for a multi-layered attack:
1. Network controls did not detect attacker intrusion activity.
2. Endpoint controls did not protect the systems, applications, services, and/or accounts.
3. Authentication, authorization, and access controls did not protect accounts and data.
4. Log monitoring controls and SIEM solution(s) did not identify the malicious activity and alert in time to stop it.

Also, keep in mind that there is never a better time to resolve these layers of security gaps than after a successful breach. In most environments, there is often a long list of known security issues that everyone knows need to be addressed. They are just waiting for a security breach to make the required leadership support and funding available.

Conversely, not identifying the root cause of the breach is a missed opportunity and an invitation for it to happen again. It will likely result in a game of Whack-A-Mole until the security gaps are resolved. Sometimes, the root causes at the various stages of the attack are only partially identified and remediated. This results in the likelihood of recurring events using the remaining attack vectors and exploit methods.

It is critical to remember that root causes are not just technological problems. It is necessary to consider causes and contributing factors within any or all of people, processes, and/or technology.

A comprehensive analysis will require stepping through each activity, artifact, and/or component of an incident. This will enable the response team to understand the cause-and-effect relationship and identify exactly what happened and how.

The 5 Why Questions

Just like children ask lots of "Why" questions to understand their world, responders need to do the same. A technique called the "5 Whys" can help peel away the layers of symptoms to identify the underlying root cause(s). 5 is an average number of whys, and greater or fewer may be required.

Example:

1. Why is the network slow? → A large uptick in outbound DNS traffic from workstations resulted in congestion.
2. Why is there an uptick in workstation DNS traffic? → It was caused by svchost.exe initiating the DNS requests.
3. Why is svchost.exe initiating a high volume of DNS requests? → An exfiltration JavaScript has called it to send user-created documents containing sensitive information over DNS to badsite.com.
4. Why is an exfiltration JavaScript running on the endpoints? → It was installed when visiting the company's externally hosted message board server.
5. Why is the company's message board server deploying malicious scripts? → Poor input validation led to an attacker being able to install an exploit kit on the server.

Note that in exploring the 5 Whys, there are multiple vulnerabilities that may be considered root causes in and of themselves for the various compromises within the layers of the affected resources. For instance, a non-comprehensive list of high-level root causes and contributing factors includes:

1. The lack of network and endpoint DRM and DLP controls permitted sensitive information to be exfiltrated.
2. The malicious JavaScript was not identified or blocked by network or endpoint security controls, and it was successfully downloaded and executed on endpoints.
3. Unauthorized scripts from the Internet are not blocked from calling svchost.exe to perform malicious activity.
4. Lack of network and application security controls on the hosted webserver resulted in the application being compromised and the installation of an exploit kit.

Key Pivot Point that Drives Response

The nature and impact of the root cause will also identify its capabilities and the access attackers may have gained. Any root cause or artifact discovered acts as a pivot point for forensic analysis and drives the identification of the upstream or downstream resources, accounts, or data affected or related to the incident.

If one examines the entire incident lifecycle, there is often a chain of events and compromised resources that extend before and after the incident is detected. These are used to facilitate the initial compromise or the exfiltration of data in such a way that it is difficult or impossible to identify the attacker's location. Once any of the root causes of the various stages is identified, it becomes a key pivot point that will drive additional investigation tasks and identify other resources that need to be investigated.

Note how, in the last example, at any phase of the incident, it was possible to pivot from any point and drive to any other point. For instance, had the incident been detected at the other end of the incident spectrum on the webserver itself, it would have been possible to identify the hosts that visited it using a combination of web server logs and customer egress firewall logs.

Informs Mitigation and Remediation

Regarding incident root causes, the vulnerabilities associated with them are not usually isolated to a single system. If an easily exploitable root cause is identified for one system, it is likely that other systems suffer from the same vulnerability and may have been exploited through the same or similar attack vector. Once identified, the vulnerabilities and attack vector IOCs should be searched, located everywhere they exist, investigated, and eradicated. Even if the compromise is an isolated incident, it is extremely unlikely that the vulnerability will be.

This can be semi-automated across the rest of the organization using endpoint security tools, such as EDR, AV/AM, vulnerability management, configuration management, and/or other capabilities, depending upon the circumstances. One or more of these tools (or others) may be required, depending upon the specific endpoint or artifact type being searched.

Trigger for Legal/Regulatory Impact

Root cause analysis is a key trigger that fuels legal and/or regulatory actions. It could affect judgments, fines, or operational restrictions placed upon the victims. Defenders get points for the adequacy of security controls they have employed and the novelty of the attack that breached them.

Conversely, the inverse will be used against them. Being compromised through significant security gaps by publicly available tools using vulnerabilities for which patches have been released is a hard situation to justify. Being compromised by unknown, custom tools using 0-day threats for which there is no known defense may be justifiable.

Typically, institutions having insufficient, ineffective security controls that result in a breach have significantly more fines, restrictions, lawsuits, and other negative impacts than those with a more plausible defense. If a company has reasonable, industry-standard security controls and no notable weaknesses, it is hard for courts, regulators, and consumer protection agencies to hold them as culpable as they otherwise might.

23 THREAT ERADICATION: UNAUTHORIZED ACCESS TERMINATION

This chapter will cover the strategy to perform unauthorized access termination and end malicious access to the customer environment. Depending upon how intruders have compromised resources and/or accounts, they can establish a wide variety of remote access methods. Each requires a different strategy to eradicate and prevent recurrence in the future.

Password Resets for in-Scope Accounts

IAM controls (such as account lockouts, password resets, forced logouts, and session termination) must be employed to secure all known or potentially compromised accounts. The typical affected account types and considerations include the following, which will be covered in more detail:

- Administrator accounts (local or domain-wide)
- User accounts (local or domain-wide)
- External entity accounts (local or domain-wide)
- Service accounts (local or domain-wide)
- Self-service password reset functions
- Force logout or session termination

Admin/User Accounts

Lock or change passwords for administrator and user accounts on systems, services, and/or applications (local or domain-wide) that have been identified as compromised or have been used on systems compromised by attackers or malware. This will address issues where credentials are currently in use on the affected system or where the credentials have been cached and may have been harvested from the system.

Local admin or user accounts (particularly those that are built-in, native to the resource, but not always used) can be hard to chase down and need to be enumerated on a resource-by-resource basis. Ideally, local accounts should be enumerated and audited on a cyclical basis and recorded in a central repository for easy access and reference during response activity.

External Entity Accounts

If resources are remotely supported or used, there is a risk to or from external entity environments or accounts. After discussion with the affected entities, change the password or lock any accounts that have been involved in or are at risk of compromise.

This will prevent exposed credentials in the external entity environment from turning into a breach of the customer environment. If existing connections are established from at-risk external entities, terminate the existing connections from their accounts and revoke MFA sessions.

Service Accounts

Lock or change the password(s) for verified affected or significantly at-risk service accounts on systems, services, and applications (local or domain-wide) that have been identified as compromised or have been used on systems compromised by attackers or malware. The logic for this is the same as for admin and user accounts. However, doing this without enough research can cause an outage. As such, an intermediary step would be to make sure that the service accounts are not remotely accessible. Ideally, these should be set to non-interactive only.

Self-Service Password Reset Functions

Validate that unauthorized, malicious individuals do not have the capability to use the customer self-service password reset function(s). Otherwise, they might once again grant themselves access to accounts in the customer environment following administrative password resets. This function should require secure, secondary validation, such as identity proofing, challenge questions, or other affirmative validation.

Force Logout/Session Termination

Following password resets of suspected or verified compromised accounts, force a logout of all accounts to terminate the existing sessions. This will make them log back in using the new password. The act of resetting passwords by itself does not end previously authenticated sessions. The session itself must be forcibly terminated.

*NOTE: If credentials are suspected to be compromised, never use the "Change password on next logon" functionality, as it could be used by attackers as well as legitimate users. After passwords are reset, ensure that compromised systems or applications are not used, or the credentials will become compromised again.

Remote Access Eradication Measures

Ingress activity from known compromised accounts and malicious source addresses must be blocked to prevent unauthorized remote access and activity. If possible, VPN devices should be integrated with threat feeds to automatically detect and dynamically block known malicious sources. The following are individual eradication considerations for remote access eradication.

Corporate User VPNs

Terminate VPN sessions for any user/administrator accounts that have been associated with unauthorized or malicious activity. Also, block the associated source IP addresses and domain names. Some specific remote access activities to block or investigate and then likely block are:

- Exposed credentials – This includes any reasonable suspicion that account credentials have been compromised or are accessible by unauthorized parties.
- Business policy/process violations – This includes any indication that an account is behaving in such a manner that violates policies, procedures, and acceptable use criteria. This may be the result of compromised accounts or authorized users behaving in a prohibited manner, such as insider threats.
- Malware activity – This includes any activity from malicious applications or sites that is detected at any phase: remote exploit, download, C2, lateral movement, exfiltration, etc.
- Known malicious source hosts – These may be identified from any detection source, threat feed, investigation activity, or manually reported.
- Connections from suspicious countries – These include any countries not having known contractors or traveling employees, especially Nigeria.
- OFAC countries – These include anything that the US Treasury Office of Foreign Asset Control has on their blocked list. These are usually dangerous and worth blocking.
- Impossible travel – These include situations where users logon from one location and then from another far away location (especially international) shortly afterward. This is a key indicator that the credentials are compromised and are being used by an unauthorized party.
- Multiple logons – These are situations where users are connected to the VPN multiple times from different locations, which is a key indicator of malicious activity.

Corporate B2B VPNs

Terminate VPN sessions for any business-to-business (B2B) account for which 1) the external entity has been identified as compromised or 2) the accounts, emails, domains, or source addresses have been associated with unauthorized/malicious activity. Also, block the source IP addresses and domain names. These should remain blocked until the external entity has completed all of 1) containment, 2) mitigation, and 3) remediation.

Corporate External Remote Administration Tools

Terminate access for all externally accessible corporate-standard remote administration tools from the compromised user and admin accounts and block the related source addresses and domain names. This includes direct, proxied, or cloud-based remote access tools used by the customer. This includes all remote administration tools that function using either inbound, outbound, or centralized access methods.

Vendor Standard Remote Administration Tools

Terminate access for all vendor-controlled remote administration tools from compromised user and admin accounts and block the related source addresses and domain names. This includes direct, proxied, or cloud-based remote access tools used by the customer, such as all remote administration tools that function using either inbound, outbound, or centralized access methods.

MFA Eradication Measures

Users may have multiple MFA tokens, depending upon the method of access granted to the respective account types. They usually include physical or soft tokens that are used either for accessing SSL/TLS or thick client VPNs.

Both hard and soft MFA tokens may become compromised using a variety of attack vectors. It is essential to validate registered MFA tokens and terminate compromised or unauthorized tokens, as well as methods used to social engineer MFA validation:

- Identify and validate all MFA tokens and access for potentially compromised accounts or tokens.
  - o Soft tokens can be compromised by copying files from the system or device that they are installed on.
  - o Hard tokens can be lost or stolen.
  - o Attacker devices can be surreptitiously registered to approve MFA requests.
- Terminate, remove, or otherwise expire compromised MFA tokens that are associated with malicious activity.
- Implement ID-proofing or other verification controls for device registration to ensure no additional unauthorized devices are added.
- Reset all MFA sessions to force re-validation once the changes have been made.

Network Eradication Measures

Depending upon the nature and phase of the malware or hacking threat, a variety of network controls may be appropriate to block and eradicate the network-based malicious activity. However, these typically only work within the security perimeter unless endpoint agents are configured with an always-on VPN client. Following are common security controls, all of which are profoundly more effective if they utilize SSL/TLS decryption to increase visibility, as well as integrate with threat feeds to increase their efficacy and value:

Traditional Firewall and IPS Capabilities

Block known malicious IP addresses, domains, network ranges, CIDR blocks, TCP/UDP ports, and/or signature-based threats. This is a stop-gap security control that is easily circumvented by attackers through the use of proxies in countries or locations that are not blocked. If the attackers are really determined, they will get around these controls and find another way in. However, it may provide the response team with additional time to implement more robust network security controls.

Next-Generation Firewalls and IPS Capabilities

Utilize next-generation firewall and IPS capabilities to block activity that is likely malicious. Specifically, block any traffic that could be an artifact of exploitation, download, C2, exfiltration, remote access, and/or persistence activity that enables attackers to maintain a foothold within the organization. Common malicious network activity includes:

- Protocol anomalies and covert tunneling – This includes a whole host of methods, including some forms of tunneling or other methods of protocol misuse that are often used for covert tunneling. The most common methods (from fastest and least covert to slowest and most covert) include HTTPS, DNS, ICMP, and SYN tunneling.
- Volumetric blocking – This includes sending out data beyond an imposed threshold, which is common for exfiltration.
- Connection time or duration blocking – This could halt connections at unexpected times or those lasting longer than a predefined time period. This behavior is indicative of exfiltration, tunneling, and C2.
- DGA blocking – This could block domains created through Domain Generation Algorithms, which are common in crimeware suites/exploit kits – especially ransomware.
- Dynamic blocking from threat feeds or other integrations – This assists in making blocking activity scalable, dynamic, and automated.
- Clandestine private VPNs and outbound remote access tools – This blocks remote access applications that are installed by unauthorized users, attackers, or malware. There are wide varieties that most commonly include remote proxy services, SSH VPNs, the TOR network, and even webmail proxies (such as Gcat, which uses Gmail for C2 and exfil).

Cloud Scrubbing

Utilize cloud scrubbing services to sanitize both ingress and egress traffic, as well as attacker and malware endpoint persistence activity. This blocks most of the malicious activity within the cloud service provider's infrastructure and requires an endpoint agent to extend coverage to off-network endpoints, like roaming laptops.

Disabling Switch Ports or Applying ACLs

Disabling network switch ports for compromised workstations and servers is typically the quickest and most definitive way to completely halt all threats related to an endpoint. It simultaneously ends malicious ingress, egress, and lateral movement activity. A variation on this is to use dynamic segmentation capabilities to apply ingress or egress ACLs to switch ports to permit only desired traffic, such as to facilitate investigative activity to and from specifically authorized systems or devices.

Virtual Infrastructure

Controlling ingress VPN traffic with virtual infrastructure can be used to block direct access to internal systems from remote access users/vendors/partners and require them to go through a jumpbox or other locked-down virtualized infrastructure. Examples of this include VDI or Citrix environments with only permitted applications published and network access enabled. It is ideal if virtual environment access is set up as the primary access method during the onboarding of relationships involving remote access. It is effectively a virtual device firewall that can significantly limit the risk of malicious activity from people or malicious processes. Moreover, it is rather cumbersome to try and bolt on during an incident, as many steps are involved in the setup for all relationships that cannot simply be severed.

Endpoint Eradication Measures

Due to the limited scope and efficacy of traditional network controls being restricted to ingress/egress activity within the security perimeter, advanced modern endpoint controls must be implemented to provide additional coverage to augment the response. If not for advanced endpoint controls, it is likely that threats on remote hosts (like for traveling employees with laptops) will not be resolved until they are brought back to the office.

This significantly prolongs the window of compromise and increases risk to the customer. The compromised laptops might not be identified until they return to the corporate environment, at which point the attackers or malware may compromise other systems, accounts, and/or data.

As such, all available endpoint security controls (especially EDR capabilities) are critical for rapid detection, response, and eradication of attacker/malware threats on endpoints. To increase EDR efficacy and value, all of the endpoint controls should be extended to systems outside the security perimeter and be integrated with threat feeds. The following are common capabilities used:

EDR Technologies

Using EDR technologies and other host-monitoring controls capable of behavioral analysis, anomaly identification, and blocking are (or can be) the most effective endpoint visibility tools. They can provide selective identification and eradication capabilities that enable legitimate activity but selectively block malicious or undesired activity. However, there are many solutions in this space, and some are significantly more capable than others, especially when it comes to the scope of activity and artifact types they monitor. Cloud-based EDR solutions provide the greatest visibility, scope of analysis, and actionability as the intelligence is centrally located within the cloud.

Application Activity

Source application traffic/activity blocking can be used to halt any activity from known malicious or manipulated processes. This is usually a method implemented through EDR and anti-malware tools but may require some manual configuration if the malicious application is not known to the tool. It can be very effective in that it enables responders to limit the manipulation of otherwise benign processes, such as limiting the behavior of user applications or script interpreters.

Traffic to/from Endpoints

Use a host-based firewall and IPS software to block IP addresses, domains, network ranges, CIDR blocks, TCP/UDP ports, and/or signature-based threats. These are legacy, host-based network capabilities that can provide selective eradication controls enabling legitimate activity but blocking malicious or undesired activity. The biggest challenge with these is that they are only as good as they are defined. There are always ways around them if attacker and malware threats are dynamic.

Account Management

Changing passwords or disabling accounts on affected workstations and/or servers should be done as soon as reasonably possible but may drag on if admin or service accounts are involved, or local accounts are unknown. Any account that has logged into or has been used on the affected system could potentially have been compromised. Local accounts, particularly local administrator accounts or clandestine accounts that have been added to the local Administrators group are of particularly significant risk and usually suffer from lack of visibility.

Host Isolation

Host isolation using endpoint agents has the advantage of blocking all network activity except that which is used for investigations by defined systems. This is typically performed with EDR, anti-malware, host intrusion protection (HIPS), or policy configuration tools. It enables otherwise compromised machines to remain network-connected for ease of investigation purposes, but it sequesters them from any other activity on the network. A good addition to host isolation is an exception list for other endpoint security and investigative tools.

Antivirus/Antimalware

Antivirus/antimalware configuration can be useful but have very low expectations. Depending upon the nature of the threat, antivirus/antimalware may be of some assistance in removing it. However, the conditions have to be exactly right. This includes 1) malware is not polymorphic, 2) a custom .dat file can be made available quickly enough, and/or 3) a custom signature can be configured. If so, AV may be useful in detecting the same infection elsewhere and stopping future examples of the same thing. However, if malware is fileless, injected, polymorphic, WMI-based, scripted, or takes the form of most modern threats, antivirus/antimalware is of little to no use. For the most part, it is a legacy concept.

Internet Service Eradication Measures

Depending upon the nature of the threat, a variety of IAM controls may be appropriate for lockout activity. These include on-prem Internet-facing services and Cloud services.

On-Prem Internet-facing Services

Unless external-facing employees and customer services have federated access for ease of management, they are difficult and time-consuming to manage. This may result in accounts that don't get disabled, credentials that don't get reset, or other missing controls. Moreover, even with federated access controls, there are still local accounts that could be manipulated by malicious insiders or using compromised credentials. When terminating access, it is critical to consider everywhere compromised credentials can be used and if there are external-facing services that could be accessed.

Cloud System/Service Access

Cloud access is often the easiest to forget to block, particularly if authentication is not federated with corporate IAM systems. For compromised credentials, it is critical to review all of the cloud access services and validate the compromised accounts/credentials have been secure to prevent unauthorized access, exfiltration, and/or tampering. These usually include a myriad of email, chat, messaging, and file repository services commonly used in redundant varieties by customers.

24 THREAT ERADICATION: MALICIOUS APPLICATION REMOVAL

This chapter will cover the strategy to perform Surgical Eradication to end malicious access to the customer endpoints. Depending upon how intruders have compromised systems, there are a wide variety of malware persistence mechanisms, backdoors, and related artifacts that need to be removed to prevent malicious activity from continuing. Surgical eradication will enable legitimate functionality to continue but halt malicious activity until more comprehensive recovery operations can be completed.

Surgical Eradication

Once potential malware activity has been identified, there is a need to stop it in order to prevent further exposure and damage. However, there are various ways to do this, and some are more impactful than others. It sounds logical to immediately take compromised systems offline when they are identified by hacking and malware alerts. However, it is not always feasible to bring down resources and block communications, particularly if there are questions about the severity of the threat, the viability of lateral movement, and whether containment may cause business impact.

Oftentimes, complete containment options are off the table until the full impact of the hacking activity is known, and it has crossed a certain threshold that the business deems appropriate to halt production systems and activity. Before that threshold is reached, partial containment (AKA Surgical Eradication) options are usually the most prudent. Surgical Eradication is a compromise that allows systems to continue to function but eradicates known threats residing on them. Known legitimate functions can continue, but other activity is blocked.

However, there are obvious risks. You don't know what you don't know. Other backdoors or persistence mechanisms may exist that are unknown to investigators and which may still be available to attackers or work in an automated manner on their own.

Malicious or Manipulated Binaries

The first step of Surgical Eradication is stopping the malicious processes, services, or drivers. This typically unlocks their respective file system artifacts and prepares them for deletion. Artifacts take a variety of different forms, depending upon the design of the malicious application. These usually include primary or supporting processes, services, DLLs, drivers, scripts, configuration files, storage files, accounts, AD artifacts, registry keys, WMI classes or subscriptions, tasks, or other artifacts and persistence mechanisms. Each of these will be addressed individually, as follows:

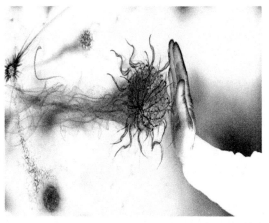

Processes

Addressing malicious processes involves killing the processes that are identified as overtly malicious or are benign (but have been compromised) and then removing the respective persistence mechanisms. However, this can occur in a variety of ways, as follows:

- Processes of known malware binaries – If known malicious binaries are identified, their processes should be killed, and the malicious binary deleted immediately afterward. Any related persistence mechanisms should also be identified and deleted.
- Processes injected with malicious libraries or functions – These processes themselves are benign but have been manipulated. The process should be killed, and all malicious persistence mechanisms must be removed. Afterward, the system and formerly injected process(es) can be restarted unmanipulated.
- Hollowed and replaced processes – These were benign processes that have been completely replaced in memory by malicious code. The original source binary, however, is usually benign. The process should be killed, and all malicious persistence mechanisms must be removed. Afterward, the system and formerly hollowed process(es) can be restarted unmanipulated.
- Processes called or manipulated by malicious processes – These processes are typically benign but are used to facilitate malicious activity as the malware lives off the land. Kill the manipulated process and then kill and delete the malicious processes and persistence mechanisms involved.

Services

Services are processes or drivers that are launched by the service control manager. If malicious services are identified, or benign services have been compromised, the process is to stop and disable or delete malicious services, remove the malicious persistence mechanism in whatever form they take, and then restart manipulated services clean.

DLLs

Dealing with malicious DLLs usually involves unregistering the respective DLLs and/or removing them from DLL search-order locations or deleting them. This will prevent them from manipulating benign processes and/or performing user-mode rootkit functionality. If malicious DLLs have replaced critical system DLLs, it is likely to result in blue-screen-of-death and the benign drivers to be replaced in Safe mode or using the Windows recovery feature.

Drivers

Malicious drivers must be uninstalled to remove suspicious or malicious drivers from the system. This will stop kernel-mode rootkits or other deep-seated malware functionality that leverage malicious drivers. If malicious drivers have replaced critical system drivers, it is likely to result in a blue screen of death, and the benign drivers must be replaced in Safe mode or using the Windows recovery feature.

Compromised Accounts/Groups

The second step of Surgical Eradication is disabling or deleting malicious user accounts and groups to prevent any additional local or remote malicious activity using compromised accounts. This will prevent attackers from remotely logging in and re-infecting sanitized systems. It will halt tasks, services, processes, scripts, or other artifacts that execute using compromised accounts and stolen passwords, provided they do not already have an active session.

Any active sessions for compromised accounts must be forcibly logged out. If the accounts are first disabled and then the sessions terminated, the attackers and malware will no longer be able to use them.

Reset Passwords

Because credentials or password hashes stored on systems are considered compromised by malware or attackers, it is mandatory to reset passwords for all accounts located on the system(s) affected or that have been used from the affected system. This includes all local or domain accounts for the system(s) or application(s) involved.

Disable Accounts

All accounts on the local systems and in applications must be validated. Delete suspicious, unverified user accounts and validate password change dates for known accounts, particularly administrator accounts.

Groups/OUs/Roles

Just as all accounts must be validated, security groups, organizational units (OUs), roles, and/or other organizational and permission-granting concepts must also be validated to verify they have not been manipulated. This includes reviewing, identifying, and remediating all suspicious, unverified changes. This is especially true for permission/rights granting methods that provide administrative or other privileged rights.

Delete File System Artifacts

Now that malicious processes are stopped, and the files are unlocked, they can be deleted. As such, the next step of Surgical Eradication is deleting the related malicious file system artifacts. The following are considerations for the common artifact types that malware commonly creates or uses to perform their malicious functions.

Binaries

Delete all malware-related binaries on the file system. This includes all PE file types, as identified either by extension (.acm, .ax, .cpl, .dll, .drv, .efi, .exe, .mui, .ocx, .scr, .sys, .tsp) or by header (MZ).

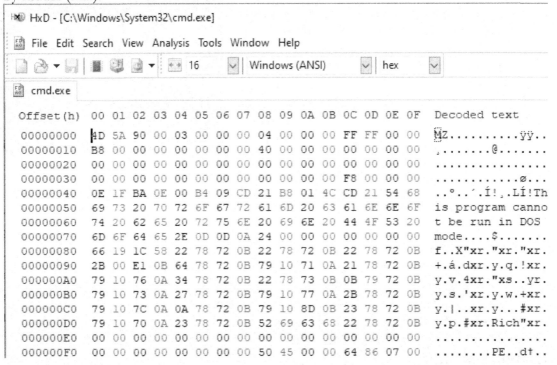

Related Files

Delete all malware-related files, including configuration files, storage files, or other operational files. It is not uncommon for attackers or malware to collect repositories of stolen information in preparation for exfiltration but not delete them when finished. Sometimes, these are not cleaned following exfiltration, or the process is interrupted by response activity.

This may result in residual risk from sensitive data stored in unauthorized locations that could cause additional exposure and disclosure. As such, following a successful breach by attackers or malware, it is important to search for inappropriately stored sensitive information on endpoints, shares, or other insecure repositories.

Scripts

Identify and delete all unverified scripts, especially those located in temporary or unprivileged user/process writable locations. The usual locations include any temp directory or any subdirectory located under the various %HOMEPATH%\AppData directories.

Malicious scripts are currently the primary malware format, which have by far supplanted binaries. All scripts residing on endpoints that cannot be verified or that have been downloaded from the Internet (which can be identified by Alternate Data Stream ZoneID=3) are highly suspect. They must be analyzed for additional IOCs, functionality, and purpose and then remediated as necessary.

Fileless Persistence Mechanisms

The next step of Surgical Eradication is deleting the related non-file-based/non-binary artifacts. These include the persistence mechanisms, configuration files, collected data files, or other artifact types. The following are key considerations and steps for the respective artifacts and/or persistence mechanisms. Typical methods of eradication in the most scalable ways involve utilizing EDR or enterprise forensics tools. However, scripts, Active Directory GPOs, or Sysinternals Autoruns will also work.

Delete Malicious Registry Entries

There are many ways that fileless malware (or any malware type) can use the Registry for persistence. Some of them are much more covert than others. In fact, depending on how deeply the persistence mechanisms are buried in the registry, it may not be entirely feasible or pragmatic to find them. Following are the most common modifications that are reasonably findable and fixable, as well as the eradication instructions for such:

- Auto-runs – Delete or sanitize known malicious or suspicious registry/autorun entries that could be used as persistence mechanisms or for malware configuration, operation, and storage. Some of them are overt, like Run entries or Services that call malicious binaries. Others are more subtle and manipulate application registry settings or other methods. There are many places where malware persistence mechanisms can hide, which can be enumerated and accessed through EDR, enterprise forensic agents, or the Sysinternals Autoruns program.
- Application compatibility shimming – Compatibility modes built into modern versions

of Windows are often manipulated by attackers to start malware or connect to malicious sites and download malware prior to application execution. Nearly any application can be shimmed to perform unauthorized activity, but applications that typically connect to the internet (like web browsers) are a favorite. These need to be identified and sanitized to remove malicious shims but still permit the intended applications to function.

- Registry resident malware – Some malware resides entirely in the registry within one or more keys and values that may be daisy-chained together. These need to be fully enumerated and then deleted. The following are the size limitations of Windows registry locations, which dictate the size of chunks that the program needs to be broken into and then reassembled in order to launch the malicious program.

Registry Element	Size Limit
Key name	255 characters
Value name	16,383 characters
Value	Available memory (latest format); 1 MB (standard format)
Tree	512 levels deep. Create up to 32 levels at a time through a single registry API call

Delete Scheduled Tasks

Identifying malicious scheduled tasks is much easier than registry entries. All scheduled tasks must be validated. If found, delete suspicious scheduled tasks that could act as persistence mechanisms that call malicious applications or launch sites. These are often overlooked and have the ability to re-infect systems at arbitrary dates in the future – very sneaky.

Delete Malicious WMI Subscriptions/Classes

Identifying malicious WMI modifications is another challenging task, as it is a very nascent space. Fileless malware mechanisms can build entire malicious applications using custom WMI subscriptions and classes, but there are no reliable automated methods to detect them.

Enumerating, identifying, and deleting these very cover persistence mechanisms leverages a combination of analyzing persistent and non-persistent subscriptions and classes. This includes a combination of file system and script-output analysis.

Once known, they can be handled by EDR tools of enterprise forensic software if they have the capabilities to interact with such. Alternatively, in Sysinternals Autoruns, this can be done very easily by right-clicking the malicious WMI database entry and selecting Delete.

Additionally, from a PowerShell perspective, it is possible to remove the WMI event subscriptions from the command line. This requires several steps to enumerate the events and objects and then delete them, depending upon the circumstances. Useful WMI functions may include Get-WMIObject, Get-EventLog, Remove-WMIObject, and others.

Moreover, it requires an understanding of what should exist. This should be augmented by a comparison of known gold-image baselines from clean systems.

Don't Stop Now

Usually, and optimally, Surgical Eradication is a temporary workaround that just buys time for the production systems to be further investigated and then restored to a known good state with no impact on availability. There will always be questions regarding the efficacy of surgical eradication. It is hard to prove definitively that all of the changes, persistence mechanisms, and backdoors were identified and remediated. There is always the possibility that the affected systems have been altered in ways that were not detected and reversed.

As such, until a more permanent and comprehensive solution can be identified, the surgically remediated systems need to be monitored and validated to ensure they do not display any additional malicious activity. There are often layers of persistence mechanisms that will download and restore the malware if primary components have been found and deleted. If the attacker determines that his tools have been removed, but he still has a foothold on a system or in the organization, he will come back with more covert tools.

Even if the system no longer has malicious functions, it may still be unstable as libraries, processes, WMI classes, or other functions may have been replaced. Depending upon what system objects the malware has modified, and what actions the responders need to take for Surgical Eradication, there is the potential that the machines will bluescreen. To be safe, recovery and restoration procedures should always be followed.

25 THREAT ERADICATION: INAPPROPRIATELY STORED SENSITIVE DATA DELETION

This chapter addresses the nuances, strategies, and considerations involved in identifying and eradicating inappropriately stored sensitive information. There are many different types of investigations, and most of them ultimately result in unauthorized access, exfiltration, encryption, deletion, or manipulation of some form of sensitive information, whether regulated data or business-sensitive information.

Data Identification, Collection, and Preservation

Following a security breach, the customer environment should be searched for source information related to the breach for which the source of compromise may not be known. Just because the information might primarily exist in one location doesn't mean it might not have been breached in another. All potential data sources need to be enumerated, and any insecure or unauthorized storage of that information should be eradicated.

Additionally, any sensitive information stored in insecure, inappropriate locations (whether or not left over from the breach) should be addressed. This will require identification, collection, and the implementation of security controls or eradication if it is unauthorized. Any unsecured sensitive information may become the subject of future breaches. As such, the content needs to be either secured or deleted.

Oddly enough, the first step of deleting inappropriately stored sensitive data is collecting it. For starters, you never want to delete something until you verify you are not about to delete the only good copy of it. There is a possibility that the copy collected by hackers or malware that is sitting in their folder of data collected for exfiltration is the only pristine version. It is possible that all other copies have been corrupted, deleted, or contaminated with malware.

Additionally, there may be legal or compliance considerations relating to inappropriately stored data that have potentially been exposed by malicious activity or unauthorized parties. As such, anything that is potentially reportable or may result in legal action should be forensically collected and preserved using forensic best practices and follow rules of evidence requirements. This will help ensure they are admissible in court.

Identifying, collecting, and preserving inappropriately stored sensitive information in most large environments typically involves using enterprise forensic or eDiscovery software to search the endpoints, shares, email, or other types of file/data repositories. This either involves searching for a known data set and/or an unknown data set. Identifying known data sets involves a combination of exact data matching using forensic hash values, partial data matching using fuzzy hash values, or using keywords to identify specific strings.

Ideally, such searching is aided via data classification tags in sensitive documents or emails. This requires a formal data classification program to be in place and for sensitive documents and emails to be properly tagged.

Identifying unknown data sets may also involve using keywords for known criteria within digital content. However, it is more likely to use regex searches to match defined patterns or formats for potentially sensitive information types, such as social security numbers, credit card numbers, patient record numbers, phone numbers, or other content that is either regulated or business-sensitive. Numeric regex strings for such data types usually create a lot of false positives, and the shorter the search expression, the greater the rate of false positives.

Fortunately, some sensitive information has a particular format that can be used to identify it and reduce the rate of false positives if the data is stored in the appropriate format. Sensitive content like credit card numbers provide additional distinction in the form of 15- or 16-digit formatted strings that are generated using the Luhn algorithm. It is a modulus 10 algorithm that makes false positives less likely, depending upon how the searching is performed.

For what it's worth, "less likely" does not mean impossible. There are still huge quantities of false positives when the Luhn algorithm is used, particularly if searches are performed on the raw files (including metadata) vs. limiting the search to the user-created content portion of the file. Interpreted searches extracting and searching native logical file content will mostly resolve this issue.

Logical vs. Physical Deletion

From a high level, there are two primary strategies for deleting data, which are logical and physical data deletion strategies. Logically (AKA soft) deleting data only marks that location on the file system or database as unallocated (AKA available) and makes it available to be used for future storage.

The data will continue to fully reside there until it is overwritten by another file, at which point it is either fully or partially overwritten. Usually, the new file that occupies the space is smaller than the previous file, and the tail portion of the original file remains on the disk in the form of file slack. Sometimes, that location on the disk might remain unallocated for months or years, depending upon the disk utilization and other factors.

Because of this, logical deletion methods are fully recoverable using forensic methods until the data has been overwritten. After the data has been overwritten, it may be partially recoverable within the file slack, from other locations on the disk, or sometimes within the page file.

Physical (AKA hard) deleting data involves not only making the space unallocated but also overwriting the entire file or record with other content, whether 0s, 1s, ransom strings, or any desired pattern. This completely eradicates the data from the last-known storage location as identified by the file system. This makes recovery of that file or content from that specific location impossible.

In the early days, best practices defined that data should be overwritten seven times to be considered fully unrecoverable. This is no longer the case, and overwriting the data in a single pass is now considered best practice, as it is unrecoverable due to modern hard drive structure.

However, due to the way some file systems operate, such as NTFS, the same or similar data from previous versions of the file might still be recoverable from other locations on the disk or possibly from the page file. As a file is created and grows in size (such as a Word document being created by the user), it may be picked up and moved around several times in order to keep the file sectors contiguous. This improves access speeds and reduces disk fragmentation.

This also happens with disk defragmentation, which moves all sectors of a file adjacent to each other in a new location. Because of this, even if files are physically deleted, it may be possible to recover an earlier version of the file or portions of its content from other unallocated or slack-space areas on the file system.

Because of this, best practices for the physical deletion of file systems involve the additional steps of wiping all unallocated clusters on the disk as well as wiping the pagefile. This can be done with various secure deletion tools. With these extra steps, the data is as close as possible to being unrecoverable. This is the level of deletion that is required in secure environments, such as to comply with DOD standards.

Depending upon the file system, repository, or structured file type, the concepts of logical vs. physical deletion take different forms and require different steps. In some cases, physical deletion is not entirely possible, such as with many structured file types. Email archives are particularly problematic in this regard.

However, for standard business purposes, physical deletion is not usually necessary. Logical deletion or the extra step of a simple overwrite of the file with 0s after collection and preservation is sufficient for most use cases. Most users will not have the ability to recover the file following these actions, and the inappropriately stored sensitive information will be out of their reach.

Endpoints

The biggest challenge an investigator may face in their career is trying to search, identify, collect, and eradicate sensitive data across all computer endpoints owned by a large customer having numerous locations and mobile users across multiple continents. This process is non-trivial, and depending upon the extant enterprise forensic capabilities, it might not even be possible.

Responders may have significant issues with endpoint detection & response (EDR), forensics, or eDiscovery agents being compatible, installed, and/or active on all targeted endpoints. There are also complications caused by systems in dispersed areas over long distances and accessed by slow network connections. Traveling users who connect to the corporate environments intermittently over VPNs complicate the issues even further.

In order to overcome these types of challenges in performing all required investigation and eradication steps on endpoints, the endpoints need to be equipped with the right types of investigative agent technologies. Responder's solutions must have agents that are compatible with all endpoint types and investigative workflows. Moreover, to support remote systems, the agents need to be capable of checking in remotely over the Internet (without a VPN), obtaining instructions, performing the search and collection activity, and then forwarding the results or uploading files to an Internet-facing system when complete (cloud or DMZ).

If remote investigation and eradication capabilities do not exist for all targeted endpoints, the workflow becomes very manual. Traveling endpoints will need to be brought into offices where forensic capabilities and members of the response team with the required skill sets reside, or qualified responders will need to travel to locations that do not have the required capabilities and personnel.

Servers create additional challenges as well. Many servers are very large, have nearly full disk capacity, and already have overtaxed utilization. Attempting to perform the full scope of searching and eradication activity on such overtaxed or large-scale infrastructure can have unintended consequences on system availability.

Additionally, depending upon the use cases for both workstations and servers in any location, it may be required to first upload decryption keys to the analysis tools for file/folder encryption technologies prior to performing search and collection for desired content, followed by the subsequent eradication steps. If the files are encrypted, the decryption keys must be used to perform the searches or the desired data will not be found. This may sometimes be agreeable to the investigative use case as the data would be considered encrypted and secured, even though the system was compromised.

To be candid, there are always a lot of factors at work with response and eradication scenarios. The path chosen from the outset should be governed by the problem that needs to be solved. This must be established at the beginning and may evolve throughout the course of the investigation. However, establishing key investigation objectives, workstreams, and action items will enable the prioritization of efforts and exclusion of unnecessary tasks.

On a side note, the easiest way to manage content stored on endpoints is to ensure that it is synced with a cloud repository and that all user-created content is kept in that folder. This will ensure that forensics and queues for eradication can be performed within the cloud environment and replicated to the endpoint. Cloud-based EDR solutions are far more effective and efficient than scan or job-based solutions or searching and eradicating every endpoint individually, which can quickly become unscalable or may not even be possible.

Network Shares and Document Repositories

Network shares and document repositories are common targets of malicious activities. They can be used for harvesting sensitive content for exfiltration, as well as lateral movement and persistence methods. The latter happens by infecting the existing files residing there. When the infected files are opened by other systems, the
infection spreads by infecting new systems or re-infecting previously infected systems.

Other common issues involving shares and document repositories are insecure permissions and unencrypted sensitive data. It is very common, particularly in large organizations, to have an unfortunately high percentage of open file shares, insecure shared repositories, and/or improperly secured sensitive information. These can become compromised by malicious (or even just curious) internal or external parties and malware. These situations can quickly turn into a full-scale response effort, followed by a need to eradicate residual or previously extant threats through formal eradication and remediation processes.

Unlike standard network shares, there are some special considerations for the large variety of document repository technologies available. These take many forms and are sometimes proprietary to each technology vendor. In order to perform searching, identification, collection, and eradication on each of these repository types, it requires the investigative technology to have connectors compatible with the document repository types. Following that, accessing them is similar to how network shares would be logically accessed.

The method of eradication to be performed will be determined by the specific data security and eradication requirements (physical or logical deletion). If logical deletion is sufficient, then using the enterprise forensic technology and the respective connectors to map shares/repositories, search and collect data, and perform logical deletions over the mounted shares or connected document repositories is sufficient.

If physical deletion is required, instead of investigating the network share content through the share itself, it should be accessed through endpoint investigative agents. Forensic agents will be able to perform all types of eradication activity from a physical level rather than being limited to the logical level.

Physical deletion on a repository will vary by each document repository type and the native capabilities. Some may not have native physical deletion capabilities through the interface and could require creative approaches to perform such. A common workaround involves logically deleting the file using the repository's administrative interface and copying all of the remaining files to new storage locations. Following that, the drives, storage containers, or other media types used by the original repository can be wiped, deleted, or otherwise destroyed to remove all traces.

This could be critical for high-security environments, such as anything having to do with classified data and government organizations. However, it is not typical for most business environments or regulatory requirements.

Cloud Services

Most organizations are making a switch toward moving key business services and storage locations into the cloud, including email, messaging, file storage, workflow, ticketing, etc. As such, the cloud is a primary attack target and evidence source requiring investigation, identification, response, and eradication activities. Just like with data repositories, evidence searching, collection, or eradication activity happens either using connector utilities within investigative tools or native functions within the cloud services administrative interfaces.

Just as with security controls, most cloud service interfaces have very limited functions for performing searching, collection, or eradication. To apply more granular, compound, Boolean, or sophisticated data searching for full or partial matching, data usually needs to be over-collected from the cloud services and pulled into the 3rd party investigative toolsets. Following that, eradication for specific items would need to be performed using either connectors integrated into the investigative toolset or native in the cloud services application.

Just as with document repository technologies, cloud services technologies typically perform logical deletion functions, and they may include versioning and backup functions that may retain the ability to recover the file later. The ability of non-administrators to recover eradicated files must be prevented.

Physical deletion or recovery from cloud services is typically impossible as there is nothing physical to work with unless the service is isolated to a particular virtual machine with a virtual physical disk dedicated to the customer. Apart from the physical limitations of artificially isolating customer data to a specific location, the nature of cloud services infrastructure is not conducive to physical deletion or recovery. So, physical deletion requires the customer data to be restricted to a single system or drive volume. If that is true, the respective files, volumes, or drives can be physically deleted.

Email

Email is a central data source for nearly any type of investigation. It could involve any cause, whether accidental or malicious and be involved at any stage of an incident. It comes up most directly in inappropriate data transmission over email, phishing, and business email compromise (BEC) incidents, as email is directly involved as a transmission vector. But it is also a subject of investigation in any hacking, malware, or credential theft incident, as these also involve the assumed compromise of anything accessible on or from the affected system or using the affected credentials.

Ultimately, email needs to be searched for evidence, and then content or attachments identified must be collected and eradicated to prevent unauthorized storage, additional threat activity, or further exposure. Email is another data source for which eradication is performed via logical methods rather than physical. This is true for on-prem or cloud-based email infrastructure and the local files stored on workstations.

Depending upon the access to the server-side email repository file and the technology used, some recovery options may be available. However, none of them are available to non-admin users, who are restricted to their email client user interface.

While it is true that in some limited cases for local, client-side email repositories, a form of physical deletion may be possible, this involves deleting the artifacts in question, compacting the file to its most compressed state, exporting all logical content to a new file, and securely deleting the original file. If the client email repository supports this, it will eliminate the ability to recover the data.

Databases

Databases are a significant source of potentially unsecured sensitive information. Depending upon the method of entry or access to the content, the data could come from a wide variety of sources and be accessible by many unintended parties or applications.

Many older databases have very limited security controls, if any. Further, the security for access to content in databases is usually implemented by the applications providing access to them. The applications also typically provide authentication, authorization, content inspection, and input validation for anything inserted into the database if those functionalities are implemented.

Encryption controls can be implemented either by the application or the database itself if encryption controls are implemented at all. Regardless of whether the application or the database implements the encryption, the application requires the decryption keys for its functional purposes. If the attacker is exploiting the application flaws to gain access through manipulation of the application, the encryption controls likely will not prevent unauthorized access.

The various formats, query languages, access methods, and encoding of the database files themselves further complicate database investigations. Unless the files can be exported to a text-based format or there is some sort of forensic connector for the database type, it is very likely that database investigations will be limited to the native query language of the database engine itself. This is a very limiting complication.

As such, from an investigation perspective, the involvement of databases introduces a significant challenge. Database forensics is a very nascent space, and encryption, encoding, varying formats, changes between versions, query languages, schema considerations, and other factors can create a significant hurdle for investigators.

Interestingly, it typically does not create the same problem for attackers who are manipulating the application. Enumerating all tables and contents in databases for exfiltration and later analysis is a lot easier than targeting searches to enumerate sensitive content.

Due to all of the complications posed by database investigations and the ability to search and identify potentially inappropriately stored sensitive information, eradication of the same information is that much harder. If the data can't be found, it's hard to delete it.

This generally means that the search and eradication methods must be performed by DBAs using specific keywords or search strings. This significantly limits the ability to perform advanced, logic-based searching for content.

Even once the content has been identified, database deletion functions for content within tables are often significantly limited. There are typically only logical deletion functions.

This is important as unless the data in the field is overwritten, it is simply marked unallocated and is potentially recoverable. However, custom scripts can be used to overwrite the content and physically delete the information.

Backups

Backups are usually perceived as the solution to data problems. However, depending on the circumstances, they may create problems as well.

If backups have the potential to restore sensitive or malicious content that was eradicated, it can result in a situation where backups are restoring previously eradicated problems. This can introduce both security and compliance issues that would need to be dealt with.

This creates a dilemma on what to do with the inappropriately stored sensitive information located in backups. This could be addressed either by deleting the specific data item in the backups (if the functionality exists in the specific solution and media type) or by creating and abiding by notes in relation to the backed-up content.

Physical Media

When it comes to physical media eradication, there are essentially two primary options. 1) The media can be overwritten with arbitrary content (0s, 1s, random strings, etc.), or 2) it can be physically destroyed. If the situation requires the need to do this, non-optical, rewritable media and devices (such as hard drives, tape

drives, etc.) can be securely overwritten, and read-only or rewritable optical media is usually destroyed.

The advent of solid-state drives (SSD) and Non-Volatile Random Access Memory (NVRAM)/Flash drives has changed these assumptions slightly, as the controllers move data around each time it is written. As such, even when overwriting the data, it may be overwritten to a different location than the original data was stored. However, the pattern used in writing data to the hard drive can make it difficult or impossible to recover the data, thus making it very close to being physically wiped.

Regardless, in high-security situations involving classified information, it is typical for all media involved to be thrown in a DOD-approved shredder if physical media eradication is required. This results in a zero percent chance of recovery.

26 THREAT ERADICATION: ENVIRONMENT, SYSTEM, AND ACCOUNT RESTORATION

This chapter addresses the response activity that must occur to begin cleaning up after an incident. Following the evidence gathering, preservation, and containment activity, it is time to restore the affected environment and resources to a known good state. There are a wide variety of considerations in doing this and a respective priority in performing such to prevent breach recurrence.

To ensure all attacker- or malware-related threats have been eradicated, all affected resources should be restored to previous, clean images or snapshots and then fully patched and hardened according to customer requirements. Additionally, all accounts that have logged into affected resources must be considered compromised and have their respective passwords reset and active sessions terminated. Groups and OUs are also a consideration in these circumstances, as they can be used to nest and hide privileged escalation and unauthorized access.

Networks

Depending upon the state of the network environment and if there is the potential for attackers or malware to compromise resources during the recovery process, it may be necessary to create a separate, clean network environment to restore resources. As such, during the recovery process, there will be at least 2 networks: 1) the original dirty network and 2) the clean network.

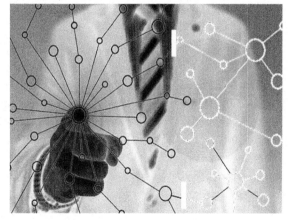

This does not require new hardware and can be established with existing systems and network devices by using VLANS. In either case, it involves moving resources from the dirty network to the clean network once sanitized. Only those resources that have been restored from known good images, factory media, or which have been affirmatively validated as clean should be placed in the clean environment. Validation methodologies must be robust and rock solid.

This process must be strictly adhered to in order to prevent compromised resources from affecting the clean environment. Known problems that complicate this process include the propensity of people to move compromised laptops in the environment or to open previously unidentified malicious emails or files, thus resulting in a compromise of the clean environment. If there are gaps in this process, it is possible that a single dirty laptop, email, or file could compromise the entire clean network, and the entire process would need to start over. It is especially critical to not allow VPN access to a clean environment until all remote systems that use the VPN have been sanitized.

Systems

All affected systems should be restored to a known good state. This will happen in a variety of ways. The main differentiation between recovery methods is between physical and virtual systems.

Physical systems (servers and workstations) are usually recovered from a gold image baseline, including the respective software and configurations required. However, sometimes a fresh installation is required, depending upon the circumstances.

A challenge that is encountered in either situation is that the resulting systems are usually far behind on patches and need to be updated prior to being placed in service. This requires that they be segregated from the larger network environment to prevent them from being compromised until updates are finished.

Internal networks can be very hostile environments. Mobile workstations, unmanaged devices, and vendor systems create significant risks. If not properly isolated during the recovery process, it is entirely likely that systems being reinstalled could be identified as vulnerable by malware scanning the internal environments. The affected systems could be compromised before security patches or other mitigating controls are applied. While this may sound fanciful, it is real and happens.

Keeping baselines for physical images up to date can be a very daunting task, especially if there are a large number of systems to maintain. The more updated the images are, the less work there is to update them post-installation, and the better protected the installation process will be.

Virtual systems (Virtual desktops (VDI) and cloud systems) are easier to recover in that they can be immediately returned to a known good snapshot state or pulled from a clean baseline image. This happens instantaneously, unlike physical systems. However, they ultimately run into the same problems with unpatched baseline images. They need to be patched before being placed in service and need to be protected in the meantime.

Devices

Devices are often overlooked during a breach investigation and the subsequent eradication activity. However, they often run outdated operating systems or firmware and could become compromised. It is not uncommon for them to be used as persistence or backdoor mechanisms. It is entirely possible for all hosts in an environment to be sanitized but then have the environment re-infected through a compromised printer, firewall, or other device that was overlooked in the eradication and recovery processes.

In addition to potential backdoors or malware persistence mechanisms, vulnerable devices are often compromised and exfiltrate sensitive information. This is commonly the case with payment or medical devices that could be leaking PCI or PHI content, respectively. As such, these devices need to be restored to a known good state and then patched to prevent re-compromise.

Software/Applications/Services

Just like systems and devices need to be restored to a known good state, so do the respective software, applications, services, and their respective components and configurations. All of these may have been tampered with by attackers or malware. Vulnerable software is just as bad as vulnerable systems and can be, for the most part, synonymous. Irrespective of whether an endpoint is compromised through a vulnerable OS or vulnerable installed software, it is essentially a matter of semantics.

Some of this will be taken care of automatically by restoring gold baseline images if they are kept current. However, as stated previously, system images may be out of date for security patches and may also have older, insecure versions of software as well. This affects both physical and virtual environments and virtual containers used for cloud services.

As such, ensuring updated software, applications, and services are on restored systems usually requires a secondary process. For physical systems, this is best performed by endpoint management software that deploys compliant program versions and manages endpoint security policy configuration to ensure compliance across the various endpoint profiles.

For virtualized or cloud systems and containers, deploying updates is best managed via updating the images and deploying new instances of the images. Directly installing updates to the deployed systems is not scalable and may result in unnecessary and expensive licensing applications if traditional endpoint configuration management tools are used.

Firmware

Firmware is essentially software that runs directly on computer hardware, network devices, peripherals, medical devices, payment devices, etc. Just like operating systems or software can be compromised and used for intrusion, persistence, and/or backdoor access, the same is true for firmware.

There are many variants of rootkits that affect firmware. These can provide very low-level, hard-to-detect backdoor access that survives a reimage/reinstall of the system and its software.

Firmware is often overlooked in the eradication and restoration processes. Managing firmware versions and deploying updates can be a challenge, especially on devices that cannot be remotely managed via configuration management.

Due to the large variety of systems and devices that may be affected, performing firmware version review, validation, restoration, and updates will require a combined approach. This typically includes using a combination of endpoint and device management utilities for all relevant systems and devices within the environment.

It may require one solution for managing firmware on servers and workstations, a different solution for network devices, another for printers and other peripherals, and yet others for medical or other types of devices. Ultimately, keeping everything up to date in a timely manner is extremely challenging and not entirely feasible, depending upon the complexity of the environment.

Password and Session Resets

In addition to the system-related components and software, all accounts used on or accessed from the affected systems or applications must be considered compromised. This includes domain, local, service, and application accounts.

During the eradication process, all accounts must be reviewed to validate they are not attacker- or malware-created backdoor accounts. The unverified or known malicious accounts must be disabled or deleted, and all valid accounts must have their respective passwords reset. This will stop access by attackers or malware using compromised credentials or malicious accounts. However, this is not a permanent solution and should be bolstered by compensating controls, such as MFA, OTP, or other secondary authentication solutions.

However, changing passwords does not necessarily block access to already established sessions. Attackers or malware may continue to be logged into accounts and have established sessions with systems and applications following the password change, so long as they do not permit it to time out. As such, the response team needs to identify and terminate/reset previously authenticated sessions.

Groups, OUs, and the respective membership must also be reviewed and validated to identify any unauthorized groups/OUs created by attackers or malware and any resulting membership changes. This often manifests as privileged groups or OUs with innocuous names to which compromised or malicious accounts have been added. Groups, OUs, and respective memberships must be reset to the state prior to infection or as required for business needs.

27 THREAT ERADICATION: VULNERABILITY MITIGATION AND COMPENSATING CONTROLS

There is a reason that security incidents happen, and it is not because customers have perfect security controls. The fact that a security breach occurred is a result of failures of security controls at multiple layers. Each of these security failures and corresponding control recommendations needs to be identified and fleshed out during the response process.

If the customer is still vulnerable to attack, the Incident Commander's job is not done. Moreover, incident response/management is incomplete unless mitigating controls have been put in place to block the threat vector. If the response actions do not at least stop the threat from being successful, the attack will soon occur again, and a game of Whack-a-Mole will ensue. This chapter provides guidance on how to avoid playing that game.

Mitigating the threats is preferably done by fully remediating them through patching and hardening resources with adequate security controls and/or configurations. Alternatively, compensating controls might be used if full remediation is not possible.

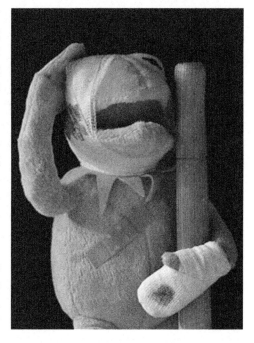

Full mitigation includes 1) updates to software, applications, and firmware and 2) implementing necessary security controls for visibility, monitoring, detection, and blocking. If done right, the combination of these two considerations will prevent further malicious activity.

No matter what controls are put in place, the mitigation steps should be validated during the testing and post-implementation stages. Performing this will require appropriate security tools and testing methodologies.

Security Patches

Unless a zero-day exploit is used, a known attack vector has most likely exploited an unpatched vulnerability or security misconfiguration. Attacks against client-side user applications and browser plugins are among the most common attacks. They have led to breaches as devastating as any external-facing server-side vulnerability.

The larger a company is, the harder it can be to keep all systems and applications up to date on security patches. This has become compounded by the complexity of patching client-side applications, browser plugins, and unmanaged or vendor-managed systems within the customer environment.

Business constraints and application development needs or timelines may also delay the deployment of patches to client-side and server-side applications, even when they are available. As such, this makes things easier for attackers, and zero-day exploits are seldom necessary.

To combat this, some environments enable automatic updates on systems with the expectation that they keep resources up to date. However, that is not an effective strategy for all security patches, especially those having to do with user applications, browser plugins, business services, web servers, databases, or anything requiring manual integration.

In response to a security breach, however, patching approvals and timelines will typically move a lot quicker. While performing vulnerability mitigation during threat eradication, it is important to use this opportunity to deploy not only patches related to the existing threats across the infrastructure but also other critical patches that could be used as alternate attack vectors.

Many of the current exploit kits will cycle through multiple vulnerabilities across various platforms until a working exploit is found. Just because malware happens to be exploiting the same vulnerability across the enterprise network does not mean that it could not just as easily exploit another one. It is critical to apply patches for all notable vulnerabilities that could permit code execution and/or privilege escalation.

For physical systems, this is best performed by endpoint management software that deploys compliant program versions and manages endpoint security policy configuration. This will ensure compliance across the various endpoint platforms, configuration types, and security profiles.

More specifically, in any large organization, there are likely to be various endpoint configurations based on the department's needs or security requirements. These are managed using dedicated endpoint configuration profiles. In this way, software versions and security patches can be deployed to all permutations in a centrally managed way.

For virtualized or cloud systems and containers, deploying updates is best managed via updating the images the virtual systems or containers are based on and deploying the new instances from the images. Updating the deployed systems is not scalable and may result in unnecessary and expensive licensing applications if traditional endpoint configuration management tools are used.

Configuration Hardening

Another primary cause, or at least a contributing factor to security breaches, is insecure client-side or server-side system and application configurations. Common failures are the lack of input validation, security configuration policies, password or hashing algorithms, lockout controls, or other types of access controls that are too voluminous to enumerate in this section.

Targeted security enhancements should be evaluated, tested, and implemented in response to a security breach and to mitigate vulnerabilities that enable threats. The types of configuration hardening controls implemented in response to a breach are usually tightly related to the security failures of the breach.

However, they often may include other foreseeable tangents or address root cause issues that reside several layers beneath the specific controls bypassed during the breach. Ideally, they should resolve entire families of attack vectors and/or exploit methods.

In any case, using the momentum created by the breach to evaluate, test, and deploy security configuration hardening controls should be maximized to block the largest variety of foreseeable threats but minimize the impact on availability. Long story short, don't play Whack-a-Mole, and never let a good crisis go to waste.

The goal is to stop attacks before they happen and to detect unauthorized access as soon as it occurs. Being successful at this requires a strong security posture and every level of technology with extreme visibility and alerting capabilities at network, endpoint, and logging. Sometimes, this visibility is a configuration function. At other times, it is an agent-based capability that is subsequently bolted on.

Deploying widespread security controls across the varied population of endpoint profiles is best performed by endpoint management software. This will not only deploy and configure approved programs but also manage endpoint security policy configuration to harden settings and ensure compliance across the various endpoint profiles.

More specifically, in any large organization, there are likely to be various endpoint configurations based on the business needs, which are managed using dedicated endpoint configuration profiles. In this way, software and configuration settings can be deployed to all supported systems and application types.

Firmware Validation

Firmware is essentially software that runs directly on computer hardware, network devices, peripherals, medical devices, payment devices, etc. Just like operating systems or software can be compromised and used for intrusion, persistence, and/or backdoor access, the same is true for firmware. There are many variants of rootkits that affect firmware. These can provide very low-level, hard-to-detect backdoor access that survives a reimage/reinstall of the system and its software.

Firmware is often overlooked in the eradication and restoration processes. Managing firmware versions and deploying updates can be a challenge, especially on devices that cannot be remotely managed via configuration management. Due to the large variety of systems and devices that may be affected, performing firmware version review, validation, restoration, and updates will require a combined approach, including endpoint and device management utilities for all relevant systems and devices within the environment. It may require one solution for managing firmware on servers and workstations, a different solution for network devices, another for printers and other peripherals, and yet others for medical or other types of devices.

Security & Compensating Controls
Hardening Access Controls

For hardening access controls, some explanations of current trends are in order. Interestingly, the concept of secure passwords has become more about secondary validation controls combined with memorable, non-weak passwords rather than long, highly complex passwords that people can meet but still be weak.

For example, a password like January2024 would likely pass most password filters, but it is easily guessable and predictable. However, even though the use of strong passwords or passphrases has been somewhat deprecated, mainly because people could not abide them, they are still a good idea if done right.

Secure IAM access controls (strong passwords, keys, client certificates, biometrics, MFA, OTP, vaulting, banned password lists, source validation, and/or other methods) must be employed to secure all known or potentially compromised accounts. Some modern guidelines are as follows:

Strong Passwords
Current standards include 8+ character passwords that are not considered to be bad, guessable passwords. However, this password length is in combination with other security controls providing additional, enhanced security and validation, such as MFA, vaulting, OTP, or other capabilities. If those are not available, the password should be substantially longer and changed at a reasonable period of time to prevent password cracking.

Banned Password Lists
This is a relatively recent attempt to eliminate bad passwords that pose as secure passwords, such as P@ssword123, Spring2024, or S3cur1ty, which are basically dictionary words with obvious number for vowel substitutions or appended with obvious number strings. Many password crackers have configuration options for this simply by checking a box.

Client Certificates
These are used to authenticate client hosts, browsers, or other client applications and are often employed by applications, VPNs, or SSH connections. They should be unique per host or user.

Biometrics
The types of biometrics controls likely used for consumer devices include fingerprints, facial recognition, and/or iris scans. However, high-security commercial or government biometrics also include palm prints, retina scans, or other advanced technologies that have lower false-positive rates.

Multi-Factor Authentication (MFA)
While both hard and soft tokens are possible and available, soft tokens on mobile devices or on computers are much more common. Hard tokens are considered more secure but are much less convenient and common. The advantage of hard tokens is that they cannot be hacked by malicious entities or applications like soft tokens can. A notable variety of malicious applications have been created to compromise soft tokens on computers and mobile devices. They either clone the configuration or intercept the OTP.

One Time Password (OTP)

OTP typically takes the form of text, voice, email, or number string from an MFA app. These are helpful but are successfully intercepted or read and possibly deleted by malicious applications. If malware can be installed on mobile devices that receive the OTP confirmation or generate the code based on a crypto seed, the OTP can be stolen and used for unauthorized purposes.

ID-Proofing

This is typically a function or integration with other identity verification controls, such as MFA or OTP. It is typically used for device registration or setting change confirmation. It makes the entity upload a photo ID to confirm they are authorized to make changes and thus ensure that unauthorized entities do not make changes to settings or add new devices.

Password Vaulting

Password vaulting is typically used by administrators and/or service accounts and implements a password-of-the-day type of functionality. The user logs in with their standard account, confirms their identity with MFA, and is then able to access the privileged account password for that day. For service accounts, password vaulting solutions can integrate with services or applications being accessed by service accounts, and the IAM solution automatically changes the password and ensures that it is updated wherever necessary.

Source Validation

Source validation is a combination of a network concept combined with IAM access controls. Users and/or systems must be authenticated from an approved location and/or IP address space. Attempts to logon from unauthorized sources would be denied.

Self-Service Password Reset Functions

Validate that self-service password reset function(s) utilize a secure process to prevent attackers from once again granting themselves access to accounts following administrative password resets. Some sort of manual verification, ID proofing, voice recognition, or other independent user verification mechanisms must exist to validate requests.

Remote Access Restrictions

Remote access, VPN, or other types of Internet ingress activity must be carefully controlled and monitored. After attackers gain valid credentials via phishing, waterhole attacks, malware, password dumps, or other methods, their next action is to logon to remotely accessible services as authorized user accounts and browse resources under the context of that account.

To assist with the identification and blocking of malicious activity, the following controls should be implemented, and all controls should be integrated with threat feeds to dynamically block known malicious hosts and suspicious connections:

Corporate User RAS VPNs

Block VPN sessions for any user/administrator account that has been associated with suspicious indicators. Some specific activities to block or investigate and then likely block are:

- Known malicious source hosts – Identified through investigation, report, or threat feed.
- Suspicious countries – Connections from suspicious countries not having known contractors or traveling employees, especially Nigeria
- OFAC countries – Anything the US Treasury Office of Foreign Asset Control (OFAC) has on its blocked list is usually dangerous and worth blocking.
- Impossible travel – If users logon from one location and then another far away location (especially internationally), this is a key indicator the credentials are compromised and being used by an unauthorized party.
- Multiple logons – If users are connected to the VPN multiple times, especially from different locations, this is a key indicator of malicious activity.

Partner/Vendor B2B VPNs

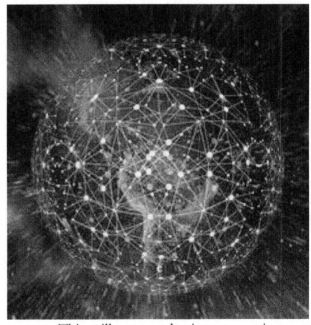

VPN connections with trusted partners should be set up as a point-to-point connection with defined IP addresses. In the event a trusted partner is found to be compromised, the connection should be easily severed until their security posture can be validated.

Virtual Desktop Gateway

Sometimes, B2B VPNs, RAS VPNs, and other direct remote access network connections must be blocked, but some form of remote access must still be provided. In such cases, a virtual desktop gateway should be used to provide secure, restricted access to a hardened virtual machine to defined resources. This will support business operations and reduce security risks. This enables externally located entities to obtain defined access to secure virtual machines that have approved applications and connect to required resources. It mitigates the risk of compromised systems spreading malware through a remote connection but enables external entities to provide services.

Network Controls

Depending upon the nature of the threat, a variety of network controls may be effective for vulnerability mitigation and/or compensating controls. However, these typically only work within the security perimeter unless endpoint agents are configured with an always-on VPN client. The following are common security controls that leverage next-generation firewalls, network IPS devices, proxies, network malware inspection, or cloud-based scrubbing controls. These either implement or have the benefit of SSL/TLS decryption to provide deep packet, protocol, and content inspection and block malicious network activity related to malware incidents.

WAFs

Protecting vulnerable web applications with web application firewalls (WAFs) can be the best way to stop most inbound malicious activity against vulnerable websites immediately. It can turn a vulnerable website with few to no security controls into a relatively secure site that has security controls that block common threats. This will enable the development team to permit a vulnerable site to function while a more secure site can be built.

Traditional Network Controls

Using perimeter firewalls and/or network IPS devices to block IP addresses, domains, network ranges, CIDR blocks, TCP/UDP ports, and/or signature-based threats is a stop-gap security control that is easily circumvented by attackers through the use of proxies in countries or locations that are not blocked.

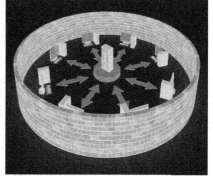

If the attackers are really determined, they will get around these controls and find another way in. However, it may buy the response team some time. Moreover, it can avoid detection and compromise from automated methods that do not try hard enough to circumvent traditional network controls, such as basic network scans.

Network DLP

Network-based Dat Loss Prevention (DLP) technologies should be implemented to identify, contain, and or delete files with targeted content as found by full-data matching, partial-data matching, specific data types (PHI, PCI, PII, etc.), or sensitive data classification tags.

While the identification of some of these data types and matching activities are automated and typically built-in (like PCI and PII), the others will require configuration to work properly. To be candid, however, all of them require some level of configuration to limit false positives and ensure that the right file formats and data sources are configured. Moreover, matching via full or partial data, enumerating PHI content, or flagging on data tags needs to be fully configured and kept up to date to ensure it is successful.

Next-Generation Firewalls

Utilizing next-generation network traffic security capabilities provides significantly greater detection, identification, prevention, and blocking capabilities over traditional firewalls. They should be integrated with threat feeds to provide additional intelligence.

Beyond looking into layer 3 and 4 network traffic socket content, next-gen firewalls and IPSs have the ability to look into traffic sources, destinations, and content. They can perform additional network traffic validation, as described in the following capabilities:

- Protocol Anomalies – The capability to perform protocol validation and anomaly detection is highly valuable, as it enables the ability to identify forms of protocol manipulation and misuse. This could enable the detection of exploitation, infiltration, C2, exfiltration, and some forms of tunneling for covert communication.

- Fraudulent sites/reputation blocking – This is helpful for preventing connections to/from any known malicious hosts or sites, as well as stopping phishing activity. However, this requires the sites to have been long enough to have developed a reputation. Alternatively, the capabilities could be integrated with network malware sandboxing solutions to analyze the sites, traffic, and files transferred to automatically detect malicious activity and classify the sites as malicious or benign. As such, the first connection to an unknown malicious site will usually be successful. However, after the analysis has been completed and the destination has been convicted, subsequent connections and activity would be flagged as malicious. All next-gen network capabilities that are integrated will then block access attempts.

- Newly registered domains and/or imposter domains – These are very common with targeted phishing campaigns and attempts to redirect traffic to imposter sites having purpose-built domains. A common example would be to use a subtle twist on a legitimate domain. A valid site (corp.com) might convincingly be phished using the domain C0RP.COM during a phishing attack. There are infinite variations on that theme, usually involving the substitution of 0s for Os, Is for ls, subtle misspellings, or methods to make them look legitimate. As such, if a domain is very new, it should at least be considered suspicious. If the domains also have imposter substitutions, they are easily convictable.

- Malicious downloads – This involves the ability to use virtual systems to visit domains and sites and/or explode files to determine whether they result in unauthorized changes to systems. This is usually a scaled-down functionality typically found in dedicated network malware sandboxing devices, which perform a similar activity with greater resources.

- Volumetric and duration blocking – This includes aggregating the quantity of connections, length of sessions, amount of data, and so forth. This may identify and enable the blocking of patterns that are determined to be suspicious or malicious based on business rules or security concerns.

- Connection time blocking – This is used to identify and block traffic that is occurring at a time it should not be, based on a user's job role.

- DGA blocking – This involves identifying and blocking suspicious domains created through Domain Generation Algorithms, which will be both new and have high entropy in the name.
- Suspicious source or destination countries – These usually include any country not having known customers, contractors, or traveling employees, especially Nigeria. This requires some preparation and documentation ahead of time in order to validate what is intended and what may be malicious.
- OFAC countries – Anything that the US Treasury Office of Foreign Asset Control (OFAC) has on its blocked list is usually dangerous and worth blocking. Any country with sanctions or travel restrictions should be blocked for inbound or outbound access unless absolutely necessary and well-defined, restricted, and monitored.
- Clandestine private VPNs and outbound remote access tools – Block user, attacker, or malware-installed remote access applications. There are wide varieties that most commonly include remote proxy services, SSH VPNs, the TOR network, and even webmail proxies, such as Gcat (which uses Gmail for C2 and exfil).

Network Malware

Utilize network malware sandbox devices to detect and block malware downloads and network traffic. This involves the ability to use virtual systems to visit domains, sites, and/or explode files to determine whether they result in unauthorized changes to systems. This usually involves dedicated hardware and large quantities of virtual machines on that hardware to scale and analyze network traffic, emails, sites, and any files  that are sent across the network. Success with network malware devices requires SSL/TLS decryption to be fully implemented and all ingress/egress methods to have coverage for such.

Dynamic Switch Port Configuration/Network Access Control

In order to limit the potential risk of systems unnecessarily and potentially maliciously communicating with and exploiting each other, the dynamic configuration of switch ports is extremely valuable, automated, and scalable. Using this technology, a system or device is identified when it is plugged in and assigned an appropriate network access profile. The switch port ACLs are automatically configured, and the system plugged in can only communicate on the network in a proscribed way. This can successfully thwart the ability of compromised hosts to cause widespread damage. However, due to switch memory limitations, sometimes these ACLs need to be significantly simplified.

Virtual Infrastructure Gateway

This should be used to limit direct access to internal systems from remote access users/vendors/partners and require them to go through a jumpbox or virtualized infrastructure, such as VDI or Citrix environment having only permitted applications published. It is ideal if virtual environment access is set up as the primary access method as part of the onboarding of relationships involving remote access. It is effectively a virtual device firewall that can significantly limit the risk of malicious activity from people or malicious processes.

Endpoint Controls

Due to the limited scope and efficacy of traditional network controls being restricted to ingress/egress activity within the security perimeter, endpoint controls can be implemented to address the same methods. Additionally, expanded sets of controls can be deployed as necessary to systems located anywhere, so long as they can communicate back to the endpoint management system, such as EDR. Endpoint controls are critical security and compensating controls providing quick detection, analysis, and containment of malware threats on endpoints. The following are common methods used.

Traditional Network Controls

Blocking via traditional endpoint-based network controls involves using host-based firewalls and IPS software to block IP addresses, domains, network ranges, CIDR blocks, implementing port restrictions, and/or implementing signature-based blocking that can and should be performed at the host level, as well as the network-level. They will protect the endpoints from malicious traffic inside or outside the corporate environment. This is highly advantageous, as it can prevent lateral movement inside the security perimeter if internal systems become compromised. It can also help defend access to sensitive ports/protocols on systems located outside the security perimeter.

EDR Capabilities

Using EDR technologies for host-based monitoring is critical for endpoint visibility and blocking. Such capabilities should include functions such as active behavior monitoring, anomaly identification, malware identification, and malicious activity blocking and prevention.

This is critical to providing the required security for systems and environments. Best-of-breed EDR solutions combine endpoint investigation and remediation capabilities with behavior-based inspection methods. This combination can provide selective containment controls, enabling legitimate activity but blocking malicious or undesired activity. It is also key for performing activity retrospection, which can enumerate accounts, processes, libraries, drivers, sites, files, and other artifacts and activity related to malware infections for systems, whether on or off the network.

This usually requires cloud-based EDR capabilities to provide a view for all Internet-connected systems, regardless of their location. Ideally, the EDR technology chosen should also be certified as an antivirus/antimalware solution in order to minimize unnecessary, superfluous agents on endpoints.

DLP

Host-based DLP technologies should be used to identify, contain, and or delete files with prohibited content as found by full-data matching, partial-data matching, data types (PHI, PCI, PII, etc.), or sensitive data classification tags.

SIEM/Log Analysis Controls

For the purposes of ongoing threat monitoring, vulnerability mitigation, and/or implementing compensating controls, a SIEM is critical for capturing, aggregating, correlating, alerting, and analyzing suspicious or malicious activity identified in logs. Creating/refining behavior-based log correlation rules, identifying malicious activity in logs, and implementing security controls to block it is an iterative process. It must happen continually, with the evolution of new threats and advancements in technologies.

The key to being successful with using logs as a compensating control and proving vulnerability mitigation is to have specific rulesets that can quickly identify and trigger secondary actions on detected threats. These secondary actions should be evidence-gathering, alerting, blocking, or other activities leading to containment.

Considering some vulnerabilities cannot be patched or threats cannot be blocked due to 1) technical, 2) business, 3) political reasons, or 4) financial reasons, sometimes they need to be as isolated as possible and then closely monitored for potentially malicious activity. Stated more succinctly, if a threat cannot be blocked, sometimes all one can do is watch and then apply additional blocking measures if there is reason to believe the resources are at risk.

Validation via Security Testing

It is essential to validate that vulnerabilities have been remediated, threats have been blocked, and attacker artifacts or manipulated content have been eradicated. This must be validated on all affected systems, devices, applications, services, repositories, accounts, and data.

Once all of the threat eradication activity has been completed, the in-scope resources must be validated via security testing methodologies to ensure they are secure and the eradication activities are complete. This includes using assessment tools and methodologies appropriate for the threat, technology types, and validation needs.

It may be performed on a system-by-system basis prior to placing systems back in service or performed holistically across the entire scope. Depending upon the circumstances, this usually requires a variety of tools to facilitate all use cases, including vulnerability assessment, penetration testing, application security, DLP scanning, endpoint management tools, change management, etc.

28 INCIDENT WORKFLOWS: INCIDENT COMMANDER-MANAGER

This chapter is the first of the workflows to be defined in detail specific to the Incident Commander role. Appendix B contains a highly summarized, quick-reference playbook for the Incident Commander role. The Incident Commander workflow provides guidance for the leading role during response functions that are performed across any or all incident response threat scenarios. The purpose is to provide insights needed for leading investigations as part of the full lifecycle incident management program. It details the considerations and incident management leadership activity that needs to be performed and documented at each phase of an incident.

Incident Notification and Details Gathering

Upon notification of an incident, the Incident Commander and other assigned response personnel should gather the required information respective to their environment, the current incident or threat activity, and the resources involved and begin building an incident response profile. The contents of the incident response profile vary by engagement but generally contain the following high-level items. It will help drive eliminating false positives or investigating a real incident:

Detection Method

Usually, threats are detected or reported from automated alerts, threat hunting, user reports, or outside entities. The associated detection, response, priority, and related processes may vary wildly, depending upon the detection method and sources involved. For the purposes of discussion, detection sources/methods will be divided between inside and outside sources, as follows.

Inside Sources

Insider detection and reporting methods are as follows. They are ordered from best to worst ways of detecting threats, meaning the most to the least desirable detection sources.

Threats are ideally detected and resolved before they become a problem, such as from security tools providing automated detection and response functions. It is best to find out about would-be threats from alerts related to blocked attempts to perform malicious activity. Less desirable sources include manual threat hunting, user-reported, or externally reported.

If any source other than security tools proactively blocking malicious activity from occurring detects a threat, it means that the threat penetrated various layers of security undetected, was successful to a certain degree, and remained active for a period of time before it was identified. The impact could range from minimal to catastrophic:

- Automated detection – These are typically system-generated alerts or hits on manual correlation rules from security technologies, such as network security, endpoint security, SIEMs, and threat feed integrations. The efficacy of these hits is as good as the signatures, IOCs, heuristics, or rules that created them. Your mileage may vary. Overall, they are likely to have both false negatives and false positives.
- Manual detection – These are usually hits on threat-hunting activity by security team members. They are generally the highest accuracy hits, as the content is (or should be) custom-crafted, tested, and validated by the threat hunter.

  Therefore, the false-positive and -negative rate is typically low if the threat hunters follow a rigorous process. Once again, your mileage may vary. If threat hunters are just duplicating what is identified on a threat feed or threat research site, this activity will essentially only be as good as the source and may as well just be integrated and automated.

  By definition, that is not threat hunting. Sadly, it often passes for it. Rather, real threat hunting requires customized research, testing, and validation for the environment, resources, and specific threats involved.
- User reported – Depending upon the type of incident or purportedly malicious activity that has been identified and reported, the validity can vary to both ends of the spectrum from low to high accuracy.

  Hacking and malware identifications can be anecdotal and inaccurate. Being as it is based on the users' experience, it will depend entirely on the user(s) involved.

  Detecting a ransomware infection is a notable exception. It is perfectly obvious if a system becomes compromised by ransomware. Anyone can get that right.

  Further, the identification of inappropriately shared, stored, or transferred information is usually very accurate. Ideally, any type of detection by end-users should be accompanied by screenshots and as much descriptive information as possible.

  However, the information they gather and share should be done in such a way as to avoid increasing risk and exposure. More specifically, avoid compromising their endpoint(s) or incurring further legal and regulatory liability from data exposures.

External Sources

If reported by or known to an outside entity, the best plan for dealing with them is to gather the information that they have to offer, but not over-engage them in the incident response processes. An exception would be for partners/vendors that are involved in joint incident response activity. With them, share IOCs, signatures, and salient findings in order to facilitate the response activity.

However, be careful not to overshare anything that could potentially introduce additional confidentiality concerns. Any findings or artifacts should be securely transferred using encrypted transfer methods to avoid creating a greater compliance incident on top of a security incident.

Moreover, if reported by or known to an outside entity, there are additional risks and action items. Public disclosure has effectively already occurred, and there are few controls over what outside entities say. Media notifications and complications are much more likely in this scenario. Typical external notifiers include the following sources:

- Law enforcement – This usually only happens if the situation is very significant or related to another case for which they need info from your environment. However, they typically won't tell you a lot. It is more of a public service notification.

  They generally will say something like: "You might want to look into the system at x.x.x.x" and then tell you nothing else. If they do provide this notification, take it seriously. There is very likely a threat there.

  However, if they want to get actively involved in the case, they are likely to take over the investigation. If they do, their goals very likely will not align with the goals of either the customers or responders.

  It is highly probable that they will want to permit malicious activity to continue for an extended period of time in order to obtain further intelligence about it and enumerate malicious infrastructure and parties involved. This will almost always result in a compromising situation for the customer, who typically just wants to clean up their environment and return to business as usual.

- Partners/vendors – This is probably the friendliest group of outsiders who will contact the customer regarding an incident. However, if they report an incident, then the service they provide is likely the source of the incident, and the systems and/or data involved may be at risk. This is usually the beginning of a lot of work.

  It is critical to obtain IOCs and malware samples that can be used to drive detections in the customer environment. It is also essential to explore whether partners/vendors have adequate in-house response capabilities or if it should be recommended/required that they retain a trusted third-party firm to assist.

- End customers/clients/patients – If the end customer complains about a security incident, there is very likely a problem, whether real or perceived. At the very least, the customer may face reputational risk.

  If the external party voices the problem to a media outlet, there is at least a public disclosure. It also probably includes exaggerations, misunderstandings, or sensationalized details provided to the media before the response team has details to refute them.

  Information, screenshots, and other available artifacts should be gathered from the external parties. However, when gathering information, it is essential not to ask them to do anything that will further jeopardize the confidentiality, integrity, or availability of related systems/data or that of others.

- Security researchers – If a security researcher escalates a vulnerability or security incident, there is definitely a problem to deal with, whether real or perceived. At the very best, they will likely try to extort the victim for a finder's fee, and at worst, they will publish an article about it or put it on their blog or podcast. In either case, there is a situation to deal with. The most innovative and effective approach the author has found to deal with security researchers who continue to probe the external environment and report issues is to put them under a short-term contract and make them sign an NDA. Either way, it is typically a bad situation. It is a catch-22. If the affected company "feeds" them, the researchers will come back for more. If the affected company doesn't feed them, the researchers will likely write negative articles or blog posts or find more public ways to monetize their findings, regardless of the true security significance of the findings. It can turn into a no-win, hostage-type situation.

Symptoms

It is particularly important to identify all of the known symptoms of a reported event or security incident in order to help validate it and begin root cause analysis. Symptoms gathered should include details about its behavior, artifacts, and impact on networks, endpoints, and logs, as well as the user experience.

Attack Vector

This may or may not be known at the early stages of a response. But, if it is, immediate steps need to be taken to mitigate the threat (such as through patching or configuration) or to implement compensating controls if mitigation is not possible.

In any case, the attack vector needs to be identified as quickly as possible so as to secure the system or environment and protect it from further exploitation. The attack vector is typically the vulnerability or misconfiguration that permitted the attack and exploitation to occur.

Exploit Method

Just like the attack vector, the exploit method should be identified as quickly as possible to prevent additional exposure. Moreover, the exploit method might apply to other attack vectors.

More specifically, the exploit method is the path by which the attack vector was compromised, such as a malicious script, buffer overflow, etc. As an example, a vulnerable version of a web browser could be an attack vector, but malicious scripts would be the exploitation method.

It usually needs to be secured separately from the actual vulnerability to prevent it from being a continued risk. This is usually where compensating controls come in.

Known Artifacts, IOCs, and YARA Rules

These need to be identified quickly and used to enumerate related threats in other locations and to implement containment controls with related security controls in any location. These are basically any definable network, system, or log artifact. However, if polymorphic malware is involved, then patterns of behavior and expressions or parameters that describe the behavior become the indicators.

Initial Scope

The initial scope usually includes locations, networks, systems, applications, etc. It is essential for performing early analysis and implementing initial containment measures to prevent the activity from spreading and limiting or blocking additional exposure, exfiltration, and/or risk. The quicker the scope is defined and containment measures go in place, the smaller the incident can be kept, and the less risk there is to the organization.

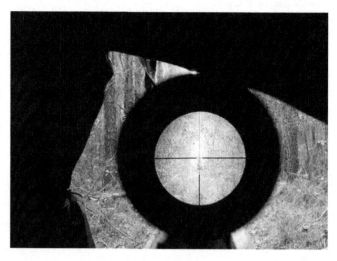

Building the Profile

Based on the details provided in the notification compared with the information known about the affected system, it is possible to make a quick assessment regarding the impact on the affected resources. If the activity is completely irrelevant and could in no way compromise the system, then the impact would be null and can be ignored. For example, benign automated scans that are part of an authorized cyclical process looking for vulnerabilities and do not perform any intrusive actions or use active exploit methods would be of no threat.

Alternatively, if the activity targeted a known, existing vulnerability on a critical system containing restricted or regulated data and successfully gained root access, the impact would be very high. In aggregate, preparing this information and enabling this analysis as early as possible will help ensure responders can hit the ground running. Moreover, it will minimize the need for additional research, which just slows down the response process.

The more research that is required at the beginning of the investigation, the longer the actual response onset is delayed. Depending upon the information required to begin, it could take hours, days, or sometimes even weeks to obtain. Delays could mean the difference between 5 systems affected or 5000 (or much more). If not for proper documentation, the information-gathering and profile-building portion of an incident can prove to be one of the most challenging phases. Without documentation, benign scans look like threats and waste time in the response process.

Incident Validation

Prior to beginning incident response activity, the team needs to validate if there really is an incident. It is very common for customers or end-users to suspect a security incident has occurred when, in fact, they just have a network, operating system, application, or other configuration issue or error.

Any time there is a disruption or negative impact on a service or some sort of misunderstood technical anomaly, it could be perceived to be the result of a security incident. It is important to not just jump immediately into incident response mode and all of the related workflows and actions when anomalous problems are reported.

Immediately assuming that reported events are true incidents will result in the team spinning up significant resources and possibly wasting a lot of time in well over half of the reported events. Most environments have a profound quantity of false positives or anomalous events, and tuning them out is a significant challenge.

As such, begin by trying to identify if there is a non-malicious technical issue that could explain the situation. It ultimately will save the response team and supporting technical teams a tremendous amount of time and effort if false incidents can be avoided through proper troubleshooting prior to escalating an incident.

This will also help preserve the team's reputation by not crying wolf on false incidents. Doing such erodes faith in the team, impacts responsiveness from the stakeholders, and ultimately delays or reduces support for response efforts.

Very commonly, the non-malicious causes for events are one or more of the following. These types of events or detections create alarm amongst users and administrators who are becoming increasingly suspicious of hacking and malware:

- Application errors
- Resource/sharing conflicts
- Browser plug-in crashes
- Endpoint slowness
- Network slowness
- Misconfigured security controls
- System updates
- Overly broad incident detection signatures
- Other unexpected error messages that raise suspicions

Incident Validation Questions

To reduce the likelihood of investigating false incidents, begin by asking probing questions with a critical approach intended to identify possible non-incident-related causes and explanations. The following are some sample questions and intended deliverables that could be used to obtain answers and artifacts that will substantiate or dismiss an event as a possible security incident. For the record, these are really just a starting place to drive discussion, and answers or deliverables will undoubtedly drive additional questions.

Question/Request	Objective/Deliverable
Why does the customer suspect an attack?	Obtain a record of observances that led to their suspicions.
What kind of suspicious behavior has been observed, and why does it stand out?	Obtain a narrative on why the customer or admin believes the activity is suspicious and how it differs from the normal state.
Gather preliminary details and artifacts.	Collect and research screenshots, events/alerts, and related artifacts that led to their conclusion.
Identify suspected incident scope and timeline based on detection and known details.	Determine how long the event and potential incident may have been occurring and begin to identify where evidence artifacts that can better establish or refute the existence of an incident may exist.
Identify and collect corroborating metrics or evidence artifacts that can confirm or refute initial suspicions and the existence of a real incident.	Identify metrics, statistics, logs, configuration files, event/incident-related files, malware samples, scripts, registry entries, or other artifacts.
Is the customer possibly mistaken or making unfounded assumptions?	Review all initially gathered information, perform research on collected artifacts, and make a determination on whether the incident is valid or a false positive.
Identify alternate explanations for the observed suspicious activity.	Enumerate potential non-security-incident sources, such as network anomalies, endpoint issues, application conflicts/errors, etc.

Incident Kick-Off

It is now game-on. Once the incident has been confirmed by the initial team evaluating the alerts, everything begins moving very quickly. It has now become real, and SLAs, SLOs, and notification or reporting timelines are typically based on the detection date/time. Alternatively, the date/time or compromise may also be used at time zero for reporting purposes.

The following bullet points identify the high-level objectives and concepts covered during the kick-off meeting, which will be covered individually in greater depth:

- The formal incident management process begins
- Conflicting objectives
- NIST 800-61 vs. reality
- Building the Incident Management Team
- Call the primary incident bridge
- Communication requirements
- Beware of unauthorized parties
- Playbooks, workflows, and objectives
- Divide and conquer
- Operational periods and status updates

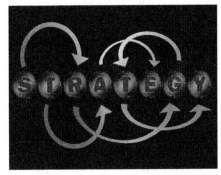

Formal IM Process Beings

From this point forward, everything counts. Every action and detail matters. It is critical to quickly establish and track changes to the incident scope, attack vector, exploit method, identified vulnerabilities, findings, impact, and the respective containment, mitigation, eradication, and remediation tasks and lessons learned.

Regarding the scope and impact, they are heavily nested concepts that include the effect of attackers and/or malware on the confidentiality, integrity, or availability of affected resources: environments, systems, devices, applications, data, employees, customers, regulatory compliance, or anything else that could be impacted by a cybersecurity incident.

While it is sometimes assumed that all data on an application or system is compromised by the attacker or malware, that is not necessarily the case. Sometimes, over-disclosures happen due to a lack of evidence to the contrary. As much as possible, the investigation should be driven to affirmatively identify exactly what happened and the specific resources and data that were affected. This will help avoid over-disclosures and unnecessary reputation loss and fines.

A challenge encountered when doing this is the work effort and time required in order to make it successful. It is possible that regulatory reporting deadlines are exhausted prior to the completion of investigative processes. This is particularly an issue when application functions and integrations need to be reverse-engineered, and large data sets need to be parsed. This is a common occurrence in web application and database breaches, as well as sophisticated malware attacks. The analysis may have to continue beyond the initial disclosure to obtain the most accurate findings possible. At the end of such, it will likely require a revision of findings, exposed data, and the affected parties.

Throughout the incident management process, the incident management team must attempt to affirmatively identify, capture, and document all relevant incident management details. These typically include the affected resources, unauthorized activity, recommendations, actions, owners, artifacts, findings, and other incident management details specific to threats or resources affected. It is important to not only address the current incident but also track the required changes needed to prevent its recurrence. These changes typically involve improvement to the security posture within people, processes, and/or technology.

Conflicting Objectives

During the response, there are at least three divergent and conflicting paths that must be followed at the same time across each of the compromised resource types. They are divergent and conflicting, because doing any of the three potentially delays or impairs accomplishing the other two. This is especially true and is magnified if complications occur or political struggles arise:

- Evidence collection – This is performed in phases and is necessary to enable the investigation and identify what happened. This is preferably done in an automated way and preserved by security capabilities, but it rarely happens that way. The need to collect evidence to understand what happened or is happening delays the ability to stop the ongoing malicious activity and to restore the system to a known good state.

- Containment, mitigation, and initial remediation efforts – This is performed to stop the attack in progress and prevent additional occurrences. The need to stop the bleeding is usually seen as paramount. The longer the unauthorized presence continues, the greater the chance that the attack will spread and that additional resources, accounts, and data will be compromised. As such, the risks and threats to the organization increase the longer the breach is active. However, rushing containment will destroy volatile evidence and impair the investigation. It may also cut off access to the system from admin teams that want to restore the system to a known good state and resume business operations.

- Restoration and recovery efforts – These are performed to enable business processes. Business units typically want to restore systems enabling business operations as soon as possible, but doing so stomps on evidence that needs to be collected and analyzed. Also, the restoration process may restore systems to the state prior to the incident, but the systems are still vulnerable and need to have vulnerability mitigation or remediation steps applied to secure them.

However, having the right capabilities in place (including people, processes, and technology) can enable all three actions to be performed without conflict. In a perfect world, they should be performed continually in an automated manner. For automated methods, the activity is continuous and simultaneous.

For a triggered or semi-automated activity that is kicked off by an event that launches an operation, it will likely be performed somewhat simultaneously or at least semi-sequentially as the jobs are queued and the response tools collect the data from the affected sources. This should take place in as rapid and orderly a manner as possible, taking proper care not to lose evidence or delay subsequent processes.

If evidence from the required data sources is always collected in real-time through continuous monitoring capabilities and integrated logging solutions and evidence repositories, then evidence collection is no longer a concern when containment is needed. The required evidence has already been collected using an automated process. If it must be triggered to run based on an automated event or a manual action, there is a risk of having to wait for evidence collection to occur prior to initiating other collection activity that is secondary or the containment procedures that must follow.

However, due to the approvals that often are required to initiate containment controls that could disrupt business processes, quick evidence-collection processes are not usually an issue. Interestingly, the more formal and streamlined or pre-defined and practiced the containment procedures become, the more likely that containment actions will be held up by evidence collection and preservation actions.

For containment, if host-based isolation capabilities are deployed, evidence collection followed by restoration/recovery can be performed without creating needless delays. This is typically implemented using endpoint controls, but it can also be performed with network controls, like dynamic segmentation.

For restoration and recovery efforts, if clean, hot-standby systems are available, or if there is a virtual solution that can be implemented, services can be restored without significant delays. Standing up a replacement environment does not need to wait on other investigative or response activities.

NIST 800-61 vs. Reality

The NIST 800-61 framework is an often-referenced standard for performing incident management. It uses the Incident Response model depicted in the image below, which shows circular processes of continuous analysis, learning, and adaptation before, throughout, and after the response is completed.

Preparation → Detection & Analysis → Containment Eradication & Recovery → Post-Incident Activity

While everything in this model is essentially true, it is overly simplified and does a disservice by omitting or collapsing critical steps in the incident management process.

As such, it needs to be expanded to include the required topics encountered and addressed in real life. Optimally, the model needs to be split out into more boxes to facilitate discussion and planning of the additional concepts and cycles of iterations. All stages have a somewhat cyclical nature and result in a series of circular flows. The following image depicts a more comprehensive break-out of the various phases of incident response planning, execution, post-incident activity, and follow-up according to the full-lifecycle incident management process. It provides a better framework for meeting the needs of incident response and incident management.

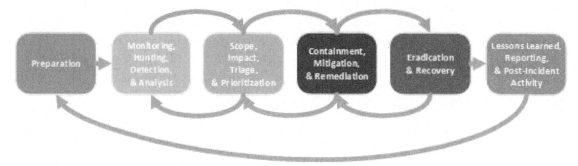

- Preparation – Informed by prior incidents, best practices, regulatory requirements, and business needs
- Monitoring, Hunting, Detection, & Analysis – Enabled by visibility tools: network, endpoint, email, SIEM, and threat feeds
- Scope, Impact, Triage, & Prioritization – Informed by analysis and awareness of affected resources
- Containment, Mitigation, & Remediation – Steps to halt attacks and prevent further malicious activity
- Eradication & Recovery – Steps to restore the affected resources to a known good state
- Lessons Learned, Reporting, and Post-Incident Activity – Closes the loop and feeds back into Preparation

Building the Incident Management Team

The team typically requires a combination of resources from technical, security, business, compliance, legal, and other leadership personnel or functional groups. With the exception of the Incident Commander/Manager and scribe, the following are very high-level categories of dynamic positions that are staffed, depending upon the needs of the specific response.

Depending upon the situation, the various roles listed below may or may not be needed. Further, if they are needed, they may be required in multiples, depending upon the resources required for the scope of activity:

Incident Commander/Manager

This is the incident leader guiding the response processes and has primary responsibility for providing the management function. All decisions and findings flow through the Incident Commander, who will coordinate investigative activity with individuals and groups in all of the required areas.

These include the various layers of leadership, business entities, technical teams, compliance personnel, and legal teams. This will ensure all investigative, business, and legal/regulatory requirements are being met during the investigative processes.

Depending upon the length and complexity of the activity, the Incident Commander role may need to be redundant or have one or more delegates. This is particularly important when investigations go on 24/7 for extended periods of time. In addition to adequate staffing, it also requires strong documentation capabilities that enable a quick hand-off process between the various Incident Commanders.

Incident Scribe

This is the incident note-taker in charge of capturing all of the activity, action items, assignments, statuses, and other details shared during incident-related meetings. They should also be responsible for building/maintaining the incident timeline, which should track all notable activity, milestones, and deliverables.

Depending upon the length and complexity of the activity, this role may need to be redundant or have one or more delegates. Just like with the Incident Commander, this is important for when investigations go on 24/7 for extended periods of time. In addition to adequate staffing, it also requires strong documentation capabilities that enable a quick hand-off process between the various Incident Commanders.

Incident Responders

There will generally be multiple dedicated technical personnel performing investigative functions and analyzing artifacts collected. They will need to have specialized knowledge of the target of investigation, such as the operating systems, applications, or data/artifact types.

All responders should be fully versed in computer forensics, network forensics, log forensics, and the broad array of information security, security architecture, and cloud computing concepts. They should also have additional specializations, as required for investigating the target of analysis.

Subject Matter Experts (SMEs)

These are the specialists responsible either for 1) The investigative capabilities, such as security resources or information technology infrastructure, or 2) The targets of the investigation, which include any resources involved in a security breach or are being analyzed in support of the response.

The investigative capabilities typically include network security, endpoint security, email security, and SIEM solutions. The targets of investigation typically include affected devices, servers, applications, and repositories of any type.

There will typically be many SMEs that will at least be involved temporarily at various phases of the investigation. Some SMEs are involved the entire way through.

There really are no specific requirements for SMEs except that they are authoritative within their respective areas of responsibility and technology types. They are people who don't normally perform an incident response function but who may be called upon to assist in various phases of the investigation.

Their job titles typically include administrators, analysts, architects, developers, consultants, etc. They will likely include a combination of internal and external parties, including vendors.

Extended Team Members

These are a highly varied combination of personnel from a broad array of sources. They will include both technical and non-technical personnel, but mostly non-technical individuals from compliance, legal, and leadership teams.

They may include vendors, contractors/consultants, business units, compliance teams (national or local), legal teams (in-house or external), leadership, and others as required for the incident response activity. As such, members of this group will be temporarily involved in the various phases of the investigation.

This group is highly dynamic, and its membership needs to be frequently evaluated to ensure unnecessary or imprudent parties are not included. This group of participants can quickly grow to be out of hand and become far broader than it should be. There will be an ever-increasing quantity of people who want to be involved or at least informed regarding incidents. The member list of this team should be closely scrutinized, managed, and trimmed to prevent over-socialization of sensitive incident details.

As such, they should be brought into the investigation (often separately or in an isolated manner), perform their function, and then be excluded if no longer needed. Many of these people will be involved in the investigation the entire way through.

Call to Primary Incident Bridge

Now, it is time to expand the scope of the response activity. This should be performed according to the applicable incident response playbook and incident response plan requirements for the respective incident type and the affected resources.

These factors will determine the application monitoring and response tools. They will help identify the knowledgeable personnel to whom notifications need to be sent and will thus ensure all required parties join the primary incident bridge.

It is strongly encouraged that the respective teams, contacts, and on-call aliases be mapped to their respective resources. These associations should be pre-configured and selectable within the ticketing and/or automated employee contact system. The ticketing and emergency contact solution should include after-hours contact information, such as personal and/or business cell phones.

It can be very challenging to try and find contact info for required personnel during an incident, especially after hours and on weekends or holidays. The better the contact information that is available for team members and SMEs, the greater the likelihood of success in getting in touch with required personnel.

The main purpose of the primary incident bridge is for response team members or stakeholders to have a place to come to obtain instructions, report back with status updates, and/or have their questions addressed. However, it is reasonable for the core response team to use it to discuss and evaluate the artifacts, findings, data, and next steps for the respective teams.

The primary incident bridge should remain continuously operational during the designated hours of operation. It should always have one or more resources manning it and performing essential functions. The essential functions include the following, at minimum.

- Capturing status
- Addressing questions
- Identifying new action items
- Maintaining a running status update
- Calling others to the bridge, as necessary

Care should be taken to ensure that the various teams do not just stay on the primary bridge and use it as a working bridge for all workflows. Each focused team should split off to their own focused bridges and come back at designated times, following the completion of "operational periods" and report in. Further, the Incident Commander and respective delegates need to have access to all of the respective bridges. This will enable them to join the discussions as necessary.

Communication Requirements

From the outset, make sure to identify communication sensitivity protocols, legal privilege, and confidentiality needs for the investigation. This includes identifying the requirements to keep incident-related discussions and details only amongst those with a need to know. As part of this, the participants need to ensure that the incident and subsequent response subject matter should not be discussed openly in public areas or in mixed company.

Communication with parties outside those designated with a need to know must be reviewed and specifically authorized by incident response leadership, the compliance teams, the legal teams, and/or other leadership as appropriate. Determining who can or will authorize additional parties is contextual, based on the communication needs, investigation sensitivity, and political landscape.

As a general rule of thumb, the need to include new groups or individuals for technical reasons to facilitate the investigation is typically authorized by the Incident Commander. The needs of the investigation need to be met without delay, if possible.

However, non-technical participants (usually requested or added for political reasons) or any outside entity need to be authorized by Compliance, Legal, and/or other leadership entities. This excludes pre-designated contractors, consultants, or companies with pre-negotiated or paid retainer agreements.

Regarding the need for legal privilege and/or regulatory concerns, if communications and work-product need to be protected by legal privilege, the activity must be requested and directed by an attorney. As such, the attorney needs to be on all of the respective communications and to direct the dissemination of the work product and information overall. The attorney should be the central point of all the activity and communications.

Unauthorized Parties

When there is a security incident, there is usually a large amount of interest. Numerous stakeholders, leadership, and various interested parties will want to join the calls, listen in, and just be informed. Many people will feel like they have a need, right, or duty to know what is happening. The desire for unnecessary parties to maintain awareness or attempt to interject themselves into incidents should be expected and strictly controlled or prevented.

Having non-essential parties involved creates significant issues for the response team in various ways. Everyone on the incident bridge must be affirmatively identified and authorized, or they must be removed. Be particularly wary of call-in users that appear as phone numbers instead of names. Also, identify those using a speakerphone and establish who else is in the room with them and listening. Following are a few of the most notable examples of looky-loos and troublemakers that will likely cause problems and may need to be dismissed:

Too Many Chefs

Having unnecessary, indirect, or lateral oversight and interference slows down the decision-making and approval processes. This will add to the level of drama without providing commensurate value.

Having too many people involved in the discussion and decision-making process adds to the political complexity of the situation. Long story short, it just makes everything more difficult, and it takes longer than it needs to. This is counterproductive when time is of the essence.

The IR team, resource SMEs, and functional owners know best what needs to be done to address threats. The fewer people involved in the decision-making process, the easier it will be, providing that the team has adequate pre-approvals or a rapid escalation path to obtain those approvals.

Loose Lips Sink Ships

Whether intentional or unintentional, permitting unauthorized parties to become aware of the sensitive details of an incident response investigation is a bad idea. People may innocently or accidentally share information that could compromise the investigation. They might overshare information to, in front of, or within earshot of people. They could include coworkers, friends, family, or passers-by.

Alternatively, they may be looking for their 10 minutes of glory and could deliberately choose to release information to the media. These people could result in a steady leak of confidential information that could jeopardize the investigation and/or damage the customer.

Any information leakage can be damaging to the investigation, the incident response team, and the customer. However, once an incident makes it into the media, it takes it to a whole new level and adds significantly to the complexity, accountability, and overall drama level of the incident. Being as it is always best to keep the level of drama in an incident to an absolute minimum, it is necessary to limit knowledge of an incident to those who absolutely need to know and can be trusted not to overshare information with unnecessary parties.

Malicious Actors/Guilty Parties

If end-users or other parties responsible for the incident gain access to the bridge and become involved in the course of the investigation, it can negatively affect the processes and outcome. This is true whether the cause was accidental or deliberate. Out of a sense of shame, guilt, or a desire to hide malfeasance, they may destroy or hide evidence.

As such, they should usually be engaged in an isolated manner, and their involvement should be kept as limited as possible. However, if they are also critical SMEs, limiting their involvement might not always be possible.

In either case, it should be emphasized that the response team is trying to investigate and resolve the security compromise, not to blame or flame people who may inadvertently have been involved. This will help minimize the problems encountered when individuals feel culpable, which inhibits their desire for cooperation.

While it is true that sometimes the investigation of personnel related to overt malicious activity must occur, this is usually the exception. Investigations into the activity and involvement of specific individuals should be a completely separate, isolated investigation and be kept as small and confidential as possible.

External Entities

Most large environments contain a significant percentage of vendor-managed devices. Or, more accurately, "vendor unmanaged devices." They are devices that are supposed to be managed by vendors but actually are unmanaged, outdated, and vulnerable.

If incidents involve these vendor (un)managed devices, there is usually a need to get vendor account and technical representation on the phone to assist with troubleshooting, containment, mitigation, and/or remediation. This should be done in as narrow of a working group as possible for a defined period of time.

Ideally, vendors should not be exposed to the full working bridge or incident scope. If they must be permitted on the working bridge, they should join at a specific time, provide their update, and then exit before the bridge before others provide information.

This will enable the external entities to provide valuable insight to assist in the investigation and response activity but will minimize the risk of data loss. Just like with everyone else, external entities should only be as involved as they need to be. Not every consultant or service provider needs to be engaged on every call. That would be a waste of resources, time, and money.

It should be mentioned, however, that some external consultants and IR providers may be exempt from this and are engaged on all calls appropriate for their scope of involvement. This is especially true if incident management resources are engaged externally, such as the Incident Commander and other critical incident response/management personnel required to track and guide the overall activity.

Playbooks, Workflows, and Objective

Each threat type should have defined steps, action items, and milestones that need to be completed, established, or dismissed for a response to be considered complete. Sometimes, this even needs to be defined individually for each threat type per resource type (like system, service, etc.) if responses for those resources are specialized.

This means that there are certain tasks that need to be performed in order to check all the boxes required to establish that a comprehensive incident response investigation has been completed. These steps will be driven by the nature of the threats, incident response best practices, security best practices, and/or regulatory compliance requirements.

These include the necessary technical and procedural action items, which include objectives and requirements involving people, processes, and technology. These are heavily nested concepts, which will need to be broken out according to the required concepts and high-level actions. This requires creating unique playbook scenarios for the most common threats and adding additional playbooks and response requirements for each new variant requiring unique or individualized response activity.

When the full response team has joined the bridge, make sure to identify the investigation path, playbook objectives, critical next steps, and action item assignments based on the circumstances. It is essential to ensure the team understands the path forward and shares the vision. Otherwise, the work performed will not meet requirements and will need to be redone.

Divide and Conquer

While it can sometimes feel tempting to keep everyone together as it can make getting status updates easy, there are too many workstreams and disparate pursuits for this to be feasible. The tasks need to be divided across the various functional areas and assigned to their respective teams (e.g., network, servers, applications, databases, workstations, email, forensics, security, recovery, etc.).

These groups need to be assigned tasks and objectives, identify their respective leadership, and then separated into teams according to their own working groups and response bridges under their own leadership to work on their respective areas. Each group representative should report to the main bridge at the designated check-in time, which is typically at the end of their operational period. However, depending on how many groups are involved, the confidentiality vs. collaboration requirements may necessitate having individual check-in times for the respective groups.

If they have questions, early status updates, or urgent findings, they or their assigned representative should come back to the main bridge at the designated time or early, as the needs dictate. This also assists with concerns around the over-sharing of information and supports the concepts of separation of duties and least privilege through compartmentalization. Just because someone is involved with an aspect of the incident response does not mean that they need to know all aspects of it and the findings from every group. All information should be shared on a need-to-know basis.

However, it should be noted that collaboration is critical to solving incidents. Oftentimes, disparate groups of people from different focus areas (like endpoint, network, and SIEM) need to work together and share findings in order to understand the behavior and resultant impact.

The more working groups are separated into functional areas, the less collaboration and cross-referenced contextual information they will have to work with. Simply stated, collaboration is inversely proportional to compartmentalization.

Action Items, Owners, and Status

Incident response and/or management nearly always involves a significant amount of project management, often under high pressure or even hostile circumstances. Larger incidents are more like extreme program management. Moreover, full-lifecycle incident management is perpetual program management that continually spins off new projects, each having action items, owners, and individual completion status.

Incidents create scores of action items and subtasks or prerequisite tasks that all need to be assigned to one or more owners, sponsors, approvers, and other required entities. All of the respective actions/tasks must be tracked to completion or other final state. Not every task results in a positive conclusion, and failed tasks usually result in alternate tasks using a different method to accomplish the desired result.

All of the resulting tasks could become the subject of an audit or other after-action activity. The ability to produce documentation proving adequate corrective activity following an incident is critical in defending audits and lawsuits, as well as avoiding compliance pitfalls and fines. Strong documentation of completed post-incident tasks to apply lessons learned is key to proving an effective response program.

Operational Periods and Status Updates

In order to get things done, the teams need to get to work. Notwithstanding the fact that the Incident Commander has divided the responsibilities and tasks into teams, sometimes there is an inclination for all the members of the extended incident response team to stay on the bridge listening to developments found by others, talking about random things, and waiting for everyone else to come up with findings.

If nothing else, it is often an exciting show and good entertainment. However, it can be a distraction for the focused areas getting work done. They can either watch or work. They need to be able to focus and work.

The Incident Commander needs to dismiss the various working groups to perform their respective functions and meet at the end of the operational period, which is the time allocated for a respective working session. An operational period can be any amount of time, but they are typically shorter at the beginning of an incident and increasingly longer over time.

Also, the higher the severity of the incident, the shorter the working periods may be. High-severity incidents will likely have half-day working sessions at the beginning that taper off to 1 day, then 3 days, then a week, and finally, the team stands down from scheduled operational periods and check-ins. The idea is that the amount of time allotted is appropriate to accomplish the assigned tasks before the next required status update or deliverable milestone is due.

After all of the objectives for the investigation and next steps have been established, work with the teams to identify the appropriate length of the operational period and set the status update schedule and respective check-in times. These may be different for the respective teams. Some teams may require longer operational periods and less frequent check-in times to allow sufficient progress for investigative tasks and preparation of findings.

Additionally, not every team needs to check in at the same time, particularly if the content they provide is particularly sensitive. It often works best to have 15-30 minute rolling timeslots for the respective teams to check in if there is a need to keep the communications separate to preserve confidentiality as much as possible. However, remember that separating the status updates inhibits collaboration and prevents other groups from keying off critical information shared in a combined status update call.

Begin Incident Artifact Preliminary Collection

Included in the early steps that the respective response teams will need to accomplish at the beginning of an incident is the requirement to identify their visibility tools and investigative capabilities. Following that, they must use them to collect and preserve evidence from their respective areas for analysis. Initial evidence gathering and preservation  typically consists of capturing live/volatile evidence, logs with a short lifespan, or other evidence that may be quickly lost or overwritten if not gathered urgently.

The initial evidence gathered is typically driven by IOCs and/or other information from the alerts or other incident notifications and then expands outward from there. This will provide a starting place for collection, investigation, and root cause analysis. It will also enable the team to understand the full scope, potential impact, and plausible containment and/or mitigation controls.

The teams should collect evidence from all visibility and/or response capabilities that the customer has regarding the compromise and subsequent activity. Depending upon the threat, some solutions work better than others or not at all. The response teams need to identify all network, endpoint, or log collection, parsing/searching, detection, and blocking capabilities that will be effective against the detected threat.

To enable evidence preservation, ensure incident responders can act without additional delay and can provide rapid identification to inform the containment of the spread of malicious applications and activity. The Incident Commander and/or response personnel should instruct the customer to ensure that all preliminary evidence is being collected and preserved and validate that there is an adequate retention period to prevent evidence from being deleted.

Very often, logs are overwritten and are lost. Preliminary evidence artifact collection locations include anything that can tell the story regarding network, endpoint, email, user, data, and malware activity:

- Network: Collect ingress/egress traffic from/to the Internet, hosts known to be involved, and sensitive environments. Targeted data sources are PCAP, NetFlow, WAF, Firewall, NIPS, HIPS, Proxy, VPN, DNS, DHCP, network-DLP, UAM, etc.
- Endpoint: Collect volatile artifacts respective to systems believed to have been involved in an attack or compromise. Targeted data sources include EDR, HIPS, host-DLP, SIEM, AD, UAM, AV/AM, etc.
- Email: Review email history, URL rewrite access, malicious attachments, spam, spoofing, etc. Targeted data sources include Email security, cloud scrubbing, AV/AM, HIPS, etc.
- User: Review user activity from any vantage point that can show/correlate activity. Targeted data sources include UAM, network/host DLP, AD, SIEM, etc.
- Data: Review data activity from any vantage point that can show/correlate activity.

Targeted data sources include network/host DLP, access/changelogs, EDR, etc.
- Malware: Identify malware samples and have them analyzed. The goal is to determine behavior, capabilities, IOCs, exploit methods, polymorphism, and mitigation techniques.

Identify and Obtain Malware or Related Artifact Samples

Malware is a key finding in any incident, as the capabilities of the malware are a strong indicator of the attacker's intent. The functions of the malware usually reflect the activities the attacker wants to perform on the affected system(s) or within the affected customer environment overall.

Every malware sample found should be analyzed to understand the capabilities and perform a threat assessment. For known malware samples, validate that there are no additional customized modules or configurations within known malware samples having public IOCs. Such modifications might materially alter the functions and capabilities of the malware and modify or enhance the respective threat.

WHEN SAMPLES ARE FOUND, IT IS CRITICAL TO INSTRUCT THE CUSTOMER AND PRACTITIONERS NOT TO UPLOAD MALWARE SAMPLES TO PUBLICLY ACCESSIBLE MALWARE ANALYSIS TOOLS, SUCH AS VIRUSTOTAL, AS THIS COULD COMPROMISE THE INVESTIGATION.

Hashes of malware can be checked against public resources (like VirusTotal). No binaries or scripts should be uploaded, as doing so could alert attackers of the customer awareness of the security breach and dedicated malware variants created for the customer environment.

Automated analysis can be safely performed within private, offline behavior analysis environments or private, segregated cloud environments. Automated analysis methods can enumerate most malware IOCs. However, if anti-reverse engineering functions are included, it will complicate the process and make automated analysis unfeasible.

Static analysis should also be performed offline, and it is the best way to fully understand malware functions and capabilities, particularly if they include anti-reverse engineering functions. In both cases, analysis should be completed to identify IOCs and/or create Yara rules that provide content for searches across the environment.

Communication & Documentation

Some of the first questions that get asked during or after an incident are about the methods used to halt malicious activity. These include the containment actions implemented to stop the ongoing activity or the mitigation steps applied to prevent new compromises. This information (including change management thereof) must be quickly identified and escalated for approval prior to a high/critical priority change being implemented.

Note that there is a significant overlap between containment and mitigation methods. The main difference is the focus and timing of the two activities. Containment is an action taken to stop malicious activity, which could be the application of mitigation controls, if appropriate. Mitigation is performed to prevent a threat from occurring.

Containment Controls and Locations

- Identity and access management (IAM) – Controls applied to secure accounts and remote access methods, such as MFA, account lockouts, remote access limitation, etc.
- System and policy configurations/hardening – Local security policy is becoming increasingly complex, with advanced capabilities for system firewall controls, application controls, account safeguards, and numerous other security restriction capabilities.
- Application configurations/hardening – Applications are becoming increasingly advanced in security configuration capabilities that can be configured out of the box to halt malicious activity, including firewall rules, certificate authentication, account safeguards, and other restriction capabilities.
- Network security devices/software – Network controls (firewalls, WAFs, proxies, IPSs, etc.) are always the go-to when it comes to blocking malicious ingress/egress activity quickly from any protected source. Containment actions involve controls implemented to inspect, validate, and/or block network access and activity on OSI model layers 2-7 as appropriate for the resources being protected or sequestered.
- Endpoint agent software – The advancements in endpoint security tools, particularly EDR capabilities, have provided amazing abilities to detect and block malicious activity from endpoints, regardless of their location, which is helpful for remote/traveling systems.
- SIEM/Log integration – These are steps taken for visibility, monitoring, and automatic triggering of secondary actions that implement security controls as appropriate to halt malicious activity.
- Threat feed – Integration of threat feeds with other security controls is critical to detecting, preventing, or blocking malicious activity in an automated way more quickly and efficiently.
- Encryption – Implementing encryption controls on files, folders, sites, network traffic, or other resources is critical to block unauthorized access at the various layers.

Mitigation Methods

- Patches and updates – Security patches and updates are always the go-to for proactively preventing malicious activity and stopping it before it starts or preventing additional exploitation.
- Configuration changes – Sometimes, patches are not the answer, but configuration settings need to change, such as hardening systems beyond default configurations.
- Compensating controls – Sometimes, there is no direct method (like patches or configuration changes) to mitigate the risk to systems, and compensating controls need

to be put in place. While these are often temporary stopgaps, they may also become permanent mitigation controls.

Root Cause

The root cause of an incident is possibly the most important item to be identified and captured during an incident. The nature of it typically drives culpability discussions and influences the outcome of lawsuits and audits, as well as the determination to impose fines or restrictions.

Large, impactful incidents caused by easily preventable root causes stemming from well-known vulnerabilities that should have been patched long ago are a recipe for disaster. It opens the affected company up to all manner of lawsuits, fines, restrictions, and government oversight.

On the other hand, a novel attack against an unknown attack vector using an undetectable exploit method would be seen much differently, and the affected company may get a pass as well as public sympathy. Moreover, affirmatively identifying the root cause of an incident will inform mitigation and remediation activity to prevent a similar incident. It will also enable auditors/regulators to make a determination on whether the entity had appropriate security controls in place at the time of the incident.

If the incident's root cause is not identified and appropriately resolved, there is a high probability of reoccurrence. What is worse is that the recurrence of the same incident and exploitation of the same vulnerability can be very hard to rationalize. It may lead to increased culpability and business or regulatory risk.

Oftentimes, identifying and documenting the root cause(s) will make the affected organization look bad. However, not putting in the effort to identify it will make the organization look even worse. It shows that in addition to the security control issues that caused a breach, there are process and other maturity issues that are sure to result in another one.

Recovery

After an incident is contained and the deficiencies are documented, the incident management process is not yet complete. While it is true that some organizations may end the process at that stage, there is still a lot left on the table that is incomplete or unresolved.

```
Ooops, your important files are encrypted.

If you see this text, then your files are no longer accessible, because they
have been encrypted.  Perhaps you are busy looking for a way to recover your
files, but don't waste your time.  Nobody can recover your files without our
decryption service.

We guarantee that you can recover all your files safely and easily.  All you
need to do is submit the payment and purchase the decryption key.

Please follow the instructions:

1. Send $300 worth of Bitcoin to following address:

    1Mz7153HMuxXTuR2R1t78mGSdzaAtNbBWX

2. Send your Bitcoin wallet ID and personal installation key to e-mail
   wowsmith123456@posteo.net. Your personal installation key:



If you already purchased your key, please enter it below.
Key: _
```

Full-lifecycle incident management also includes oversight and review of the recovery and service restoration processes and the capabilities or gaps identified therein. As an example, there is nothing quite like a pervasive incident involving ransomware or wiperware worms to test a company's ability to recover systems/data and restore services.

Many organizations develop their BC/DR capabilities based on natural disasters, power outages, single/multiple system failures, or other fairly isolated and contained circumstances. Moreover, network or cloud backup solutions have made significant progress in replacing physical media backups due to the automated simplicity of the process.

As a result, many organizations have no offline backups on physical media. If all goes according to plan and circumstances do not stray from the expected BC/DR recovery scenarios, offline backups from physical media are simply not needed, and they are more trouble than they are worth.

As an extreme but plausible example, any organization would struggle with highly successful ransomware or wiperware that made significant inroads into their systems. However, if the malware takes out the network backup servers or the network backups themselves, it could become an unrecoverable incident due to BC/DR capability gaps.

New vulnerabilities permitting new exploits utilized by new malware or existing exploit kits come out all the time. They could affect any or all types of systems, devices, services, or applications. Any business-critical resource should have an adequate BC/DR plan to address foreseeable incident types, especially destructive malware incidents and catastrophic failures of the environment.

Lessons Learned
Just like a plane crash, every successful hacking incident is a result of layers of security failures from defense-in-depth. Each layer must have failed at every stage along the way, or perhaps it was non-existent to begin with.

At the very least, the technology must have failed at the following stages:
1. Network controls did not detect attacker intrusion activity
2. Endpoint controls did not protect the systems, applications, services, and/or accounts
3. Authentication, authorization, and access controls did not protect accounts and data
4. Log monitoring controls and SIEM solution(s) did not identify the malicious activity and alert in time to stop it.

There is never a better time to address these deficiencies or failures than after a successful breach. There is a window of time following a breach when people are supportive of making changes and willing to make the sacrifices that go along with them. Making these changes requires documentation of the related gaps and appropriate planning to overcome the issues.

Moreover, not enumerating and remediating deficiencies that led to a breach is a missed opportunity and an invitation for it to happen again. It will likely result in a game of Whack-A-Mole until the security gaps are resolved. Sometimes, hacking threats are only partially identified and remediated, resulting in recurring events using the remaining attacker backdoors, which maintain perpetual access and perform attacker-directed functions.

It is critical to remember that remediation needs are not just new technology or configuration changes. It is necessary to consider the need for changes within any or all of people, processes, and/or technology. Changes in each of these categories involve a lot of time and usually money. Each one of these areas has its own respective challenges requiring planning, collaboration, and funding to overcome.

- People – Additional personnel may be required to assist with security program development, implementation, monitoring, identifying unauthorized activity, and responding to alerts. Moreover, all staff may require training on the security program to prevent future events. However, making changes or additions to human resources is a significant change that involves leadership at all affected levels, human resources, recruiting, and funding to pay for it all.

- Process – If systemic security events occur, there are likely process or process enforcement-related problems. Clear guidance must be created and provided for security and response programs and all of their sub-components. This process must be trained, monitored, and enforced. Making changes or additions to company processes requires extensive collaboration, coordination, notification, training, and auditing to ensure changes are put in place without significant impact or risk to the organization.

- Technology – To support people and processes in the security and response programs, the right technology needs to be in place to identify and respond to threats. This needs to be in place at IAM, network, endpoint, and SIEM/log monitoring levels. Depending upon the state of technology within the affected environment and the extant ability or inability to implement needed detection and blocking controls, this can become very expensive. If threats continue to be successful, all of the technology controls should be evaluated to assess their ability to detect, respond to, terminate, and prevent security threats. New or replacement hardware, software, and licensing can be very expensive, often totaling 7, 8, or even 9 figures. Sometimes, these changes involve years of architecture, budgeting, planning, testing, implementation, and training.

Remediation

The last mile of the full-lifecycle incident management process, which brings the reactive activity back to the proactive process, is remediation. All of the identified deficiencies, recommendations, and lessons learned need to be distilled into remediation items, which are developed into proactive tasks to improve the customer's security posture.

Remember, incidents that recur based on known vulnerabilities result in increased risk. This is because the organization knew about them and did not fix them. This is somewhere between difficult and impossible to successfully defend during audits, regulatory investigations, and lawsuits.

The risk is only reduced when the known security gaps are fixed or at least when reasonable compensating controls are applied to mitigate the compromise of the extant threats. Meaning, the final solution does not have to be in place, but reasonable compensating controls must be applied to mitigate the threat(s), even if they are only temporary solutions.

As part of the program or project planning, some of the tasks to fix these gaps can be completed in the short term. However, many will need to be developed into long-term project plans and holistic solutions that require funding and management as multi-year projects.

All of this requires detailed planning and supporting content. Source materials required for this include specific examples and metrics from past incidents. This will demonstrate the need for security engineering support and the creation of optimal solutions.

Program and/or project managers should be assigned to ensure the proper resources are brought to bear. This includes the resources required to engineer/architect solutions, formally document plans, assign resources, and track action items through completion.

It is sometimes tempting to have the incident management team track the remediation processes through to completion. However, that is a mistake considering the prolonged, sticky nature of remediation activity.

Think of it this way: if a fireman puts out a fire at your home or business, you don't ask him to come back and design or build you a new house. While he may have some expertise in how this should best be done, he is not the ideal candidate to do such.

Moreover, proactive activity is a huge distraction from performing reactive work. If the response team must do both, one or the other will always suffer. More specifically, if the response team is too busy project managing post-incident activity, the urgent incident response functions will suffer, or the post-incident activity will not be completed in a timely manner. Ergo, handing off post-incident activity through a formal process involving dedicated project/program management personnel is an absolute must.

Investigation Findings

The actual investigation findings, type of data affected, and quantitative impact will ultimately be the biggest headline in an incident. This includes the quantity of customers, users, data, records, etc.

Headlines and data breach reports are full of these metrics stack ranked in descending order of magnitude. Moreover, the type of data and quantity of records impacted are the most discussed data elements and the biggest drivers for regulatory impact, fines, and lawsuits. However, there is a lot more data than that, which ultimately needs to be included in the investigation's findings for the documentation to be complete. Each of the sections listed in the template are key artifacts that need to be communicated, captured, and documented, if applicable. Some of the sections will not apply to an incident, depending on the situation.

Incident Response Report Template

- Cover page
- About Document and Audience
- Document Control
- Executive Summary
- Background and Scope
- Incident Notification
- Incident Timeline
- Attack Overview and Root Cause Analysis
- Resources Analysis
- Network Traffic Analysis
- Volatile Metadata Analysis
- Data Analysis
- Data Restoration
- Malware Analysis
- Investigative Findings
- Containment Actions Taken
- Remediation Plan
- Incident Participant List
- Point of Contact

Deficiencies and Recommendations

No response is adequate or complete without documenting a list of deficiencies and recommendations pertaining to the people, processes, and/or technology that led to the compromise. The recommendations should also include both short- and long-term suggestions to accommodate business needs and financial constraints. Oftentimes, short-term recommendations will consist of compensating controls to temporarily address security concerns using existing technologies that will be reconfigured in different ways to address deficiencies until the intended solution(s) can be put in place.

The template shown in this section will typically expand out like an accordion when all of the deficiencies, recommendations, action items, and prerequisites are blown out to accommodate all of the people, processes, and technology and are fully documented. If these items are not captured or acted upon, they are likely to repeat and increase the legal and regulatory risk to the organization. The following contents should be captured and documented:

Deficiency and Recommendations Summary

1. Date detected
2. Date resolution required
3. Detection Source: User reported/Security Tool/Threat Intel
4. Person Reporting: Employee Name (or outsider)
5. Deficiency Summary: Brief summary of the problem
6. Recommendation Summary: Recommended solution or course of action
7. Deficiency Remediation Details:
    7.1. Scope:
        7.1.1. Environments
        7.1.2. Networks
        7.1.3. Systems/Devices
        7.1.4. Accounts
    7.2. Urgency:
        7.2.1. Risk: High/Medium/Low
        7.2.2. Priority: High/Medium/Low
        7.2.3. Business Value: Explanation
        7.2.4. Regulatory Impact: PCI/PHI/PII/SOX
        7.2.5. Actionability: Explanation
    7.3. Owner(s)/Sponsor(s): List of owners and roles
    7.4. Action Item(s): List of actions and details to be defined for each action
        7.4.1. Description
        7.4.2. Status
        7.4.3. Prerequisite(s)
        7.4.4. Assignee(s)
        7.4.5. Individual Steps/Components – if appropriate

See the INCIDENT COMMANDER located in APPENDIX B for the consolidated quick-reference role playbook and easy-to-use guidance.

29 INCIDENT WORKFLOWS: COMBINED INCIDENT RESPONSE METHODOLOGIES

This workflow is an introduction to the common investigative themes that run across the spectrum of hacking-related incident workflows. This workflow combines all of the investigative steps discussed for threats affecting the customer environment and the corresponding response workflows (from identification through reporting).

This combined workflow is intended to provide a baseline of shared insights, concepts, and activities that run across all incident workflows and provide instruction on investigative actions that need to be considered holistically for most incident types. Moreover, it identifies evidence types, data sources, and collection methodologies. These insights can be used for response planning or execution.

Incident Notification/Detection Method

Upon notification of a potential incident, the Incident Commander should work with a focused team possessing the ability to perform incident validation and investigative capabilities. The team members usually consist of the NOC or SOC team members who received the alert and the on-call members of the incident response team.

Depending on the subject of the alert and threat type, sometimes the smaller group investigating and validating the alert needs to bring in subject matter experts to assist with the validation process prior to engaging the full incident response team. This typically starts as small as possible and grows from there based on the needs of the investigation.

The initial team will gather the required information respective to the incident detection or threat activity, the customer environment, the computer resources involved, and the extant security controls to begin building an incident response profile. All of this content will be used to validate if there is actually an incident (not a false positive caused by a misperception or technical issue) and will also be used to formulate the incident response strategy, including engaging the right resources.

The contents of the incident response profile vary by engagement and will build over time. The goal at the beginning is to gather enough content to inform the analysis and determine if there is a real incident or eliminate observations and findings as false positives. There are a wide variety of detection methods, as follows:

Automated Detection

These involve system-generated alerts or hits on manual correlation rules from security technologies, such as network security, endpoint security, SIEMs, and threat feed integrations. The efficacy of these hits is as good as the signatures, IOCs, heuristics, threat feeds, or other rules that created them.

Your mileage may vary. Overall, they are likely to have both false negatives and false positives. Developing accurate detection capabilities requires significant tuning and refinement of visibility and alerting solutions and all of the rules, alerting, and exclusions involved.

Manual Detection

These involve hits on threat-hunting activity by security team members. These are generally the highest accuracy hits, as the content is custom-crafted and validated by the threat hunter.

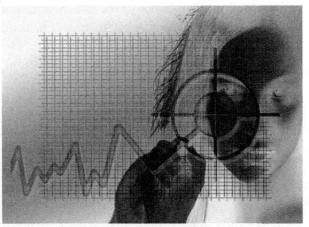

Therefore, the false-positive and - negative rate is typically low if the threat hunters follow a good identification and validation process. Once again, your mileage may vary. If threat hunters are just duplicating what is identified on a threat feed as opposed to doing manual research and testing, this activity will essentially only be as good as the threat feed and may as well just be integrated and automated.

User Reported

Depending upon the type of incident, purportedly malicious activity that has been identified and reported by the end-user, department manager, or support team can vary to both ends of the spectrum from low to high accuracy. Hacking and malware identifications can be anecdotal and inaccurate, based on the user experience, unless ransomware is involved.

However, the identification of inappropriately shared/stored/sent information is usually very accurate. Ideally, any type of detection by end-users should be accompanied by screenshots and as much descriptive information as possible. A note or warning is in order, however. The information they gather and share should be done in such a way as to avoid compromising their endpoint or incurring further legal and regulatory liability.

Externally Reported

If reported by or known to an outside entity, the best plan for dealing with them is to gather the information that they have to offer, but not over-engage them in the incident response processes. An exception would be for partners/vendors that are involved in joint incident response activity. With them, IOCs and salient findings need to be shared in order to facilitate the response activity.

But, be careful not to overshare anything that could introduce additional confidentiality concerns. Any findings or artifacts should be securely transferred using encrypted transfer methods to avoid creating a greater compliance incident on top of a security incident.

Initial Scope

The Initial scope, as identified in the notifications, typically consists of several of the following content types. These include key objects, artifacts, and considerations, including the respective locations, networks, systems, devices, applications, services, accounts, repositories, and the associated data and potential regulatory impact.

- Locations – A specific region, site, or building
- Networks – A specific network segment, VLAN, or virtual network
- Systems – An individual workstation, server, virtual machine, or container
- Devices – Any type of purpose-built computerized device or appliance that operates with firmware, software, or embedded operating system and is not intended to function as a personal computer
- Applications – Programs that run on servers and workstations and provide client-side or server-side functionality

- Services – Persistent server-side applications that can be accessed at any time by clients to perform individual functions, like network services (DHCP, DNS, etc.), communication services (email, messaging, telecom, etc.), file & print services, etc.
- Accounts – Any user, admin service, or application account, whether local or domain-wide
- Repositories – Any type of data repository, including file servers, databases, email archives, etc.
- Data – The content that is being digitally created, transmitted, or stored
- Regulatory – The regulatory compliance requirements that govern the data type, security requirements, and disclosure protocols

The initial scope is essential for collecting initial artifacts, performing early analysis, and implementing initial containment measures. These are required to prevent the activity from spreading and limiting or blocking additional exposure, exfiltration, and/or risk.

The smaller the incident and scope can be kept, the less risk there is to the organization. While the initial scope may or may not turn out to be the full scope, the quicker the full scope is defined and containment measures go into place, the less likely it is to grow.

In aggregate, preparing this information and enabling this analysis as early as possible will help ensure responders can hit the ground running. It will minimize the need for additional research, which just slows down the response process.

The more research that is required at the beginning of the investigation, the longer the actual response onset is delayed. Depending upon the information required to begin, it could take hours, days, or weeks to obtain. Delays could mean the difference between 5 systems affected or 5000.

Initial IOCs/Artifacts

Initial artifacts typically found in the alerts can come from any network security device, endpoint monitoring technology, or from analysis and correlation rules on a SIEM. All of this technology can be significantly augmented using multiple threat feeds, as well as correlations from multiple data sources and rulesets between them. The detections, notifications, indicators, and artifacts often include the following components:

Network Indicators

Automated alerts and IOCs usually contain lists of IP addresses, domain names, FQDNs, URLs, and the respective ports and protocols they use. This socket information could be related to any part of the attack lifecycle or activity type. Network device detection ability is enhanced through next-generation firewalls implementing SSL/TLS decryption and application awareness. This will identify script and application activity, as well as hand-off to 3rd party inspection tools. Key indicators include:

- Exploitation – The initial compromise
- Malware download – Downloading either primary or secondary malware tools
- Exfiltration – Transferring stolen content outside the victim organization
- Known malicious signatures – Pre-determined IOCs, YARA rules, hashes, etc.
- Known malicious site connections – Any known malicious external host/site
- Unusual foreign connections – Any ingress/egress traffic from suspicious countries
- C2 connections – Outbound connections to hosts associated with malware command and control (C2)
- Protocol anomalies – Any protocol manipulation used to hide traffic and/or facilitate covert communications
- Tunneling traffic – Any protocol encapsulation and/or encryption method used to hide traffic from detection and blocking capabilities
- Connection time or duration anomalies – Any uncharacteristic connections that are off-hours, last too long, or are otherwise suspicious
- DGA detection – Any use of domain generation algorithms other than known, legitimate sources
- Newly registered domain connections – Any newly created domains that could be used to facilitate nefarious purposes
- Suspicious connections to domains that have just changed ownership – Malicious purpose and re-use of previously legitimate domains

Memory Indicators

Alerts may contain suspicious memory artifacts that render systems or applications within the scope of the investigation. If the attacker is using fileless threats over encrypted network connections to perform attack activity, it is possible that the only indicators that may be found are in memory. These include the identification of key objects and malicious activity indicators, such as:

- Malicious hosts (domains, hostnames, and IP addresses)
- Encryption keys – Memory is usually the easiest way to obtain way to obtain them
- Golden tickets – Forged TGTs
- Silver tickets– Forged service tickets/TGSs
- Skeleton keys – Manipulation of the LSA process on domain controllers

- Credentials (usernames and passwords) – Enable decryption of attacker files and tools
- Commands and communication – Enumerate attacker or malware activities
- Data streams and exfiltration traffic – This can result in the identification of key indicators
- Function calls – Related to malware and respective objects
- Calls to file system or registry objects – Identify all objects compromised processes or functions interact with
- Process injection – Carve out injected components
- Process hollowing – Carve out the entire binary
- Malicious scripts – Show decoded/decrypted contents
- Other fileless memory-based anomalies – Unlimited possibilities

Commands and Scripts Indicators

Automated alerts can identify malicious client-side, server-side, or network activity at any type of command interface with the required visibility tools and monitoring logic capable of recovering command history. This can be anything from system command-line interfaces, API or instrumentation query interfaces, script interpreters, or database commands. Commands and scripted actions are high-value threat activities and should be monitored for malicious intent. They can be key to identifying fileless malware activity.

WMI Indicators

Alerts may include references to malicious WMI classes or backdoors that can be persistent, asynchronous, and/or fileless in nature. Windows enables the creation of fully functional fileless applications using WMI, including custom WMI classes and subscriptions. As with anything, this feature can be used for benign or malevolent intent. While these should be considered immediately in the scope of investigation when found, this is another nascent space that is hard to detect and easy to circumvent detections.

Log Indicators

If logs are configured to record and preserve the right activity, they can be critical for quickly identifying unauthorized or malicious activity from the vantage point of the log source. However, by default, logs typically do not capture all of the information needed to inform incident response investigations.

Moreover, the efficacy of logs is a balance between the verbosity of activity tracked and the capacity of storage and searchability. Being as log storage capacity is finite, if too much data is captured, it will reduce the length of the window of live storage below the minimum online retention period.

Also, storing log data that is not helpful during an investigation is effectively just noise that takes up storage space, incurs unnecessary expense, and complicates the search and review process. Alternatively, not capturing the right events needed for an investigation will effectively result in the logs being blind to the required information.

For best results and to reduce the likelihood of tampering, logs should be sent to a central location within a SIEM for collection, correlation, searching, alerting, and archival. Having all critical logs in a central location enables powerful rules to be created to identify, correlate, and trigger automated events for malicious activity.

Endpoint File System and Volatile Metadata Indicators

Automated alerts and IOCs typically contain a listing of artifacts, such as files, processes, services, and registry entries, involved in the detection or that are commonly associated with the detected malware variant. Obviously, these need to be considered in-scope and searched across other systems in the environment to expand the scope of the response, as necessary.

However, the data in the alerts is just a starting place. Usually, there are additional or possibly different files, processes, services, and/or registry entries involved. Sometimes, alerts just provide templatized content based on public IOCs when one or more components are identified. When enough IOC elements are identified to associate the activity with a particular threat, the alerts often include the rest of the commonly associated artifacts. This enriched data may or may not be applicable to current detection.

As such, some of the content may be inaccurate, and the specific malware behavior on any given system might be completely different. Any or all of the artifacts might change, depending upon the circumstances. This is particularly true with modern polymorphic and/or scripted malware, which commonly modifies many aspects of itself from system to system to avoid detection.

This polymorphism can be used against itself using EDR capabilities that can identify unique processes, drivers, or targeted file types that should be consistent, or at least non-unique, across the organization. As an example, a unique process on a suspect system is highly suspicious and should be considered in the scope of the investigation.

IOCs and YARA Rules

Sometimes, artifacts or indicators are identified in groups, such as IOCs and/or YARA rules. These include any definable network, system, or log artifact in all their varieties, colors, and flavors.

However, if polymorphic malware is involved, then the patterns of behavior and expressions or parameters that describe the activity become the indicators. Examples include the pattern of file and folder names and locations, such as the character set, length, and path of such.

Fortunately for IOCs and YARA rules, not all artifacts are polymorphic, particularly in the later phases of an attack. Oftentimes, attackers utilize standard toolkits, which can be found on the file system. It is common to identify dual-purpose/potentially unwanted programs (PUPs), like security testing tools, pen-testing tools, administration tools, password reset tools, network sniffing/MiTM tools, or covert communication/tunneling tools. PSEXEC is a good example.

Symptoms of the Attack – User Reported

If a user is detected, it is important to identify all of the user-identified symptoms of the incident in order to help validate it and develop situational awareness. Considering that user-reported symptoms are highly anecdotal, the most reliable of user-identified symptoms are the effect or impact of hacking rather than the actual hacking methods themselves. Commonly observed higher-fidelity (but not perfect) user-reported symptoms include.

- Website defacement
- Inappropriately stored sensitive data
- Browser redirections
- Suspicious emails

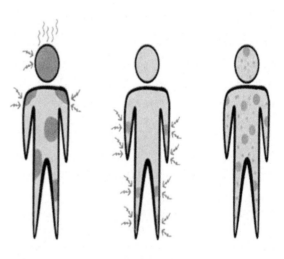

Less reliable user-reported symptoms include:

- Application crashes
- System errors
- Blue screens
- Unexpected browser windows
- Zero-size browser windows
- Unexpected command shells
- Slowness
- Freezing
- Non-user-initiated mouse movement

Very commonly, there can be either malicious or non-malicious, benign causes for suspicious events. The most common sources include:

- Application errors
- Resource/sharing conflicts
- Browser plug-in crashes
- Endpoint slowness
- Network slowness
- Misconfigured security controls
- System updates
- Overly broad incident detection signatures
- Other unexpected error messages that raise suspicions

Any of these items might be unexpected and raise suspicions that are perceived either rightly or wrongly as indicators of an incident. Just like with IOCs or other detection methods, symptoms can be false-positive or false-negative. For this reason, user-reported symptoms for highly technical attackers or malware activity may be unreliable starting places for threat detection and/or root-cause analysis. However, they can be invaluable for identifying the artifacts and impacts.

It is unlikely that user-reported symptoms would be helpful in identifying that their machine was affected by a malicious JavaScript exploit. But, they could describe perfectly well that their web browser is being redirected to a website with inappropriate content or one that contains scareware.

Obtaining exact details for each symptom is key to the investigation. Symptomatic details gathered should include specifics about the behavior, artifacts, messages, and impact on networks, endpoints, and logs. Taking screenshots and collecting both endpoint and network-related telemetry are very helpful in this regard.

The details should also include a description of the impact on the user's experience. However, without empirical data and evidence artifacts, user-reported symptoms can often be too vague and nebulous to be acted upon.

A note of caution is in order, however. While gathering specific details for each user-reported symptom, make sure not to ask users to do anything that will place their systems at risk or further expose sensitive data. This includes opening files that are either possibly infected or may contain regulated or other sensitive content.

Some screenshots will need to be sent using encryption to protect the confidentiality of the content. Standard processes and instructions to facilitate this should be set up and available ahead of time.

Symptoms of the Attack - System Reported

Malicious activity is more reliably detected using system-generated means informed by behavioral analysis, threat feeds, IOCs, real-time activity monitoring, retrospection, etc. Collecting both endpoint and network-related telemetry can be extremely helpful in this regard. This provides overlapping views of the same activity from different perspectives, which is ideal for facilitating investigative activity and root-cause analysis.

System resource utilization metrics are also key symptoms for identifying malware and related activity. This includes memory utilization, processor utilization, disk I/O, network utilization, etc.

These metrics may or may not be decisive indicators of malware. They also may be false positives, having benign causes. Application memory leaks, AV scanning, system/application updates, or cloud syncing may cause the same type of activity and utilization as seen with malware. This is why it is so important to have multiple, overlapping views from different vantage points of the same suspicious activity.

Each of the identified symptoms is an important piece of the overall puzzle in identifying attacker activity, functions, and capabilities. If an intrusion is affirmatively identified on a system and spikes in resources are identified, it is possible to identify the likelihood of certain types of malicious activity. This includes:

- High memory utilization – Non-specific; could apply to numerous malicious use cases and malware actions
- High processor utilization – possible password cracking or crypto mining
- High disk I/O – possible mass file read/write (ransomware, wiperware, mass-copy, etc.)
- High network utilization – possible data exfiltration or worm

Attack Vector

The attack vector is a fairly broad concept typically consisting of a vulnerability and path that can be used to exploit systems, devices, applications, or other resources. For many incident types, the attack vector is usually related to a vulnerability or misconfiguration that is exploited to grant unauthorized access. They can be remote or local and could occur over any operating system, application, service, port, protocol, application, firmware, data entry, interface, or hardware type.

Any method of inputting data, running code, loading files, or interpreting content could conceivably be used as an attack vector to run an exploit. Yes, this means that they may also apply to Mac and Linux systems. No platform is immune.

Attack vectors are most often vulnerable applications having a network listening service (if threats are directly targeting a system) or vulnerable endpoint applications or browser plugins (if threats are targeting an employee using a vulnerable system or device). Direct attacks typically start with a vulnerability scanner and end with an exploit tool to deploy the payload of choice. Indirect attacks may take several steps to social engineer a user into compromising their own machine through whatever methods the attacker can devise. These indirect attack methods often involve waterhole attacks, phishing, malicious removable media, etc.

The attack vector needs to be identified as quickly as possible so as to secure the system or environment and protect it from further exploitation. The longer an attack vector remains available, the greater the risk of exploitation by attackers or malware.

If the attackers or malware are found and eradicated, but the attack vector remains, there is nothing to stop the same or worse activity from happening again. In fact, if it is the same attack group, the next time they come back, it will be with more covert methods.

Exploit Method

Just like the attack vector, the exploit method(s) should be identified as quickly as possible to prevent additional exposure. The exploit method is the other half of the equation and is the specific means by which the attack vector is exploited/compromised.

Moreover, the exploit method might apply to other attack vectors and needs to be secured separately to prevent it from being a continued risk. This is usually where compensating controls can be immensely helpful in reducing the efficacy of exploits.

Exploit methods targeting client endpoints are typically delivered by email or hosted on malicious websites. They are typically cross-platform and multi-layered or nested with various components, exploit types, and scripting languages to increase target compatibility and efficacy.

Malicious scripts often use exploit methods (such as JavaScript) to target attack vectors that work on multiple platforms. JavaScript enjoys broad support across all platforms and runs automatically when the browser visits a website. The malicious JavaScripts can contain other script types (Powershell, VBScript, BASH, etc.), shellcode, and employ various layers of malicious code to provide the greatest "compatibility" and impact for all host types.

As such, the same script can have multiple exploits capable of compromising numerous browsers, versions, and operating systems. This means that a compromised website could be infected with a single script that could work on most of the systems that visit it. A common, frequently used exploit method is to deploy a malicious JavaScript (which runs on every major browser) to exploit browser vulnerabilities that then calls embedded scripts (PowerShell for Windows, BASH for Linux and Mac, etc.) to make system changes and/or extract shellcode to deliver malicious binaries in a format that will run on the local operating systems.

To make the code hard to detect, the exploits often utilize polymorphic techniques, encoding, encryption, or other obfuscation methods. These are often combined with anti-detection/anti-reverse-engineering safeguards to effectively disrupt the code if breakpoints are inserted during reverse engineering and prevent the code from decrypting or decoding. So, inserting breakpoints changes the code, which effectively makes it corrupted and unreadable garbage. Meaning, the code only runs if the script is unaltered. If it is altered by breakpoints, the script will not decrypt. It is a clever tactic but not insurmountable.

Potential Impact

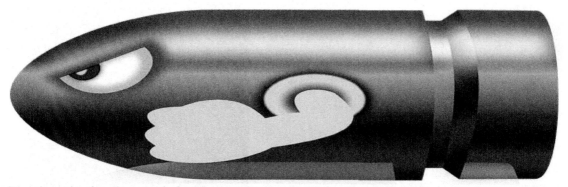

Based on the details provided in the notification compared with the information known about the affected system (such as version, configuration, data, use, and/or regulatory applicability), it is possible to make a quick assessment regarding the impact on the affected resources, severity assignment for the incident, and resources to be allocated to the response.

If the activity is completely irrelevant and could in no way compromise the system (like automated scans looking for any vulnerability but not using anything that would be successful), then the impact would be null. This activity is quite common, with most of the full-suite automated scanning functionalities built into automated scanners, exploit kits, and malware. They often throw everything at a target and see what sticks.

On a personal note, when he was a system admin decades ago, the author used to get great joy out of changing the TCP stack and webserver application headers on Internet-facing Windows systems in the DMZ to identify as those from their Linux counterparts and vice-versa for the Internet-facing Linux systems. In this way, the Windows webservers would get hit with automated Linux attacks, and the Linux webservers would get hit with automated Windows attacks. Because of this, nearly all of the attacks that targeted the webservers had zero chance of success, and only attacks that were for the correct operating systems and applications were of any note.

Alternatively, if the activity is intelligent and targets a known, existing vulnerability on a critical system containing restricted, regulated data and successfully gained root access, the impact would be remarkably high. An example of this would be a targeted attack against a PCI POS server using an existing vulnerability for which the successful attack and subsequent malware C2 traffic is detected by an out-of-band IDS monitoring the network segment. This would go straight to red alert for a PCI compromise. It would be the same for any other type of restricted data or regulatory requirement.

Any compromised resources containing or having access to regulated data are of high impact and need to be handled with elevated priority and urgency. This would typically involve implementing expedited containment, blocking, or other compensating controls.

Begin Incident Artifact Preliminary Collection

Using the best available visibility tools and investigative capabilities, the teams need to begin to collect and preserve evidence from their respective areas for analysis.

Initial evidence gathering and preservation typically consists of capturing live/volatile evidence, logs with a short lifespan, network traffic, or other evidence that is lost quickly over time and ensuring logs are not overwritten. The initial evidence gathered is typically driven by IOCs and/or other information from the alerts. Alternatively, there may be other incident notification sources, and evidence collections would then be driven based on observations.

This will provide a starting place for collection, investigation, and root cause analysis. It will also enable the team to understand the full scope, potential impact, and plausible containment and/or mitigation controls.

The teams should collect evidence from all visibility and/or response capabilities the customer has respective to the compromise and subsequent activity. Depending upon the threat, some solutions work better than others or not at all. The response teams need to identify all network, endpoint, or log collection, parsing/searching, detection, and blocking capabilities that will be effective against the detected threat.

It is critical to enable evidence preservation, ensure incident responders can act without additional delay, and provide for the rapid identification and inform containment measures to prevent the spread of malicious applications and activity. As such, the Incident Commander and/or response personnel should instruct the customer to ensure that all preliminary evidence is being collected and preserved and then validate they have an adequate retention period to prevent the destruction or deletion of evidence.

Very often, logs quickly overwrite and are lost. Moreover, some automated evidence collections are time or size-based, and the content expires, eats its tail, or is otherwise unrecoverably lost. Rolling network traffic captures, native log files, and misconfigured SIEMs are all common sources of these problems.

Preliminary evidence collection artifact locations include anything that can tell the story regarding network, endpoint, process/application, email, user, data, and malware activity. Preliminary evidence collection and analysis usually casts a broad net across a wide variety of visibility tools. It collects surface-level information using known indicators in order to identify the scope of malicious activity and all objects involved. Following are the evidence artifact and data sources/target types for preliminary collection activity:

- Network: Collect ingress/egress traffic from/to the Internet, hosts known to be involved, and sensitive environments. Targeted data sources are PCAP, NetFlow, WAF, DLP, Firewall, NIPS, HIPS, Proxy, VPN, DNS, DHCP, network-DLP, UAM, etc.

- Endpoint: Collect volatile artifacts respective to systems believed to have been involved in an attack or compromise. Targeted data sources include EDR, HIPS, host-DLP, SIEM, AD, UAM, AV/AM, etc.
- Process/Application: Collect volatile artifacts respective to processes/applications believed to have been involved in an attack or compromise. Targeted data sources include EDR, HIPS, host-DLP, SIEM, AD, UAM, AV/AM, etc.
- Email: Review email history, URL rewrite access, malicious attachments, spam, spoofing, etc. Targeted data sources include Email security, cloud scrubbing, AV/AM, HIPS, etc.
- User: Review user activity from any vantage point that can show/correlate activity. Targeted data sources include UAM, network/host DLP, AD, SIEM, etc.
- Data: Review data activity from any vantage point that can show/correlate activity. Targeted data sources include network/host DLP, access/changelogs, EDR, etc.
- Malware: Identify malware samples and have them analyzed. The goal is to determine behavior, capabilities, IOCs, exploit methods, polymorphism, and mitigation techniques.

Order of Evidence Collection/Preservation
Live Data – best captured before containment

1. Network packet captures – The most volatile of all evidence is network traffic, which can be make-or-break information for determining the actual exposure.
2. Preserve all logs – Logs can shortcut the investigative process by telling who did what and when. However, they are surprisingly volatile and may disappear quickly if not properly configured or captured, offloaded, and preserved. This is frequently true with logs stored locally on systems or applications where the logs are in a default state, having inadequate storage space for the volume of activity, and where logs are not forwarded to a SIEM.
3. Volatile metadata – The term volatile metadata is used to describe information in memory related to processes, libraries, drivers, connections, live registry, and the respective details and interconnectivity, which changes from moment to moment.
4. Full memory and page file – The full memory dump includes the metadata and the respective content stored in memory at the moment of collection, which is useful for finding decrypted or decoded information, extracting decryption keys or passwords, identifying hidden processes, and enumerating content that could not otherwise be obtained.

Note: This is the ideal place for containment if host isolation is available, which should limit affected system connectivity to block outbound connections and only permit inbound connections from investigative systems.

Static Data – *is unlikely to change and can wait until after containment*

5. Targeted files, registry locations, or other artifacts – Each operating system and threat types have a certain limited subset of system artifacts that are most helpful in understanding what happened. These vary by circumstance but could expedite the investigation if collected before the system is contained.

***Note: This is the ideal place for containment if host isolation is not available.**

6. Full file system artifacts/disk images – Making disk images and doing a full forensic collection is usually done offline but can also be done online if host isolation is enabled.
7. Email servers/repositories – These are data elements in email servers or cloud repositories that need to be exported or imported, possibly converted, and then parsed.
8. Databases, repositories, and structured data files – These are artifacts stored on the file system or in various data repositories, which need to be converted, imported, and parsed.

Network Packet Captures

For the network-enabled incident workflows, capturing network traffic is very important for understanding what happened at many of the various states of the attack. Using the 7 stages of the Lockheed Martin Kill Chain and assuming encryption and decryption are not issues, 6 of the 7 stages would be observable over the network if network methods are used for the attack:

1. Reconnaissance (Partial Visibility) – Scanning and casing activity could potentially be identified on the wire, but it would be hard to distinguish. Other out-of-band reconnaissance activity would not be visible or detectable from any network monitoring solutions.
2. Weaponization (No Visibility) – Coupling the exploit with the payload happens on the attacker's machine and would not be detectable on the wire.
3. Delivery (Partial Visibility) – The network delivery of the weaponized exploit bundle to the target would be observable. However, not every delivery method uses the network.
4. Exploitation (Partial Visibility) – The exploitation of vulnerabilities and execution of code may be detected if the exploitation happens remotely, such as a remote code injection type of exploit. However, for it to be visible, it must NOT have already pushed a binary or script to the endpoint to run locally upon being triggered.
5. Installation (Partial Visibility) – The installation of malware and backdoors can also happen either locally or remotely, depending on how it is pushed. Remote code injection of those that call the C2 server whenever the system is launched or logged into are good examples. Secondary exploits or modules are often downloaded at this time from C2 servers and are detectable.
6. Command & Control C2 (Full Visibility) – C2 is almost always detectable over the network, except in rare cases when the malware uses removable media or other mechanisms to communicate. However, even removable media C2 ultimately uses the network at some point unless it is an on-prem attack, which is not covered in the

Lockheed Martin model.

7. Actions and Objectives/Persistence (Full Visibility) – Like C2, this final persistence phase (which also includes lateral movement and beginning the activity all over again on other machines) often involves sending lots of data over the network and can be detected.

However, if network traffic is not being captured, this info will be lost. Once network traffic is sent, it is gone. Unless there is a fragment of it in memory or it is being recorded via some type of network traffic recording system/device, there will be no usable record of it.

The only artifact that might still exist would be firewall or IPS logs, primarily consisting of socket information and not data. Some companies store NetFlow information, which is not much better than metadata. It is essentially network traffic metadata + metrics.

A rolling window of network ingress/egress traffic should be collected at all times, but this is less common than it should be. Many organizations only implement full packet captures for the purposes of troubleshooting or when an incident is in progress. At the very least, when an incident is suspected, all ingress/egress traffic from all POPs should be collected and preserved until the incident response activity is completed.

This could turn into many, many terabytes of PCAPs. Adequate storage needs to be provided.

It is also critical to collect the traffic from an un-NATed location and for outbound traffic SSL/TLS decryption to be implemented ahead of time. The best place to do this is on next-gen perimeter firewalls with capabilities for inline SSL/TLS decryption and decrypted traffic hand-off to secondary capture and analysis tools.

If this does not happen, the traffic is mostly useless. It will consist mostly of encrypted data from unknown sources, and all that will be discernable from it is the external socket information (IP Addresses and ports) and the volume of traffic sent or received.

Preserve All Logs

For all incident workflows, capturing and preserving logs is critical for understanding what the attackers did on the affected resources. Depending upon the nature of an attack, any logs could provide value. However, if the systems are compromised by an attacker with admin credentials, the log data is at risk of deletion or manipulation.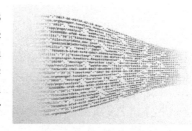

Also, it probably seems counter-intuitive that logs would be considered a live or volatile data source. The reason for this is that, in and of themselves, logs are often surprisingly volatile and can evaporate quickly. If they are left in the default configuration within large organizations, they may only last for seconds before overwriting. Active Directory logs are notorious for this, but any locally/natively stored log source for systems or applications could be affected by this. Essentially, if the log storage allocation is small and the volume of activity is high, the logs may only preserve moments of information.

This means that IT and Security teams need to make sure that all logs from any source are being preserved, including systems, devices, applications, services, databases, etc. The best thing about this task is that it can easily be farmed out to all of the respective subject matter experts (SMEs) with little to no impact on the responders' resources. Essentially, the responders can define and guide the SMEs, which can go their own way and make the changes as necessary.

However, it must usually be clarified with the action owners that "all logs" really means ALL LOGS, without exception. It is not completely possible to determine which logs will be needed from the outset of the response process to identify or clarify malicious activity. Usually, a combination of logs from disparate resources are required, depending upon the specific threats involved and the targets affected. It is much better to over-collect logs and not need them than to need them for an unforeseen aspect of a case and not have them.

Moreover, it is not just enough to capture and retain logs. The logs themselves need to collect the right content. Often, only certain failure events are logged, but success events are not. More specifically, by default, in many cases, if an attacker tried to logon 100,000,000 times and failed, but the next attempt was successful, the logs would only show the 100M failed attempts, not the successful attempt.

This makes it difficult to identify if attackers were actually successful or not in their attempts without a much deeper forensic analysis. Further, depending on the artifacts left behind (or not), a deep-dive forensic examination might not yield any meaningful results. Affirmatively identifying access is more about logging activity than about file system analysis.

The ideal method for doing log collection and preservation is to push all logs to a central location (such as a SIEM) where use cases can be correlated and searches queried across all data sources. The data should be kept available for the entire retention period.

Even better, it is ideal if all this is set up ahead of time. This will lengthen the window of searchability and enable the investigative team to view activity retrospectively back to the time of exploitation across all relevant data sources. This provides the best view of malicious actions.

Volatile Metadata

Name	PID	Status	User name	CPU	Memory (p...	Command line
svchost.exe	15320	Running	Colby	00	576 K	C:\Users\Colby\AppData\Local\Microsoft\Network\svchost.exe
svchost.exe	21616	Running	SYSTEM	00	1,324 K	C:\WINDOWS\system32\svchost.exe -k netsvcs -p -s wlidsvc
svchost.exe	9684	Running	SYSTEM	00	1,284 K	C:\WINDOWS\system32\svchost.exe -k SDRSVC
svchost.exe	18128	Running	SYSTEM	00	2,192 K	
svchost.exe	720	Running	SYSTEM	00	504 K	c:\windows\system32\svchost.exe -k dcomlaunch -p -s PlugPlay
svchost.exe	1028	Running	SYSTEM	00	14,028 K	C:\WINDOWS\system32\svchost.exe -k DcomLaunch -p
svchost.exe	1136	Running	NETWORK...	00	9,392 K	c:\windows\system32\svchost.exe -k rpcss -p
svchost.exe	1188	Running	SYSTEM	00	2,120 K	c:\windows\system32\svchost.exe -k dcomlaunch -p -s LSM
svchost.exe	1432	Running	SYSTEM	00	1,272 K	c:\windows\system32\svchost.exe -k localsystemnetworkrestricted -...
svchost.exe	1440	Running	LOCAL SE...	00	1,300 K	c:\windows\system32\svchost.exe -k localservicenetworkrestricted -...
svchost.exe	1520	Running	LOCAL SE...	00	13,236 K	c:\windows\system32\svchost.exe -k localservicenetworkrestricted -...
svchost.exe	1640	Running	LOCAL SE...	00	7,240 K	c:\windows\system32\svchost.exe -k localservice -p -s nsi
svchost.exe	1716	Running	LOCAL SE...	00	1,784 K	C:\WINDOWS\system32\svchost.exe -k LocalService -p
svchost.exe	1752	Running	LOCAL SE...	00	1,344 K	c:\windows\system32\svchost.exe -k localservicenetworkrestricted -...
svchost.exe	1872	Running	NETWORK...	00	3,608 K	c:\windows\system32\svchost.exe -k networkservice -p -s NlaSvc
svchost.exe	1880	Running	SYSTEM	00	5,640 K	c:\windows\system32\svchost.exe -k netsvcs -p -s Schedule
svchost.exe	1984	Running	LOCAL SE...	00	2,856 K	c:\windows\system32\svchost.exe -k localservice -p -s netprofm

The term volatile metadata is used to describe the memory information and related processes, libraries, drivers, network connections, live registry keys/values, open files, and the respective details and interconnectivity, which changes from moment to moment. It is the quickest way to put together the story of what is happening right now (meaning the time of the snapshot) or during a selected period of time if real-time monitoring is used and the period of time is captured. This will enable the investigators to track the activity on any or all monitored machines and view the activity as the hacker moves throughout the environment.

Volatile metadata is fast, detail-rich, and contains most of the data needed for IR-related information unless it has been manipulated by malware-hiding techniques. For most incident workflows, capturing volatile metadata is important for understanding malicious activity. This includes identifying malicious applications, C2 network connections, and attacker/malware-related file activity at the moment that the volatile metadata snapshot was taken.

Alternatively, if volatile metadata is continuously monitored across all endpoints, it will reveal all activity across all monitored systems for the entire incident window. While volatile metadata is good when collected at the time of an incident, there is still a lot of data lost unless it is continually collected starting before an incident and captures all activity throughout the incident lifecycle.

The only way to affirmatively identify what happened during an incident, from exploit to exfiltration, is to record the activity from every source and artifact and then display that data on a retrospective timeline. This includes the activity of every process, script, file read/write, registry read/write, WMI modification, and network connection.

Once correlated and displayed through a process activity tree, this will tell the story of what happened in short order. More importantly, they can be used to identify or block similar activity based on behavior and IOCs.

There are a lot of technologies that do this, but their capabilities differ significantly between the various solutions. Most of them look similar in their front-end interface, but the way they monitor and capture information underneath the hood can be profoundly different. These architectural differences may be invisible from a user interface perspective, but they can result in profound variances in efficacy and usability.

The most powerful of the real-time volatile data monitoring solutions are cloud-based and capture all activity and volatile content using direct memory interrogation rather than Windows API calls. This provides depth, breadth, and visibility into systems, whether on or off the corporate network.

With this capability, investigations are significantly expedited, and deeper dive forensics may not even be required unless sensitive data has been compromised. All of this can be done orders of magnitude faster than using the conventional forensic analysis approach, especially since it does not have to wait until systems are contained and acquired. It has become the only way to keep up with emergent threats. Moreover, using the real-time method of collection, the evidence is continuously collected and unaffected by containment activity. As such, containment can happen at any time.

The network connections portion of the volatile metadata is particularly important and distinct, as it will identify all network traffic. This includes internal traffic, such as between workstations or traffic from servers to workstations. These traffic types are atypical and generally a sign of malicious activity, such as lateral movement, self-replicating malware, etc.

The downside of volatile metadata snapshots is that they can be easily manipulated using various memory tampering and hiding techniques, depending on how they are collected. If they rely on APIs vs. direct memory interrogation, they can be easily manipulated by malware. If relied upon solely, they can create a false understanding of the current state of activity if the hiding techniques are successful.

Moreover, volatile metadata completely lacks content and, therefore, lacks context. This is another reason for collecting other evidence, including a continuous capture of volatile activity with retrospective capabilities, as well as the collection and analysis of a full memory dump and full disk acquisition. Moreover, using this method of collection, the evidence is continuously collected and unaffected by containment activity.

Full Memory and Page File

For most incident workflows, capturing full memory captures, including the pagefile, can fill in many of the details missing in the volatile metadata. This includes some of the substance and the respective context of open files, executed commands, live processes, network traffic content, and malware. All of this can be used to understand the attacker's activity and assist in analysis prioritization.

For the sake of clarity, the memory dump provides pointers and arrays of data but very little data content. The pagefile contains the actual content and substantive data that is being pointed to.

The full content of memory and pagefile is useful for finding decrypted or decoded information (such as encryption keys, passwords, scripts, chats, files, commands, or other data) and is the best way to identify hidden processes or artifacts that are manipulated by malware. This may be the only place where certain types of data reside and could be found during an investigation.

A good data example of this is encrypted chat communications that do not log conversations to disk and cannot be decrypted on the wire. The full text of the conversations and files transferred may be available to be carved out of memory with the correct parsing methodology.

A good malware-related example of memory being the only place to identify artifacts includes hollowed process or script-based activity that does not leave evidence on the file system. It also speeds up cryptography, credential harvesting, and decoding efforts by making them unnecessary. Everything is first decrypted or decoded in memory prior to use or execution. Rather than having to use exhaustive methods to decrypt or decode content or artifacts, it is available for the taking in its clear-text state in memory.

This may be a good time to pull malware samples out of memory, particularly if they are injected into other processes, libraries, or drivers. These samples should be provided to the malware analysis team (whether internal or contracted) for analysis to identify the capabilities and identify the IOCs.

Even if the investigator does not have a parser capable of harvesting the sought-after content or the knowledge of where to find it, these details can be worked out later. It is critical to capture this content prior to the containment of the system in order for it to provide maximum value.

If it is collected post-containment, data related to active network connections and associated processes may be lost. Disconnecting the network port will end the network connection, which may close the respective application and delete the data in memory.

Notwithstanding the volume of data, memory only contains limited data. Only recently accessed or proactively loaded information is available. At some point, file system artifacts are needed.

Targeted Files, Registry Locations, or other Artifacts

For most incident workflows, capturing some basic file system artifacts prior to containment can make all the difference in expediting an investigation and understanding the actual impact of the attacker on the affected system. Considering that limited data is stored in memory and a full-disk acquisition takes far too long, a common alternative is to gather the live evidence, as well as limited static evidence, required to establish the facts of an incident. This is a middle ground that collects minimal evidence to provide the most likely content for an investigation without running an overt risk of handicapping it, but also without over-collecting content that can probably wait.

Each threat type and affected operating system or application has a certain limited subset of related artifacts that are key to establishing root cause(s), exploit methods, and impact. These vary by circumstance but could expedite the investigation if collected before the system is contained. Most of this data will remain unchanged post-containment unless there is some sort of logic that deletes artifacts when the network connection is severed. These types of malware functions exist, but they are not commonly seen and are more likely associated with nation-state activity than commoditized cyber threats. Some common examples of targeted forensic artifacts include the following, which manifest differently on each operating system type:

- Account/group/role configuration – Identify unauthorized accounts, group memberships, and/or other changes made by the attackers to elevate privileges or create backdoor accounts.
- File system catalog ($MFT, FAT, Inode table, etc.) – Capture the entire file system catalog to obtain a listing of files, folders, metadata, and deleted content.
- Recently created/written binaries and scripts – Create a file system timeline to identify changes from attacker activity and malware installation. This includes the enumeration of all recently created or written binaries and scripts to inform targeted collections.
- Deleted file history – Identify any files/folders that were deleted either from the directory catalog, Recycle bin, and/or folder records
- Targeted MRU history – View recent activity across desired MRU locations to identify the most recently used sites, files, applications, searches, mapped drives, printers, etc.
- Program execution configuration settings – Identify tampering of application execution, such as shimming the execution of other programs or scripts first or specifying custom parameters that change the functions at execution.
- Prefetch files – Enumerate all prefetch files to identify application execution history, suspicious/malicious files executed, and the respective prefetch settings for malicious files: C:\Windows\Prefetch
- Internet browser history – Enumerate websites visited, scripts executed, and files downloaded or opened.
- Network settings – Enumerate all network interfaces and settings to identify any unauthorized interfaces or configurations that could be used for surreptitious access.
- Temporary/AppData file locations – Enumerate non-privileged user-writable locations and identify any files, binaries, or scripts downloaded to temp, AppData, or other public subdirectory locations and perform targeted collections.
- WMI or other fileless application configuration – Identify fileless programs added to the

system, such as custom WMI classes utilized by Windows, typically located in the default location: C:\Windows\System32\wbem

- Auto-runs and services configuration – Enumerate any programs or services that run on startup or login, which may identify malicious applications.
- Scheduled tasks – Enumerate all scheduled or recurring tasks, which may identify malicious applications, scripts, or functions.
- Targeted event logs – Collect key event logs from the system and/or applications, such as Security logs.
- Link files – Capture link files to enumerate recently accessed files, programs, removable drives, or shares that may provide quick evidence of previous activity.
- USB device history – Enumerate all removable devices inserted into the system and their respective details about the devices and the users that inserted them. Default locations include the following registry keys:
  - SYSTEM/CurrentControlSet/Enum/USBSTOR
  - SYSTEM/MountedDevices
  - NTUSER.DAT/Software/Microsoft/Windows/CurrentVersion/Explorer/MountPoints2
  - SYSTEM/CurrentControlSet/Enum/USB

Out of this targeted detection, collection, and analysis, malware and/or malicious script samples may be identified and made available for analysis.

Ideal Place for Containment

In a perfect world, this is the ideal place for containment and halting malicious activity. The team now has enough substantive evidence to investigate the attack, identify related activity, and implement containment without slowing the investigative process down.

The key is to be able to do this without slowing down the containment activity. Considering containment measures usually require approval, the preliminary evidence collection can be done if the process is well defined, visibility is available at all data sources, and well-trained/tested teams move quickly to collect the data.

It is strongly advised that adequate people, processes, and technology are employed to make the pre-containment evidence collection as invisible and seamless as possible. It is even better if the evidence collection is automated based on a continuous process or triggered by specific activities.

This is possible to do but not necessarily easy. It requires proper correlation, configuration, and pre-defined triggers on and integrated between security capabilities. These typically include firewalls, IPSs, EDR tools, SIEMs, threat feeds, etc.

Cloud-based network and EDR tools with activity recording and retrospection automate most of it. They could even potentially automate all of it, depending upon the circumstances and evidence artifacts desired.

Moreover, depending upon the nature and speed of the threat, all of the manual evidence collection steps may fly out the window, and urgent containment measures may need to be applied. In such cases, the only data that will be immediately available for investigation will be on devices that already store it, and any further evidence will come from post-containment activity, which will suffer a certain amount of data loss.

Selective Preservation and Surgical Eradication

Once potential malware activity has been identified, there is a need to stop it in order to prevent further exposure and damage. However, there are various ways to do this, and some are more impactful than others.

It sounds logical to immediately take compromised systems that are identified by hacking and malware alerts offline. However, it is not always feasible to bring down resources and block communications, particularly if there are questions about the severity of the threat, the viability of lateral movement, and whether containment may cause business impact.

Oftentimes, complete containment options are off the table until the full impact of the hacking activity is understood, and it has crossed a certain threshold that the business deems appropriate to halt production system and activity. Before that threshold is reached, partial containment (AKA Surgical Eradication) options are usually the most prudent. Surgical Eradication is a compromise that allows systems to continue to function but eradicates known threats residing on them. Known legitimate functions can continue, but other activity is blocked. It involves the following.

- Positive identification of threats and the respective IOCs
- Collection of associated artifacts related to the threats:
  - Files
  - Process
  - Memory
  - Registry entries
  - Network traffic
  - Scheduled tasks

    o   Auto-start locations
- Eradication of the threat and related artifacts
  - Kill processes
  - Stop services
  - Delete files
  - Delete registry entries
  - Terminate connections
  - Delete auto-start entries and scheduled tasks
  - Make configuration changes
- Validation and monitoring to ensure that the threat has been addressed and malicious activity does not recur

Usually (and optimally), Surgical Eradication is a temporary workaround that just buys time for the production systems to be further investigated and then restored to a known good state with no impact on availability. There will always be questions regarding the efficacy of Surgical Eradication, such as:
- Were all of the changes made by the attacker identified and reversed?
- Were all of the attacker's backdoors identified and remediated?
- Were the systems altered in ways that were not detected?
- Have all of the risks been mitigated?

Even if the system no longer has malicious functions, it may still be unstable. The libraries, processes, WMI classes, or other functions could have been replaced. To be sure, full recovery and restoration procedures should always be followed.

Preliminary Analysis

For all incidents, it is urgent to get inside the attacker's head and ascertain as soon as possible the "who, what, when, where, why, and how" questions pertaining to the incident and root cause. Not all of this will be identifiable right away.

The initial evidence collected will allow the response team to identify (or know where to go to identify) the rest of the story. Preliminary analysis workflows include:
- Perform timeline analysis by pulling together as much detail as initially available from notable activity and multi-artifact timeline builders, such as Log2Timeline. Log2Timeline has dozens of plugins for various artifact types. Common sources include:
  - Alerts
  - Files
  - Browser history
  - Logs
  - Registry
  - Processes

o Network connections
- Aggregate, correlate, and analyze all collected evidence to identify associations.
- Identify attacker activity, tools, methodology, artifacts, connections, infrastructure, files, and impact.
- Analyze collected evidence and activity for the scope of external/internal attacks and expand the activity timeline of events to include new findings.
- Identify additional targets of internal/external attacks and use the timeline artifacts and all indicators identified.
- Review affected systems for indications of successful exploitation and methods used.
- Enumerate affected systems, applications, and data sets and the respective sensitivity/confidentiality of each.

Prioritizing Response Efforts

If an attack targets multiple machines, not every affected resource will be able to be investigated first. While it may be possible to investigate more than one at a time using multiple investigators on a team, at some point, the team will run out of personnel to investigate affected resources in parallel.

Moreover, in addition to affected systems, each artifact, data source, and analysis type is technically a separate workflow that needs to be prioritized. This turns into a significant math problem if everything must be analyzed for every affected system.

Ultimately, a judgment call must be made regarding what takes priority, and making the wrong choice delays key findings and the containment of malicious activity. Some activities come first, and others will have to wait for their turn.

Triaging and prioritizing response and containment efforts is a highly contextual judgment call. It varies from one organization to another based on their business operations, customer impact, regulatory needs, and data sensitivity.

Ultimately, everything has a priority, and some priorities are higher than others. The context of the threat and respective impact on each system, device, application, user, function, and/or data will inform the response priority and containment requirements. Usually, business criticality, regulatory impact, and the respective nature of the threat vector play the most significant role in prioritization. In addition to the contextual priority developed by organizations, there are also innate prioritization considerations that should be evaluated:
- Actively spreading malware threats – These threats have the potential to bring down the entire environment and resources therein.
- Systems that support life – These systems are very high priority and should be contained ASAP to prevent malicious impact.

- Systems with regulated data – Regulated data exposures can be very costly, including > $242 per record lost, and they may compromise the health and longevity of the company. Halting them to minimize impacted records is critical. Even worse, the highest per-record cost is $429 and affects the health industry in the United States.
- Critical systems and networks supporting business operations – While these systems may sound more critical than 4th on the list, the functionality of these resources will usually be sacrificed to prevent impact on higher priority items listed. Moreover, the longer these systems are online, the more sensitive data may be collected and add to the problem.
- Ancillary systems – These systems seem obvious as a 5th priority, but they may also be someone's favorite system or application, and there may be political pressure to elevate the priority.
- Not known to be affected systems – These are another example of types that may seem obvious as a low priority but often result in a political issue wherein there may be a desire to elevate the priority to prove a negative. Meaning, there may be a need to perform an investigation to prove that nothing malicious happened to these systems.
- Inaccessible systems – Some systems may be extremely urgent for response and restoration purposes, but for whatever reasons, there is no ability to access, analyze, or act upon them. The best thing to do with these is to build a containment wall around them using network controls. This inability could be the result of any reasons, including:
  o Externally managed
  o Externally hosted
  o Highly sensitive
  o Unstable
  o Inaccessible or untouchable by existing teams
  o Not immediately actionable

IAM Containment Measures

Depending upon the nature of the threat, a variety of IAM controls may be appropriate for lockout activity:
- Remote access restrictions – Lock down remote access to all environments:
  o Corporate remote access tools – Terminate access to all corporate standard remote administration tools, including direct, proxy, or cloud-based access tools.
  o Block user-installed remote access and administration tools – Blocking these requires first identifying tools and communication methods the actor is using.
  o Corporate VPNs – Terminate access to corporate VPNs for all malicious actor accounts and tokens.
  o Accounts – Administrator, user, service, and application accounts, including local or domain accounts.
  o MFA tokens – Users may have multiple MFA tokens (such as physical or soft tokens used either for SSL or thick client VPNs) depending upon the method of access granted to the respective account types.

- Private VPNs or network tunneling tools – Blocking these requires first identifying tools and communication methods the actor is using.
- Cloud system/service access – This access is often the easiest to forget to block, particularly if authentication is not federated with corporate IAM systems.
- Accounts – Lock down all accounts that are considered at-risk or known to be compromised:
  - Lock or change passwords for administrator and user accounts (local or domain-wide) - Local accounts can be hard to identify at the time they are required and need to be enumerated ahead of time for optimal response time.
  - Change passwords for service accounts (local or domain-wide), but only after careful planning and investigation. Doing this without enough research can cause an outage. As such, an intermediary step would be to make sure that the service accounts are not remotely accessible. Ideally, these should be non-interactive only.
  - Lock or change passwords for application accounts – Just like local accounts, these should be tracked in change management or IAM tools. If not, they can be really hard and time-consuming to find at the time of investigation and lockout when urgency is required.
  - Deregister MFA tokens so they no longer function on anything – These need to be bricked.
- Kerberos – Remove Kerberos persistence mechanisms.
  - Golden tickets – Reset all admin passwords, especially KRBTGT (2 times), to invalidate any golden tickets/TGTs.
  - Silver tickets – Configure PAC validation to deny forged service tickets/TGSs.
  - Skeleton keys – Identify and remove any persistence mechanisms creating skeleton keys.

Network Containment Measures
Depending upon the nature of the threat, a variety of network controls may be appropriate to block the internal or external hacking activity. However, these only work within the security perimeter. The following are common methods used:

- Protecting vulnerable web applications with web application firewalls (WAFs) – This can be the best way to stop most inbound malicious activity against vulnerable websites immediately. It can turn a vulnerable website with few to no security controls into a relatively secure site that has security controls that block common threats. This will enable the development team to permit a vulnerable site to function while a more secure site can be built.
- Using perimeter firewalls and/or network IPS devices to block IP addresses, domains, network ranges, CIDR blocks, TCP/UDP ports, and/or signature-based threats – This is a stop-gap security control that is easily circumvented by attackers through the use of proxies in countries or locations that are not blocked. If the attackers are really determined, they will get around these controls and find another way in. But, it may buy the response team some time.

- Using network-based DLP technologies to identify, contain, and or delete files with targeted content as found by full-data matching, partial-data matching, data types (PHI, PCI, PII, etc.), or sensitive data classification tags. Encrypted data will be a challenge, particularly if it was encrypted by a malicious actor.
- Utilize Next-generation firewall capabilities to block:
  - Protocol anomalies – This includes a whole host of things, including some forms of tunneling or other methods of protocol misuse.
  - Fraudulent sites/reputation blocking – This is common with non-targeted, commoditized malware, particularly if the threats have been around a little while.
  - Newly registered domains – This is common with targeted attacks having purpose-built domains, such as being a subtle twist on a legitimate domain.
  - Malicious downloads – This is common with known malware C2, phishing domains, waterhole attacks, etc.
  - Volumetric blocking – This includes sending out data beyond an imposed cap, which could indicate exfiltration or tunneling.
  - Connection time or duration blocking – This could halt connections at unexpected times or those lasting longer than a predefined time period, which could indicate exfiltration or tunneling.
  - DGA blocking – Block domains created through Domain Generation Algorithms, which are often used for C2 or exfiltration.
  - Dynamic blocking from Threat feeds or other integrations.
- Utilize cloud scrubbing services to sanitize inbound traffic and prevent hacking, malware, and volumetric attacks – This blocks most of the malicious activity within the service providers' infrastructure.
- Utilize reputational services to prevent unauthorized, compromised, or defaced versions of websites/applications from being visible to customers – This places a cached proxied layer between the client on the Internet and the web/application server that only permits authorized versions of content to be displayed by anyone visiting the domain/URL. However, it can be bypassed by going directly to the web/application server IP address.
- Disabling network switch ports for workstations and servers – This is typically the quickest and most definitive way to completely halt all threats related to an endpoint.
- Block direct access to internal systems from remote access users/vendors/partners and require them to go through a jumpbox or virtualized infrastructure, such as VDI or Citrix environment, with only permitted applications published. It is ideal if virtual environment access is set up as the primary access method as part of the onboarding of relationships involving remote access. It is effectively a virtual device firewall that can significantly limit the risk of malicious activity from people or malicious processes. Moreover, it is rather cumbersome to try and bolt on during an incident as many steps are involved in the setup for all relationships that cannot simply be severed.

Endpoint Containment Measures

Due to the limited scope and efficacy of traditional network controls and the function existing primarily for ingress/egress activity within the security perimeter, endpoint controls can be implemented to address the same methods.

Additionally, they can add an expanded set of controls on systems located anywhere. The following are common methods used:

- Using a host-based firewall and IPS software to block IP addresses, domains, network ranges, CIDR blocks, TCP/UDP ports, and/or signature-based threats – This is a host-based network control that can provide selective containment controls enabling legitimate activity. But blocking malicious or undesired activity.
- Using host-based monitoring and EDR technologies capable of behavioral analysis and anomaly identification and blocking – This is a behavior-based method that can provide selective containment controls enabling legitimate activity but blocking malicious or undesired activity.
- Using host-based DLP technologies to identify, contain, and or delete files with targeted content as found by full-data matching, partial-data matching, data types (PHI, PCI, PII, etc.), or sensitive data classification tags.
- Source application traffic/activity blocking is used to halt any activity from known malicious processes. This is usually a method implemented through EDR and anti-malware tools, but it may require some manual configuration if the malicious application is not known to the tool.
- Changing passwords on workstations and/or servers – This should be done as soon as reasonably possible, but it may drag on if admin or service accounts are involved.
- Disabling user accounts on workstations and/or servers – This should be done as soon as reasonably possible, but it may drag on if admin or service accounts are involved.
- Performing host isolation using endpoint agents – This is typically performed with EDR, anti-malware, or policy configuration tools. It has the advantage of blocking all network activity except that which is whitelisted for use by security or investigation purposes.
- Antivirus configuration can be useful, but you should have very low expectations – If a .dat file is available or a signature can be configured, AV may be helpful in detecting the same infection elsewhere and stopping future examples of the same thing, but polymorphism usually negates the efficacy of this.

Threat Feed Integration/Correlation for Containment

In order to provide scalability to the detection and blocking of suspicious or malicious activity, the following activity monitoring, alerting, and blocking should be integrated with threat feeds and/or cross-integrated or correlated to leverage detection and blocking IOCs across as many response technologies as reasonably possible. This will protect critical systems (if not all systems) and quickly identify or automatically contain, block, or otherwise prevent malicious activity.

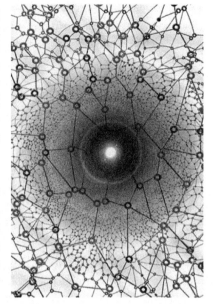

Specifically, multiple threat feeds should be integrated into the detection and blocking capacities within all network, endpoint, and SIEM tools to identify emergent threats as quickly as possible. No single organization can have the breadth of reach and exposure necessary to obtain the required insight on evolving threats to enable them to stay ahead of them.

As such, threat intelligence should be crowd-sourced as much as possible, and intelligence from crowdsourcing should be integrated with detection and blocking technologies at all levels.

- Actors/Toolsets/IOCs/Methods/Infrastructure – Threat feeds with web interfaces that allow for research and pivoting to related indicators are key for providing quick insight into other related tools, artifacts, and activities. Meaning, if one piece of the puzzle is identified (such as an IP address), that IP address could be linked back to the attacker and potentially identify other IP addresses, malware, methodologies, or other useful details. Essentially, any linked indicator can theoretically be tied back to any other linked indicator.
- Domains and IP addresses – The easiest stage of an attack to identify is usually the communication with domains or IP addresses involved in malicious downloads or C2 traffic. This is because endpoint indicators are more polymorphic than network indicators for commoditized attacks that affect a broad swath of non-targeted entities. Targeted attacks often use unique virtual infrastructure per targeted entity.
- Processes/services/drivers/functions/WMI classes – IOCs for volatile metadata, whether hidden or not, can be found in memory. Even if polymorphic, threat feeds can identify indicators about the function and behavior of the malicious processes, services, or WMI classes and subscriptions that can be identified by EDR or anti-malware technologies.
- Files/folders/registry entries/auto-start methods – File system and registry IOCs from threat feeds can be helpful for identification and blocking if there are non-polymorphic artifacts or patterns for the naming convention that can be uniquely identified. Auto-start

methods are particularly helpful for finding persistence, and regardless of whether they are polymorphic, they may stand out as anomalous.

- Internet Access and Artifacts – Internet access to malicious sites is obviously the primary attack vector to compromise endpoints, which have become the primary target of attackers. The myriad of browser plugins and vulnerable endpoint applications integrated with browsers or having direct Internet access leads to a large attack surface, difficulty in timely patching, and a strong likelihood of exploitation.

Because of this, the inside is the new outside, and the Internet is full of overtly malicious sites, compromised legitimate sites, and waterhole attacks that automatically compromise vulnerable endpoints. All outbound access to the Internet must be monitored, tracked, and validated as much as possible, and malware artifacts should be analyzed to identify methods used to bypass security controls.

This is particularly important in the modern fileless malware environment that utilizes various scripts, WMI classes, and memory-resident capabilities. This is best done through a combination of firewall/proxy, network traffic, EDR, and endpoint forensic technologies. All of these can utilize the latest threat intel to enhance detection, alerting, and containment capabilities.

- Email Activity, Links, Attachments, and Other Artifacts – Malicious emails are essentially an extension of malicious Internet activity and the bundling of selected attack vectors or pointers to them into a discrete package. All email access should be tightly restricted, monitored, and controlled to identify and prevent malicious attachments, links, spoofing methods, and other activity.

All attachments and links should be automatically analyzed to identify malicious intent, and links should be rewritten to identify end-user access to simplify the investigative process. Moreover, the ability to crowd-source phishing campaigns based on the most current threat intel can dramatically reduce the efficacy of such attacks.

- Process/Application Behavior – modern EDR capabilities provide the ability to monitor, validate, and provide retrospection for processes and applications to validate that they are acting within normal bounds and not behaving maliciously. This is usually done through a variety of methods, including profiling normal behavior and flagging deviations therefrom or from identifying malicious activity based on a chain of events.

A simple example of this would be "an uncategorized application starts an instance of svchost.exe that initiates a connection with a known attacker C2 site. Therefore, the uncategorized application is malicious." Alerts pertaining to this type of activity should be quickly investigated to rapidly halt malicious activity.

Moreover, the retrospective functionality and activity linking of many EDR solutions make for quick identification of root cause(s). This can be greatly expedited and simplified through the use of threat intel as other entities likely saw it first and can provide information on how to detect and proactively contain it.

- User Behavior Monitoring – By utilizing a combination of User Activity Monitoring (UAM), Data Loss Prevention (DLP), access logs, and firewall logs, it is possible to get a reasonable idea of what entities are doing and business logic, privacy, and security rules should be developed, integrated, or otherwise implemented to identify suspicious, prohibited, or malicious activity.

Malware threats often appear as suspicious user activity. A combination of understanding normal/expected behavior combined with solid threat intel identifying expected malicious activity can assist in the early detection of unauthorized or malicious behavior.

- Repository/Share/File Activity – By utilizing a combination of User Activity Monitoring (UAM), Data Loss Prevention (DLP), Identify and Access Monitoring (IAM) solutions, and access activity logs, it is possible to detect and track malicious actions attack groups or by malicious applications acting under the legitimate user's context (such as ransomware or wiperware). Keeping these detection signatures relevant is really only possible with automated methods like threat feed integration.

- Configuration Changes and File Integrity Monitoring – Through the use of endpoint software that performs configuration management and file integrity monitoring, it is possible to identify unauthorized activity by entities or malware making potentially malicious changes. Configuration changes are made both by malware and scripts. Being able to identify them in an automated manner can speed up initial detection and simplify root-cause analysis. The detected activity can be correlated with threat feeds to identify malware families or variants potentially involved and trigger alerts or containment actions accordingly.

- Site/Web Application/Database Activity – All external-facing and sensitive internal websites and corresponding databases should be monitored and validated via WAFs and database activity monitoring software. These systems are ideal for identifying unusual, suspicious, and/or malicious activity as they learn the objects they are monitoring and identify deviations from normal.

Known malicious activity that appears successful should be immediately investigated. While it is true that these methods aim toward taking a behavioral whitelisting approach, it is also true that they are always doing a certain amount of learning and do not block activities they cannot convict. Specific, crowd-sourced knowledge regarding the malicious nature of activities will expedite the conviction process.

- Volumetric Activity – Some malicious activity does not appear overt and can only be detected by identifying an excessive number of connections or activity to a service or protocol. As such, all Internet-facing, business-sensitive, and administration applications, services, and access methods should implement rules to identify excessive volumetric activity that could be related to DoS, DDoS, scanning activity, or other malicious actions. Considering the evolving nature of volumetric attacks, threat feed integration is essential to identify new methods of DoS/DDoS and the known sources involved in campaigns.

Divide and Conquer

Oftentimes, response teams make the mistake of being single-threaded in analysis and not employing enough personnel to ensure response tasks are completed in a timely manner. There are too many workstreams and disparate pursuits for single-threaded analysis to be feasible. Under-assignment of resources creates the risk of rushing through or skipping analysis tasks and failing to meet response needs. Either is a recipe for failure.

The tasks need to be divided across the various functional areas and assigned to their respective groups (e.g., network, servers, applications, databases, workstations, email, forensics, security, recovery, etc.) under the direction of the Incident Commander. This will ensure the most qualified personnel are engaged in their key response areas, working on completing incident management assignments and accomplishing goals.

These groups need to be assigned tasks and objectives, identify their respective leadership, and then separated into teams according to their own working groups and response bridges under their own leadership to work on their respective areas. Each group representative should report to the incident management leadership on the main bridge at the designated check-in time, which is typically at the end of their operational period.

Full File System Artifacts/Disk Images

Depending upon the nature of the threat, this step may be optional. Incident response has been trending away from full-disk forensic investigations since remote, enterprise-wide volatile metadata and memory collection and analysis became possible around 2004. Since then, the practice of collecting disk images has become more selective over time to the point that it is no longer the norm, based on the current threat landscape.

However, for incidents where the goal is typically to steal data on the targeted systems and where regulated/restricted data may be affected, disk images and full forensic analysis are typically required. For instance, if a server containing unencrypted PHI was breached by malware or an attacker to gain access and exfiltrate information, a full-disk acquisition absolutely must be performed in order to preserve the state of the system and data for further investigation. This acquisition and any other that may be turned over to law enforcement, subject to legal action, or involve regulatory compliance must be handled according to forensic best practices and should utilize chain of custody evidence tracking.

To complicate matters, some systems have storage that is too large to be collected remotely, or they may not be compatible with enterprise forensic and remote evidence collection capabilities. This results in the need for local teams to perform the evidence collection, but they might not be qualified.

This forces a difficult decision whether to 1) have remote teams ship evidence to locations that have qualified personnel, 2) have unqualified personnel perform the collection using instructions written by qualified personnel, or 3) send qualified personnel on-site to perform the collection. There aren't any perfect solutions to this problem, and it is a classic conundrum. Regardless of which option is chosen, keep in mind that sensitive, regulated data should not be mailed without proper security controls (such as encryption) to prevent unauthorized access if the data is lost in transit.

Evidence handling procedures and testimony activity must comply with the most recent updates to or interpretation of the Federal Rules for Civil Procedure and the Federal Rules of Evidence, specifically Rules:

- 1001-1008 (Best Evidence Rule)
- 902 (Evidence that is Self-Authenticating)
- 901 (Authenticating or Identifying Evidence)
- 802 (The Rule Against Hearsay)
- 702 (Testimony by Expert Witnesses).
- Other rules relating to discovery and evidence production also apply but typically apply later in relation to subsequent legal action. These include Rules 26, 33, 34, 37, and 45.

Email/Messaging/Cloud

For the incident workflows involving email, the forensic collection system utilizes connectors to pull the targeted content directly from a live evidence source or utilizes a server-side dump of mailboxes for analysis. The forensic collection options permit more granular filtering, culling, and Boolean logic as it is effectively a live collection queried from structured data sources.

The collection should include affected email boxes and any Internet-accessible repository that is accessible with the same credentials. If an O365 account is compromised, the same credentials may be used to access Teams, Skype, OneDrive, SharePoint, or other external cloud access repositories that use the same credentials.

Being as companies often use Single Sign-on, the credentials between disparate internal or external users may be linked and potentially exposed. As such, all external repositories need to be evaluated for unauthorized access. If unauthorized access is suspected or verified, the repositories need to be collected and forensically analyzed to ascertain the impact. Each repository should include its own chain of custody, and if a breach is identified, this content will be discoverable.

This type of forensic collection and analysis resides somewhere between forensic analysis and eDiscovery. Pragmatically, this portion of the collection and analysis is usually farmed out to members of the forensic and eDiscovery teams and should include keyword, regex, and calculated (Luhn) searches looking for any type of regulated content: PHI, PCI, PII, SOX, etc. Identification of such will drive reporting and disclosure requirements.

Databases, Repositories, and Structured Data Files

For the incident workflows requiring full forensic analysis, capturing this last category of evidence collection happens in a variety of different ways, depending upon the data source. The workflow typically involves either:

1. Secondary processing of full-disk images for targeted file types (such as databases, email file repositories, file shares, etc.) that can be pulled from the file system of the target collections or respective load files
2. The forensic collection system utilizes connectors to pull the targeted content directly from a live evidence source.

Option 2 permits more granular filtering and Boolean logic as it is effectively a live collection queried from structured data sources. These typically include databases, email file repositories, file shares, etc.

This type of forensic collection and analysis resides somewhere between forensic analysis and eDiscovery. Pragmatically, this portion of the collection and analysis is usually farmed out to members of the forensic and eDiscovery teams and should include keyword, regex, and calculated (Luhn) searches looking for any type of regulated content: PHI, PCI, PII, SOX, etc. Identification of such will drive reporting and disclosure requirements.

Each of the evidence drives associated with the respective content (if there is more than one) will have its own separate chain of custody forms, and all evidence handling should be conducted according to forensic best practices. This content is likely to be discoverable, and respective evidence and analysis methods/findings will need to be archived for the life of the retention period.

Identifying Hacking Impact and Key Artifacts

Now that all of the evidence has been collected, it is time to do a comprehensive analysis to identify all malicious activity, methodology, tools, and artifacts related to it. The artifacts and methodology that will be analyzed are too exhaustive to enumerate for this section. However, the objectives of the analysis are the identification of attacker activity as follows:

- Exploit methods – Identify methods used to obtain unauthorized access and the vulnerabilities or misconfigurations that allowed them to be successful.
- Malicious Activity – Identify all malicious activity on the devices, systems, applications, and data sources, whether performed by malware, attackers, or compromised user accounts.
- Accounts/Groups – Identify all compromised or unauthorized user accounts and/or groups.
- IAM/Directory services – Identify malicious, suspicious, or unauthorized activity from any infrastructure controlling single or multi-factor authentication and/or authorization of accounts, resources, and data on systems, devices, applications, services, and shares.
- Files/Content – Identify all files/content on the system and enumerate the contents. Specifically, identify any files added, modified, deleted, or collected. Regulated content (PHI, PCI, PII, SOX, etc.) is of particular interest as it may be reportable.
- Applications/Services – Identify all applications or services that were added or modified.
- Malware/attack tool components – Identify all malware, scripts, backdoors, fileless programs, or other forms of surreptitious applications added to the systems, devices,

firmware, or hardware.

- Persistence mechanisms – Identify all mechanisms that make malware persistent and enable attackers to regain access to systems, devices, applications, or accounts.
- Lateral movement – Identify all lateral movement activity and all systems that have been affected by the activity.
- Full Incident Timeline – Update the known incident timeline with notable findings of salient activity and artifacts identified during the course of analysis.

Patch Review and Vulnerability Assessment

Understanding vulnerabilities that permit attack vectors is critical in any response investigation. This information is used to identify root cause(s), mitigate threats, and affect needed changes to the security posture.

Depending on various factors, the associated vulnerability may or may not initially be known. This depends on various factors:

1. The specific alert
2. The method of detection
3. The attack vector
4. The exploit method
5. The stage of the attack in which the alert occurred

Moreover, even if an attack vector and specific vulnerability are identified, there may be additional vulnerabilities that are notable and need to be documented and remediated. If there is one critical vulnerability on affected systems, there are likely other vulnerabilities or systems with the same vulnerability that are exploitable.

As such, during the forensic analysis, the system and application patch status should be enumerated to identify security gaps that need to be identified via changes to people, processes, and technology. If the attack vector was not identified previously, the forensically performed vulnerability assessment would identify investigative tasks to pursue and artifacts to gather and analyze. Each type of vulnerability has its own set of artifacts and associated forensic processes to follow.

The results of the forensic vulnerability assessment should be compared with known vulnerability scans performed prior to and/or after the security breach. This will help identify the efficacy of the vulnerability management technologies and processes in place.

Root Cause Analysis

Establishing the root cause for an incident during the forensic investigation is a critical data point that drives incident and post-incident activity. It will shape the investigation activity, inform mitigation and remediation steps, and be used as a trigger in regulatory or legal actions to dictate whether the customer had effective security controls or not.

Regarding incident activity, if an easily exploitable root cause is identified for one system, it is likely that other systems suffer from the same vulnerability and may have been exploited by the same attack vector. Once identified, the vulnerabilities and attack vector IOCs should be searched, identified, and addressed across the rest of the organization using EDR, AV/AM, vulnerability management, and/or other capabilities.

The nature of the vulnerability will also identify the access that the attackers may have gained and the resources potentially affected. Once identified, this will drive additional investigation tasks and resources that need to be investigated.

Being compromised through significant security gaps by publicly available tools using vulnerabilities for which patches have been released is a hard situation to justify. Being compromised by unknown, custom tools using 0-day threats for which there is no known defense may be justifiable.

Typically, institutions having insufficient, ineffective security controls that result in a breach have significantly more fines, restrictions, lawsuits, and other negative impacts than those with a more plausible defense. If a company has reasonable, industry-standard security controls and no notable weaknesses, it is hard for courts and regulators to hold them accountable.

Evidence of Data Exfiltration

For any system, application, or account that has suffered a security breach, it is assumed that all of the respective data on the system suffering unauthorized access has been exfiltrated until proven otherwise. There is an immediate assumption of guilt that requires forensic best practices and good preparation to overcome it successfully.

Proving a negative (meaning that data was not exposed) is challenging as all the enabling factors must be in place to affirmatively identify that data was not viewed or transmitted. Security capabilities and evidence sources include network packet captures, SSL/TLS decryption, enhanced access logging, EDR, DLP, SIEM, and other tools with enough visibility to trace the path of the threat within the environment. It requires a full analysis of the respective activity, resources, accounts, data, and related logs and security measures to enumerate the content and identify evidence of access or blocking by mitigating controls that would have prevented it.

If it is not possible to prove data was not exfiltrated, identifying evidence of what specifically was exfiltrated and the affected companies, people, and data elements is critical. It is the key driver for regulatory fines, lawsuits, and imposed restrictions. The larger the breach, the greater the impact, as the quantity of records breached is typically used as the multiplier to assess the fines.

If it cannot be proven what specifically was exfiltrated or that nothing was, it is usually assumed that all data contained on or accessible by affected resources was compromised. Correspondingly, the data and its respective details and affected entities need to be enumerated and evaluated to determine if sensitive/regulated is affected and could be subject to notification.

This is also a key time to identify inappropriately stored sensitive information, which resulted in a breach. If sensitive, regulated data was stored with insufficient security controls and was compromised by attackers and/or malware, more secure sensitive data handling policies, procedures, and technologies need to be implemented. This will result in eradication, mitigation, and remediation activities.

Any findings involving the breach of sensitive/regulated information should immediately be reported to Legal to obtain their guidance in handling and transferring findings and to preserve legal privilege. While it is true that legal is often included from the beginning of an investigation, if they are not, this is the best place to involve them.

Threat Eradication, Restoration, and Recovery

Following the evidence gathering, preservation, and containment activity, it is time to restore the affected environment and resources to a known good state. There are a variety of considerations in doing this.

All systems, devices, virtual machines, and containers should be restored to previous, clean images or snapshots and then fully patched, hardened, and validated via security testing methodology to validate they are secure. This includes updates for software, firmware, and applications and for implementing necessary security controls for visibility, monitoring, detection, and blocking to prevent further malicious activity.

For anything that cannot be hardened, compensating controls should be implemented to augment the security profile. Common occurrences of this include websites, web apps, or any form of network applications or APIs for which hardening may involve some sort of re-design that may take too long.

In such cases, an intermediate network monitoring, detection, and blocking device should be implemented to permit benign, intended traffic but block anything suspicious, malicious, or outside the intended profile. Web Application Firewalls (WAFs) are particularly good at this for websites/web apps and various other application-aware Next-Gen firewalls and/or API firewalls that exist to protect web traffic and other network applications, services, and protocols.

Data must also be restored to a known good state and validated to ensure sensitive data is not stored inappropriately. It is essential to validate that no attacker artifacts or manipulated content are left behind, such as collections of sensitive data for exfiltration or modified, malicious versions of seemingly benign files that may cause the environment to be re-infected. It is best to restore everything to a recent backup and then validate that the contents are supposed to be there and do not constitute unauthorized storage.

Investigation Findings

Following the completion of a high-severity response activity, particularly if there are notable security deficiencies or reportable findings, it is critical to create an after-action report to document all of the circumstances, activity, and findings. The after-action report will be the official document detailing the specifics of the incident and subsequent investigation. It will be the primary artifact of the investigation that may become discoverable and shared if there are legal or regulatory actions following the incident.

The actual investigation findings, type of data affected, and quantitative impact (including the number of customers, users, data, records, etc.) will ultimately be the biggest headline in an incident. Headlines and data breach reports are full of these metrics, which are typically ranked in descending order of magnitude. Moreover, the type of data and quantity of records impacted are the most discussed data elements and the biggest drivers for regulatory impact, fines, and lawsuits.

However, there is a lot more data than that, which ultimately needs to be included in the investigation findings for the documentation to be complete. Each of the topics listed in the template in this section are key artifacts that need to be communicated, captured, and documented, if applicable. Some of the sections will not apply to a given incident, depending on the situation.

Incident Response Report Template

- Cover page
- About Document and Audience
- Document Control
- Executive Summary
- Background and Scope
- Incident Notification
- Incident Timeline
- Attack Overview and Root Cause Analysis
- Resources Analysis
- Network Traffic Analysis
- Volatile Metadata Analysis
- Data Analysis
- Data Restoration
- Malware Analysis
- Investigative Findings
- Containment Actions Taken
- Remediation Plan
- Incident Participant List
- Point of Contact

A key consideration for the investigation findings and reporting is that the incident timeline is not completed until at least the containment and mitigation steps have been completed. Early remediation steps may also be listed if completed by the date of the final report.

Once completed, the after-action report and supporting documents will typically be maintained by legal and/or compliance teams, who will typically use them as the basis for external reporting purposes. To protect the confidentiality of the after-action report and to preserve legal privilege as much as possible, it should be labeled as: "Privileged and Confidential – Prepared at the Direction of Counsel."

See APPENDIX C: COMBINED RESPONSE PLAYBOOK for the consolidated playbook template.

30 INCIDENT WORKFLOWS: EXTERNAL ENTITIES

This chapter addresses incident response for security breaches involving external entities, including vendors, partners, and affiliates. This workflow involves situations where the breach is purely in the external entity's environment but which may pose a risk to the customer environment or data. As such, the customer is limited to 1) blocking access to/from the affected external entity for the purposes of containment and 2) making investigative requests, which are sometimes bolstered by regulatory requirements and/or contracts.

The cooperation and overall quality of assistance provided by vendors are driven heavily by 1) contractual requirements and 2) legal or regulatory requirements. At best, you get what you have under contract, but that is not guaranteed. Sometimes, customers have to settle for what is required by legal or regulatory statutes. However, even that is not guaranteed. Good luck with that!

Moreover, sometimes external entities are entirely uncooperative and provide nothing at all. Legal, regulatory, and contractual provisions may not be honored if the risk of breaking them is less than the risk of honoring them. The risk of abiding by contractual requirements, obeying the law, and keeping customers happy might outweigh the reward of doing such if there is a significant liability associated with being culpable for the breach.

Incident Notification/Detection Method

There are a handful of common methods for detecting or reporting the compromise of external services. For obvious reasons, these are much more limited than internal security breach detection methods, as there is little to no telemetry for such.

Automated/Manual Detection

Hopefully, customers do not identify breaches of external entities they do business with and with whom they have VPN connections or integrations from automated or manual detections within the customer environment. If so, that would mean that malicious activity has jumped from the affected entity environment across the VPN or integration and is threatening customer resources, accounts, and data.

This is basically a worst-case scenario, as it may be too late to stop it from infecting the customer network. The external entity's breach has effectively become the customer's breach, and all networks, systems, applications, accounts, and data are at risk. This obviously has profound relationship, business, and legal implications.

Affected External Entity Reported

The best source from whom to be informed about a breach regarding an external entity that the customer has a business relationship with is the external entity itself. Ideally, the external entity should quickly notify customers, collaborate on the investigative, share information as prudent, and work quickly to implement containment, mitigation, and remediation needs. There should be language in contracts that ensures that notification happens in a timely manner, as driven by security and regulatory concerns and requirements.

Media

If customers learn about breaches of contracted external entities from the media, this is a bad situation as it usually means that contractual or regulatory breach notifications have failed to occur. It also highly likely means that the breach occurred at some time in the past, and the response has been going on for some time.

Breaches aren't necessarily immediately disclosed to the media, and sometimes, the notification of such can lag behind for months. Therefore, in addition to the security risk associated with delayed breach notification coming from media sources, there may also be regulatory risks from the late reporting of such.

Initial Scope

The Initial scope for external entity-related incidents and affected resource(s) may include anything in the external entity's environment or under their control. This includes their networks, systems, applications, services, accounts, repositories, and associated data. For each of these resources, there are also detection and alerting considerations based on potential regulatory impact.

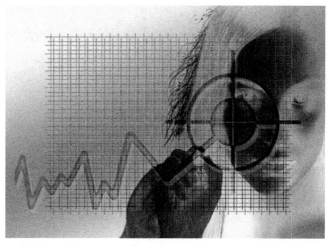

Also of scope consideration are any customer networks, systems, services, or accounts that the affected external entity connects to, integrates with, or shares accounts with. Any form of connection between a compromised resource and a resource in the customer environment could be an attack vector between the two that can be exploited.

As such, all accounts, connections, remote access, system access, and/or data transfer between the customer environment and the compromised external entity environment or users may be blocked until the matter is resolved. To do this requires an enumeration of all related connections, resources, and accounts.

This section will not address the threat vector of malicious access from external entities to customer networks, systems, applications, etc., as they are hacking and lateral movement incident workflows and are covered in the combined incident response workflow chapter. As such, this section will focus on the relationship and requests with the external entity and protecting the customer environment from the same.

Potential Impact

At a high level, identifying the impact of hacking activity against external entities involves an assessment of several considerations, including:

1. The significance of the breach within the external entity environment
2. The impact of allowing compromised external entities to continue to have access to the customer environment
3. The impact of customer data in the compromised external entity environment

Significance of External Entity Breach

Identifying the potential impact of a security incident is critical to everything else that follows. Some threats are relatively meaningless in the context of regulatory disclosure and reporting, while others can be catastrophic.

Just like with internal threats, if a resource has been compromised by an attacker or malware that has enabled the attacker to run arbitrary commands or access any data on the system, it is immediately assumed that the attacker has done so, and all accounts and data on the resources have been compromised. This is a "guilty until proven innocent" situation, and it takes a defensible forensic process to establish a "low probability of exposure" to prevent the hacking incident from being reportable.

Moreover, because it is no longer possible to truly outsource risk, a breach in the external entity environment of customer data is effectively the same from a regulatory perspective as a breach of data within the customer environment. The customer must perform due diligence to ensure that the external entity can secure and be trusted with their data. If the data has been breached in the external entity environment, the due diligence was not adequate, and the customer is accountable for the breach.

Something that can create even more problems than a significant compromise of regulated data is the specific way it happened and the residual effects within the external entity's environment. A couple of examples are in order:

Scenario 1

Ransomware running under the context of an employee's user account encrypts all of the user-created files on the local system and mapped network shares. The encrypted files contain a mixture of personal and business content, and some of it is considered sensitive.

Scenario 2

An Active Directory Domain Administrator account was compromised, and it was used to spread ransomware via scripts and malicious GPOs to every Windows workstation, server, and file share in the entire environment. All files have been encrypted, including those on network backup servers.

In Scenario 1, the isolated, user-mode threat is quickly recoverable through a combination of password resets, workstation re-imaging, and file restoration from a known good backup. The damage can be reset back to a known good state in a single day's time by a handful of personnel (maybe even just one). This means that the threat from the external entity to the customer is quite small, and any impact on the service could be restored relatively quickly.

In Scenario 2, the Domain Admin account compromise is a Keys to the Kingdom type of threat that likely could mandate rebuilding the entire Windows Active Directory infrastructure. However, even if the entire AD infrastructure is rebuilt, there will always be questions about data leakage that occurred, encryption keys that were compromised, and backdoors or exploit kits that might still remain. Even after an exhaustive analysis, there will always be questions regarding whether everything was truly found and remediated.

Further, it gets a lot worse than that. Considering the online backups were encrypted, this situation might be a near-total loss. Unless offline backups are available, the customer data may be unrecoverable.

As such, scenario 2 could result in the complete loss of viability of the affected company and could drastically affect all of the respective customers/partners if they were relying upon the company to provide BC/DR.

Admittedly, it is unreasonable and unrealistic to expect external entities to burn down their entire computing environment completely and start from scratch with entirely new infrastructure. Therefore, based on the threat vector and the applicable regulatory frameworks, guidance, and data impacted, the customer legal, compliance, and response teams must identify criteria to establish the probability of exposure and conditions for re-establishment of service.

External Entity Access to Customer Environment

The threat or impact of the external entity's access to customer's networks, systems, devices, applications, services, and accounts in and of itself has two separate concerns that are diametrically opposed:

1. The impact of blocking or terminating access to the affected external entity
2. The impact of allowing access to continue

It may seem a logical choice to block remote system or VPN access to sensitive resources from compromised external entities. However, what if their access is critical for business operations, and blocking their access would be detrimental to the customer environment? Some environments, like healthcare, rely on external partners and affiliates to perform services that help keep patients alive. It is possible that blocking access to key vendors who have suffered a compromise could potentially result in the death of a patient.

This creates a no-win situation. Blocking access could result in patient death. However, allowing it to continue could permit malware to jump from the external entity environment to the customer environment, compromise systems, and possibly result in patient death. Either way, patients could die. Both situations are highly impactful and require significant consideration to navigate. Oftentimes, careful planning and compensating controls are required to create some sort of middle ground.

Customer Data in Vendor Environment
The threat or impact of the customer's sensitive information that is stored in the external entity's environment has significant security and/or regulatory concerns, depending upon the situation. Of primary considerations are the following, which will be explored in more detail:
1. The nature of the threat
2. The sensitivity of the target/data
3. The probability of exposure
4. The threshold for breach set by regulatory requirements

Threat Assessment
Identify the likelihood of the threat to be successful in exploiting the targeted resources (networks, systems, services, applications, repositories, accounts, data, etc.) and what could be compromised if the attack were successful.

Target Sensitivity
Identify the respective business, security, or regulatory compliance sensitivity (PHI, PCI, PII, SOX, etc.) of the resource and the risk created by exposure.

Probability of Exposure
Identify the likelihood that sensitive resources have been exposed in relation to the threat activity. For example:
- External DoS attack against exhausting TCP connections – There is a very low probability of impact on data or accounts on the system.
- Exploit kit installed on PCI system granting arbitrary access – There is a very high probability of impact on payment data and accounts on the system.

Regulatory Requirements

Understanding regulatory requirements is critical as they contain definitions, thresholds, and triggers created by legal statutes or program requirements for sensitive data handling and exposure. However, the requirements or guidance are sometimes overly vague and technically ambiguous. This is particularly true with older requirements that have not been updated or those that are meant to apply to either technical or non-technical workflows.

Additionally, many of the requirements have been written in a way that they don't make sense at a technical level. The Health and Human Services (HHS) Office of Civil Rights (OCR) ransomware guidance is a good example of something that is highly specific, but at a technical level, it has many incongruities and seems to have been written by people who don't understand the nuances of malware, ransomware, or related components. As of the completion of this book (January 2024), it has not yet been clarified, corrected, or challenged in court. But, the general consensus from technical, security-minded people is that it would be indefensible from a technical perspective.

Irrespective of that, regulatory requirements are effectively the law or are at least required to use the service or data type and dictate reporting requirements. While it may be true that they are full of technical flaws, they are still formidable and will have their day in court if they are to be challenged and overcome.

Analysis and Reporting

Considering all of the response activity must be done by external entities in their own environment and the customer essentially must take their word for it, it makes the investigation and reporting process much more difficult and less definitive. The customer has no true control over the situation and must trust the thoroughness of the investigation and the accuracy of findings reported by the external entity.

If the external entity does not do a thorough investigation, it could result in inaccurate findings that expose the customer to additional legal or regulatory impact. Moreover, working through a rather biased external entity to perform an investigation that could prove them culpable makes proving a negative significantly harder, less conclusive, and more subjective.

In these circumstances, the probability of exposure or exfiltration will have to be determined by the thoroughness of the external entity's response and analysis processes performed either by their internal personnel or 3rd party contractors. As much as possible, the customer should push the external entity to engage a mutually agreeable 3rd party contractor to perform the investigation and provide independent attestations from the same. Specifically, the following investigative findings must be addressed and answered by the trusted 3rd party:

- Incident root cause/exploit method – Identify how the attack occurred within the external entity environment, which will inform follow-up questions about how they addressed the attack vector and if the situation is contained, mitigated, and remediated.

- Attacker/malware methods and IOCs – This will inform the investigation of the customer environment, looking for the same threats.
- Risk to customer environments/resources/accounts – This will also inform investigation in the customer environment and drive containment activity.
- Containment measures – Determine if the malicious activity has been satisfactorily blocked or if the external entity needs to do more.
- Mitigation and remediation activity – Determine if the vulnerabilities in people, processes, and technology have been satisfactorily resolved.
- Impact on customer data – Determine the scope of data impacted and all respective details and attributes.
- Data exfiltration – Identify the specific data that has been exposed.

Evidence of Data Exfiltration

For any external entity resources (systems, services, applications, accounts, and/or data) that have suffered a security breach, it is assumed that all of the respective data on the resource suffering unauthorized access has been breached and exfiltrated until proven otherwise. This is true whether the breach happens manually by attackers targeting it or automatically by malware that happened to compromise a system having it. There is an immediate assumption of exposure that requires forensic best practices and good preparation in order to overcome it successfully.

Proving a negative (meaning that data was not exposed) is challenging. All the enabling factors must be in place to affirmatively identify that data was not viewed or transmitted, which is not usually the case for externally provided services.

Security capabilities and evidence sources that can help forensically prove a negative include network packet captures, SSL/TLS decryption, enhanced access logging, EDR, DLP, SIEM, WAF, and other tools with enough visibility to trace the attacker's activity. It requires a full analysis of the respective activity, resources, accounts, data, and related logs and security measures to enumerate the content and identify evidence of access or blocking by mitigating controls that would have prevented it.

It is especially hard with an external entity, as the customer must trust them or their 3rd party contractor to perform a thorough investigation. Moreover, any findings they provide are inherently prone to bias and likely self-serving.

There is a conflict of interest in the external entity performing or paying for a thorough investigation. Thoroughly investigating all evidence sources could either 1) conclusively identify evidence of exfiltration or 2) establish a low probability that it could have occurred based on a preponderance of evidence showing there is no compromise.

Alternatively, not paying for a thorough investigation likely results in a lack of conclusive evidence and/or findings that a breach occurred principally because the investigators were not paid to look broadly enough. So, by performing a cheap, bad investigation, external entities might be able to demonstrate that "nothing bad happened" simply because they didn't find it. This is based on the logical fallacy that "the lack of evidence that a breach occurred is evidence that it didn't happen." It is not true, but it is a common misconception.

As such, the cost of performing a thorough analysis is expensive, and any evidence discovered in the process could either prove or disprove data exfiltration. If it results in proving sensitive data was accessed by attackers and exfiltrated, things just get more expensive from there. Therefore, external entities have an inherent incentive to perform a bad investigation and find as little as possible if they feel they can get away with it.

If the surface-level investigation performed by the external entity does not identify data exfiltration, they will likely be tempted to stop there. If they continue investigating and identify potential exfiltration activity, they may be considered culpable, and the evidence they paid extra to find could be used against them in legal or regulatory actions. As such, if the initial investigative activity does not identify exfiltration activity, there is a motivation for them to stop.

However, if initial evidence does identify possible exfiltration, there is a strong motivation to conclusively identify precisely how many records were compromised in order to reduce the potential data set from "all customer records." This means that if it is not possible to prove a low likelihood that data was not exfiltrated, identifying conclusive evidence of what specifically was exfiltrated and the affected companies, people, and data elements is critical.

It is the key driver for regulatory fines, lawsuits, and imposed restrictions. The larger the breach, the greater the impact, as the quantity of records breached is typically used as the multiplier to assess the fines.

If it cannot be proven what specifically was exfiltrated or that nothing was, it is usually assumed that all data contained on or accessible by affected resources was compromised. Correspondingly, the data and its respective details and affected entities need to be enumerated and evaluated. If sensitive/regulated is determined to be affected, the breach, affected parties, and data are typically subject to notification per a pre-defined reporting deadline, which varies per state and regulatory body.

Ultimately, all the customer has is the attestation of findings provided by the external entity. However, the customer and response team should be involved as much as possible to ensure that the response, legal, and compliance teams have the best information possible to address legal and regulatory notification and reporting concerns. The more involved the customer is in the investigation, the more the external entity is held accountable for performing a thorough investigation that can be supported in the post-incident regulatory and legal processes.

This is also a key time to identify poor data handling practices and inappropriately stored sensitive information in the external entity communications, transactions, or environment, which resulted in a breach. If sensitive, regulated data was sent to them via email or other insecure protocol or stored with insufficient security controls and was compromised by attackers and/or malware, a more secure sensitive data handling policy, procedures, and technologies need to be implemented. This will result in eradication, mitigation, and remediation activities.

Any findings involving the breach of sensitive/regulated information should immediately be reported to legal and compliance teams to obtain their guidance in handling and transferring findings, as well as measures best employed to preserve legal privilege. While it is true that legal is often included from the beginning of an investigation, if they are not, this is the best place to involve them.

See APPENDIX D: EXTERNAL ENTITIES PLAYBOOK for the consolidated playbook template.

31 INCIDENT WORKFLOWS: EXTERNALLY HOSTED SERVICES

This workflow addresses incident response for externally hosted infrastructure. These types of vendors offer ease and speed of provisioning services, but there is usually limited potential to implement security controls and detect or respond to breaches in infrastructure. This includes hosted solutions providing virtualized systems, containers, or individual services, such as web hosting, databases, file storage, or other repositories and/or other networked services. At best, you get what you pay for and the contractual requirements of the same. However, this is still not guaranteed.

It should be assumed that no cooperation or access that is not documented under a written contract will be provided when needed. It should also be expected and planned that not even contractual provisions will be honored if the risk of breaking the contract is less than the risk of honoring it. This sounds pessimistic, but it is often true. As such, it is incumbent on the customer to have mandatory security controls and the necessary visibility, monitoring, and detection capabilities for sensitive resources located in external environments.

Incident Notification/Detection Method

The following are common methods for detecting or reporting the compromise of external services. For obvious reasons, these are much more limited than internal security breach detection methods, as there is little to no telemetry for such.

Automated Detection

There are typically much fewer automated threat detection and response capabilities available in external environments as compared to internal environments. The following are common security capabilities that are available if procured either within the hosted solution or outside of it.

- Identity and Access Management (IAM) – This is only feasible if there are federated sites, services, applications, and administration access to hosted resources that control IAM from a centralized location within the corporate environment.
- Network – Security alerts may come from hosting service security controls, such as firewalls, IPS devices, or other network monitoring capabilities, if these functions are available. This usually comes at an extra cost.

  However, customer-accessible network monitoring may not be available, considering hosted solutions are typically shared. It is very common for a single physical or virtual system to be used for dozens of customer environments. These alerts may not be directly accessible to a specific customer simply because it is hard to associate the alerts with specific customers. Separating network traffic is even harder.
- Cloud scrubbing – There are a variety of cloud-based network security solutions that network traffic can be routed through to provide customer-managed SSL/TLS decryption with a variety of network traffic inspection and blocking capabilities. These typically include next-generation firewalls, WAF, IPS, DLP, and reputation protection services to prevent unauthorized access and changes to websites, services, and applications.
- Logs – The on-demand/user-accessible logs from hosted environments are likely to be very limited, as hosting environments have numerous customers. As such, logs that intermingle data are typically only available via special request and will be provided via support personnel. These logs are not accessible over self-serve means.

The on-demand/user-accessible logs that are directly available to the customer typically contain logons to the administrative interfaces and changes made respective to administering the environment. However, depending on the hosting solution, other options may be available. Some solutions enable the porting/forwarding of specific logs to company log aggregation/SIEM solutions.

- Application security plugins – The various website and web application technologies may have various plugins that provide enhanced access, security, monitoring, input validation, and logging controls. Some of the application security plugin solutions also enable the porting/forwarding of logs to company log aggregation/SIEM solutions.

Manual Detection

Unauthorized changes and potential hacking discovered through scans or code audits performed by security team members during assessments are likely to be the highest accuracy and most actionable findings as they can be very specific and highly conclusive. Additionally, if they visit the page and see that it has been vandalized or materially altered, it will be perfectly obvious that attackers have compromised it.

User Reported

Hacking activity, such as website defacements, malware deployments, or other malicious activity that has been identified and reported by the site/application users is highly anecdotal, as it is based mostly on the user's subjective experience. As such, it can be very unreliable unless it is very obvious (such as defacements).

There may be a lot of false positives inherent in these detections. As such, the reports should be accompanied by screenshots or other user-created evidence to substantiate the observations.

False negatives for unauthorized changes to websites are even higher. However, if users run across malicious artifacts and start clicking on things, they are entirely likely to infect their systems and make things worse, particularly if they activate self-replicating malware. Extreme caution should be exercised when utilizing end-users to gather incident-related details.

Externally Reported

If reported by or known to an outside entity, the best plan for dealing with them is to gather the information that they have to offer. However, do not over-engage them in the incident response processes. There is always an inherent risk in communicating too candidly and overly involving  external entities. This is true even if they are trusted parties under contract, with non-disclosure agreements, and performing a defined function. It is best to engage them only for their function.

Another exception would be for partners/vendors that are involved in joint incident response activity. With them, IOCs and targeted, salient findings need to be shared in order to facilitate the joint response activity. However, be careful not to overshare anything that could introduce additional confidentiality concerns. Any findings or artifacts should be securely transferred using encrypted transfer methods to avoid creating a greater compliance incident on top of a security incident.

Initial Scope

The Initial scope for incidents involving externally hosted services, as identified in the manual or automated notifications, is much more limited than that for on-prem resources. If there are any notifications at all, they typically involve telemetry provided for the hosted environment. This includes sources such as systems, applications, services, integrations, accounts, repositories, and associated data. For each of these resources, there are also detection and alerting considerations based on potential regulatory impact.

Also of scoping consideration are any networks, systems, services, or accounts that the affected hosted resources connect to, are integrated with, or share accounts with. Any form of connection between compromised externally hosted resources and internal resources could be used as attack vectors between the two, which could be exploited.

Initial IOCs/Artifacts

Initial artifacts typically found in the alerts for externally hosted service hacking incidents often include the following components and malicious activity indicators.

Network Data

Network monitoring detections and alerts are rare for externally hosted environments. However, they might be available if the customer has implemented a cloud scrubbing/WAF service or has paid for network security monitoring from the hosting provider.

If available, automated alerts for network indicators of hacking incidents and associated data might include only partial information. This is particularly true for cloud scrubbing solutions that require specific routing to function.

The traffic must be routed as intended via DNS resolution that resolves to the cloud scrubbing solution and then forwards the traffic to the externally hosted site. If that process is not followed, such as by accessing the hosted site by the external IP address, then no protections or detections are available. The security is bypassed. As such, direct access to the external IP addresses of the sites protected by cloud scrubbing should be blocked.

The hosted solutions might offer firewalls, IPS/IDS, DLP, or other inline security controls. If offered, these would be less likely to be bypassed. However, they are probably not as robust as the security capabilities provided by cloud scrubbing options.

In any case, assuming all of the typical network security controls, monitoring, and alerts are available, the alerts would be similar to on-prem solutions. Malicious activity detections and alerts would contain ingress/egress data or metadata, such as IOCs of malicious IP addresses or domain names, manipulated/unauthorized URLs, and the respective ports and protocols they use. This network data information could be related to any part of the attack lifecycle or artifact type. Key activity, artifacts, and indicators that are highly suggestive of this unauthorized activity include:
- Positive hits on known malicious traffic signatures or threat feed data
- Connections to known malicious domains or IP addresses
- Suspicious outbound traffic
- Unusual foreign connections, particularly to OFAC countries

Commands/Script Activity

Automated alerts from network devices can identify malicious server-side activity at any type of command interface with the required visibility tools and monitoring logic. The activity could include anything from system command-line interfaces, API or instrumentation query interfaces, script interpreters, or database commands. Commands and scripted actions are high-value threat activities and should be monitored for malicious intent. This is particularly true with dynamic content performing SQL queries to databases that can enumerate content or perform command execution:
- Executable downloads to clients
- Suspicious script execution on clients
- Injection attacks
- Remote command execution (RCE)

Logs

Automated alerts from logs that identify hacking activity can run the gambit across all log sources and will often require correlation rules to link them together to assemble an activity timeline. As attackers or malware move through the affected systems and applications, the logs could be identified in the respective systems, applications, network devices, and security capabilities therein.

Files

Automated alerts and IOCs typically contain a listing of identified files (such as binaries, scripts, or web shells) involved in malicious activity. Anything detected should be considered in-scope and searched across other resources in the environment to expand the scope as necessary. However, the data in the alerts is just a starting place, and usually, there are additional signs of malicious activity and unauthorized changes. Just because one artifact is detected, it does not mean that it is the only one. Suspicious file system indicators include:

● Unauthorized website changes and/or addition of new pages, files, scripts, or binaries
● Suspicious changes in file size
● Detection of web shells

Attack Vector

For externally hosted service hacking incidents, the attack vector is usually related to a vulnerability or misconfiguration that is exploited to grant unauthorized access. They could occur over any Internet-accessible port, protocol, application, logon function, or data entry interface. Any method of inputting data, uploading/running code, loading files, interpreting content, or entering credentials could conceivably be used as an attack vector to run an exploit.

Delving into the details of specific attack vectors for Internet-facing services is beyond the scope of this course. However, there are many excellent, freely available resources and projects dedicated to this. The OWASP Top Ten Project is possibly the most famous and well-maintained.

Some of the most common attack vectors exploited in relation to externally hosted services are the myriad of free or cheap website development tools, especially those that are PHP-based. They are notorious for being compromised, especially if automatic updates are not turned on. And, even if updates are enabled, they are still notorious for being compromised.

WordPress might be the most notorious and commonly exploited of website development tools. There are numerous publicly available WordPress vulnerability scanning applications and exploit tools with exploits for scores of insecure plugins included in WordPress. In fact, there are continuous scans occurring across the Internet trolling for vulnerable WordPress sites, particularly on known web hosting platform address space. It is not unlikely for a vulnerable WordPress site to be hacked within minutes or even seconds of being published on the Internet.

For the most part, attacks on externally hosted services involve direct attacks. Direct attacks involve those where an attacker directly goes after the target of interest, such as a specific system, service, or application. For systems and applications, this would typically start with a vulnerability scanner and end with an exploit tool to deploy the payload of choice against the vulnerable target identified. Targets are usually network-enabled services or data entry forms. An example of an Indirect attack in this instance could involve masquerading as a system, service, or API that the hosted resources connect. Alternatively, it may involve using DNS poisoning and posing as a service in such a way as to engineer unauthorized access into the system(s). This could involve intercepting credentials that the hosted resource connects with and then using them on the hosted resource.

Regardless of the type, the attack vector needs to be identified as quickly as possible so as to mitigate the threat and secure the hosted resource(s) from further exploitation. The longer an attack vector remains available, the greater the risk of exploitation by attackers or malware. Moreover, if the attackers or malware are found and eradicated, but the attack vector remains, there is nothing to stop the same or worse activity from happening again. In fact, if it is the same attack group, the next time they come back, it will be with more covert methods.

Potential Impact

At a high level, identifying the impact of hacking activity against externally hosted services involves an assessment of the particular threat, the sensitivity of the target/data, the probability of exposure, and the threshold for breach set by regulatory requirements. There is a lot of detail nested in this description, as follows:

- Threat assessment – Identify the likelihood of the threat to be successful in exploiting the targeted resource (system, service, application, container, account, etc.) and determine what could be compromised if the attack was successful.

- Target sensitivity – Identify the respective business, security, or regulatory compliance sensitivity (PHI, PCI, PII, SOX, etc.) of the resource and the risk created by exposure.

- Probability of exposure – Identify the likelihood that sensitive resources have been exposed in relation to the threat activity. For example:
  - External DoS attacks against Internet-facing services that exhaust TCP connections – This can be annoying, but there is a very low probability of impact on data or accounts on the targeted system. However, it may be a smokescreen to draw your attention away from other systems targeted by more invasive threats.
  - Web shells installed on websites or web apps granting arbitrary access – There is a very high probability of impact to data and accounts on the system, as well as the compromise of the system itself.
  - Malicious/unauthorized software distribution – Compromised sites can potentially impact the clients that visit the affected resources if the attackers have turned it into a waterhole site for distributing malware.

- Regulatory requirements – Set thresholds for data exposure (which sometimes don't make sense, but they are effectively the law) and dictate reporting requirements.

However, if a resource has been compromised by an attacker or malware that has enabled the attacker to run arbitrary commands or access any data on the system, it is immediately assumed that the attacker has done so, and all accounts and data on the resources have been compromised. This is "a guilty until proven innocent" situation, and it takes a defensible forensic process to establish a "low probability of exposure" to prevent the hacking incident from being reportable.

As such, any compromised resources storing or having access to regulated data are of high impact and need to be handled with elevated priority and urgency. This would typically involve taking the system or service offline or implementing expedited containment, blocking, or other compensating controls to prevent further exposure as soon as possible in the investigation.

Begin Incident Artifact Preliminary Collection

In most hosted environments, resources are typically virtualized, and the systems and services have multi-tenancy. As such, there is not a clean separation of either live or static data and artifacts, such as network traffic, volatile metadata, memory contents, web application logs, file systems, databases, etc.

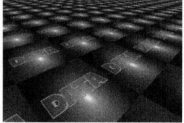

Because of this, it is usually not possible for customers to directly access live data or static file system data unless they have a court order. Therefore, there are no pre-containment data collection tasks that can be performed, and post-containment data collection options are very limited. Considering the timing involved and the length of time between an attack, the detection, getting a court order, and finally getting evidence, live/volatile data is not really feasible unless the systems are dedicated to the customer and there is a pre-defined agreement for the hosting company to provide such.

Order of Evidence Collection/Preservation

1. Freeze the virtual container or disable services for the customer instance – this will take the service offline and preserve it in its current state.
2. Preserve all available logs – Customer access is typically limited to access and changelogs for the provisioned web service and admin interface.
3. Collect web or shared files – Download all files and folders associated with the service provided by the hosted instance.
4. Collect database files – Export and collect all database-related files associated with the service provided by the hosted instance.

Preliminary Analysis

For incidents involving the hacking of externally hosted services, it is critical to be able to identify unauthorized changes to accounts and content on hosted services, including files, databases, links, scripts, or other items.

As such, more information must be obtained in order to establish the facts of the case. This requires evidence. The evidence collected will allow the response team to identify or know where to go to identify the rest of the story. Analysis workflows include:

- Data Sources – Enumerate all hosted virtual machines, containers, repositories, cloud services, and other hosted resources.
- Network traffic – Identify all network sources, destinations, protocols, and access methods.
- Accounts – Enumerate all accounts involved in suspicious or malicious activity.
- Log sources – Identify all monitoring controls that can identify any activity related to the hosted environment or access thereof by external or customer-owned systems.
- Evidence collection - Collect evidence from all initially known sources, including all externally hosted systems, virtual machines, files, databases, logs, and any internal data sources of all types known to be involved.
- Timeline analysis – Pull together as much as initially possible from notable activity and multi-artifact timeline builders (such as Log2Timeline): alerts, files, browser history, logs, registry, processes, network connections, etc. Log2Timeline has dozens of plugins for various artifact types.
- Identify associations – Aggregate, correlate, and analyze all activity to understand patterns of activity involving data and enumerate all accounts, data movement, and locations that contain sensitive data in whatever format it takes.

Deep-dive Forensic Analysis
Identifying Hacking Impact and Key Artifacts

Now that initial information has been gathered and some attacker activity and artifacts are known, it can be used as pivot points to inform the deep-dive analysis. This will better identify all hacking-related activity, methodology, tools, and artifacts related to it. The artifacts and methodology that will be analyzed are too exhaustive to enumerate for this section. However, the objectives of the analysis are the identification of attacker activity as follows:

- Exploit methods – Identify methods used to obtain unauthorized access and the vulnerabilities or misconfigurations that allowed them to be successful.
- Malicious Activity – Identify all malicious activity on the devices, systems, applications,

and data sources, whether performed by malware or compromised user accounts.

- Accounts/Groups – Identify all compromised or unauthorized user accounts and/or groups.
- IAM/Directory services – Identify malicious or unauthorized activity using IAM/directory services controls governing authentication and authorization of accounts and access to resources within the hosted environment. For the most part, this will be logon and logoff activity, but if available, it could include access or changes to objects and data. It is especially beneficial if access controls are federated and logged to a SIEM. If they are not, then only web hosting account management logs will be available.
- Files/Databases/Content – Identify all data on the system and enumerate the contents. Specifically, identify any files added, modified, deleted, or collected. Regulated content (PHI, PCI, PII, SOX, etc.) is of particular interest as it may be reportable. Business-sensitive content (such as intellectual property or other confidential data that has been exposed) should be enumerated and analyzed.
- Applications/Services – Identify all applications or services that were added, modified, or vulnerable and used to gain access to the system.
- Malware/Web shells/Exploit Kits – Identify all malware, scripts, web shells, backdoors, fileless programs, or other forms of surreptitious applications added to the hosted sites, VMs, containers, or other services.
- Persistence mechanisms – Identify all mechanisms that enable attackers or malware to access and remain persistent or regain access to hosted sites, services, accounts, or content.
- Lateral movement – Identify all lateral movement activity and all spreading mechanisms, environments, networks, and systems that have been affected by the activity.
- Full Incident Timeline – Update the known incident timeline with notable findings of salient activity and artifacts identified during the course of analysis.

The identification of this information will provide the substance for the findings in the final report. It will also inform additional analysis to identify any attacker-related artifacts, attack tools, web shells, backdoors, or at-risk data. These findings will provide content for short- and long-term remediation actions, training activity, and other security improvements.

Root Cause Analysis

Establishing the root cause for a successful attack during the forensic investigation is a critical data point that drives incident and post-incident activity. It will shape various phases of investigation activity, inform mitigation and remediation steps, and be used as a trigger in regulatory or legal actions. The findings of root cause analysis will identify whether the customer had effective security controls or not. It will also influence the potential for fines, restrictions, penalties, lawsuits, and regulatory actions.

Regarding incident activity, if an easily exploitable root cause is identified for one system, it is likely that other hosted systems, services, or applications suffer from the same vulnerability and may have been exploited by the same attack vector. Once identified, the vulnerabilities and attack vector IOCs should be searched, identified, and addressed across the rest of the hosted or on-prem environments. This is easiest to do using vulnerability management tools, source code management tools, manual code reviews, and/or other capabilities appropriate for an extant in the externally hosted environment.

The nature of the vulnerability will also identify the access that the attackers may have gained and the scope of resources affected. Once identified, this will drive additional investigation tasks and resources that need to be investigated.

Being compromised through significant security gaps by publicly available tools using vulnerabilities for which patches have been released is a hard situation to justify. Being compromised by unknown, custom tools using 0-day threats for which there is no known defense may be justifiable.

Typically, institutions having insufficient, ineffective security controls that result in a breach have significantly more fines, restrictions, lawsuits, and other negative impacts than those with a more plausible defense. If a company has reasonable, industry-standard security controls and no notable weaknesses, it is hard for courts and regulators to hold them accountable.

Evidence of Data Exfiltration

For any systems, services, applications, or accounts that have suffered a security breach (whether by attackers targeting it or by malware that happened to compromise a system having it), it is assumed that all of the respective data on the hosted resource suffering unauthorized access has been breached and exfiltrated until proven otherwise. There is an immediate assumption of exposure that requires forensic best practices and good preparation in order to overcome it successfully.

Proving a negative (meaning that data was not exposed) is challenging as all the enabling factors must be in place to affirmatively identify that data was not viewed or transmitted. This is not usually the case for externally hosted services.

Security capabilities and evidence sources that can help forensically prove a negative include network packet captures, SSL/TLS decryption, enhanced access logging, EDR, DLP, SIEM, WAF, and other tools with enough visibility to trace the attacker's activity. It requires a full analysis of the respective activity, resources, accounts, data, and related logs and security measures. These are used to enumerate the content and identify evidence of access or blocking by mitigating controls that would have prevented it.

Considering externally hosted solutions don't offer most of the visibility and monitoring tools previously listed, it makes proving a negative significantly harder and more subjective. In these circumstances, the probability of exposure or exfiltration will have to be determined by all available logs, forensic analysis of artifacts, method of intrusion, and the capabilities of attacker tools.

If it is not possible to prove a low likelihood that data was not exfiltrated, identifying evidence of what specifically was exfiltrated and the affected companies, people, and data elements is critical. It is the key driver for regulatory fines, lawsuits, and imposed restrictions. The larger the breach, the greater the impact, as the quantity of records breached is typically used as the multiplier to assess the fines.

If it cannot be proven what specifically was exfiltrated or that nothing was, it is usually assumed that all data contained on or accessible by affected resources was compromised. Correspondingly, the data and its respective details and affected entities need to be enumerated and evaluated. If sensitive/regulated is determined to be affected, the breach, affected parties, and data are typically subject to notification per a pre-defined reporting deadline, which varies per state and regulatory body.

This is also a key time to identify inappropriately stored sensitive information, which resulted in a breach. If sensitive, regulated data was stored with insufficient security controls and was compromised by attackers and/or malware, a more secure sensitive data handling policy, procedures, and technologies need to be implemented. This will result in eradication, mitigation, and remediation activities.

Any findings involving the breach of sensitive/regulated information should immediately be reported to Legal to obtain their guidance in handling and transferring findings and to preserve legal privilege. While it is true that legal is often included from the beginning of an investigation, if they are not, this is the best place to involve them.

Threat Eradication, Restoration, and Recovery

It is now time to restore the affected environment and resources to a known good state. There are a variety of considerations in doing this.

All resources should either be rebuilt from scratch or restored to their previous known good state and then fully patched, hardened, and validated via security testing methodology to ensure they are secure. This includes updates for all affected technology and resource types and implementing necessary security controls for visibility, monitoring, detection, and blocking to prevent further malicious activity.

For hosted environments, this usually involves virtual machines, virtual services, and/or publishing sites via web development platforms. Some content management/website building platforms (like WordPress) integrate site changes made by developers with dynamic content changes made by site users. All changes from all sources are included and merged together from version to version. It can become difficult to impossible to separate the site development changes from user content changes.

This becomes incredibly frustrating when malicious content is inserted into the site, and developers are unable to distinguish between benign and malicious content. For this reason, these types of sites must usually be completely rebuilt from scratch rather than recovered from a previous state.

Moreover, all passwords related to affected resources must be changed, as there is the potential for those passwords to be cracked and used later. If users synchronize the same passwords on the affected externally hosted resources and internal resources, the passwords for their internal accounts should be changed as well.

For anything that cannot be hardened, compensating controls should be implemented to augment the security profile. Common occurrences of this include websites, web apps, or any form of network applications or APIs for which hardening may involve some sort of re-design that may take too long.

In such cases, an intermediate network monitoring, detection, and blocking device should be implemented to permit benign, intended traffic but block anything suspicious, malicious, or outside the intended profile. Web Application Firewalls (WAFs) are particularly good at this for websites/web apps. Various other application-aware Next-Gen firewalls and/or API firewalls exist to protect web traffic and other network applications, services, and protocols. As such, this is a good opportunity to bring hosted services in-house, where better security controls can be applied.

Data must also be restored to a known good state, as well as validate that sensitive data is not stored inappropriately. It is essential to validate that no attacker artifacts or manipulated content are left behind.

This includes the identification and eradication of sensitive data collected for exfiltration or seemingly benign files that were modified or replaced with malicious versions that may cause the environment to be re-infected if the files are opened. It is best to restore everything to a recent backup and then validate that the contents are supposed to be there and do not constitute unauthorized storage.

Investigation Findings

Following the completion of a high-severity response activity, particularly if there are notable security deficiencies or reportable findings, it is critical to create an after-action report to document all of the circumstances, activity, and findings. The after-action report will be the official document detailing the specifics of the incident and subsequent investigation. It will be the primary artifact of the investigation that may become discoverable and shared if there are legal or regulatory actions following the incident.

The actual investigation findings, type of data affected, and quantitative impact (including the number of customers, users, data, records, etc.) will ultimately be the biggest headline in an incident. Headlines and data breach reports are full of these metrics stack ranked in descending order of magnitude. Moreover, the type of data and quantity of records impacted are the most discussed data elements and the biggest drivers for regulatory impact, fines, and lawsuits.

However, there is a lot more data than that, which ultimately needs to be included in the investigation findings for the documentation to be complete. Each of the sections listed in the template in this section are key artifacts that need to be captured, documented, and communicated if applicable. Some of the sections will not apply to a given incident or will typically require vendor assistance with evidence collection, analysis, and investigation, depending on the situation.

Incident Response Report Template

- Cover page
- About Document and Audience
- Document Control
- Executive Summary
- Background and Scope
- Incident Notification
- Incident Timeline
- Attack Overview and Root Cause Analysis
- Resource Analysis
- Network Traffic Analysis – Will require vendor cooperation
- Volatile Metadata Analysis – Will require vendor cooperation
- Data Analysis
- Data Restoration
- Malware Analysis – May require vendor cooperation
- Investigative Findings
- Containment Actions Taken
- Remediation Plan
- Incident Participant List
- Point of Contact

Once completed, the after-action report and supporting documents will typically be maintained by legal and/or compliance teams, who will typically use them as the basis for external reporting purposes. To protect the confidentiality of the after-action report and to preserve legal privilege as much as possible, it should be labeled as: "Privileged and Confidential – Prepared at the Direction of Counsel."

See APPENDIX E: HOSTED SERVICES PLAYBOOK for the consolidated playbook template.

PART 3 – POST-INCIDENT ACTIVITY

32 VALIDATION TESTING

This section addresses the ongoing post-incident process of ensuring containment and mitigation controls are holding and preventing new occurrences of malicious activity that could impact customer resources. It involves searching for the recurrence of previously identified indicators and the identification of vulnerabilities or attack vectors that could be used to exploit resources. It requires an ongoing process of testing to validate that threats have not re-emerged, unforeseen consequences have not arisen, and a rapid process to escalate and resolve issues as they are identified.

Security Validation

Following the eradication stage of any incident or as part of a pre-incident to prevent impending malicious activity, it is critical to continuously search and validate that vulnerabilities, indicators of compromise, or inappropriately stored sensitive data do not suddenly recur or present themselves anew. A network environment is anything but static. Systems that were previously dormant, remote/traveling, contractor/guest-owned, or new might suddenly appear on the network in a vulnerable or compromised state. This presents a significant risk to the customer environment or to the systems themselves.

It is essential to validate that no unpatched or misconfigured systems, malware, attacker artifacts, or manipulated content left behind once again appear on the network and re-introduce the same threat. This includes collections of sensitive data for exfiltration or modified, malicious versions of seemingly benign files that may cause the environment to be re-infected.

Each new incident the security team is responding to, or threat they are preparing for, adds to the continual process of applying lessons learned and preventing future compromises. This involves searching, identifying, and remediating threats from any known source, whether reactive or proactive, to sustain a continuous improvement process.

Ongoing Validation Testing Indicators

Ongoing validation testing involves a multitude of tools and processes to be successful. In addition to functional testing to ensure resources are fully available, ongoing security-related tests should also be performed.

These include a combination of vulnerability assessment, IAM, Network security, Endpoint security, and SIEM/log analysis tools to tie everything together and create use cases for alerting and automatic triggers. The following are the monitoring criteria:

- Vulnerabilities and misconfigurations – This involves using endpoint and configuration policy management tools or vulnerability assessment and management tools to identify unpatched applications or insecure, non-compliant configurations on active systems. This is somewhat dynamic as the tools may be limited to internally located systems that are currently reporting in.

  An unpatched system can connect to the network at any time without notice and be at risk of being compromised by another system infected by malware that is actively exploiting that vulnerability. Ensuring that all systems are patched and/or have compensating controls to mitigate the risk of compromise protects them from emergent or known threats.

- Network Data – Network monitoring devices at ingress/egress locations and critical choke points or VLANS/networks to identify malicious activity, including IOCs from prior incidents. Ingress/egress traffic should be augmented by SSL/TLS decryption, and decrypted data can be offloaded to other security devices.

- Commands/script activity – Identify malicious client-side, server-side, or network activity at any type of command interface with the required visibility tools and monitoring logic. The activity could include anything from system command-line interfaces, API or instrumentation query interfaces, script interpreters, or database commands.
- Logs – Automated alerts from manual use cases or automated alerts on SIEMs that identify the recurrence of malicious activity can run the gambit across all log sources and will often require correlation rules to link log sources together.
- Files/Processes/Services/Registry/WMI – Automated alerts and IOCs to identify files, processes, services, registry entries, or WMI classes involved in malicious activity or containing inappropriately stored sensitive information.
- IOCs and/or YARA rules – Alerts based on combined lists of indicators for malware or attack tools having known artifacts or indicators.

If any of the monitoring and detection mechanisms from any source identify signs of the recurrence of malicious activity, it needs to be stomped out as soon as possible. This will minimize the possibility of spread and reduce the potential impact.

In some cases, the cleanup activity may be a rinse and repeat of the previous containment and eradication activity. This will likely be true of automated threats that are deploying static malware.

However, if malware is polymorphic or if the customer is suffering an APT-style attack, then the threats will change and require more in-depth analysis to identify all of the related Tactics, Techniques, and Procedures (TTPs). In a worst-case scenario, it might require all of the response activity to begin anew.

33 CONTINUOUS IMPROVEMENT

An incident management program is never finished. It will always be a work in progress in continual flux. Any change in anything requires other changes to compensate.

Due to the evolution in the threat landscape, advancements in technology, changes within the customer environment, and findings from lessons learned identified in each incident, the incident management program must be updated to remain relevant. The longer it remains stagnant, the less relevant it will become.

Just like a plane crash, every successful hacking incident is a result of layers of security failures from defense-in-depth that missed the mark at every stage or were non-existent to begin with. At the very least, the technology must have failed at one or more of the various stages.
1. Network controls did not detect attacker intrusion activity
2. Endpoint controls did not protect the systems, applications, services, and/or accounts
3. Authentication, authorization, and access controls did not protect accounts and data
4. Log monitoring controls and SIEM solution(s) did not identify the malicious activity and alert in time to stop it.

There is never a better time to address these deficiencies or failures than after a successful breach. There is a window of time following a breach when people are supportive of making changes and willing to make the sacrifices that go along with them. Making these changes requires documentation of the related gaps and appropriate planning to overcome the issues.

Moreover, not enumerating and remediating deficiencies that led to a breach is a missed opportunity and an invitation for it to happen again. It will likely result in a game of Whack-A-Mole until the security gaps are resolved. Sometimes, hacking threats are only partially identified and remediated, resulting in recurring events using the remaining attacker backdoors, which maintain perpetual access and perform attacker-directed functions.

It is critical to remember that remediation needs are not just new technology or configuration changes, but it is necessary to consider the need for changes within any or all of people, processes, and/or technology. Changes in each of these categories involve a lot of time and usually money.

Each one of these areas has its own respective challenges requiring planning, collaboration, and funding to overcome.

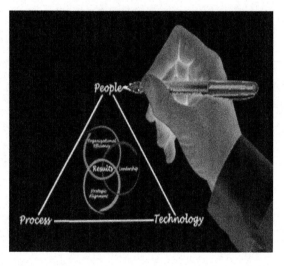

- People – Additional personnel or training may be required to support the security program development, implementation, monitoring, identifying unauthorized activity, and responding to alerts. Moreover, all staff may require training on the security program to prevent future events. However, making changes or additions to human resources is a significant change that involves leadership at all affected levels, human resources, recruiting, and funding to pay for it all.
- Process – If systemic security events occur, there are likely process or process enforcement-related problems. Clear guidance must be created and provided for security and response programs and all of their sub-components. This process must be trained, monitored, and enforced. Making changes or additions to company processes requires extensive collaboration, coordination, notification, training, and auditing to ensure changes are put in place without significant impact or risk to the organization.
- Technology – To support people and processes in the security and response programs, the right technology needs to be in place to identify and respond to threats. This needs to be in place at IAM, network, endpoint, and SIEM/log monitoring levels. Depending upon the state of technology within the affected environment and the extant ability or inability to implement needed detection and blocking controls, this can become very expensive. If threats continue to be successful, all of the technology controls should be evaluated to assess their ability to detect, respond to, terminate, and prevent security threats. New or replacement hardware, software, and licensing can be very expensive, often totaling 7, 8, or even 9 figures. Sometimes, these changes involve years of architecture, budgeting, planning, testing, implementation, and training.

34 AFTER-ACTION REPORTING

This section addresses the key considerations and details that should be included in the incident after-action reporting in order to comply with regulatory requirements and security best practices. Breaches of regulated data typically result in some sort of disclosure, notification, or reporting to the media, customers, or regulators. They may also incur fines or restrictions for the compromised company or end up in court pursuant to legal actions filed by affected customers, regulatory, or government agencies, resulting in costly judgments.

Even if there is no regulatory impact, there are numerous circumstances where after-action reports are either required or desirable. Quite often, the need for reporting is political and necessary to influence change in the environment and push the remediation for deficiencies and recommendations captured during the incident.

For all of these use cases, it is critical to have all salient facts and findings documented. Long story short – details matter. It is incredibly important for any response activity resulting in a breach of sensitive information (particularly regulated information like PHI, PCI, PII, or SOX data) to be captured in an after-action report.

This section identifies all of the typical content that often goes into an after-action report, provided the various sections are relevant. It is expected that some sections may not be applicable, depending on the circumstances.

Note that it does not include sections to identify security gaps, recommendations, or lessons learned during the investigation or identify how to improve the security posture of the environment. For best practices, that type of content involving any sort of enumeration of weaknesses should be separated into a separate document and fleshed out for the entire problem space and solution set.

It is important that the AAR is tightly focused on what specifically happened during the incident, the resources involved, and what was done during the course of the investigation. This section will go through each one of these sections in detail.

Key After-Action Reporting Details:

- Cover page
- About Document and Audience
- Document Control
- Executive Summary
- Background and Scope
- Incident Notification
- Incident Timeline
- Attack Overview and Root Cause Analysis
- Resources Analysis
- Network Traffic Analysis
- Volatile Metadata Analysis
- Data Analysis
- Data Restoration
- Malware Analysis
- Investigative Findings
- Containment Actions Taken
- Remediation Plan
- Incident Participant List
- Point of Contact

Cover Page

Cyber Security Incident Response Team

Incident Response After Action Report
<INCIDENT NUMBER - NAME>
Privileged and Confidential – Prepared at the Direction of Counsel

Status: <Draft / Final>
Version Number: <##.##>
Version Date: <YYYY-MM-DD>

For starters, the cover page is important. It immediately identifies the sensitivity of the document and the protections it is under. Of particular importance is the "privileged and confidential – prepared at the direction of counsel" statement, which indicates that it is part of a work-product request for an activity directed by an attorney. This will somewhat protect the document from discovery or will at least keep it from being immediately discoverable.

Note that for this to be true, an attorney must be involved from the beginning, guiding the overall process and deliverables. Pragmatically, however, the nature and contents of this document often result in it being discoverable, and as such, the content is highly focused on narrowly answering questions on exactly "what happened during the investigation."

In addition to discovery protection, the tagging and confidentiality statement are a clear warning to any individual who inadvertently comes across the document that it is a protected document that they should not read without authorization. It further identifies what needs to happen if someone finds or receives it in an unintended or unauthorized manner.

The cover page also serves to clearly identify the document, the incident details, the status of the document (draft or final), the version number, and the respective version date. This makes all the most germane document tracking information immediately identifiable.

Sometimes, these reports are so sensitive that they need to be watermarked for individuality per recipient (like having the recipient's name or employee ID on each page of the document) and other protections, such as "Do not copy, forward, print, or share." This is difficult to manage, however. It is typically only done in the most serious of situations.

About Document and Audience

About this Document

This document provides details regarding a security incident and the respective response activity, attack vectors, containment measures, and focused remediation activity. It represents a point-in-time snapshot of the security posture of the organization as investigated.

Document Audience

This document is privileged and confidential and is prepared at the direction of counsel. The audience for this report is limited to decision makers and technical personnel on a need to know basis. It includes selected parties within Information Security, business leadership, executive management, and other areas as needed and approved by the Legal Department and Compliance Office. It provides information at varying levels (from summary to technical) and enables the readers to be able to drill down to sufficient depth within the document to address any questions they may have.

This document is restricted only to limited distribution, as authorized. Please do not forward or share without the prior approval from the Legal Department and the Compliance Office.

For readers, regulators, compliance, and legal purposes, it is important to clearly identify the purpose of the document and the intended audience. It helps define the intentions of the document and provides a framework for understanding its contents. It also makes a good artifact for regulatory compliance audits by showing the customer has sufficient documentation supporting adherence to the incident response reporting requirements within the various regulatory criteria.

Note that the document audience includes technical and leadership personnel, which is a disparate group having very different communication needs. As such, the subsequent sections will begin with an executive summary to leadership, followed by a deeper dive into specific details for more technical personnel.

Document Control

Document Control

This report has been approved to be distributed to the following individuals by the <Legal Department> and the <Compliance Office>. Approval authority for dissemination of this report resides with the <Legal Department> and the <Compliance Office>.

Document Author:	Name, Title
	name@domain.com
	Cell: ###.###.####

	Draft Version	0.1	Name	Date
	Peer Reviewed	0.5		
Document Revision:	Initial Release	1.0		
	Revised Release	1.1		
	Final Release Candidate	1.2		
	Final Release	1.3		

	Person 1	Title, Department
Document Distribution List:	Person 2	Title, Department

The Document Control section contains basic information for the author(s), tracking of versions, and the intended distribution list. This section will often get expanded depending on the distribution list and the quantity and nature of revisions it has to go through.

It is important to keep documents in a draft phase until all key parties agree it is completed. Documents marked as DRAFT are not held to the same standard as FINAL documents, and they are significantly less relevant if produced during the discovery process. Long story short, the contents of draft documents are easily refuted as simply being unfinished and still under development and review. Once a document is marked final, however, it carries significantly greater weight in discovery and the subsequent review by legal, judicial, and regulatory entities.

Executive Summary

The executive summary is possibly the most important section of the document, as it is all that some of the readers will ever see. It is not just for executive audiences. It should provide all of the information the reader needs to get the gist of the situation.

The executive summary is effectively a condensed version of the entire document that identifies all of the most important details presented on a single page. This includes identification and a brief explanation of the who, what, when, where, why, and how respective to the incident. More specifically, in a non-technical way, it identifies the incident detection/notification, scope, timing, attack vector, root cause, impact, and containment or remediation activity performed.

To do this, it needs to be very succinct and matter-of-fact. It is essentially written like a news article with meaningful content highly condensed and distilled into succinct sentences. There should be no wasted words. The following topics should be succinctly addressed:

- Detection/notification
- Scope
- Timing
- Attack vector
- Root cause
- Impact
- Containment/remediation performed

Background and Scope

This section identifies the relevant background and scope information about the affected resources. This should include the purpose, usage, and potential impact concerning the respective networks, systems, devices, applications, services, accounts, and/or data affected by the incident. This is not an enumeration of findings but a description of the resources at risk. The outline template includes the following sections:

- Purpose
- Usage
- Potential impact
    - Networks
    - Systems
    - Devices
    - Applications
    - Services
    - Accounts
    - Data

Incident Notification

Notification Methods	Incident ticket escalated by SOC
Severity Level	Sev 3
Date/Time Detected	2019-8-11.18.59.16
Date/Time of Notification	2019-8-11.19:23:07
Detection Method	FireEye Network Malware; PAN egress firewall
Symptoms	Outbound network traffic to malicious site; malware download by JavaScript downloader and malware callback; User credential entry exposed password
Attack Vector	Browser and endpoint configuration vulnerability; social engineering for password theft
Exploit Method	Malicious JavaScript downloader with embedded PowerShell; attackers attempt credentials on VPN
Known Artifacts, IOCs, and Yara Rules	Polymorphic - no consistent IOCs

The Incident Commander should capture and retain all incident notification and escalation content to detail the facts surrounding the threat detection and reasons for escalation. The contents of the incident notification details will vary by detection but generally contain the following high-level items. When aggregated, the following will inform metrics and drive changes in people, processes, and technology:

- Notification methods – Identify how the incident was reported. Oftentimes, this part of an incident circumvents standard processes and needs more maturity.
- Severity – The particular definition of severity needs to be defined ahead of time in the incident response policy/plan and should be chosen in the notification based on the respective definition.
- Date/time – This varies in meaning depending upon the circumstance. It is typically the date of compromise. However, if that cannot be determined, the Date/Time will be the date of detection. Alternatively, if the compromise occurred some time ago and was not detected until recently, the window of compromise (date of compromise → date of containment) should be identified.
- Detection method – This is usually from automated alerts, threat-hunting activity, user-reported observations, or externally reported events. If reported by or known to an outside entity, there are additional risks and action items. Media notifications and

complications are much more likely in this scenario. Identifying and documenting this is important, as it will set the tone for communications and whether public relations/media, compliance, and legal teams need to start right away with working on external communications. It will also assist in documenting the efficacy of automated detection tools.

- Symptoms – Briefly describe the symptoms experienced, which indicate the initially observable impact of the incident.
- Attack vector – Provide details on attack vectors (AKA vulnerabilities). This will need to be addressed later in the report via patching, mitigation, configuration, and/or containment or compensating control activities.
- Exploit method – Just like the attack vectors, the exploit methods should be identified and addressed later in the document to demonstrate the method for resolution.
- Known artifacts, IOCs, and YARA rules – Reference the known signatures used to identify and/or block attacks, which should be included in detail within an appendix.

Incident Timeline

Date (UTC)	Time (UTC)	Activity	Actor	Internal System	External System	Datasource / Control	Comment
8/11/2019	18:58:11	User visits compromised website and enters credentials	Dave.Smith (user)	LVWS295843	p0wn3dsit3.com	PAN Firewall (LV)	not detected
8/11/2019	18:58:25	Malicious java / Powershell script downloaded	Dave.Smith (user)	LVWS295843	malicious-site.com	FireEye NX	subsequently detected, not blocked
8/11/2019	18:59:16	Malware callback detected on endpoint	Dave.Smith (user)	LVWS295843	malicious-site.com	PAN Firewall (LV)	Initial detection
8/11/2019	19:15:12	Attackers attempt VPN logn	Nigerian actors	NA	<Nigeran IP>	PAN Firewall (LV)	
8/11/2019	19:23:07	Event reviewed by SOC and escalated	Jack Frost (SOC)				Event escalation
8/11/2019	19:35:21	user credentials reset	Dave Rambo (CERT)	LVWS295843		IAM system	reset comprmised creds
8/11/2019	19:43:11	Capture volatile data	Dave Rambo (CERT)	LVWS295843		EnCase	Initial data collection
8/11/2019	20:05:49	Implement endpoint isolation	Dave Rambo (CERT)	LVWS295843		FireEye HX	Containment
8/11/2019	20:55:17	Capture logical disk image (key artifacts)	Dave Rambo (CERT)	LVWS295843		EnCase	Full evidence collection
8/11/2019	21:05:51	Authorize LVWS295843 for reimging by IT	Dave Rambo (CERT)	LVWS295843			Sal Smith took possesion
8/12/2019	14:27:41	Forensic analysis completed	Arny Swartz (CERT)	LVWS295843			No PCI/PHI/PII data
8/13/2019	10:33:08	Forensic report completed	Arny Swartz (CERT)	LVWS295843			Report completed
8/13/2019	11:08:44	Evidence archived / ticket closed	Arny Swartz (CERT)	LVWS295843			Ticket completed

The incident timeline needs to start early and be maintained all along the way, or data will be lost. It is not that hard if an individual is assigned to assist the Incident Commander by taking notes and tracking notable events and milestones on the incident timeline. Moreover, considering the high volume of information flow during significant incidents, the tracking of notable observations, developments, findings, activity, action items, assignments, and statuses, a dedicated resource should be assigned to track all of this activity, which can be distilled into an incident timeline with related artifacts and details.

This example shows a simplified set of data elements that are not intended to be comprehensive. The contents may need to be adjusted to capture details respective to relevant data sources or actions, depending upon the circumstances.

In order for the timeline to make sense, all data sources should utilize synchronized NTP servers to avoid time drift, and all entries should be displayed in UTC to show a true sequence of events. These two requirements are essential, or the timeline becomes meaningless and unusable.

The span of this timeline example is highly simplified to succinctly show key milestones during the investigation. In a real incident, there will likely be many more steps along the way. This example clearly and cleanly shows the start and endpoints with key milestones for this type of investigation.

Attack Overview/Root Cause Analysis

The root cause of an incident is possibly the most important item to be identified and captured during an incident. The nature of it typically drives culpability discussions and influences the outcome of lawsuits and audits, as well as the determination to impose fines or restrictions.

Large, impactful incidents caused by easily preventable root causes stemming from well-known vulnerabilities that should have been patched long ago are a recipe for disaster. It opens the affected company up to all manner of lawsuits, fines, restrictions, and government oversight.

On the other hand, a novel attack against an unknown attack vector using an undetectable exploit method would be seen much differently, and the affected company may get a pass as well as public sympathy.

Moreover, affirmatively identifying the root cause of an incident will inform mitigation and remediation activity to prevent a similar incident. It will also enable auditors/regulators to make a determination on whether the entity had appropriate security controls in place at the time of the incident.

If the incident's root cause is not identified and appropriately resolved, there is a high probability of reoccurrence. The recurrence of the same incident is very hard to rationalize and leads to increased culpability and business risk.

Oftentimes, identifying and documenting the root cause(s) will make the affected organization look bad. However, not putting in the effort to identify it will make the organization look even worse. It shows that in addition to the security control issues that caused a breach, there are process and other maturity issues that are sure to result in another one.

Resources Analyzed

For evidence tracking processes, there are a significant quantity of details that need to be captured for each evidence item that is analyzed. Not all of these will be applicable for every evidence item, and sometimes additional fields may need to be added, depending upon the circumstances:

- Location (address/building/office)
- Owner (company/person/custodian/account)
- Numbers (Evidence tracking/Model/Serial)
- Type (server/workstation/share/VM/device - many types)
- Hostname | UNC path
- IP Address
- MAC Address
- Description
- Operating system/application/service
- Management ownership
- Administration access
- Sensitivity/impact

  - Regulatory compliance (PHI, PCI, PII, SOX, etc.)
  - Business operations
  - Customer services

There may also be a significant amount of variability in the type of content collected for each field, depending on the resource type. Meaning, a server and a workstation have similar data fields, but they vary significantly from that of a network share or a medical device.

If there is a legal or regulatory impact on the systems involved, the chain of custody information should also be included. This should include all storage media and document appropriate hash values for each physical or logical drive image.

Network Traffic Analyzed

Capturing and analyzing network traffic is very important for understanding what happened at many of the various stages of the attack. In a perfect situation, network traffic could identify almost everything from intrusion to exfiltration. Considering attackers could go in or out through any network connection, network traffic should be analyzed, and the salient findings must be identified and reported from key vantage points. These include:

1. Every ingress/egress point of presence (POP)
2. All internal chokepoints for sensitive environments, such as PCI, PHI, PII, SOX, etc.
3. All business-sensitive networks, such as development, executive, servers, etc.
4. Specific traffic captured for any system that was believed to have been compromised

This section contains the standard details that are captured respective to network activity. The report should document the most notable investigative details, metrics, malicious files, exfiltrated data, C2, and/or other notable observations identified in network traffic. It will usually require accompanying attachments to document the full details of notable activity identified:

- Location
- Network device
- Date/time
- Socket information
  - Source host/port
  - Destination host/port
- User/account
- Activity detected
  - Infection/exploit
  - Download
  - C2
  - Exfiltration
  - Lateral movement
- Detection method (numerous)
- Files/scripts/commands/injection
- Quantity of data inbound/outbound
- Connection duration

Volatile Metadata Analysis

- Hostname/device
- Process/PID
- Process hash
- Parent process/PPID
- Process tree
- Process owner (account)
- Drivers
- DLLs/libraries
- Handles
- Start time
- Snapshot time/retrospection window
- # of instances
- Full path
- Current directory
- Command-line

- Open files
- Autostart locations
- Live registry keys/values
- Strings
- Named pipes
- Threads
- Company
- Certificate
- Injection activity
- Hidden
- WMI classes
- Network connections
- VirusTotal score
- Threat feed score

Capturing and documenting volatile metadata, especially along a timeline, illustrates the activity of attackers and malware and could potentially identify the most notable activity between compromise and exfiltration if captured with the right types of continuous monitoring toolsets. The report should include details from key moments in time and the pattern of activity over the attack lifecycle if available through retrospective analysis tools.

The report should describe the malicious artifacts and activity, including processes, libraries, drivers, network connections, live registry keys/values, open files, and the respective details and interconnectivity to provide an understanding of what attackers did and the tools they used. It should discuss the malicious activity on or across monitored machines and demonstrate how the attacker or malware moved throughout the environment and affected resources.

Volatile metadata should also be used to identify least-prevalent processes or other artifacts related to the attack that are indicative of polymorphic malware, which would be unique in each instance within the environment. This functionality is even more useful if it can be extended to other artifact types, such as malicious polymorphic scripts.

If visible from the EDR solution providing the view into volatile metadata, it should identify any rootkits, backdoors, hiding techniques, or covert mechanisms in place that enable the attacker or malware to remain hidden and/or maintain unauthorized access within the environment. Depending upon the solution employed, this may or may not be possible with volatile metadata alone.

Data Analysis

The data analysis sections describe the notable data stored or accessed on systems, devices, shares, repositories, email stores, or other resources impacted by an incident. The report must document notable affected files and data that have been affected by the malicious activity, identify at-risk sensitive information, and determine the respective impact. The following fields are notable but not comprehensive:

- Evidence tracking number
- Location
- Hostname/device/UNC
- Description
- File/folder
- File type/format
- MACB times (modified, accessed, $MFT changed, born)
- Sensitivity/impact
- Regulatory compliance (PHI, PCI, PII, SOX, etc.)
- Business operations
- Information security
- Customer services
- Quantity exposed records
- Data fields

Not all of the data-related fields and sensitivity/impact types in this section will be used for every situation, and there is the potential that more may be required, depending upon the circumstances. However, these are the most common. Breaches of regulated data typically result in some sort of disclosure, notification, or reporting to the media, customers, or regulators. They may also incur fines or restrictions for the compromised company or end up in court pursuant to legal actions filed by affected customers, regulatory, or government agencies, resulting in costly judgments.

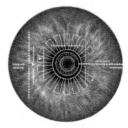

All of these actions and consequences are driven by the quantity and type of data exposed, for which this section will provide the respective metrics. This will typically be enumerated in a spreadsheet contained in an appendix or provided separately containing all affected individuals and the respective sensitive data elements exposed. In this way, the impacted individuals and the relevant regulatory agencies can be notified of the breach and the respective data related to it.

For all of these use cases, it is critical to have salient facts and findings documented in a single, easily referenceable location that tracks the notable evidence artifacts. Three key data fields in this section that drive most of the regulatory reporting are:
1. Location
2. Regulatory compliance
3. Data fields

This section will typically require accompanying attachments to document all of the related information. The length of the attachments is usually longer than the length of the report.

For any sensitive file(s) with regulated content identified on compromised systems, devices, or repositories, the most important response task is to determine whether the content was exposed, exfiltrated, or altered and if it can be conclusively proven it was not. Some of this can be done on the endpoint with the necessary endpoint visibility tools, like DLP and EDR, but it will need to be bolstered by applicable network controls as well.

Data Restoration
This section is less about the investigation and more about documenting the content that needs to be recovered. This is important for tracking the remediation and recovery activity, which can also be an important compliance concern where data availability is a factor (such as for HIPAA). It is especially important if files were affected by ransomware and had to be restored due to them being encrypted. Per the HHS\OCR ransomware guidance, the fact that the files were encrypted means that they were under the control of an unauthorized entity. Completing this section will usually require accompanying attachments to document all files recovered.

The following are typical data fields that need to be documented, at minimum.

- Hostname/Device
- File/Folder/Share
- File Purpose
- Recovery Reason
- Recovery Time

Malware Analysis

The malware analysis section should document the methodology used to analyze the malware and the functions, artifacts, and findings related to it. This will likely require supplemental attachments and/or appendices to detail the in-depth technical analysis.

The high-level objectives of the analysis are the identification of malware-related activity and artifacts as follows:

- Malware family/variant – Identify the particular malware discovered on the system.
- Components – Identify all malware components, files/folders, scripts, backdoors, fileless programs, or other forms of surreptitious applications added to the systems, devices, firmware, or hardware.
- Persistence mechanisms – Identify all mechanisms that make malware persistent and enable attackers to regain access to systems, devices, applications, or accounts. This may include multiple forms of persistence mechanisms, often involving registry keys/values, scheduled tasks, WMI classes, etc.
- Accounts/Groups – Identify all compromised or unauthorized user accounts and/or groups created or used by the malware.
- Exploit methods – Identify methods that the malware used to obtain unauthorized access and the vulnerabilities or misconfigurations that allowed them to be successful.
- Malicious Activity – Identify all malicious activity performed by malicious applications or the accounts compromised by it.
- Applications/Services – Identify all applications or services that were added or modified by malware.
- Exfiltration – Identify all malware exfiltration activity and capabilities.
- Lateral movement – Identify all lateral movement functions or spreading activity exhibited by the malware.
- Configuration/Modules – Identify the respective malware configuration, the modules that it is configured with, and the respective capabilities for which it is enabled.

Investigation Findings

The investigation findings section of the report is a distilled, non-technical summary of all key findings from all investigative sections of the report. The investigation findings section of the report is a distilled, non-technical summary of all key findings from all investigative sections of the report. It does not go into as much detail or show specific analysis steps as other individual analysis sections do. It is a roll-up of the salient findings from all sections organized by the resources involved, ordered by the likelihood that the resources may have been compromised (based on facts and analysis in all responsive areas), and documents the impact associated with compromise of the respective resource.

It will enumerate the type of resources, data affected, how they were affected, and both the qualitative and quantitative impact. This includes the type and quantity of customers, users, data, records, etc. These will be the biggest drivers for regulatory impact, disclosure, notification, fines, lawsuits, and restrictions. The following outline should be populated:

- Networks
- Remote access methods
- Systems
- Devices
- Applications
- Repositories
- Data
- Users
- Customers
- Vendors

Leadership, stakeholders, auditors, regulators, compliance teams, and legal entities should be able to read the investigative findings section and understand the full scope, impact, and legal potential of a security breach.

Containment

The containment section of the incident after-action report identifies all of the security controls implemented during the response to halt the ongoing malicious activity and prevent further exploitation using the same or similar attack vector. Containment activity is often limited to security technologies already extant in the environment prior to the start of the incident that can be configured during the response to halt the unauthorized activity. However, they could also include anything that is implemented following the detection of an incident, such as by the external incident response provider or which was quickly purchased and implemented to contain the problem.

This usually includes a combination of blocking measures within the following capabilities as appropriate for the circumstances. Note that the following capabilities are very high-level, and there is a significant variety of controls nested beneath each section:

- Network – Controls are implemented to inspect, validate, and/or block network access and activity on OSI model layers 2-7 as appropriate for the resources being protected or sequestered.
- Endpoint – These are controls implemented to inspect, validate, and/or halt activity on endpoints, including user or process behavior, network connections, or file access.
- Identity and access management (IAM) – Controls applied to secure accounts and remote access methods, such as MFA, account lockouts, remote access limitation, etc.
- Mitigation – This involves patching vulnerabilities or applying configuration changes as required to mitigate threats.
- SIEM/Log integration – This involves the steps taken for visibility, monitoring, and automatic triggering of secondary actions that implement security controls as appropriate to halt malicious activity.
- Threat feed – This involves the integration of threat feeds with other security controls to more quickly and easily detect, prevent, or block malicious activity in an automated way.
- Encryption – This involves implementing encryption controls on files, folders, sites, network traffic, or other resources to block unauthorized access.

Remediation Plan

The remediation plan is very similar to containment in that it may include the introduction or modification to any or all of the same security capability types, with the exception that those changes will continue beyond the active incident. The remediation plan addresses issues identified during the incident that leadership wants to continue to associate with the incident for remediation purposes.

Care should be taken to carefully select items for the remediation plan that can and will be completed. They should be of a highly focused nature, not overly broad, and not go into significant detail about vulnerabilities or security gaps. The discussion and focus should be on specific, achievable changes directly related to the incident that need to be made and avoid reasons and justifications as to why. The reason for this is that the after-action report might be provided to outsiders and should not include too much detail about security gaps and respective scope that may or may not be fixed in a timely manner.

The remediation plan leads into post-incident processes and may continue for months or years, depending upon project approval, financial budgeting, design, architecture, planning, and implementation considerations. In addition to the security capability types mentioned in the containment section, the remediation plan also includes additional, more in-depth considerations as follows:

- Compensating controls – Due to the fact that it is usually not immediately possible to implement the desired information security controls, there is usually an interim step between containment and full remediation. More specifically, remediation steps are usually divided between short- and long-term remediation goals. Short-term remediation goals may consist primarily of compensating controls that hold the environment in a state of acceptable security until the long-term (or full-remediation plans) can be completed.
- Security program/project development – In its scope, it includes any or all elements in whole or in part of people, processes, and technology design, development, and implementation.
- Cybersecurity architecture – This involves developing a secure program or project design requirements for specific technologies, services, capabilities, or integrations.
- Secure code development – This involves developing secure code to replace vulnerable sites, services, applications, or other custom code identified as being vulnerable.
- Training – Design, develop, and deploy a training program that addresses the required security concepts, capabilities, and workflows.
- Testing – Perform functional, security, workflow, and tabletop testing of all aspects of security capabilities, policies, procedures, and the overarching security and response program.

Incident Participant List and Point of Contact

Undoubtedly, one of the most important and difficult actions in and sometimes after an incident can be identifying the system/device/application owners, admins, and contacts. If this is not known ahead of time, it can be the hardest and most frustrating part of an incident. Carefully documenting this info as it is identified will be critical through the various stages of the incident management lifecycle and post-incident activity.

It is essential to identify and document at least the following types of contacts and stakeholders during the response process and include them in the final report. They are typically required to assist with response activities, including access, investigation, containment, remediation, and post-incident activity respective to their particular stewardship, and follow-up activity from compliance, legal, or audit teams will need to contact the individual parties involved with questions. Each of these entities and groups are described in the explanation in the following bullet points:

- Incident Commander – The Incident Commander leads the investigation and is the primary source of contact for approved questions and discussions regarding the investigation.
- Cybersecurity leadership – Cybersecurity leadership has overall responsibility for the

security controls, investigative process, and approval of all reports and recommendations associated with the incident.

- Investigative team members – These are the team members involved in performing the incident response and forensic activities.

- SOC team members – These are the team members responsible for the monitoring, detection, and escalation to the investigative/response team.

- Compliance team – These are the national or regional compliance team members responsible for providing regulatory guidance during the incident.

- Legal team – These are the national or regional legal team members responsible for providing legal and statutory guidance during the incident.

- Business owners – These individuals will need to be consulted and usually obtain their approval before any type of changes can be made to the production environment. These are the people who are ultimately accountable and have to pay for the changes. They are also most affected by the related outages.

- Department heads – Department heads need to be advised, as taking systems offline could impact business processes, customer services, etc. Additionally, even if there is no service disruption, there are likely to be financial impacts that will need to be approved.

- Change approvers – It will be critical to have the specific change approvers for resources documented, who may or may not be the same as business owners, department heads, system/application owners, or others. These entities will need to be in communication throughout the response process and be provided access to reports.

- System owners/admins – It is important to involve system owners/admins as they will (hopefully) be able to answer specific questions regarding the affected resources. Typical questions include: 1) How they work, 2) What the legitimate capabilities/functions are, 3) What data is stored on them, 4) Identify what artifacts may need to be examined, 5) identify unauthorized changes, and 6) be able to assist in the system restoration, hardening, and recovery processes.

- Application owners and development personnel – Application owners/developers will (hopefully) be best able to answer application deep-dive questions regarding the capabilities and functions of affected applications. They should be able to assist with determining data elements, files, configurations, and other artifacts that need to be examined. They are also key to the restoration, hardening, and recovery processes.

- IT support personnel – IT support is usually of the most value when trying to take possession of or make changes to the physical aspects of the system, such as unplugging a system, locking it in an IT closet with an appropriate label, and holding it for examination. These individuals are typically the start of a chain of custody.

- Network personnel – The regional/local network team is important to document as they will be able to implement and remove network containment measures as well as define what is permissible or typical for network traffic to/from affected resources. Using network containment methods is typically the fastest way to contain threats.

- Vendor relationship owners – Many organizations have relationship owners who manage or laisse contacts with vendors and through which all contact must flow. It is critical to identify and document these individuals. They can simplify the process of navigating the vendor environment, identify the vendor account managers, and obtain vendor support team contacts to help understand the history of the resources.

- Vendor support team – Viable vendor contacts can be one of the most difficult contact types to maintain. However, it is critical to have them documented and updated, as they will be consulted throughout the incident management process. They are essential as they typically understand their systems/applications/devices better than onsite support teams and will often need to assist with updates or configuration changes.

35 SECURITY DEFICIENCIES AND RECOMMENDATIONS ANALYSIS

This section addresses the considerations and details involved in capturing and documenting security deficiencies and the associated lessons learned and recommendations. This will drive changes to improve the customer's security posture.

As a result of incidents, tabletop activities, penetration tests, the evolving threat landscape, or in response to security best practices, there can be a large variety of security deficiencies identified that need to be addressed. They have a large variety of impetus but typically have overlapping needs. Ultimately, the same solutions can address many different use cases and solve a variety of common problems.

In order to give the security deficiencies and respective recommendations adequate analysis, they should be separated from the impetus and looked at holistically. The scope and impact of a specific security deficiency are likely much larger than the context within which it was identified.

The ultimate scope addressed during the full remediation process is not restricted to the scope of vulnerability identified by proactive assessments or reactive response activity. The nature of the issues to be addressed may be systemic across the entire organization, whereas the scope of the assessment or response activity was limited to a subset of systems.

For example, if a single workstation was compromised due to an application vulnerability, the problem is likely more widespread than that specific workstation or even that class of workstations. It is possible that the entire endpoint management program needs to be evaluated and revised. The same is true for penetration test findings or any other reason a deficiency is being evaluated. As such, this analysis requires a framework with sufficient detail to identify the needs, enumerate the specific tasks, and categorize all of the findings.

Cover Page

Cyber Security Incident Response Team
Security Deficiencies and Recommendations Form
<DOCUMENT NAME>
Privileged and Confidential – Attorney Work Product
Prepared at the Direction of Counsel

Status: <Draft / Final>
Version Number: <##.##>
Version Date: <YYYY-MM-DD>

CONFIDENTIAL – FOR AUTHORIZED USE ONLY

This document is the property of <COMPANY>. It contains information that is proprietary, confidential, or otherwise restricted from disclosure. Any dissemination, distribution, copying or unauthorized use of this document in whole or in part by anyone other than the intended recipient is strictly prohibited without prior written permission from the <Legal department> and the <Compliance Office>. If you are not an authorized recipient, please return this document to a member of the <COMPANY> legal department, the <Compliance Office>, and/or destroy any and all copies of the document in your possession.

For starters, the cover page is important. It immediately identifies the sensitivity of the document and the protections it is under. Of particular importance is the "Privileged and Confidential – Attorney Work-Product" "Prepared at the Direction of Counsel" statement, which indicates that it is part of a work-product request for an activity directed by an attorney.

Another key concept is that this document must not be specifically related to an incident, penetration test, or other specific security activity. If they are, the document runs the risk of being discoverable if the discovery of documents related to the security activity has been authorized by court order.

The legal tagging and separation from other activities will somewhat insulate the document from discovery or will at least keep it from being immediately discoverable. Note that for this to be true, an attorney must be involved from the beginning, guiding the overall process and deliverables.

In addition to discovery protection, the tagging and confidentiality statement are a clear warning to any individual who inadvertently comes across the document that it is a protected document that they should not read without authorization. It further identifies what needs to happen if someone finds or receives it in an unintended or unauthorized manner.

The cover page also serves to clearly identify the document, the incident details, the status of the document (draft or final), the version number, and the respective version date. This makes all the most germane document tracking information immediately identifiable.

Sometimes, these reports are so sensitive that they need to be watermarked to uniquely identify each recipient. For instance, place the recipient's name or employee ID on each page of the document and identify other protections that apply to their use case, such as "Do not copy, forward, print, or share." This is difficult to manage, however. In the private sector, it is typically only done in the most serious of situations. This is more likely to be seen in government or military high-security use cases.

About Document and Audience

For readers, regulators, compliance, and legal purposes, it is important to clearly identify the purpose of the document and the intended audience. It helps define the intentions of the document and provides a framework for understanding its contents. It also makes an easy read for regulatory compliance audits by showing the customer has sufficient documentation supporting adherence to the incident response reporting requirements within the various regulatory criteria.

Note that the document audience includes technical and leadership personnel, which is a disparate group having very different communication needs. As such, the subsequent sections will begin at a summary level and then drill down as far as appropriate and necessary to satisfy the needs and recommendations of the various stakeholders and audiences.

About this Document

In any Information Security organization there needs to be a common communication channel to ensure threats, issues, and recommendations are known and progress is made. This is important for the overall security, compliance, communication, and documentation of efforts for the organization. This document provides an assessment of deficiencies found within <COMPANY>'s information security and incident management programs. It includes recommendations for improvements within all elements of people, process, and technology that could be made for future prevention, detection, response, and blocking capabilities for malicious activity. This document includes details regarding vulnerabilities, gaps, security needs, recommendations, action items, and statuses.

Document Audience

This document is privileged and confidential. The audience for this report is limited to decision makers and technical personnel on a need to know basis. It includes selected parties within Cybersecurity, information technology, business leadership, executive management, regulatory compliance, legal, and other teams and individuals as required for the success of the efforts. It details security deficiencies, remediation recommendations, and lessons learned that should be acted upon to improve <COMPANY>'s security posture.

This document is restricted only to limited distribution, as authorized. Please do not forward or share without the prior approval from the Legal Department and the Compliance Office.

Document Control

The Document Control section contains basic information for the author(s), tracking of versions, and the intended distribution list. This section will often get expanded depending on the distribution list and the number of revisions it has to go through.

It is important to keep documents in a draft phase until all key parties agree it is completed. Documents marked as DRAFT are not held to the same standard as FINAL documents and are significantly less relevant if produced during the discovery process.

Long story short, the contents of draft documents are easily refuted as simply being unfinished and still under development and review. Once a document is marked final, however, it carries significantly greater weight in discovery and the subsequent review by legal, judicial, and regulatory entities.

Document Control

This report has been approved to be distributed to the following individuals by the <Legal Department> and the <Compliance Office>. Approval authority for dissemination of this report resides with the <Legal Department> and the <Compliance Office>.

Document Author:	Name, Title name@domain.com Cell: ###.###.####			
	Draft Version	0.1	Name	Date
	Peer Reviewed	0.5		
Document Revision:	Initial Release	1.0		
	Revised Release	1.1		
	Final Release Candidate	1.2		
	Final Release	1.3		
	Person 1	Title, Department		
Document Distribution List:	Person 2	Title, Department		

Deficiency and Recommendations Summary

This section is obviously the meat of this chapter. These contents are highly focused on defining the problem to be solved and providing high-level recommendations on how to solve it.

However, there are several steps that come after this that will determine how best to solve it at a lower level and enumerate all of the analysis and details involved in the specific solution(s). The deficiencies and recommendations document will identify a gap, such as "the service/application employs only single-factor authentication (SFA), and sensitive information can be accessed by unauthorized parties if they have obtained user's credentials."

An example of the high-level solution presented would be:

It is recommended that a multi-factor authentication (MFA) solution be implemented and required for all remote access to the service/application and that the specific MFA solution provide:

1) *A mobile application performing the authentication*
2) *Device verification to ensure the mobile device is legitimate/approved*
3) *Identity Proofing be required for all device changes and/or password resets*
4) *A One-Time-Password (OTP) be sent to the original device if externally initiated changes are to be made to devices or configurations*
5) *Detection and blocking of impossible travel times to prevent unauthorized remote parties from having access to stolen credentials and the ability to social engineer users into granting MFA access.*

Note that this recommendation just provides basic requirements that could be satisfied by any MFA product, and it stops short of identifying a specific vendor or product to provide the MFA solution. Identifying the specific technology requires significant research and cybersecurity architecture in order to enumerate all of the functional and compatibility requirements needed to integrate the MFA solution into all technologies and use cases.

It also requires significant project management, tracking, product evaluation, user acceptance testing, etc. All of these tasks are far outside the scope of the incident management process and have transitioned into the cybersecurity architecture and information security program development workflows.

As such, the deficiency and recommendations summary should inform the subsequent workflows, but it is not the definitive document providing the final solution. This document identifies the need(s) and informs the subsequent workflows that will identify how those needs will be addressed and the program/project management-related considerations. Following is an explanation of all the data elements in this document:

- **Dates Detected/Compromised** – Hopefully, these two dates are the same, but not necessarily. Oftentimes, there is a dwell time between the two. Both dates are relevant as they drive regulatory requirements and can influence the "**Date Resolution Required By.**"
- **Date Resolution Required By** helps drive the sense of urgency and respective timeline according to business needs, regulatory requirements, budgeting decisions, and project plans.
- **Detection Source** helps drive and inform the analysis and planning processes that may require modification or integration with downstream activity.
- **Person Reporting** identifies who to return to for follow-up questions and additional information.
- **Deficiency Summary** is where the team defines the problem statement at a high level and could involve any problem source, such as vulnerabilities, misconfigurations, missing capabilities, etc.
- **Recommendation Summary** is where the team identifies the high-level solution(s)
- **Deficiency Remediation Details**:
  - **Scope** - Identify all of the affected locations, resources, and artifacts involved
    - Environments
    - Networks
    - Systems/Devices
    - Accounts
  - **Urgency** – Perform business analysis to identify all of the driving factors and sense of urgency
    - Risk: High/Medium/Low
    - Priority: High/Medium/Low
    - Business Value: Explanation
    - Regulatory Impact: PCI/PHI/PII/SOX
    - Actionability: Explanation
  - **Owner(s)/Sponsor(s)** – Identify a list of owners, sponsors, and technical roles at any level that are required for the project in any phase
  - **Action Item(s)** – Identify the list of actions and details to be defined for each action (multiple)
    - Description
    - Status
    - Prerequisite(s)
    - Assignee(s)
    - Individual Steps/Components – if appropriate

36 EVIDENCE HANDLING, RETENTION, AND DESTRUCTION

This section will go through incident management best practices with evidence collection, handling, storage, and subsequent disposal. This has many use cases, techniques, and data sources. Depending upon the investigation type and the company's respective business, regulatory, or legal drivers, there are a wide variety of considerations that may cause evidence to be treated differently.

Post-incident activity is the wrong time to start thinking about proper considerations for the evidence lifecycle. However, this is typically when most environments and responders start getting serious about creating documentation, evidence labels, chain of custody, storage, etc.

Evidence Labeling

When collecting physical evidence, care should be taken to first photograph and document the respective evidence details and apply appropriate labeling before doing anything else with it. When doing so, it is important to photocopy or photograph the face of the hard drive, showing the manufacturer label with the manufacturer, model, and serial numbers. Other computers, devices, peripherals, and other components should also be photographed, including the manufacturer's labels and serial numbers.

To make the evidence items quick and easy to identify, place an evidence label with a unique evidence number on each evidence item. If components are removed from a larger evidence item, such as multiple hard drives from a computer, each drive/component should receive its own evidence number and label and be associated back to the parent evidence item.

It is never acceptable to analyze original evidence, as the evidence may become damaged, corrupted, or altered. Several copies of original evidence (OE) must be made and verified forensically to be identical, and then the forensic copy of the OE is analyzed. The copies should share the same evidence number as the original but be distinguished using an Evidence#.Copy# notation. This enables quick identification.

In situations where physical evidence cannot be obtained without compromising the evidence, a logical image of the physical devices must be created. This becomes a child of the parent item and should be tracked as such. The parent device is the OE, but a logical image of the physical device is also treated as OE, as the physical device may need to be returned to service. This makes the designated copy of the logical evidence the best evidence available. This often applies to striped RAID arrays, integrated hard drives, or other restrictive configurations for which the physical drives may be unusable as evidence.

Careful notes, pictures, and documentation should be captured regarding the exact configuration of the drives or other artifacts within the parent evidence item. Evidence tracking documentation must make allowances for parent/child relationships between evidence items and respective labels. Bar-coded evidence labels should also include the actual evidence number for easy identification. Evidence information, including the following, should be collected for each evidence item and entered into the evidence tracking system:

- Case number
- Evidence number
- Parent evidence number
- Child evidence numbers
- Quantity of copies
- Customer name
- Brief description
- Location collected from – all information down to the room number
- Custodian
- System/device purpose
- Collection date/time
- Collected by – investigator
- Manufacturer
- Model number
- Serial number
- Version number

Chain of Custody

Evidence that may be turned over to law enforcement, subject to legal action, or involve regulatory compliance must be handled according to forensic best practices and should utilize chain of custody, as well as standard evidence tracking. The chain of custody form tracks the movement of evidence between entities.

This usually starts with the original custodian or customer representative who provided the evidence to the investigator. It then tracks movement between investigators and/or to the shipper (sent by delivery to the lab), to the lab tech, and to the evidence storage location, law enforcement, or other locations. Each time the evidence is checked out and checked in (such as for analysis in the lab), the chain of custody is updated, and the evidence tracking system must be updated with the current location and custodian of the evidence item.

Chain of Custody Form

The purpose of the Chain of Custody Form is to record the initial receipt and movement of evidence items. The Chain of Custody Form is used to document all transfers of evidence and help account for the location of any given time.

Incident Tracking Number:	
Item Name or Description:	

Chain of Custody Log

Date (YYYY-MM-DD)	Time (HH:MM AM/PM, Timezone)	Action and Reason	New Location of Evidence	Released By (Name & Signature)	Received By (Name & Signature)

In this way, an individual can speak to the disposition of the evidence at any point in time. To maintain the chain of custody, evidence must not be left unattended in an unsecured location. Pragmatically, evidence must always be attended to and monitored (if in use) or securely locked in a controlled area for storage. All movements must be logged.

Evidence Handling and Testimony

Evidence handling procedures and testimony activity must comply with the most recent updates to or interpretation of the Federal Rules for Civil Procedure and the Federal Rules of Evidence. The most directly applicable sections include:

- 1001-1008 – Best Evidence Rule
- 902 – Evidence that is Self-Authenticating
- 901 – Authenticating or Identifying Evidence
- 802 – The Rule Against Hearsay
- 702 – Testimony by Expert Witnesses
- Other rules relating to discovery and evidence production also apply, but typically later in relation to subsequent legal action. These include Rules 26, 33, 34, 37, and 45.

Evidence Transportation

Evidence files or logical drives must be encrypted and meet current encryption best practices prior to shipping. The decryption keys or passwords must not be shipped with encrypted drives to avoid them being used if the evidence is intercepted.

The evidence must be placed within an unmarked, locked container and placed in a shipping box marked Fragile. It is preferred to have the evidence shipped expedited via 1st- or 2nd-day delivery and to avoid ground shipping if at all possible. It must have a requirement for tracking in transit and signature upon delivery.

Some important safety tips to mention are 1) Never ship OE via a mail/package carrier unless absolutely necessary, 2) Never ship your only copy of evidence – meaning always make sure the responders or the lab have at least one copy, and 3) make as many copies as necessary to ensure at least one is always safe and can be used as best evidence if all evidence in shipping is lost.

Evidence Lab and Storage Vault

For evidence labs and storage rooms or vaults, all access must be strictly controlled and monitored. The evidence lab should be a secure room with camera monitoring and badge control for ingress/egress access.

The evidence storage room or vault is a hardened room within the evidence lab with similar access and monitoring controls. As such, it should be a secured room within a secured room. Common evidence lab and storage room or vault requirements include:

- Floor through plenum hardened walls built to current construction materials specifications
- Hardened, vaulted doors built to current design specifications
- Internal room with no windows is preferred
- Security system w/ motion detection & alarm system is required
- Secured HVAC vents are required
- Other hardening protocols per evolving federal, state, and local requirements and best practices

Retention and Destruction

In most cases, evidence should not be stored indefinitely. This is for legal and logistical reasons. As a matter of policy and procedure, evidence retention and destruction should have a pre-determined retention date and subsequent destruction process.

Retention time frames are typically based on legal and regulatory requirements, such as dictated by the type of data stored or ongoing legal actions. However, even when the retention time expires, it is advisable to verify that the data should be deleted or the evidence destroyed before doing so.

If evidence is to be destroyed, but the drives are to be repurposed for future cases, the evidence drives should be securely wiped. Alternatively, the respective evidence items should be physically destroyed to prevent reuse or access of any kind. Either way, it must be rendered unrecoverable.

Physical destruction should be performed through a certified device destruction/degaussing service. Such services will typically provide a certificate of destruction, which should be added to the chain of custody. This is a key artifact that may be required for legal or compliance purposes.

After the retention period has expired, evidence destruction has been authorized by legal/compliance teams, and the evidence has been destroyed, the evidence tracking system should also be updated with the ultimate destruction status and evidence destruction method. This will be the final resting place for the chain of custody, certificates of destruction, and other information or documents related to the evidence and its final disposition.

For internal cases, Compliance and Legal teams typically authorize evidence destruction, but individual circumstances may differ per entity. For consulting relationships, authorized individuals within the customer environment should be consulted to direct the evidence destruction or request continued retention.

APPENDIX A: DIRTY DOZEN QUICK REFERENCE

Process	Parent Process	Local User	Start Time	# of instances	Image Path
csrss.exe	smss.exe	Local System	w/in seconds of boot	2 or more	%SystemRoot%\System32\csrss.exe
explorer.exe	userinit.exe	Logged-on user(s)	1st instance w/ logon	1+ per user	%SystemRoot%\explorer.exe
lsaiso.exe	wininit.exe	Local System	w/in seconds of boot	0 to 1	%SystemRoot%\System32\lsaiso.exe
lsass.exe	wininit.exe	Local System	w/in seconds of boot	1	%SystemRoot%\System32\lsass.exe
RuntimeBroker.exe	svchost.exe	Logged-on user(s)	varies	1+ per user	%SystemRoot%\System32\RuntimeBroker.exe
services.exe	wininit.exe	Local System	w/in seconds of boot	1	%SystemRoot%\System32\services.exe
smss.exe	System	Local System	w/in seconds of boot for master instance at at time of each session	1 for master instance and 1 child per session	%SystemRoot%\System32\smss.exe
svchost.exe	services.exe	varies	varies	multiple	%SystemRoot%\System32\svchost.exe
System	N/A	Local System	at boot	1	
taskhostw.exe	svchost.exe	varies	varies	1+	%SystemRoot%\System32\taskhostw.exe
wininit.exe	smss.exe	Local System	w/in seconds of boot	1	%SystemRoot%\System32\wininit.exe
winlogon.exe	smss.exe	Local System	w/in seconds of boot for master instance at at time of each session	1+	%SystemRoot%\System32\winlogon.exe

The playbooks contained in the following appendices are trifold, double-sided quick reference playbooks. They are intended to be photocopied or cut out and copied double-sided and then folded and distributed to team members for reference as necessary. **The owner of this book is provided a limited license to distribute these quick reference playbooks for use inside of their organization or within the scope of their professional services engagements for active incident response, incident management, incident command, or training purposes. Recipients of the original or copies are not permitted to make copies in any manner for any use unless they are also owners of this book or other Cyber Security Masters Guides containing the same.**

An illustration of how to fold the pamphlets is below:

APPENDIX B: INCIDENT COMMANDER PLAYBOOK

1A) PROCESS PREPARATION
- Establish CIRT members
- Develop / provide CIRT training
- Identify assets, attributes, ownership, and escalation
- Perform and maintain recent system and application vulnerability assessments to quickly identify security gaps, misconfigurations, and potential exposure
- Document and maintain network and application logical diagrams and with traffic and data flow
- Document visibility, monitoring, detection, and blocking capabilities for the computing environment
- Identify business and resource stakeholders, team or group aliases, SMEs, and 24/7 contact methods
- Establish roles and responsibilities quick reference
- Establish break-the-glass pre-requisites & procedures
- Create and socialize IR policy, procedures, and plans
- Perform continuous threat intelligence monitoring

1B) TECHNOLOGY PREPARATION
- User access and monitoring—IAM, UAM, UBA, UEBA
- Network (all ingress/egress)—firewalls, proxies, VPNs, SSL/TLS decryption, packet capture, malware sandbox, IDS/IPS, DLP, WAF, or other gateways
- Endpoint—firewall, packet capture, EDR, IDS/IPS, DLP, DRM, antivirus/anti-malware, policy and configuration management, patch management, and vulnerability assessment
- Email security—monitor, inspect, block, quarantine
- Cloud scrubbing—customer managed network security functions with SSL/TLS decryption, next-gen firewall, WAF, IPS, DLP, and reputation protection, etc.
- SIEM—log aggregation, correlation, use cases, alerts, integration, action triggers, and threat feeds

Note: It is important to map out the computing environment, crown jewels, business critical infrastructure, sensitive information, and critical operations vs. the visibility and blocking coverage of deployed security capabilities. This will determine areas of strengths and weaknesses for security controls involved in incident response processes.

2A) IDENTIFICATION
- Automated detection from technology
- Manual detection, Threat hunting, compliance search
- Business / user / admin / contractor reported
- Externally reported:
  • Law enforcement
  • Partners, vendors, affiliates, contractors
  • Customers
  • Security researchers
  • Threat feeds, security bulletins, media

2B) NOTIFICATION
- CIRT on-call list, aliases, ticketing groups...
- SMEs, technical leads, vendors, retainer agreements...
- Leadership, business owners, stakeholders...
- Compliance, legal, customers, regulators, media...

2C) SCOPING
- Locations
- Networks
- Systems
- Devices
- Applications
- Cloud services
  • Accounts
  • Repositories
  • Files
  • Email / chat
  • Databases
  • Regulatory

2D) VALIDATION
- Validate incident is real before beginning full-scale response efforts or sending leadership notifications
- Enumerate symptoms from observable vantage points: users, endpoint, email, network, logs...
- Rule out technical problem or false positive detection misidentified as incident
- Do not assume incident if technology complication, failure, or misconfiguration is reasonably possible
- Identify potentially likely incident root causes and contributing factors that could complicate response

3A) INCIDENT KICK-OFF MEETING
- Identify key SMEs, groups, and build response team
- Determine need for Legal/Compliance personnel
- Start incident bridge and invite critical personnel
- Verify that only authorized personnel are on bridge
- Identify and follow appropriate incident playbook
- Enumerate investigative tasks and assign to teams responsible for respective technologies
- Define operational periods, objectives, and check-ins

3B) TRIAGE AND PRIORITIZATION
- Actively spreading malware
- Compromised credentials
- Systems that support life
- Externally vulnerable resources
- Systems with regulated data
- Critical for business operations
- Other affected resources

3C) CONTAINMENT (*Perform in parallel*)
- User access and monitoring—block account access, reset passwords, harden permissions, require MFA
- Network (ingress/egress/internal)—block locations, domains, IP addresses, subnets, VLANs, and/or hosts
- Endpoint (physical or virtual)—block traffic, isolate host, delete artifacts, GPO policy, patch deployment
- Email security—inspect, validate, block, quarantine
- Cloud scrubbing—inspect, validate, sanitize, block
- SIEM—integration, use cases, threat feeds, triggers

3D) EVIDENCE COLLECTION (*only as applicable*)
Note: Live evidence must be collected pre-containment to ensure that it is not altered or lost by containment
- Live: Network traffic
- Live: Memory
- Live: Processes
- Live: Registry
- Live: WMI
- Live: Commands
- Live: IOCs and YARA rule matches
- Live: Logs
- Static: Logs
- Static: File systems, shares, and repositories
- Static: Databases
- Static: Archives
- Static: Cloud file, email, and data repositories

4A) INVESTIGATION & ROOT CAUSE ANALYSIS

- Attack vectors
- Exploit methods
- Malicious activity
- Vulnerabilities
- Systems and devices
- Applications / services
- Accounts / groups / directory services
- Shares, folders, files, data, records, contents, details
- Malware, toolkits, webshells, backdoors, keyloggers
- Phishing emails, malicious sites, links, attachments
- Persistence mechanisms / auto-start locations
- IOCs and YARA rules
- Attacker/malware C2 traffic
- Lateral movement activity
- Exfiltration activity
- Compromised business operations
- Compromised business sensitive data
- Compromised regulated data (PHI, PCI, PII, & SOX)
- Incident timeline

4B) MITIGATION / REMEDIATION

- Access controls and permission hardening
- Patch installation and configuration management
- System /GPO policy hardening
- Application or operating system scripting controls
- Application hardening / input validation
- File integrity controls, white listing, and validation
- Network and endpoint encryption controls
- Email and chat security controls
- Internet traffic inspection security controls
- Compensating controls (network, endpoint, or other)
- Validation testing
- Install or configure additional security technologies, infrastructure, controls, and capabilities
- Develop and implement needed policy and processes
- User security training, testing, and attestations

5A) ERADICATON / RESTORATION / RECOVERY

- Surgical eradication (preliminary)
  - Kill malicious processes, services, and drivers
  - Delete malicious arti- facts, binaries, libraries, and scripts
  - Remove attacker / mal- ware persistence mechanisms and back- doors
- Reinstall, re-image, or restore all affected devices, servers, workstations, virtual machines, containers, applications, network services, directory services, files, databases, and data to a known-good state.
- Reset compromised passwords for affected accounts
- Delete unauthorized accounts (local, domain, app)
- Remove directory services threats, such as golden tickets, silver tickets, skeleton keys
- Identify and remove all exfiltration artifacts and/or inappropriately stored sensitive information from workstations, servers, email, file-shares, databases...
- Validation testing: systems, applications, accounts...

5B) LESSONS LEARNED / REPORTING

- Document investigative steps and observations
- Finalize incident and response activity timeline
- Identify root cause and enabling factors
- Document all investigation findings, affected systems, devices, applications, services, accounts, and data
- Identify impact to cyber security, regulated data, members, and business operations
- Implement and document monitoring and blocking of identified threats related to the incident to pre- vent a similar attack or using the same infrastructure
- Create after action report documenting activity, find- ings, and review with leaders, legal, and compliance
- Enumerate security gaps related to the incident
- Identify recommendations pertaining to each area of people, process, and technology
- Document all lessons learned and create tickets for task tracking through completion for each

COLBY CLARK ENTERPRISES, LLC

Full Lifecycle
Incident Management
Playbook

INCIDENT COMMANDER

< CUSTOMER_NAME >

<Primary Business Address>
<Address Line 2>
<Address Line 3>
<Address Line 4>

Phone: <CUSTOMER_PRIMARY_PHONE>
Fax: <CUSTOMER_FAX>
Email: <CUSTOMER_EMAIL>

All Rights Reserved © 2020 Colby Clark
Phone: 208.553.3266
colby@colbyclarkenterprises.com

Note: Steps and within each section are not necessarily linear and are often performed in parallel by teams of responders, subject matter experts (SMEs), contractors, and vendors.

APPENDIX C: COMBINED RESPONSE PLAYBOOK

1A) PREPARATION

- Establish CIRT members
- Develop / provide CIRT training
- Identify assets, attributes, ownership, and escalation
- Perform and maintain recent system and application vulnerability assessments to quickly identify security gaps, misconfigurations, and potential exposure
- Document and maintain network and application logical diagrams and with traffic and data flow
- Document visibility, monitoring, detection, and blocking capabilities for the computing environment
- Identify business and resource stakeholders, team or group aliases, SMEs, and 24/7 contact methods
- Establish roles and responsibilities quick reference
- Establish break-the-glass pre-requisites & procedures
- Create and socialize IR policy, procedures, and plans
- Perform continuous threat intelligence monitoring

1B) TECHNOLOGY

- Identity and Access Management (IAM)
- User behavior/activity monitoring (UAM/UBA/UEBA)
- Network—firewalls, proxies, SSL/TLS decryption, packet capture, malware sandbox, IDS/IPS, DLP, WAF, or other gateways
- Endpoint—firewall, packet capture, EDR, IDS/IPS, DLP, antivirus/anti-malware, policy and configuration management, patch management, and vulnerability assessment
- SIEM—log aggregation, correlation, use cases, alerts, integration, action triggers, and threat feeds

2A) IDENTIFICATION

- Automated detection:
  - ▣ IAM
  - ▣ UAM/UBA/UEBA
  - ▣ Network
  - ▣ Endpoint
  - ▣ SIEM
- Manual detection / Threat hunting
- Business / user / admin reported
- Externally reported:
  - ▣ Law enforcement
  - ▣ Partners / vendors
  - ▣ Customers
  - ▣ Security researchers
  - ▣ Threat feeds / security bulletins

2B) NOTIFICATION

- CIRT on-call list, aliases, ticketing groups...
- SMEs, technical leads, vendors, retainer agreements...
- Leadership, business owners, stakeholders...
- Compliance, legal, customers, regulators, media...

2C) SCOPING

- Locations
- Networks
- Systems
- Devices
- Applications
- Services
- Accounts
- Repositories
- Data
- Regulatory

3A) TRIAGE AND PRIORITIZATION

- ▣ Actively spreading malware
- ▣ Systems that support life
- ▣ Systems with regulated data
- ▣ Critical for business operations
- ▣ Ancillary systems
- ▣ Not known affected systems
- ▣ Inaccessible systems

○ NOW
○ Later
○ Today
○ Tomorrow

3B) CONTAINMENT

- IAM controls—MFA, password resets, restrictions...
- Network devices—blocks, host isolation, disable ports, socked-based restrictions
- Endpoint controls—firewalls, EDR, HIPS, AV/AM, DLP, policy & configuration management...
- Cloud / hosted controls—virtual system/network
- SIEM—custom use cases, correlation, dashboards, integration, and automated blocking triggers

3C) EVIDENCE COLLECTION

- Live: Network traffic
- Live: Memory
- Live: Processes
- Live: Registry
- Live: WMI
- Live: Commands
- Live: IOCs and YARA rule matches
- Static: Logs
- Static: File systems
- Static: File and email repositories
- Static: Databases
- Static: Archives

4A) INVESTIGATION / ROOT CAUSE ANALYSIS

- Attack vectors
- Exploit methods
- Vulnerabilities
- Malicious activity
- Systems and devices
- Applications / services
- Accounts / groups / directory services
- Files / data / records / contents / details
- Malware and components
- Persistence mechanisms
- IOCs and YARA rules
- Lateral movement
- Incident time line
- Security, business, legal, and regulatory impact

4B) MITIGATION / REMEDIATION

- Patch installation
- System policy hardening / scripting controls
- Application hardening / input validation
- Encryption controls
- Configuration management
- Compensating controls
- Validation testing
- Install / configure additional security infrastructure, controls, and capabilities:
  - IAM
  - UAM/UBA/UEBA
  - Network
  - Endpoint
  - SIEM
- Develop and implement needed policy and processes

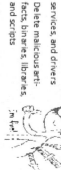

5A) ERADICATON / RESTORATION / RECOVERY

- Surgical eradication (preliminary)
  - Kill malicious processes, services, and drivers
  - Delete malicious arti- facts, binaries, libraries, and scripts
- Remove attacker / malware persistence mechanisms and backdoors
- Reinstall, re image, or restore all affected devices, servers, workstations, virtual machines, containers, applications, network services, directory services, files, databases, and data to a known-good state.
- Delete unauthorized accounts
- Reset compromised passwords for affected accounts
- Remove directory services threats, such as golden tickets, silver tickets, skeleton keys
- Identify and remove all exfiltration artifacts and/or inappropriately stored sensitive information from workstations, servers, email, file-shares, databases...
- Validation testing: systems, applications, accounts...

5B) LESSONS LEARNED / REPORTING

- Document investigative steps and observations
- Identify root cause and enabling factors
- Articulate all investigation findings, affected systems, devices, applications, services, accounts, and data
- Identify business, security, and regulatory impact
- Enumerate security gaps
- Identify recommendations pertaining to each area of people, process, and technology
- Implement monitoring and blocking of identified threats related to the incident to prevent a similar attack or using the same infrastructure
- Create final report and provide to legal team
- Document all lessons learned and create tickets for task tracking through completion for each

COLBY CLARK ENTERPRISES, LLC

Full Lifecycle Incident Management Playbook

GENERAL / ALL COMBINED

<CUSTOMER_NAME>

<Primary Business Address>
<Address Line 2>
<Address Line 3>
<Address Line 4>

Phone: <CUSTOMER_PRIMARY_PHONE>
Fax: <CUSTOMER_FAX>
Email: <CUSTOMER_EMAIL>

colby@colbyclarkenterprises.com
Phone: 208.553.3266

Note: Steps and within each section are not necessarily linear and are often performed in parallel by teams of responders, subject matter experts (SMEs), contractors, and vendors.

APPENDIX D: EXTERNAL ENTITIES PLAYBOOK

1A) PREPARATION
- Establish CIRT members
- Develop / provide CIRT training
- Create and socialize IR policy, procedures, and plans
- Establish vendor contracts with supporting security and incident response/management requirements
- Identify and document vendor managed resources, attributes, contacts, and escalation paths
- Identify and categorize sensitive content stored in on-prem vendor systems or in the vendor environment
- Perform and maintain recent system and application vulnerability assessments to quickly identify security gaps, misconfigurations, and potential exposure
- Document and maintain network and application logical diagrams and with traffic and data flow
- Document visibility, monitoring, detection, and blocking capabilities for the computing environment
- Identify business and resource stakeholders, team or group aliases, SMEs, and 24/7 contact methods
- Establish roles and responsibilities quick reference
- Establish break-the-glass pre-requisites & procedures
- Perform continuous threat intelligence monitoring

1B) TECHNOLOGY
- Identity and Access Management (IAM)
- Network—dynamic segmentation, dedicated vendor VLANs, VPN, least privileged access
- Endpoint—host/application vulnerability assessment
- Email security—monitor, inspect, block, quarantine
- SIEM—use cases, alerts, integration, & auto-triggers

Note: it is important to map out the architecture of the hosted environment, as well as the sensitive information vs. the visibility, monitoring, and blocking coverage of available security capabilities. This will determine areas of strengths and weaknesses for security controls involved in incident response processes.

2A) IDENTIFICATION
- Legal / compliance reported
- Business / user / contractor reported
- Externally reported:
  - Customers
  - ISAC groups
  - Partners, vendors, or affiliates
  - Threat feeds or security bulletins
  - Media outlets or blocks
  - Security researchers

2B) NOTIFICATION
- CIRT response teams: CIRT Bridge alias
- Cyber Security SMEs / technical leads: Team on-call lists or ticketing groups, alert groups, or team aliases
- Leadership, business owners, stakeholders
- Compliance, legal, customers, regulators, media...

2C) SCOPING

Vendor Environment	Customer Environment
Locations	B2B VPN
Environments	RAS VPN
Networks	Citrix
Systems	External servers/Cloud
Devices	Portals
Applications/services	Email
Email	Vendor integrations
Confidential data	Vendor accounts
Cloud services	Vendor on-prem systems/devices
3rd party contractors	Regulatory concerns
Regulatory concerns	

2D) VALIDATION
- Gather and review risk assessments, contracts, and agreements with outside entity and determine risk
- Perform interview and verify outside entity's access to sensitive data and enumerate methods of access
- Identify remote access to VPNs, networks, systems, cloud services, applications, and portals

Warning: The breach of vendor environments and resources is usually isolated to the content stored within the vendor locations and the customer data they store. However, if the vendors have remote network access (VPN, VDI, third-party proxied access, or otherwise) to the customer environment or if the service provided includes integration between systems in the various environments, the attackers or malware may spread internally and turn into a full-blown breach.

3A) TRIAGE AND PRIORITIZATION
1. Vendor VPN connections
2. Vendor remote access accounts
3. Vendor system/service integrations
4. Vendor systems in customer environment
5. Vendor contracts / agreements
6. Vendor websites / external facing services
7. Vendor emails to customer
8. Customer data in the vendor environment

NOW
Later
Today
Tomorrow

3B) CONTAINMENT
- IAM controls—vendor password resets, disable accounts, access restrictions.....
- Network—block ingress/egress traffic for vendor integrations, services, and Internet infrastructure
- VPN—block vendor VPN connections; limit remote access to secure portal of VDI infrastructure
- Email—perform vendor email filtering & quarantine
- Data—Halt sending sensitive data to vendor
- SIEM—custom use cases, correlation, dashboards, integration, and automated blocking triggers

Warning: Until vendor environments, resources, accounts, and connections can be validated as clean, secure, and no longer a risk, no network connections, integrations, remote access, or unvalidated data transfer should be permitted.

3C) EVIDENCE COLLECTION
- Live: Internal or external network traffic to or from vendor and/or related on-prem, external, or hosted systems, services, applications, and infrastructure
- Live or Static: Vendor IOCs, YARA rules, or malware samples, or related artifacts
- Static: All vendor documentation, contracts, and agreements
- Static: IAM
- Static: Vendor accessible apps
- Static: SIEM/Logs
- Static: Firewall/IPS
- Static: Proofpoint and TAP
- Static: Vendor related email
- Static: Files with employee or member data stored in compromised vendor environments, networks, systems, services, or applications
- Static: Investigation and analysis reports affected vendor or third-party investigative services provider

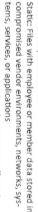

4A) INVESTIGATION / ROOT CAUSE ANALYSIS

- Attack vectors
- Exploit methods
- Vulnerabilities
- Malicious activity
- Accounts and directory services
- Systems, applications, and services
- Files / data / records / contents / details
- Malware, attacker toolkits, and components
- IOCs and YARA rules
- Persistence mechanisms
- Lateral movement and integration impact
- Incident time line
- Security, business, legal, and regulatory impact

Note: Investigation and root cause analysis will need to be conducted by the affected vendors or their third-party incident response provider(s). Third parties are preferred.

4B) MITIGATION / REMEDIATION

- Vendor dedicated VLANs and dynamic segmentation
- System & application hardening / input validation
- File integrity controls
- File and network encryption controls
- Compensating controls
- Install / configure additional security infrastructure, controls, and capabilities:
  - IAM
  - Network
  - Endpoint / VDI
  - SIEM
- Develop or refine security and incident response & management vendor contracts, policies, and procedures

5A) ERADICATION / RESTORATION / RECOVERY

- Validate that vendor has resolved the root cause attack vector and exploit method
- Validate that vendor has restored all compromised resources to a known good state
- Validate that vendor has fully patched and hardened production infrastructure
- Replace, reimage, or restore all affected on-prem vendor resources a known-good state
- Validate removal of threats to directory services such as golden tickets, silver tickets, skeleton keys...
- Validate removal of malware and backdoors
- Identify and delete unauthorized accounts
- Reset compromised passwords for affected accounts
- Identify and remove all exfiltration artifacts and/or inappropriately stored sensitive information from workstations, servers, email, file-shares, databases...
- Validation testing: systems, applications, accounts...

5B) LESSONS LEARNED / REPORTING

- Document investigative steps and observations
- Identify root cause and enabling factors
- Articulate all investigation findings, affected systems, devices, applications, services, accounts, and data
- Identify business, security, and regulatory impact
- Enumerate security gaps
- Identify recommendations pertaining to each area of people, process, and technology
- Implement monitoring and blocking of identified threats related to the incident to prevent a similar attack or using the same infrastructure
- Create final report and provide to legal team
- Document all lessons learned and create tickets for task tracking through completion for each

VENDOR-PARTNER-AFFILIATE

COLBY CLARK ENTERPRISES, LLC

Full Lifecycle Incident Management Playbook

<CUSTOMER_NAME>

<Primary Business Address>
<Address Line 2>
<Address Line 3>
<Address Line 4>

Phone: <CUSTOMER_PRIMARY_PHONE>
Fax: <CUSTOMER_FAX>
Email: <CUSTOMER_EMAIL>

All Rights Reserved © 2020 Colby Clark
Phone: **208.553.3266**
colby@colbyclarkenterprises.com

Note: Steps and within each section are not necessarily linear and are often performed in parallel by teams of responders, subject matter experts (SMEs), contractors, and vendors.

APPENDIX E: HOSTED SERVICES PLAYBOOK

1A) PREPARATION

- Establish CIRT members
- Develop / provide CIRT training
- Identify assets, attributes, ownership, and escalation
- Perform and maintain recent system and application vulnerability assessments to quickly identify security gaps, misconfigurations, and potential exposure
- Document and maintain network and application logical diagrams and with traffic and data flow
- Document visibility, monitoring, detection, and blocking capabilities for the computing environment
- Identify business and resource stakeholders, team or group aliases, SMEs, and 24/7 contact methods
- Establish roles and responsibilities quick reference
- Establish break-the-glass pre-requisites & procedures
- Create and socialize IR policy, procedures, and plans
- Perform continuous threat intelligence monitoring

1B) TECHNOLOGY

- IAM - Federated access controls and monitoring
- Network—hosted SSL/TLS decryption prior to inspection and /or packet capture by firewalls, proxies, IDS/IPS, DLP, WAF, or other security gateway capabilities
- Cloud scrubbing—customer managed network security functions with SSL/TLS decryption, next-gen firewall, WAF, IPS, DLP, and reputation protection, etc.
- SIEM— log aggregation, correlation, use cases, alerts, integration, action triggers, and threat feeds
- Application security—App security/logging add-ins

Note: It is important to map out the architecture of the hosted environment, as well as the sensitive information vs. the visibility, monitoring, and blocking coverage of available security capabilities. This will determine areas of strengths and weaknesses for security controls involved in incident response processes.

2A) IDENTIFICATION

- Automated detection:
  - IAM
  - Network (on-prem or hosted)
  - Cloud scrubbing
  - SIEM
  - Application security add-ins
  - Ancillary resources
- Manual detection / threat hunting
- Business / user / admin / contractor reported
- Externally reported:
  - Law enforcement
  - Partners / vendors
  - Customers
  - Security researchers
  - Threat feeds / security bulletins / media

2B) NOTIFICATION

- CIRT on-call list, aliases, ticketing groups...
- SMEs, technical leads, vendors, retainer agreements...
- Leadership, business owners, stakeholders...
- Compliance, legal, customers, regulators, media...

2C) SCOPING

- Systems
- Applications
- Services
- Integrations
- Accounts
- Repositories
- Data
- Regulatory

3A) TRIAGE AND PRIORITIZATION

- Webshells, rootkits, backdoors, or other malware...
- Resources with regulated data
- Accounts with elevated privileges
- Critical for business operations
- Admin systems/interfaces

3B) CONTAINMENT

- IAM controls—password resets, disable/terminate accounts, account restrictions...
- Network—source and destination host, service, and port filtering
- App add-ins—traffic filtering, input validation, password strength requirements, app security controls
- Cloud scrubbing—decryption, inspection, malicious data and traffic blocking (next-gen firewall, protocol inspection, WAF, IPS, DLP, and reputation protection)
- SIEM—custom use cases, correlation, dashboards, integration, and automated blocking triggers

Note: Collection and containment in the externally hosted environments is effectively done at the same time by pausing web-services and databases and collecting related files.

3C) EVIDENCE COLLECTION

- Live: Network traffic
- Live: Commands
- Live or Static: Logs
- Static: Logs
- Static: File systems
- Static: Databases
- Static: Archives

Warning: The breach of externally hosted websites/services is usually isolated to the content stored in the hosted resources. However, if internal passwords are used on the hosted infrastructure, or if the infrastructure has network integrations, the attackers or malware may spread internally and turn into a full-blown breach.

4A) INVESTIGATION / ROOT CAUSE ANALYSIS

- Attack vectors
- Exploit methods
- Vulnerabilities
- Malicious activity
- Systems
- Applications / services / containers / interfaces
- Accounts / groups / directory services
- Files / data / records / contents / details
- Malware, webshells, attacker toolkits, & components
- Persistence mechanisms
- IOCs and YARA rules
- Integrations / lateral movement
- Incident timeline
- Security, business, legal, and regulatory impact

4B) MITIGATION / REMEDIATION

- System, site, application, service, and container patching and policy hardening
- Non-persistent virtual images
- Immutable directories and files
- File and network encryption controls
- Compensating controls
- Validation testing
- Install / configure additional hosted / cloud-based security controls and capabilities:
  - IAM
  - Network
  - Application add-ins
  - Cloud inspection and scrubbing
  - SIEM
- Develop and implement needed policy and processes

5A) ERADICATON / RESTORATION / RECOVERY

- Surgical eradication (preliminary)
  - Kill and block malicious activity and connections
  - Remove unauthorized changes, delete attacker artifacts, and scripts
  - Remove attacker / malware webshells, persistence mechanisms and backdoors
- Reinstall, reimage, or restore all affected, virtualized systems, containers, applications, services, directory services, files, databases, and data to a known-good and/or secure state.
- Delete unauthorized accounts
- Reset compromised passwords for affected accounts
- Identify and remove all exfiltration artifacts and/or inappropriately stored sensitive information from file systems, databases, and storage repositories
- Validation testing: systems, applications, accounts...

5B) LESSONS LEARNED / REPORTING

- Document investigative steps and observations
- Identify root cause and enabling factors
- Articulate all investigation findings, affected systems, devices, applications, services, accounts, and data
- Identify business, security, and regulatory impact
- Enumerate security gaps
- Identify recommendations pertaining to each area of people, process, and technology
- Implement monitoring and blocking of identified threats related to the incident to prevent a similar attack or using the same infrastructure
- Create final report and provide to legal team
- Document all lessons learned and create tickets for task tracking through completion for each

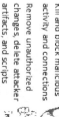

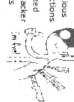

EXTERNALLY HOSTED SERVICES

COLBY CLARK ENTERPRISES, LLC

Full Lifecycle
Incident Management
Playbook

<CUSTOMER_NAME>

<Primary Business Address>
<Address Line 2>
<Address Line 3>
<Address Line 4>

Phone: <CUSTOMER_PRIMARY_PHONE>
Fax: <CUSTOMER_FAX>
Email: <CUSTOMER_EMAIL>

All Rights Reserved © 2020 Colby Clark
Phone: 208.553.3266
colby@colbyclarkenterprises.com

Note: Steps and within each section are not necessarily linear and are often performed in parallel by teams of responders, subject matter experts (SMEs), contractors, and vendors.

Printed in Great Britain
by Amazon